THE EVOLVING ROLES OF THE STATE, PRIVATE, AND LOCAL ACTORS IN RURAL ASIA

by

Ammar Siamwalla

with contributions by

Alex Brillantes
Somsak Chunharas
Colin MacAndrews
Andrew Macintyre
and
Frederick Roche

OXFORD
UNIVERSITY PRESS

OXFORD
UNIVERSITY PRESS

Oxford University Press is a department of the University of Oxford.
It furthers the University's objective of excellence in research, scholarship,
and education by publishing worldwide in

Oxford New York

Athens Auckland Bangkok Bogotá Buenos Aires Cape Town
Chennai Dar es Salaam Delhi Florence Hong Kong Istanbul Karachi
Kolkata Kuala Lumpur Madrid Melbourne Mexico City Mumbai Nairobi
Paris São Paulo Shanghai Singapore Taipei Tokyo Toronto Warsaw

with associated companies in Berlin Ibadan

Oxford is a trade mark of Oxford University Press

First published 2001
This impression (lowest digit)
1 3 5 7 9 10 8 6 4 2

Published in the United States
By Oxford University Press Inc., New York

© Asian Development Bank 2001

All rights reserved. No part of this publication may be reproduced,
stored in a retrieval system, or transmitted, in any form or by any means,
without the prior permission in writing of the Asian Development Bank.

This book was prepared by the staff of the Asian Development Bank,
and the analyses and assessments in this volume do not
necessarily reflect the views of the ADB's Board of Directors
or the governments they represent. The Asian Development Bank
does not guarantee the accuracy of the data included in this publication
and accepts no responsibility whatsoever for any consequence for their use.
The term "country" does not imply any judgement by the Asian Development
Bank as to the legal or other status of any territorial entity.

This book is sold subject to the condition that it shall not, by way of trade or otherwise, be lent,
resold, hired out or otherwise circulated without the publisher's prior consent in any form of
binding or cover other than that in which it is published and without a similar condition
including this condition being imposed on the subsequent purchaser.

Published for the Asian Development Bank by
Oxford University Press

British Library Cataloguing in Publication Data
available

Library of Congress Cataloging-in-Publication Data
available

ISBN 019-592456-8 (Paperback)
ISBN 019-592455-X (Hardback)

Printed in Hong Kong

Published by Oxford University Press (China) Ltd.
18th Floor Warwick House East, Taikoo Place, 979 King's Road, Quarry Bay
Hong Kong

TABLE OF CONTENTS

THE EVOLVING ROLES OF THE STATE, PRIVATE, AND LOCAL ACTORS IN RURAL ASIA

Foreword	....	ix
Preface	....	xiii
Chapter I	**The Evolving Paradigms and Patterns of Rural Development** .... *By Frederick Roche and Ammar Siamwalla*	1

Development Issues and Trends Underlying
   the Study   1
        Agriculture and Food Supply   4
        Rural Nonfarm Growth   9
        The Macro and Global Environment   10
        Demographic, Social, and Political
        Developments   15
The Asian Financial and Economic Crisis   16
Reader's Guide   19

Chapter II	**Roles and Actors in the Provision of Rural Goods and Services** .... *By Ammar Siamwalla*	23

Types of Collective Action: Demand-Side Roles   24
        Goods and Services and their
        Characteristics   24
        Macroeconomic Stability   27

Poverty Reduction and Social Justice	27
Rules and Property Rights	28
Actors: The Supply Side of Collective Action	36
Central Government	36
Local Governments	53
Nongovernment Organizations	60
For-Profit Private Sector	64
Multilateral Lending Agencies	67
Interactions between Actors and Roles	70
Comparative Advantage	70
Coproduction	72
Social Capital	73
Governance	78
Conclusions	80

Chapter III Devolution and Decentralization   83
    By Colin MacAndrews, Alex Brillantes, and Ammar Siamwalla

Introduction: Why Devolve?	83
Country Experiences	87
Indonesia	87
The Philippines	102
The PRC	114
Lessons Learned	119

Chapter IV   The Changing Character of Technology and its Impact on Research and Extension   123
    By Ammar Siamwalla

Patterns and Trends in Technology Development	123
A Typology of Factors that Shape Agricultural Technology	124
Genetic Improvement before Biotechnology	126
Biotechnology	134
Intellectual-Property Protection	143

	Research to Improve Resource Management	158
	Mechanization	167
	Who Will Undertake and Who Will Pay for the Research?	168
Extension		173
	Traditional Extension	173
	Private Contract Farming as a Means of Extension	175
	The Role of NGOs in Extension	177
	Devolution of Extension Services: a Wave of the Future?	178
Conclusions		180

Chapter V   Irrigation Management Under Resource Scarcity 183
By Ammar Siamwalla and Frederick Roche

Introduction	183
The Landscapes of Irrigation Management	185
Upper Basin and Small Floodplain Irrigation	186
Large Floodplains	192
Basin-wide Considerations	198
Supply Augmentation	200
Administered Rationing of Supply Among Water Users	201
Demand Management Through Pricing Mechanisms	203
Upper Watershed Management and Common Property Rights	206
Donor Roles: Doing More by Doing Less?	207
Summing Up	209

Chapter VI The Political Economy of Food grain and Fertilizer Distribution 213
By Ammar Siamwalla and Andrew MacIntyre

Introduction: Why Are Foodgrains Special?	213
Asia's Models of Market Intervention and	
Food Price Stabilization in a Risky World	215
Intervention in Foodgrain Markets	
before 1970	215
Intervention in the Fertilizer Market	218
Stabilizing Output Prices: the Southeast	
Southeast Asian Style of Intervention	226
Rationing and Targeted Consumer	
Subsidy: The South Asian Model	234
Assessment of the State Roles	239
The Politics of Agricultural Policy Making	243
The Importance of Institutions and Political	
Dynamics	243
Thailand	247
Malaysia	254
Indonesia	261
Political Institutions and Agricultural	
Policy: Lessons for Policy Analysts	268

Chapter VII Rural Human Capital 271
By Frederick Roche, Colin MacAndrews, and Somsak Chunharas

Rationale for State Intervention	271
Trends in Education and Health	275
The Provision of Education	278
Access	280
Effectiveness and Quality	282
Improving Access and Quality	284
Resource Allocation, Efficiency, and	
Mobilization	286

Education Management and Decentralization	294
Nonformal Education	296
The Provision of Health Services	296
Reform in Public-Sector Financing	299
Decentralization and Health	301
The Private Sector, NGOs, and Village Health Workers	302
Community Financing	305
Human Resource Leakage in Health Care	305
Health Research and the Distribution of Health Technology	307
Health Insurance	312
Promoting Good Health	313
Water Supply, Nutrition, and Child Development	314
Rural Water Supply and Sanitation	315
Nutrition and Early Child Development	318
Impacts of the Asian Economic Crisis	328
The Case of Indonesia	329
Evidence from Other Countries	333
Donor Roles in Human Capital Development	335
Summing Up	336
Appendix Table	340

Chapter VIII Conclusion 351
By Ammar Siamwalla and Frederick Roche

Responding to Historical Experience	351
New Actors in Old Roles	352
New Roles for an Old Actor	357
Fitting Actors Into Roles: A Guide for the Policy Analyst	360

References 363

Indexes 389

Author Index	389
Subject Index	395

Foreword

An economic transformation has occurred in much of rural Asia since the Asian Development Bank (ADB) last undertook a survey of the region in 1976. The rural economy has become increasingly linked to a rapidly integrating world economy and rural society in Asia faces new opportunities and challenges.

The transformation of rural Asia has also been accompanied by some troubling developments. While large parts of the region have prospered, Asia remains home to the majority of the world's poor. Growing inequalities and rising expectations in many parts of rural Asia have increased the urgency of tackling the problems of rural poverty. The rapid exploitation of natural resources is threatening the sustainability of the drive for higher productivity and incomes in some parts of rural Asia and is, in general, affecting the quality of life in the entire region.

These developments have altered the concept of rural development to encompass concerns that go well beyond improvements in growth, income, and output. The concerns include an assessment of changes in the quality of life, broadly defined to include improvements in health and nutrition, education, environmentally safe living conditions, and reduction in gender and income inequalities. At the same time, the policy environment has changed dramatically. Thus, there has arisen a need to identify ways in which governments, the development community at large, and ADB in particular, can offer more effective financial and policy support for Asian rural development in the new century.

Therefore, ADB decided to undertake a study to examine the achievements and prospects of rural Asia and to provide a vision for the future of agriculture and rural development in Asia into the next century. The objective of the study was to identify, for ADB's developing member countries in Asia, policy and investment priorities that will promote sustainable development and improve economic and social conditions in the rural sector.

The study was designed as a team effort, using ADB staff and international experts under the guidance of an ADB interdepartmental steering committee. To address the diverse issues satisfactorily and in a comprehensive manner, five thematic subject areas were identified to provide the analytical and empirical background on which the study's recommendations would be based. Working groups comprising ADB staff were set up to define broadly the scope and coverage of each of the themes. The five working groups acted as counterparts to international experts recruited to prepare the background reports, providing guidance to the experts and reviewing their work to ensure high quality output.

A panel of external advisers from the international research community was constituted to review and comment on the approach and methodology of the study and the terms of reference for each of these background reports. The external advisers also reviewed the drafts of the reports. In addition, external reviewers, prominent members of academe and senior policymakers, were appointed to review each of the background reports and to provide expert guidance.

The preparation of the background reports included four workshops held at ADB's headquarters in Manila: an inception workshop in May 1998; two interim workshops, in November 1998 and January 1999, respectively, to review progress; and a final workshop in March 1999, at which the background reports were presented by their authors to a large group of participants comprising senior policymakers from ADB's developing member countries, international organizations, international and locally based nongovernment organizations, donor agencies, members of academe, and ADB staff.

The five background reports, of which this volume is one, have now been published by Oxford University Press. The titles and authors of the other volumes are

Transforming the Rural Asian Economy: The Unfinished Revolution
Mark. W. Rosegrant and Peter B. R. Hazell

The Growth and Sustainability of Agriculture in Asia
Mingsarn Santikarn Kaosa-ard and Benjavan Rerkasem with contributions by Shelley Grasty, Apichart Kaosa-ard, Sunil S. Pednekar, Kanok Rerkasem, and Paul Auger

Rural Financial Markets in Asia: Policies, Paradigms, and Performance
Richard L. Meyer and Geetha Nagarajan

The Quality of Life in Rural Asia
David Bloom, Patricia Craig, and Pia Malaney

The results and recommendations from the study were presented at a seminar during ADB's 32nd Annual Meeting in Manila. These have since been published by ADB as a book titled *Rural Asia: Beyond the Green Revolution*.

The findings from the study will provide a basis for future discussion between ADB and its developing member countries on ways to eradicate poverty and improve the quality of life in rural Asia. The volumes in this series should prove useful to all those concerned with improving the economic and social conditions of rural populations in Asia through sustainable development.

The analyses and assessments in this volume do not necessarily reflect the views of ADB's Board of Directors or the governments they represent. The term 'country' does not imply any judgement by ADB as to the legal or other status of any territorial entity.

Tadao Chino
President
Asian Development Bank

Preface

This volume reflects the work of numerous persons to whom due credit must be apportioned. First, I wish to thank my colleagues and immediate co-authors—Alex Brillantes, Somsak Chunharas, Colin MacAndrews, Andrew MacIntyre, and Frederick Roche. In addition to contributing directly to all chapters, Fred chaired the ADB Working Group that oversaw the preparation of this volume.

In addition, I would like to thank Pratima Dayal, Naved Hamid, Chongshan Liu, Arthur McIntosh, Patricia Moser, and Robert Siy, members of the ADB Working Group; Yoginder Alagh, Ha-Joon Chang, Merrill Williams, Justin Lin, Klaus Lampe and Obaidullah Khan, external reviewers; and participants in the March 1999 Workshop held at ADB. All made valuable suggestions to improve the contents of this volume. Robert Herdt, Paul Teng, and Benjavan Rerkasem kindly read Chapter IV and shared generously of their insights. I am also indebted to Dr. Benjavan for sharing the US patent document on basmati rice discussed in that chapter. Susan Horton and Jay Ross gave valuable comments on the discussion of malnutrition in Chapter VII. ADB's Charles Currin and Takako Yasukawa also provided detailed suggestions on Chapter VII, while Antonio Perez and Carl Amerling commented on Chapter IV. Finally, recent events in Indonesia have led to significant changes in the role of the National Logistics Agency (BULOG); I thank Steven Tabor and ADB's Mark Mitchell for updating our knowledge in this area for Chapter VI. Naturally, the authors must plead guilty to all remaining errors.

Elsewhere in ADB, Messrs. Yang Weimin, Akira Seki, Muhammad Tusneem, and Hans-Juergen Springer chaired the Steering Committee for the Rural Asia project. Their dedication and tireless guidance in this effort are greatly appreciated. Shahid Zahid and Bradford Philips, as day-to-day task managers of the project, displayed the great virtue of patience, even though they were at times sorely tested.

In Bangkok, thanks are due to Tiensawang Thamwanich and Jiraporn Plangpraphan for their able research assistance, and to Napaporn Mekdumrongruks for her logistical management. In Manila, excellent research and administrative support were provided by Elizabeth Tan, Laura Britt, and Lisbeth Perez. Sara Medina did a fine job as editor, hopefully integrating the style of six authors in relatively seamless fashion.

Ammar Siamwalla
December 1999

I The Evolving Paradigms and Patterns of Rural Development

> These are people who have lost their fear of the state. They saw from their experience... that the state has nothing to give them... they'll want to create something new, a new consciousness... I don't know if they can succeed, but it's a very interesting development.
>
> –Ahmet Altan, Turkish newspaper columnist, commenting on the earthquake victims of August 1999 (IHT 1999a).

DEVELOPMENT ISSUES AND TRENDS UNDERLYING THE STUDY

Most economic development literature and practice through the 1960s assumed as a matter of course that central governments would plan, initiate, motivate, and finance economic development. This approach doubtless had many origins, beginning with the Keynesian perspectives on the macroeconomic roles of government that underlay the creation of the Bretton Woods institutions and the reconstruction of post-World War II Europe. Intense international attention to the problems of underdevelopment ensued in the early 1950s, when Europe was on the road to recovery and the era of independence in the former European colonies was well under way in Asia and Africa. The operations of the World Bank and, subsequently, the regional development banks were based in part on the notions that the accumulation of capital, both

2 The Evolving Roles of the State, Private, and Local Actors

physical and human, was critical to economic growth; that this growth had to be balanced and therefore planned; and that only central governments were suited to lead the process. Hence the capital and technology transfers financed by international and bilateral development organizations have been and continue largely to be channeled through central governments.

When most developing countries emerged from their centralized colonial heritage, their existing private enterprises had neither the capital nor the motivation to accelerate the processes of investment and growth. What strength existed in public institutions—and in this there was considerable variation among countries, depending upon their colonial legacy—was concentrated at the Center. Moreover, outside the enclaves of modernized production and trade in the export-oriented sectors and the towns, economic activity focused on the subsistence production of food crops. Rural technology was stagnant. Thus, the initial development strategies focused on centrally planned, urban-based, industry-led, and often inward-looking capital accumulation and growth, upon which economic progress and "modernization" were expected to follow.[1]

At the outset, development economists saw the main role of the Government in the countryside as extractive, providing "wage goods" (i.e., cheap food), surplus labor, and taxes to support urban-based development. It was really only with the green revolution of the early 1970s that economists and planners came to recognize universally the contributions of a progressive agriculture sector to overall economic growth. Because much greater food security came within reach, the extractive approach to agriculture was arrested. Governments, as never before, lavished resources on the rural areas in the form of subsidies to fertilizer, irrigation, and other inputs. But even by then, rural development was largely equated with, or at least considered to be derived from, the growth of

---

[1] See Arndt (1987) for an excellent history of the evolving concepts of "development" up to the early 1980s.

agriculture. And the principal model of agricultural development, which the State was again deemed best suited to lead, consisted of spreading the adoption of a simple seed, chemical, and water technology, often augmented by directed, subsidized credit.

Dawning in the late 1960s and growing with increasing force to this day has been the cognizance that poverty has persisted in the developing countries.[2] Poverty reduction has become a major development objective in and of itself. It is understood now that poverty is largely rural and, indeed, became increasingly so during the decade before Asia's present financial and economic crisis, due to the much more rapid income growth in the urban areas. A second and related policy objective has evolved from the realization that increasing per capita incomes goes only part of the way toward achieving rural development. Improving the overall quality of life of rural Asians is a broader goal that encompasses health, education, gender equality, and political participation. The increasing concern with these issues, as well as with poverty reduction in general, has led to the recognition that development must be measured by social as well as economic indicators. Moreover, households, communities, and local administrations must play a far greater role in designing, implementing, and sustaining development interventions.

Thus, the world today has become quite a different place since ADB's last Rural Asia Study (ADB, 1977). Within the international community, views about the efficacy of past development approaches and the critical constraints to growth have evolved considerably during the past two decades as the result of profound, interrelated changes in agriculture and food supply, the broader rural economy, the macroeconomic and global environment, and society and politics. Developments

---

[2] In Arndt's account, a key event was the address by Robert McNamara, the World Bank's President, to his Board of Governors in late 1972 on the theme of "Social Equity and Economic Growth." This was followed by great attention to the possibilities for "redistribution with growth," in which literature the book by Chenery et al. (1974) was among the most influential.

in each of these areas have led to a new orthodoxy about the roles of the public, local, and private sectors (including not only for-profit private enterprises, but also civil society and nongovernment organizations) in rural development,[3] even while development best practices—the "how to do it"—are often still catching up with the orthodoxy.

This brief chapter serves two purposes. First, it describes the principal sources of rural dynamism in order to set the stage for the subsequent analyses of public-sector, local, and private-sector roles. Second, it provides a reader's guide to the coming chapters.

Agriculture and Food Supply

As the result of the green revolution, food production (especially cereals) is no longer as pressing a concern as it was two decades ago. Most of Asia, and particularly the largest countries, have dramatically improved their domestic food security as compared with the 1972–74 period of food and energy crises (Figure I.1). The main exceptions include the fastest-growing countries of East Asia (where agriculture's economic role is now minor), the post-Soviet economies of Central Asia (which were never a part of the green revolution), and much of South Asia outside India (where , in part because of rapid population increase, agricultural growth per capita has been relatively slow). Overall, because incomes have risen rapidly due to growth in the nonagricultural sectors, the argument for a focus on agriculture as the source of wage goods has weakened considerably. Household budget shares for food have declined and, with them, the sensitivity of food consumption to price movements.

Nonetheless, at a global level, foodgrain supplies must increase by an estimated 1.5 percent annually during the next 25 years to maintain aggregate food security, as compared to

---

[3] The rationale for a greatly changed view of the role of the State in development is most comprehensively presented in World Bank (1997).

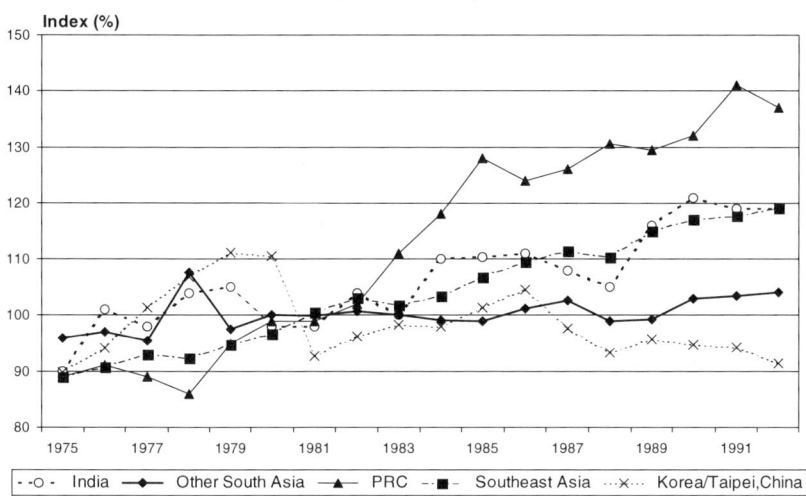

Figure I.1 Index of the Real Value of Agricultural Output Per Capita (1980/81=100)

[Line chart showing index (%) from 1975 to 1991 for India, Other South Asia, PRC, Southeast Asia, and Korea/Taipei,China]

Source: FAO (1995).

the growth rate of 3.0 percent achieved during the peak years of the green revolution (IFPRI 1995). In rapidly growing regions such as East and Southeast Asia, feedgrain demand will place additional pressure on the agriculture sector. But the 1970s model of agricultural growth—seed, chemicals, and water—is rapidly losing momentum. Rates of growth of foodgrain yields declined during the past decade, while the difference between experimental yields and yields on Asia's best farms has gradually narrowed (see the first volume in this Rural Asia study, Rosegrant and Hazell [1999])

It is generally accepted that the limits of agricultural extensification have largely been reached in Asia. The potential for intensive agricultural practices in suitable rainfed lands is limited. Further, some of Asia's best agricultural lands are being paved over for nonagricultural uses due to the steady encroachment of urban and industrial development. Emerging water scarcity is likely to significantly influence irrigated agriculture, by far the largest (although by no means the least efficient) user of water. As detailed in Volume 2 of this Rural Asia Study (Mingsarn and Benjavan [1999]), most of Asia's forests and watersheds are degraded, while the region's coastal and marine fisheries have been substantially depleted.

There had been, at least until the economic crisis beginning in 1997, an unprecedented period of income growth and urbanization, particularly in East and Southeast Asia. Through the expression of consumer preferences, an even more rapid change in the relative market demands for staple and nonstaple foods occurred. The production of income-elastic noncereal commodities—e.g., horticulture and poultry—responded rapidly in the faster-growing countries. But while national and international public agencies led the big push for technological change in cereal production, technological change and growth in the production of most other commodities has usually been led by the market and the private sector.

Beyond the changes within the agriculture sector, there has been a continuing secular decline in agriculture's terms of trade with the nonagricultural sectors, as well as in agriculture's shares of GDP and employment; the decline in the latter has been much slower than that in the former. Along with stagnating technology, declining rates of growth in yields, and declining terms of trade, the rate of growth in agricultural labor productivity has also tended to decline. In countries that enjoyed high rates of growth propelled by exports of manufactured goods, the previously tight link between food adequacy and domestic agricultural production has loosened considerably. Because they enjoy high export earnings, these countries can comfortably afford to meet any food shortfall by means of imports. Despite a possible interlude due to the Asian economic crisis (see below), agriculture will continue to decline in relative economic importance, but the sector must also continue to provide livelihoods and assure food security and is central to concerns about poverty and natural resource management. Agriculture's strategic role will be most prominent in Asia's low-income, slower-growing countries.

Poverty has persisted among resource-poor regions and socioeconomic groups. The green revolution and many of the subsequent, market-induced sources of agricultural growth largely bypassed Asia's rainfed agriculture. The principal exception has been in those upland areas that, because of temperature, soils, and proximity to markets, are suited to horticulture. But where this has occurred, it has almost invariably been a spontaneous, market-led phenomenon. Estate crops such as oil palm have also done well, again largely because of private-sector investment, complemented in some countries by public-sector research.

For a variety of reasons, the development resources channeled traditionally to agriculture through the public sector have become increasingly scarce, particularly for irrigation, which formerly accounted for the lion's share of State capital expenditure in agriculture (see the review in Von Braun et al. [1993]). National and international budgets for agriculture are now much more seriously constrained (Figure I.2). The financial subsidies lavished on fertilizers and irrigation during the green revolution and the costs of major public interventions in foodgrain markets will be more difficult to justify in the future.

The above developments have significant implications for Asia's agriculture-sector strategies and programs. Given the finite base of land and other natural resources, technological change and improved productivity have become the cornerstones of agricultural growth. The green revolution has run its course, both as a technology to be diffused and as a model of State-led development. With public resources becoming scarcer, private actors, both local and international, must increasingly finance research and investment in agriculture. Indeed, the development of the newest and most promising agricultural technologies—hybrid seed and biotechnology applications—is even now being driven by the private sector. In the United States, annual private-sector spending for agricultural research and development grew from $177 million in 1960 to more than $3.3 *billion* in 1992 (James 1997a). Much of the increase has been concentrated in developing crop varieties and other inputs associated with biotechnology. The level of private investment in the U.S. now dwarfs the total operational budget—about $325 million in 1997—for all institutes of the Consultative Group for International Agricultural Research.

Thus, the State will need to reconsider its priorities and comparative advantages in the agriculture sector. First and

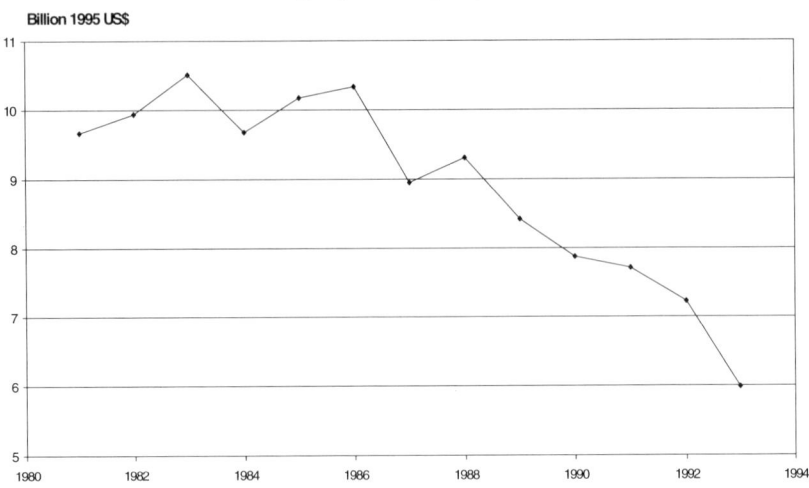

8 The Evolving Roles of the State, Private, and Local Actors

Figure I.2 Real External Assistance to Developing Country Agriculture

Source: FAO (1995).

foremost, it must finally be acknowledged that agriculture, unlike other economic sectors, is fundamentally unyielding to direct State planning and control. Agricultural production is inherently risky, while the dispersed nature of rural communities greatly complicates any attempts at centralized control. This is in stark contrast to other sectors of the economy, where a few key decision makers, often in State-owned enterprises, are responsible for the level of output and, as a result, simple administrative instructions are sufficient to implement the State's development plans and policies. Unlike other sectors of the economy, the patterns and growth of agriculture are determined not by fiat, but more indirectly by the *incentives* that motivate farmers, communities, and other private actors through the economic, legal, and institutional environment.

During the coming decades, the State's new challenges in agriculture are likely to be threefold:

- Creating an appropriate incentive and regulatory structure to encourage private-sector investment and

sustainable, market-led growth. Concerns about the environment and sustainability have led, on the one hand, to much greater attention to community roles in the management of natural resources. On the other hand, the incentives and externalities associated with common-property resources such as water and forests are likely to require new or enhanced State roles in regulating property rights and resolving intersectoral conflicts over water allocation. The emergence of private actors in agricultural research and technology development may force the State to establish more effective legal and regulatory frameworks, ranging from intellectual property protection to biosafety regulations.
- Decentralizing public research and extension systems so that they focus on technologies suited to the location-specific agroecological conditions and resource constraints of both irrigated and nonirrigated areas.
- Focusing direct public interventions increasingly on the bypassed regions and commodities that are of little interest to the private sector.

Rural Nonfarm Growth

The green revolution, growing rural incomes, and urban-industrial growth linkages have engendered rural dynamism through the expansion of rural nonfarm production. This has mostly comprised nontradables produced by households and microenterprises (e.g., food processing, housing, retail trade, and services). However, in a few East Asian countries—most notably Taipei,China; the Republic of Korea; Japan; and the People's Republic of China (PRC)—rural industrialization has extended to larger-scale, often export-oriented production of goods such as textiles and metal products.

The central feature of Asia's rural nonfarm growth is that it has been led almost entirely by the market and the private sector. State efforts to promote rural industrialization directly have largely failed (the PRC's township and village enterprises are the primary exception; see Chapter II), despite the appeal of the arguments for enhancing efficient employment creation, alleviating rural poverty, reducing rural-to-urban migration, and containing the external costs of excessive urbanization. Rural industrialization has been most successful in countries possessing the requisite managerial and labor skills, ready markets for inputs and outputs (including financing), and good infrastructure, particularly as regards transport costs (Otsuka 1998). The State's provision of infrastructure—roads, power, and telecommunications—has obviously facilitated this component of rural dynamism. More broadly, rural nonfarm growth has been most rapid in countries possessing a vibrant agriculture sector.

Providing infrastructure is likely to remain the State's major role in facilitating future rural growth in both nonfarm and farm activities. An issue for the future will be the scope for decentralizing and possibly privatizing the provision and management of rural infrastructure, as has occurred in urban areas. Also of major importance is the State's role in providing the enabling legal, policy, and regulatory environments for the growth of private commercial banking in the rural sector (see Volume 3 of this Rural Asia study, Meyer and Nagarajan [1999]). Rural education—also seen heretofore mainly as a State responsibility—is of critical importance if the transition is to be made from simple village technologies to more sophisticated nonfarm activities having higher value added. However, expanded education may encourage an even greater exodus to urban areas unless it is accompanied by other measures that foster rural industry. Besides physical infrastructure, a supportive policy and legal framework must exist in the areas of business licensing, taxation, rural finance (including property rights that determine small enterprises' access to loans), and relevant labor regulations (Islam 1997).

The Macro and Global Environment

A fundamental role of the State has been, and will continue to be, the provision of basic macroeconomic stability. Until very recently, macroeconomic policies were generally believed to be sound in Asia's more mature market economies, as evidenced by the fundamentals of prudent monetary and fiscal policy and sound exchange rates. In the most rapidly growing economies, two decades of sustained growth lent credence to the adage that "if it ain't broke, don't fix it." Now, however, the Asian financial and economic crisis has prompted a rethinking of the State's roles in managing capital and financial markets, in providing the so-called "social safety net," and, more fundamentally, in providing "good governance."

The 1980s saw the rise of Reaganomics, Thatcherism, and the gospel of "the magic of the marketplace." With considerable financial and intellectual support from the international community, there has been in Asia an almost universal liberalization of markets, reduction of barriers to foreign investment and capital flows, and movement to privatize State-owned enterprises. Private financial flows to ADB's developing member countries have, since the early 1990s, come to dwarf the official flows provided by multilateral and bilateral agencies (Figure I.3). With the sole exception of the Korean Democratic People's Republic, all of Asia's centrally planned economies have undergone far-reaching, but as yet incomplete, programs of privatization and market-oriented reform. During the medium term and beyond, the trend toward declining direct State economic interventions is expected to continue throughout most of Asia.

This decline can be seen in the changing levels and composition of central government expenditure. Although it is difficult to assemble consistent time series for all of Asia, central government expenditure has certainly declined as a percentage of GDP in many, if not most, countries during the last decade. The decline has been most pronounced in the transitional economies of Central and Southeast Asia, remains more gradual in South and Southeast Asia from the 1980s onward, and seems to have begun in the high-income economies of East Asia only in the early 1990s (Figure I.4). The decline reflects, *inter alia*, the effects of growing private-sector roles in previously State-dominated sectors, the difficulties central governments face in raising revenues, and and the trend toward more decentralized revenue generation and expenditure.

12   The Evolving Roles of the State, Private, and Local Actors

Figure I.3. Real Net External Capital Flows to ADB Developing Member Countries

• Official Flows from all Sources   • Net Private Flows from all Sources   — Total

Source: ADB (various years). *Key Indicators of Developing Asian and Pacific Countries.*

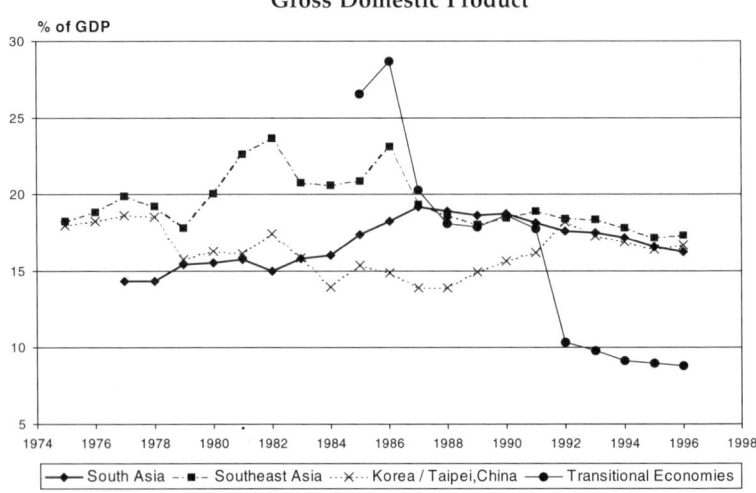

Figure I.4. Central Government Expenditure as a Share of Gross Domestic Product

—◆— South Asia   --■-- Southeast Asia   ⋯×⋯ Korea / Taipei,China   —●— Transitional Economies

Notes: South Asia includes Bangladesh, India, Nepal, Pakistan, and Sri Lanka. Southeast Asia includes Indonesia, Malaysia, the Philippines, and Thailand. Transitional economies include PRC, Kazakhstan, Mongolia, and Viet Nam. Grouped countries are weighted by GDP.
Sources: data compiled from (all various years) ADB Statistical Database System, ADB Key Indicators of Developing Asian and Pacific Countries; and IMF, Government Finance Statistics Yearbook.

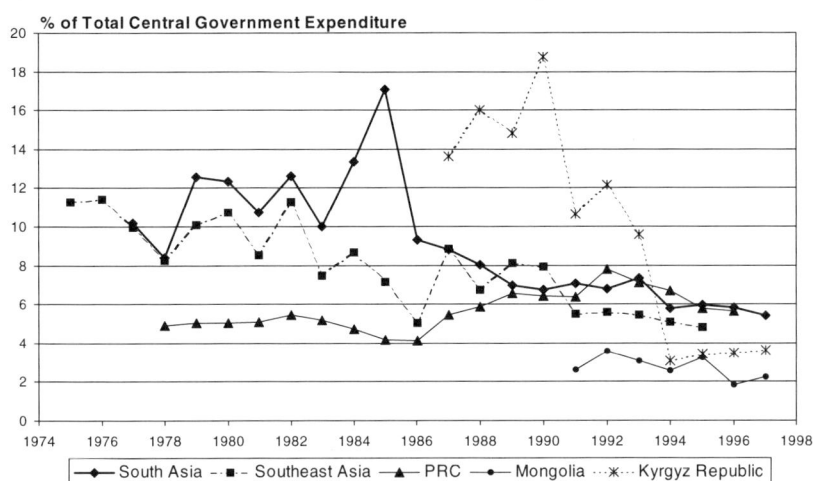

The Evolving Paradigms and Patterns of Rural Development 13

Figure I.5. Central Government Expenditure on Agriculture as a Share of Total Government Expenditure

Notes: South Asia includes Bangladesh, Nepal, and Sri Lanka. Southeast Asia includes Indonesia, Malaysia, and the Philippines. Grouped countries are weighted by GDP.
Source: IMF (various years). *Government Finance Statistics Yearbook*.

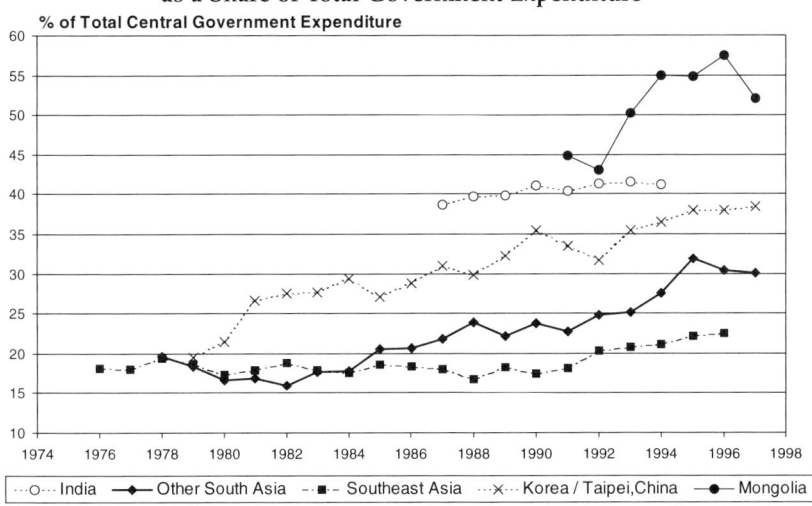

Figure I.6. Central Government Expenditure on Social Services as a Share of Total Government Expenditure

Notes: Social services include education, health, housing, social security, and welfare. Data for Indonesia and Sri Lanka exclude housing. Other South Asia includes Bangladesh, Nepal, and Sri Lanka. Southeast Asia includes Indonesia, Malaysia, and the Philippines. Grouped countries are weighted by GDP.
Source: IMF (various years). *Government Finance Statistics Yearbook*.

Aside from the possibilities for profitable State-owned enterprises, government revenue-generating capacity in Asia has been, and for the foreseeable future will remain, constrained by the capacity to tax and borrow (see Chapter II). In any event, it is not possible for the State to satisfy all competing demands, even in the wealthiest and best-administered societies. Hence, this volume focuses on the issue of how to best allocate society's scarce resources among sectors and actors for the betterment of rural Asia.

By sector, the share of agriculture in central government expenditure has often declined, to be replaced in part by larger expenditure shares for social services such as education, health, housing, and the social safety net (Figures I.5 and I.6). In many countries, the status of agriculture on the totem pole of State development priorities has dropped significantly during the last decade. At the same time, the urban areas have captured a disproportionate share of social expenditures.

In the transition economies of Southeast Asia (the Lao People's Democratic Republic [PDR] and Viet Nam) and, more recently, in Mongolia and Central Asia, the separation from the life-support systems of the former Soviet Union led to major macroeconomic disequilibrium, hyperinflation, and the sharp erosion of purchasing power and employment. The PRC, fortunately, avoided this adjustment. In the PRC and Viet Nam, the relatively brief interlude of central planning and the persistence of the age-old tradition of family farming allowed agriculture to respond rapidly once most farm decision making was returned to the farmer and market incentives were improved. In Mongolia and much of Central Asia, however, agriculture's response has been much slower. State directives originally developed much of the agriculture on large-scale collective farms, often in agroecological conditions unlikely to permit sustainable farming in a market economy. The former large-scale farms have so far proven unprofitable, despite their privatization and the liberalization of markets.

Globally, and most particularly within Asia's fastest-growing economies, there has been rapid growth in international trade as a share of GDP, with manufactured and services exports growing rapidly as a share of total trade. In the future, the World Trade Organization, which will implement the General Agreement on Tariffs and Trade, holds promise of further liberalization of trade that will encourage growth through specialization by comparative advantage within participating countries. Within Asia, promoting such growth has been one of the main motivations for the creation of regional agreements under the auspices of the Association of Southeast Asian Nations and the Asia Pacific Economic Cooperation forum. The potential downside of the growth of trade as a factor in GDP is increasing economic interdependence among countries and regions. Trade links are often cited as one of the sources of "contagion" of the Asian financial and economic crisis.

World markets are increasingly global. At its "shallow" level, globalization entails the liberalization and eventual elimination of trade barriers. At its more profound, or "deep," level, globalization implies economic integration of investment and production across countries, which in turn requires accelerated liberalization and improved governance in areas such as competition policy; government procurement; tax and commercial laws; and environmental, labor, and product standards.

Demographic, Social and Political Developments

Rapid urbanization has been the central demographic feature of Asia during the past decade. Improved transportation and communications have fostered much greater rural labor mobility, especially among the educated young. Urbanized economic development is doubtless straining traditional community and family values and cohesiveness.

A second feature is that much of Asia has entered the final phase of the demographic transition: human fertility is gradually declining to match the decline in mortality that began during the 1960s. Across countries, the rate of fertility decline is positively correlated with the rates of economic growth, urbanization, and social development (as measured by infant mortality, education, and female labor-force participation). Nonetheless, because of the momentum of the young age distribution, Asia's population continues to grow rapidly; school leavers entering the labor force are the immediate economic and political concern.

Until the pause caused by the region's economic crisis, Asia's middle class had grown rapidly, albeit from a small initial base. Although largely urban, this growth has also occurred to a degree in Asia's more prosperous rural and periurban areas. Rising incomes and education levels and better health standards have improved the quality of Asia's human resources, but have also engendered rising aspirations and sociopolitical demands. More broadly, televisions, radios, and printed media now reach almost every village as the result of income growth and developments in communications technology. With the greater accessibility of international media, it is becoming harder for governments to keep secrets from their subjects.

As compared to the economic scene, change in Asia's political institutions has been less widespread, but where change has occurred, it has often been very significant. In East Asia and parts of Southeast Asia, democratic institutions and more competitive politics have attained seeming permanence. Rising aspirations have led to demand for greater "voice." The human rights movement, encouraged by international, bilateral, and nongovernmental organizations, has added to the impetus for greater openness and accountability and in some countries has contributed to grudging, but ultimately meaningful, political change.

Development—an inherently dynamic process—has engendered profound social changes that have necessitated and will continue to necessitate progressively increasing local participation. As centralism and autocracy decline, governments will perforce become more open and accountable.

THE ASIAN FINANCIAL AND ECONOMIC CRISIS

Almost completely unforeseen by economists, the Asian financial and economic crisis that began in 1997 has arrested growth in much of the region, with ripple effects that are still being felt worldwide. Depending upon the country, the downturn may have consumed between 20 percent and 30 percent of the GDP that would, at past growth rates, have otherwise accumulated in Asia's most rapidly growing economies. The social and political repercussions of the crisis—most prominent in Indonesia—have indeed been serious. The potential for instability was high, particularly insofar as the economic downturn reduced the incomes of significant numbers of people.

An optimistic prognosis underlies this discussion, however. The ripple effects of the crisis may be painful for the next two to three years, but Asia will recover fully. Future growth may be slower than that of the last decade. But if lessons about the causes of the crisis can be learned and incorporated into Asia's development strategies and policies, the future growth path should also be more stable and sustainable.

In the context of this volume's theme, several major implications of the crisis for Asia's rural areas can be identified.[4] First, one of the immediate impacts of the crisis has been a loss of employment in urban and periurban areas, forcing many workers to return to their rural villages. Thus, village economies are under greater pressure than ever to provide viable employment and incomes.

Second, the crisis has been accompanied by depreciated exchange rates that are likely to persist for some time. This has caused a fundamental shift of profitability in favor of tradables produced with few imported inputs; this in turn provides the opportunity for agriculture and other labor-intensive industries to contribute to labor absorption, economic recovery, and growth. The relative decline of agriculture's economic role could be slowed or even reversed during the medium term. To equate agriculture with salvation in any given country would probably be wrong, however, because the exchange-rate declines have occurred

---

[4] This listing is not meant to be exhaustive. Please refer to the companion volumes in this Rural Asia study for additional discussion.

broadly in the region and thus individual countries confront a common competitive environment.[5]

Third, national and international resources for agriculture and rural development, already on a downward trend, will be even more limited. Even if this were not the case, the traditional public-sector interventions in agriculture—research, extension, and irrigation—are of lengthy gestation and would be difficult to mobilize during the short run. Thus, the crisis underlines the conclusion that future growth in agriculture must increasingly be driven by the private sector. Public resources for social services have also been stretched thin by the crisis. Therefore, households, communities, civil society organizations, and the private sector may play an increasing role in the provision and financing of education, health care, and water supply and sanitation—all of which are essential for improving the quality of life in rural Asia. The challenge for Asia's governments will be to nurture and guide these processes.

Fourth, the crisis has eroded confidence in government and intensified attention to four principles that are now accepted—among many donors, at least—as building blocks of good governance: accountability, participation, predictability, and transparency (ADB 1995a). The Asian economic crisis has shown clearly that the loss of confidence and credibility can have an extremely rapid impact on capital flows and investment. Just as important, *loss of confidence* erodes the State's capacity to guide development, regardless of the State's potential *competence* to provide goods, services, and technologies. Transparency, accountability, and reliable application of laws and rules are all essential for confidence in government and to achieve this, participation is a prerequisite.

---

[5] Moreover, in analyzing the Thai situation, Ammar and Orapin (1998) note that adopting a recovery strategy based on a return to agrarian roots would be, in effect, to reject the urban-industrial growth path that had been so successful during the previous two decades. Instead, they argue that Thailand's response should involve a redoubled emphasis on education and human resource development so that the recovery and return to growth are placed on a more secure footing.

In conclusion, there is now a window of opportunity for the traditional "lead actors" in rural development—central governments and, prominent in the background, the donor community—to reconsider their roles in the context of the causes and consequences of the Asian crisis. This makes the present volume timely and, we hope, useful and relevant.

READER'S GUIDE

The reader should recognize at the outset what this book is and what it is not. Many of its themes fall under the general rubric of participation, whether it is by the private sector, local communities, civil society, or the economically and socially disadvantaged. It is hoped that it will provide a reasonably comprehensive review of current thinking in the development profession about selected problems related to participation in Asian rural development. But there is no pretense at providing a blueprint for the solutions. In part, this is because the paradigms and practices of development have evolved considerably during the past decade, so that the targets being aimed at have always been in motion. More important, to have blueprints and predetermined solutions is incompatible with the very idea of participation! The search for practical approaches to eliciting participation is greatly complicated by the diversity in Asian history, cultures, and institutions: one size *does not* fit all, in stark contrast to what the green revolution provided. At the same time, many principles of rural development have endured since ADB's last Rural Asia study; some of these are highlighted by the quotations that begin many of the following chapters.

The volume is written from a variety of disciplinary standpoints. Overall, the thrust—somewhat in contrast to the intentionally provocative quote that opens this chapter—is that the State will, for the foreseeable future, retain many of its lead roles in rural development. Concurrently, the State must also develop new roles to both encourage and regulate the emerging private sector, to define and enforce property rights, and to nurture the participation and initiative of local communities and civil society. The trial-and-error evolution of these new roles will doubtless require reforms of public administration and governance, which in turn will constitute one of the main development challenges during the coming decades.

Chapter II begins with an economic taxonomy of the goods and services provided or produced by the public, local, and private sectors, including the provision of largely intangible regulatory and legal frameworks governing rural economic activity. Poverty alleviation and environmental preservation are discussed as social objectives that justify public intervention in otherwise private markets. Attention then turns to a taxonomy of the various institutions or "actors" in rural development, ranging from national political bodies down to nongovernment and community-based organizations. The roles that these actors play, the incentives that motivate them, and the constraints that they face are analyzed. Finally, the principles whereby actors acquire their roles are outlined.

Chapter III investigates the devolution and decentralization of public administration. The forces precipitating decentralization are examined, including the growing social and political demands for local control and autonomy and the roles played by national governments, the international community, and nongovernment or civil-society organizations. The processes and experiences of decentralizing public administration are then examined in three countries: Indonesia, the Philippines, and the PRC. As should be expected, decentralization processes have taken many forms in these and other countries, as a result of their highly varied social and physical geography, resource endowments, and political environments, to name just a few distinguishing characteristics. Nonetheless, the chapter concludes by synthesizing the political, social, financial, and institutional prerequisites for successful decentralization in the future.

The next four chapters deal in detail with the provision of four types of rural goods and services: agricultural research and extension (Chapter IV); water and irrigation (Chapter V); the marketing and storage of rice and fertilizer (Chapter VI); and education and health as the two key components of rural human capital (Chapter VII). These specific goods and services have been chosen for two main reasons. First, they were instrumental to the agricultural growth and the improvement in quality of life that have occurred in Asia over the last two decades. Second, they lend themselves to a variety of alternative provision systems involving the State, local governments, rural communities and community organizations, and the for-profit private sector.

The objective of these case studies is to analyze how resource scarcities, market forces, and institutional dynamics are transforming public-sector, local and private-sector roles in financing and provision. In the case of rice marketing, Chapter VI, for example, analyzes in detail the political economy of rice-price stabilization, illustrating how the political benefits and the structure of political power are of equal or greater importance than economic considerations in the policy-making process. In general, the studies take the perspective that, from the standpoint of the efficiency and quality of the goods and services, rural productive activities should be privatized and localized wherever possible. A specific goal of the case studies is therefore to assess what the residual roles of the State will be in creating and sustaining an appropriate enabling environment that is consistent with the objectives of efficient growth, equity, and environmental sustainability.

Land constitutes a fifth "good" that is central to agriculture and to rural welfare more generally. Chapter II discusses land in the context of property rights and the incentives of alternative land-tenure arrangements for productivity and sustainability. In addition to the *incentive* issue associated with land, there is the *equity* issue of land as the major determinant of rural income distribution. The equity issue prompted land reform efforts in a number of Asian countries from the 1950s to the early 1980s, including the PRC, Viet Nam, the Philippines, and the states of Kerala and West Bengal in India. The equity and efficiency effects of land ownership and tenure received considerable attention in the previous Rural Asia study (ADB 1977 and appendices). Since the 1980s, however, the political impetus for land reform has largely waned. In this paper, therefore, the incentive issue is the focus in Chapter II.[6]

Rural industry is not examined here, since this has been led almost entirely by the private sector. Rural roads, energy, and telecommunications are also instrumental to Asian rural development, but the State will remain the dominant actor in both the provision and maintenance of such infrastructure for the foreseeable future. However, there is, as noted above, possible scope for private-sector provision of rural infrastructure. In addition, rural communities already play a significant role in the maintenance of village roads. Finally, this volume does not question the primacy of the State in areas such as disaster prevention and management of national defense, although community participation is inherent in both.

Chapter VIII briefly summarizes the study's conclusions and recommendations, drawing primarily from the case-study findings to assess what might be done to improve future rural development outcomes. However, it is stressed that sweeping recommendations are inappropriate, due to the wide variability in resources and institutions among ADB's developing member countries.

---

[6] Readers interested in a relatively recent assessment of land reform in a variety of developing countries are referred to El-Ghonemy (1990).

II Roles and Actors in the Provision of Rural Goods and Services

When I asked them about local issues they wished the new member of Parliament to resolve, they shook their heads: the best-dressed person among them... said that there was no problem at all... It was only when my exasperated driver introduced me as a journalist and urged them to tell me the truth that the old man began to speak.

The others prompted him, whisperingly at first, and then everyone spoke at once. The village was privileged in having a tube-well for drinking water, but, they said, the nearest hospital was nine miles away, and though the government has installed an electric line, there had never been any current. The biggest problem related to the government primary school: it had been around for several years, but the teacher came only once a week from Allahabad and even then only for a couple of hours. There was no way of knowing when he would come and so the boys and girls dressed each morning for school and spend most days waiting for the teacher outside locked doors. That wasn't all: the teacher swallowed all the rice the government sent for the students each year. He had also carved out for himself personal profits from the building of the new one-room school for girls...

– Pankaj Mishra (1999)

Chapter I provides the context of development thinking and experience in Asia during the past two decades. For most of that period, the very words "policies" and "policy making" were associated with acts of the central Government. During the last decade, however, the automatic assumption that the central Government is the fount of all policies and policy making has been steadily undermined. More actors are making themselves heard and are more active in shaping the policies of Asian societies. This chapter examines these newly vocal actors.

But before these new actors are listed, it is important to define the various types of collective action required for rural development. Throughout this volume, "collective action" is essentially an antonym for private action. It is action that has to be undertaken either by the State or by a multiplicity of individuals. The reasons prompting such action are referred to as the demand side of collective action. Who undertakes the action, and, in the case of non-State actors, what form their association takes, constitutes the supply side. The types of collective action are the roles that the actors are expected to play. Choosing to describe the roles first reflects the thesis that these are the fundamental needs of any society, while the actors are merely instruments by which the needs are to be met. The means by which one or more of the actors and one or more of the roles become synthesized is discussed in the later sections of the chapter.

TYPES OF COLLECTIVE ACTION: DEMAND-SIDE ROLES

Goods and Services and their Characteristics

For a rural economy to function and develop there must be goods and services. Rural households require goods and services of various kinds. As a first step, they can be divided into three basic categories.

- PUBLIC GOODS AND SERVICES. Public goods partake of two major characteristics: *nonrivalry* (what one person

consumes does not subtract from what another person has available to consume) and *nonexcludability* (if the goods have been produced, it is impossible to prevent people from consuming them). The classic example of a pure public good is national defense.
- LOCAL PUBLIC GOODS. For rural areas, which are by definition spread out geographically, most public goods, i.e., those characterized by nonrivalry and nonexcludability, have an impact only over limited geographical distances and therefore over a much smaller subset of people than the whole nation. An example of local public goods is sanitation services that limit the spread of infectious diseases. These types of goods will feature importantly in the discussion below.
- PRIVATE GOODS AND SERVICES. These are the conventional goods and services, characterized by rivalry and excludability, that are normally bought and sold in various markets.

These categories can seldom be neatly and sharply distinguished. Many public goods have the characteristics of private goods and vice versa. Water, for example, would appear to be a pure private good: the consumption of water by the crop in a farmer's field would appear to preclude other individuals' using it. But because of the way irrigation systems are constructed in Asia, when a farmer irrigates his fields, he cannot prevent other farmers from obtaining some water as well. Similarly, when he sprays his crops with insecticides, normally considered a private good, the total number of insects may decline and neighboring farms may benefit. Such mutual interactions in the consumption of goods, which are not purely nonrivalrous or nonexcludable, will be termed *externalities*. Negative externalities may also occur; e.g., the insecticide may drive the insects from one farm to the next.

Apart from those three categories of goods and services, there are two more important groups of goods and services. These are (nonexhaustive) subcategories of private goods:

- MERIT GOODS. A household's consumption—its effective demand—of any good is limited by the size of its income. But society may consider that while some households do not have enough income to acquire adequate levels of certain significant goods, consumption of these goods is too important to be limited by purchasing power. Thus, society may deem that a household must have access to or is entitled to a minimum level of, say, food, health care, housing, or education, regardless of income. If a household's effective demand is inadequate for this minimum, then society may have to find other means to ensure that the household can acquire it.
- GOODS AND SERVICES WHERE THE BUYERS AND SELLERS HAVE ASYMMETRIC INFORMATION. In transactions involving these private goods, the buyer has an informational advantage over the seller about his demand, or the seller about his product or service. Such asymmetric information makes it difficult for a transaction, certainly an arm's-length transaction, to develop naturally. Even though both parties might gain from the transaction, something has to happen to force it to take place. A good example is health insurance. Most consumers would like to have health insurance. It is difficult for a private health-insurance market to develop, however, because if a policy is offered with specified payments, the provider will be flooded with buyers who are already prone to disease, while the healthier part of the population will stay out (a phenomenon known as adverse selection). Furthermore, once buyers have policies, they will not take sufficient care to limit their medical treatment, since they know that the insurer will pay for it (a situation called moral hazard). Without a forced pooling of risks, a competitive health insurance market is unlikely to emerge. The market for health insurance is discussed in Chapter VII. For now it should be noted that

several kinds of insurance would increase people's welfare, but asymmetric information makes it very difficult for suppliers of insurance to enter the market and be assured of a profit.

Quantitatively, more than three fifths of the resources of an economy are used to produce private goods and services. In most Asian countries this is taken care of by the market system. Important as they may be quantitatively, these goods and services will not be much discussed here, unless the State or the community becomes involved in their production or distribution, unless they are merit goods, or unless they involve some degree of asymmetric information.

Besides depending upon physical goods and services, rural Asia's development also has a number of more abstract foundations in which the State's role is, and will remain, paramount. These include macroeconomic stability, socioeconomic equity, and rules and property rights.

Macroeconomic Stability

Macroeconomic stability may appear at first to be removed from the problems of rural areas. However, since the agricultural sector produces mostly tradable goods, it is important that variations in the aggregate price level and real exchange rates be kept within bounds. Therefore there is a need for the macroeconomy to become and remain stabilized. While the efficacy with which the task is done is of the utmost importance to the rural population, there has been little question that the central Government and its various organs, including the central bank, should be performing this task. Discussion of the relative roles in macroeconomic management of various organs within the central Government is beyond the scope of the present volume.

Poverty Reduction and Social Justice

Most societies would like to prevent inequalities of income among their members from becoming too large and have built in mechanisms, both voluntary and involuntary, to transfer incomes to the disadvantaged. This again can be thought of as a form of public good, but for our purposes, it is best considered as a separate role to be filled. Intimately connected with the issue of poverty reduction is the provision of merit goods or the fulfillment of basic needs, for it is recognized that many households in rural Asia are unable to meet these basic needs because of poverty (Harberger 1984). The issue of basic needs will be returned to at various points in this volume, but not poverty reduction as a policy.

Poverty reduction is but one subcategory of broader concerns with "social justice" that provide the rationale for State intervention in otherwise private economic and social activities. Concerns with women's roles, disadvantaged or neglected social groups, involuntary human resettlement, and the effects of natural disasters also fall under this category. In this volume, such social concerns are dealt with primarily in the context of rural human capital in Chapter VII.

Rules and Property Rights

For a society to function effectively and to produce desirable outcomes, there is a need for rules to limit people's behavior in various ways. A country's legal system is one set of limiting rules. Others include the rules adopted by local communities about access to forest products or allocation of water.

Property rights are yet another kind of rules, which assign the rights of control over or access to something to an individual or a community. This has particular relevance for rural Asia and will therefore be subject to somewhat more detailed treatment. Three questions can be posed with respect to property rights: To whom are they assigned? Over what resources do the rights assign control? And who undertakes the task of assigning?

- TO WHOM ARE THE PROPERTY RIGHTS ASSIGNED? The most common kind of property rights in market economies is private property rights, which are assigned to individuals. At the other extreme there are State property rights. In between there are communal property rights, which are assigned to a defined set of individuals. Communal property rights must be distinguished from what is sometimes called common property or, as it is called in this volume, open-access resources. With communal property, the asset is assigned to a community whose membership is clearly defined, together with rules of entry and exit, e.g., through the sort of kinship and/or marriage rules that are much beloved of anthropologists. Among members of the community, access to the resource whose rights are defined will be according to rules set by the community. Open access, on the other hand, is the absence of any property rights; no one is prevented from having access to the resource. In many Asian countries water remains an open-access resource. Historically, when the population density was lower, land and the forests on it were also open-access resources.

  In most instances, private property holders have the freedom to alienate their property to someone else through sales or gifts. State property and communal property, on the other hand, cannot be alienated by individuals.
- OVER WHAT KINDS OF RESOURCES DO PROPERTY RIGHTS ASSIGN CONTROL? Most commonly, property rights are assigned to physical assets that can be made to yield income over an extended period. The assignments are rarely absolute but are hemmed in by restrictions or rules imposed by contract, custom, or law. Rules and regulations introduced by policies almost always restrict property rights in some respect. Outside these restrictions, the proprietor can do what he pleases. This power exerted by the owner of property is known

as residual control rights. It is a crucial element in the economic theory of property rights (Hart 1995) and clearly has important implications for the distribution of power. In the case of landed property, for instance, the landowner not only uses his rights to generate income for himself, but in many instances also acquires a great deal of power over the tenants or laborers who toil on his land, because his residual control rights allow him to eject them at will—unless of course there is a law that protects tenants' rights. Where the distribution of land is grossly unequal and the landowners have large estates, as is true particularly of the Philippines, this could be the basis of political power (Sidel 1994). Land tenure rights probably affect the lives of rural people more directly than any other form of property rights. In many parts of Asia, property rights in land that have legal clarity and are properly enforced are still rare, even in market economies (see Box II.1). Only in South Asia and the Philippines, and in the latter only in the older settled areas, are there clear legal bases of property rights in land, but even there colonial legacies have left structures of land ownership that are unequal. After a massive land reform under communist governments, transitional economies are now undergoing the process of reestablishing private property rights in land (see Box II.2).

Technically, property rights in land are among the easiest to establish. The problems of establishing clear property rights over water, however, are tougher by orders of magnitude than in the case of land. As the population increases, and with it the severity of conflicts over resources, there is the need for devolution of control over water from the State (see Chapter V). Asian governments will most likely have to grapple with the legal ramifications of this extremely difficult issue well into the 21st century; the discussion in Chapter V suggests merely the first few tentative steps that can be taken.

The extension of property rights to an intangible resource such as intellectual product is even more difficult, but here the problem goes beyond merely technical questions, although these are difficult enough. With property rights in land or water, the issue is driven by the national interest in having a good management system for these two crucial resources, which are almost always in one country's territory (although there are international problems with water in some river basins). With intellectual property rights, on the other hand, what a country does or does not provide in the way of protection has immediate international ramifications. The national interest in the provision of this form of protection can and does come into conflict with the demands of the international community—and within the international community, the developed countries are the noisiest advocates. Developing countries are being dragged into providing intellectual property rights protection in areas such as biotechnology, possibly well before it is in their national interest to do so and certainly before many of them have a good legal and social framework for making such protection useful (see Chapter IV).

- WHO ASSIGNS THE PROPERTY RIGHTS? Property rights, once assigned, must be followed by enforcement. Enforcement of property rights necessarily entails the exclusion of those not having the rights from having access to or using the property in question. Since the State has the monopoly of coercive power, and since coercive power is necessary for exclusion, the State ultimately has to be involved in the assignment of property rights. The growth of property rights thus has an intimate connection with the power and capability of the State. Thus, one author states flatly, "a theory of property rights cannot be complete without a theory of the state" (cited in Eggertsson 1990). True, the existence of the State is not necessary for some rudimentary

> **BOX II.1: The Ecology of Property Rights in Land in Thailand**
>
> For a perspective on the problem of property rights in land, it is necessary to look first at the peripheral part of Thailand, the hill country. There property rights in land are still designed for a land-extensive form of shifting agriculture known as slash-and-burn. This agricultural system is pervasive throughout the hills of Southeast Asia, stretching from Assam in India to parts of northern Viet Nam. In this system, property rights are vested in the community: an individual household can only choose a plot with the approval of the village council or headman; once it has cleared the land, it still possesses only temporary usufruct rights (Boserup 1965, Van Roy 1971, Keyes 1977). Among these communities the concept of "property rights" is somewhat loose; it survived as long as it was viable under the condition of low population density and as long as the central Government did not intrude into the arrangement---two not entirely unrelated events.
>
> In the rice-growing wetlands, private property rights had become the norm by the end of World War II. In the colonized Asian countries, the imperial power superimposed the Western concept of property rights on a myriad of practices that existed in the precolonial states, but independent Thailand also adopted the system of private property. It is interesting to note that in traditional Thai law, all land belongs to the King, but households can occupy the land to farm. Note the similarity to the communal concept among the hill tribes, where the headman (or council) assigns the land that each household can farm. This concept of land ownership arose
>
> (continued next page)

property rights to come into existence (Eggertsson 1990). In particular, the social arrangements concerning the use of land in areas with shifting cultivation preceded the arrival of the State (see Box II.1); these remain independent of, and sometimes even antagonistic to, the laws of the country. Similarly, rules concerning the allocation of water within an irrigation system are sometimes created and maintained by communities independent of the State.

Box II.1 (continued)

during a time when Thailand was an underpopulated country with surplus land.

With population increases accelerating after World War II, people began to move to upland areas and clear new land. Until about 1970, much of this pioneering occurred on good agricultural land that was under forest cover. Unfortunately for the farmers, the Thai Government never made up its mind as to what to do with these lands and began to issue various sorts of certificates of occupancy. By the mid-1980s, there were no fewer than ten different kinds of titles and certificates of occupancy issued by four separate government departments (Feder et al. 1988). Most of these titles cannot be used as collateral, as they do not permit the alienation of the property (a restriction designed to prevent moneylenders from taking over land). At that time, of the 24.7 million hectares of land occupied by private individuals, only 13.2 million had clear titles or certificates that could be used as collateral with banks. Of the remaining 11.5 million hectares, 6.2 million had some sort of certificate, but none that could be put up as collateral, while 5.3 million were held by squatters, who were occupying and no doubt farming "forest lands."

An analysis of the consequences of this messy situation done in the 1980s shows that, surprisingly, the main source of inefficiency was not insecurity of tenure. Rather, the main loss arose from the farmers' inability to put up land as collateral, thereby making it difficult for them to invest in land improvements (Feder et al. 1988).

Throughout this study ways and means are explored by which central governments can decentralize and privatize their activities. One way of evaluating the alternatives for reform is to look at them conventionally in terms of their impacts, the efficiencies of the various parties in performing the tasks currently done by governments, and the regulatory framework that is necessary to ensure the quality of the activities after the

(Text Continued on page 36)

BOX II.2: Reestablishing Private Property Rights in Transitional Economies: the PRC and Viet Nam

The establishment of property rights in the People's Republic of China (PRC) and Viet Nam followed slightly different paths. In 1978 in the PRC, the first step in what turned out to be a series of far-reaching reforms was the introduction of the household responsibility system. This reform effectively restored the family farm as the basic production unit in the PRC. It began with the production teams' making contracts with their member households for specific tasks. There were many forms of contracts (see Perkins and Yusuf [1984], but the most common was used to distribute the team's resources, particularly land, among households. Each household was assigned a share of the output quota, taxes, and other obligations of the team, which it had to meet. Use of variable inputs, such as seeds, fertilizers, and labor, was at the discretion of the participating households.

At the beginning, the reform did not have the full official blessing of the Center. In 1978, a few local authorities agreed to let some production teams engage in such contracts. When spectacular yield increases ensued, the central Government came around to accepting this practice, finally giving it the official stamp of approval in 1981. By 1983, 98 percent of the production teams had adopted the household responsibility system. This also contributed to the collapse of the commune system, which had outlived its economic function: in 1983, the township government was restored to take over administrative work and some economic functions from the commune, while the village committee replaced the production brigade.

A reason for the central Government's reluctance at the beginning, and its acceptance in the end, is the ambivalent nature of land ownership under the new system. Transfer of outright land ownership to individual households would have been (and

(continued next page)

Box II.2 (continued)

still is) deemed incompatible with socialist principles. Under the new system, land is still owned social by the village; the production teams merely contract with the households to have the latter operate on the land and produce the requisite quota.

Viet Nam began to decollectivize its agriculture in 1981, when the cooperative land was allocated to individual households. In 1988, land belonging to the cooperative was divided up among households in proportion to the size of their labor force. Each farm household was given a long-term lease of up to 15 years, with the sole obligation to pay taxes, which were and remain quite high relative to Viet Nam's Asian neighbors (approximately 10 percent of the gross output).

The 1988 reform still requires land use to be in conformity with land-use classifications; in particular, paddy land must be used to grow paddy rice. More importantly, the 1988 reform prohibited "sale, purchase, seizure and lease of land for rent." This portion was lifted, however, by the enactment of a land law on 1993 that allowed transfers, exchanges, leases, and mortgages subject to the approval of the People's Committees at the village and district levels.

The one point where Viet Nam was even more radical than its neighbors was in the allocation of forest lands. The condition for receiving forest land is that the household reforest it by private means within two or three years after the allotment. Whether the household can meet the condition is assessed by the cooperative. Once the village and district People's Committees approve the cooperative's decision, the household receives a 50-year lease on that forest land. It will than have to provide the cooperative a share of the timber harvested. For the trees that the household plants, it must give the cooperative 20 percent of the harvest; for the trees that were there prior to the lease, it must give 50 percent. Field visits indicate that the arrangement has apparently proved successful and land has been reforested (Hayami 1993).

reform. Although this will be the main approach adopted in this volume, another approach that will be occasionally touched upon is to look at the reform as a change in the system of property rights and to ask how to impose restrictions on property rights of the various firms and individuals so as to yield efficient outputs of the desired quality.

ACTORS: THE SUPPLY SIDE OF COLLECTIVE ACTION

Fulfilling the needs of societies as listed above can be thought of as roles that must be filled by certain actors. This section lists the candidates—people and institutions—that might fill the various roles. In playing those roles, each set of actors faces its own structure of incentives devised by society. These incentives are embodied in formal constitutions, rules, and regulations, or have influence informally through various forms of social conventions. The performance of the various actors within the constraints set by the rules is the first theme of this section.

Other than the constraints set by rules and conventions, actors are also constrained by their resources and where they procure them. In addition to the description of the structure of incentives, it is necessary to consider the *budget constraints* that actors have to work under, which are specific to each set of actors. This will be the second theme of this section.

Central Government

Governments in Asia come in many different forms, shaped by the history of their countries. Thus, we have countries that have market economies and countries whose economies are transitional but whose political systems remain dominated by communist parties. Among countries with market economies, there are those that have electoral processes with varying degrees of competitiveness. Some have a presidential system of government, with or without a prime minister, such as the Philippines, the Republic of Korea, and Taipei,China; others, like Thailand and Malaysia, have parliamentary systems. Analysis of these forms is complicated by the fact that for social reasons, there are governments of each type that are highly stable and others that are not. Some countries not only have unstable governments, they also change constitutions quite frequently.

It is not the intention of this chapter to present a compendium of the various forms of government. But all political systems have politicians and bureaucrats, who are clearly distinct from one another (except possibly in the transitional countries). Their relationships to each other and to those they rule significantly affect the policies and strategies that they formulate. It is worthwhile to examine the changes that have been taking place among these actors and relationships, despite the difficulties in covering a huge and highly amorphous mass of literature.

Politicians

Not only is Asia characterized by a diversity of political forms of government, but as pointed out above, the states also differ a great deal from one another in their informal structures. Furthermore, politics is intimately tied up with the question of leadership, so individual personalities also matter. Here again, Asian political leaders come in all shapes, sizes, and political orientations. It helps to divide Asian governments into two types, depending upon the degree of political competition. In the first, leadership is a function of an individual, a small group (junta), or a political elite; it suffers little or no constraint on the exercise of political power or the implementation of policies, either because of the outright authoritarian nature of the regime or because the main political party is so dominant that it wins every election. In the second type, there is strong electoral competition, so leaders are constrained by the need to win votes. This is not to say that in the first set of countries the leaders are free of constraints. They merely have more flexibility to change policies. In addition, the two types of leadership overlap in some areas and undergo similar political experiences, although usually for different reasons and with different outcomes.

The approach to tackling the mass of very diverse literature on the subject of Asian politicians is first to consider the case of politicians in countries where there is little electoral restraint on the exercise of political power. The focus here is the PRC, although its experience will be compared with that of other countries that have also experienced periods of minimal political competition. This will be followed by an examination of India as an example of the second, electorally competitive type of leadership. India is unique in that upon achieving independence, its duly elected Government enjoyed overwhelming electoral support and experienced little competition, but its electoral politics have become fiercer over the decades. Thus, India provides a longitudinal look at the changes that take place as the leadership's freedom to maneuver becomes increasingly circumscribed. As the description of the Indian evolution approaches the present, the Indian experience is compared with that of other countries that have had more competitive politics, mostly in recent times.

In the PRC, the Maoist revolution (together with the previous half-century of chaos, conflict, and foreign invasion) had destroyed almost the entire web of relationships that permeated Chinese rural society before 1949. Mao Tsetung and his colleagues, on assuming power, erected an entirely new set of social units, such as mutual aid teams, collectives, and communes. Further, and more importantly, people could not move or socialize across these "cells" on account of various restrictions on movements of people and on commerce, leading to what has been called "social cellularization" (Shue 1994). In agriculture, the old elite—the landlords—was eliminated as a class. The farms were collectivized and units much larger than households carried out production. All produce not consumed by the farms was sold to the State, thus cutting off commercial relations with other areas of the country. This was also true of social relations. All prerevolutionary linkages, such as lineage associations, temple associations, and traders, were swept away and replaced by mass organizations such as peasant associations, labor unions, and women's federations, all mediated by the party-State. In the terminology that is described a little further along, it can be said that the Communists erased the prerevolutionary social capital altogether.

Nonetheless, while formal civil organizations had little room to grow, rural people did have needs and demands. These were articulated, if not formally, then informally, giving rise to informal patron-client networks, an old social phenomenon reincarnated in the totally different social landscape created by communism. These networks became the essential interface that linked individuals to the State and party apparatus. (Huang 1998). A second informal phenomenon, much decried by the authorities but nonetheless pervasive throughout the PRC between 1949 and 1978, was the localism within the party and State apparatuses themselves. Local officials and local cadres had to interpret central policies and adapt them to local conditions. Given the PRC's vast size, these conditions were too diverse to be covered in detail by Beijing's directives. Consequently, the officials found room to yield more to the needs and particularities of the area in which they served, rather than to the literal dictates of the central authorities (Shue 1994; Huang 1998). Clearly, though, there were limits to what the local cadres could do, particularly while Mao held supreme power.

The extreme social cellularization of the Maoist period allowed the Communist Party (particularly its leader) to pursue its own agenda without the need to compromise with civil society. A key item in that agenda was the pursuit of national growth by means of forced-pace industrialization. The logic of that decision led ineluctably to a policy of keeping food prices low in order to accelerate the pace of industrialization, particularly in heavy industry. Food prices were kept low by two means, which had opposite effects on rural welfare. The first was by a policy of extracting the surplus from the agricultural sector by means of collectivization and forced procurement (Lin, Cai, and Li 1996). The second was by means of investments in rural infrastructure.

Unfortunately, however, most of the "financing" for these investments was forced from the rural population in the form of underpaid labor and artificially low levels of rural consumption. The rural population thus had inadequate incentives to increase agricultural production. When reforms were implemented that substantially reduced the penalty on higher productivity, the response was dramatic.

Every change in the policies of the Chinese Communist Party from 1949 onward, whether it was the land reform of the 1950s, the Great Leap Forward, or the Cultural Revolution, arose primarily as the result of struggles among its top leadership. Throughout the Maoist period, rural people paid a heavy price for these policies. (The Cultural Revolution of 1966–76, on the other hand, appeared to affect urban areas more severely than rural areas [Huang 1998].) However, the upheavals wrought by these twists and turns in policies undermined the capacity of the central party and government apparatuses, particularly in the area of economic planning (Shue 1994). Local and provincial officials were strengthened by the leadership struggles during the Cultural Revolution and thereafter, as different factions within the party tried to attract their support. Their strength was further reinforced as a result of the reforms introduced by Deng Xiaoping in the late 1970s, when regional officials became a major influence in the Central Committee (Shirk 1993). One consequence was that power began to be decentralized from the central Government in the late 1970s and early 1980s (see Chapter III).

While Deng's reforms, as with every policy change since the revolution, were initiated from the top, they were enthusiastically received in the countryside, which had had enough of the frequent upheavals wrought by the various Party campaigns. The new regime appeared to the rural population to give individual households considerable autonomy and therefore provided them with some buffer space against drastic changes dictated from the top. To be sure, rural people in the PRC, like those everywhere else, remained wary of directives from above. Despite the dispersal of decision making—as in the introduction of the household responsibility system, the key reform of the early Deng regime—the Center still retained through the Party apparatus considerable power to implement unpopular policies, e.g., the one-child policy (Huang 1998).

Forced-pace industrialization was not the monopoly of left-wing authoritarian regimes. The Republic of Korea under President Park Chung Hee, who ran the country between 1961 and 1979, started along a path that was to be phenomenally successful for the next three decades. During the first decade of his rule, he continued his predecessors' extractive policies toward agriculture, but began to reverse that policy in the early 1970s (Moon 1975). There was a similar switch in other authoritarian countries such as the Philippines under President Ferdinand Marcos (1966–1986) and Indonesia under President Suharto (1965–1998). The external factor that elicited these responses was the food crisis of 1972–74, during which the countries experienced both a drop in their domestic production and a sharp run-up in international cereal prices. Further, new technology in the form of the green revolution had become available and this opened up a new option for these regimes.

Aside from the need to provision the cities, which was a major factor leading to a turnaround in policies (see Chapter VI), there was a political side to this increased attention to the rural population. Though these regimes were thoroughly authoritarian, and though their support may have been based mainly on other sources such as the armed forces, such regimes had to garner support from the rural areas as well. This need arose because these regimes chose to organize elections at which voters were expected turn out and vote for the government's ticket.[1] Control over the countryside had to be exerted. State organs such as the police were by themselves inadequate for this purpose, since many of these countries, such as the Philippines and Thailand, were also subject to communist

---

[1] Why did these governments need the elections, since many of them could keep power easily enough without them? The need to have the "show" of elections was, and in many countries remains, useful to counter critics' accusations of dictatorship. Criticism came not only from domestic urban-based intellectuals and students, but also international public opinion, which found their repression abhorrent.

insurgency, which employed the Maoist technique of using the countryside to capture power.

A technique used by most of these regimes was to set about their own organization of the countryside. Thus, in the Republic of Korea President Park initiated the Semaul Undung, a self-help organization that was to serve as a vehicle for rural development programs. In the Philippines, President Marcos set up the Samahang Nayon, a pre-cooperative to which all would-be beneficiaries of land reform had to belong. The armed forces in Thailand organized the Village Scout Movement. A consistent theme in Indonesian President Suharto's rural policies was the support and attention lavished on the cooperatives.

All of these organizations and movements were supposed to subscribe to the ideology of self-help, but they were subverted by the need of the regimes to use them as vehicles of political support. And in their quest for this support, the regimes concentrated on the rural elite. Unlike the PRC Communists, who erased and then refashioned the preexisting social order to suit their purposes, these regimes accepted the existing social structure as the basis for these artificial organizations. The result of these exercises was the continued survival of vertical patron-client relationships, which were to prove an important tool during the succeeding democratic periods in these countries. This problem is discussed further below.

Interestingly, India, which along with Sri Lanka has enjoyed democratic politics longer than any other Asian nation, also underwent similar changes in its policies toward rural people. However, the political developments that led to the changes were far more complex than in the cases discussed above. The politics of India have several idiosyncrasies. The first results from its sheer size. The second is its diversity, but in this respect, India is certainly not unique: many smaller countries are blessed (or cursed) by as much diversity. The third aspect that merits mention is the presence of castes, an important influence on Indian politics: in this respect India *is* unique. Finally, post-independence India was dominated by two very strong personalities, namely Jawaharlal Nehru and Indira Gandhi.

India began its independence in 1947 with the dominance of Nehru as *the* unchallenged political leader. Note that this dominance was tempered by countervailing sources of power: in the Cabinet, in the party, in the parliament, and among the states. There was also the dominance of his Congress Party. The rural support that sustained Nehru's and his party's dominance was derived from the "vote banks," that is, voting blocs mobilized and delivered by the Congress Party machine. The Nehru period was an atypical interlude in Indian political history, during which the competition at the Center was essentially only among the elite at the head of the Congress party (Kohli 1994)—a situation very similar to that obtaining in authoritarian states like the PRC. The masses of the Indian population, particularly those in the rural areas, had little input into the process of policy setting required in Nehru's planned economy.

This allowed the Indian Government at the time to pioneer a series of economic policies that became the model for the rest of the developing world (however wrong-headed those policies may appear in retrospect, particularly with respect to agriculture). As a result, grand, well-thought-out plans were formulated away from the hurly-burly of electoral politics. They were indeed taken seriously and implemented and set India on a path of development that was to continue well into the 1980s, although by then most of the planning exercises had lost their potency. The most troublesome legacy that India has to grapple with to this day is the overgrown system of controls that was necessary in the planned economy devised by Nehru's Government.

While the economic system that Nehru and his advisors had put together lingered on, the political scene in India changed enormously after his death. The key event that led to the change was in 1969, when Indira Gandhi split the Congress party by going over the heads of the "Syndicate"—the grandees that ran the party after the departure of Nehru—and mobilizing the population for a radical program of reforms (Frankel 1978). These reforms had as their guiding theme the removal of poverty. This direct appeal to the population for a political program was something new in post-independence

India and was to leave an ineradicable imprint on the Indian body politic. Interestingly, despite the claimed goal of removing poverty, Mrs. Gandhi's radical platform concerned the nationalization of the banking and insurance industries and the taming of the corporate sector, yet was silent on what would have had far greater impact on rural poverty, namely land reform. Despite the presence of economic planning and its cadres of highly sophisticated analysts, there was very little linkage between the policies proposed and the claimed result in removing poverty.

Political scientists now argue that the legacy of Mrs. Gandhi lay in mobilizing India politically as it never had been before (Kohli 1994, Khilnani 1997). At the same time, precisely because of this mobilization, politics at the grass roots became highly fragmented. This political mobilization has had its costs. In a country riven by castes, religions, and language groups, the mobilized population was moved in different directions, destructive as often as constructive. The lower classes and castes no longer submitted to the preferences of their betters, as had been the case with the old Congress Party. The instability that has characterized the Indian polity of the 1980s and 1990s, not to mention its susceptibility to emotional (and dangerous) appeals by castes and religion, is the consequence.

The above history divides post-independence India into two distinct parts. Before 1969, there was a political system that was not highly mobilized, but thereafter it became so. Political mobilization *per se*, however, did not lead to a governmental system that was responsive to the desires of the people, nor did it imply the existence of the machinery to implement programs around which politicians mobilized their support, particularly for a radical economic platform.

> The reason is in part that it is very difficult for any state to reach out into the nooks and crannies of a society and hope to restructure social relations in a manner that would benefit the weak at the expense of the socially powerful. Next to making war, redistributive reform is probably the most difficult task a state can undertake. If leaders use

standard operating procedures, such as pass laws, and hope the bureaucracy implements them, land reforms do not get implemented... If such reforms are to be implemented, what is needed instead is much more of a political intervention, one that can simultaneously strengthen the weak by organizing them, and utilize politicized implementing agents, usually party cadres, that more readily respond to the decisions of rulers than bureaucrats. (Kohli 1994).

Paradoxically, therefore, despite being (temporarily) immensely popular, the populist rhetoric of Mrs. Gandhi, and later her son Rajiv, did not translate into effective programs. By concentrating power into their own hands, they destroyed the old political machine and the second and third tiers of leadership and therefore made it impossible for their programs to find the support and resources necessary for implementation.

This political history of India does, in a way, illustrate the experience of other Asian countries. Thus, in most of Asia, the rural population still remains largely unmobilized, as was the case in India before 1969. Politicians with a rural base, or those campaigning on rural themes, seldom do so with clear economic platforms that propose decisive measures aimed at achieving predictable results. The sole exception in Asia in this respect is the ruling party in Malaysia, but this country's pro-rural policies carry a decisive ethnic bias.

By and large, rural politicians succeed better in the legislatures by using the power of the purse to bring back resources from the central Government. The pressure of electoral competition has led to an emphasis on bricks and mortar and, more generally, on construction projects. Since legislators do not control the bureaucracy itself, however, the problem of operations and maintenance (O&M) is not seriously addressed. A great deal of investment has indeed flowed into rural Asia from central governments through this process: thus road networks are now extensive, access to electricity is much more widespread than before, and irrigation structures are erected. But all too often, the roads are not maintained. Little is done to ensure that aggregate power supply is adequate to meet demand (and when there is need to ration the supply, rural areas are inevitably pushed to the end of the line). And while sophisticated irrigation structures have entailed enormous investments, their use remains grossly inefficient (see Chapter V). The exceptions are found in countries whose economies have had a high growth rate and hence whose fiscal revenues are also ample.

Critical to this game of milking the center by rural politicians is again the role of the local, rural elite. The local leaders in the constituencies are able to control a sizable portion of the votes that can be delivered to themselves or the candidates of their choice—much like the "vote banks" in India. The job of these leaders and also of the candidates is not to present their policies and elicit the voters' preference for one set over others. In fact, specific policies matter little in most Asian elections, with most political parties clustering themselves around anodyne promises. Rather, the local leaders' or candidates' job is to act as entrepreneurs, bet on whichever horse on the national ticket will win, and position themselves in the prospective winner's party so as to achieve the coveted executive positions or to be able to significantly influence the executive branch.

Translated from the Indian experience, this voting pattern still shows an unmobilized voting bloc in the rural areas. A hypothesis may be ventured that mobilization in India was facilitated by the existence of castes, which provided an organizing principle for the rural population that is missing in other societies. The rural population outside India has seldom been politically mobilized, except by left-wing insurgency movements such as in Sri Lanka, Thailand, and the Philippines. In none of these countries did the rural movements succeed in overthrowing the governments, South Viet Nam being the last Asian country where a rurally-based insurgency prevailed. The political order has been overturned in many Asian countries—Thailand in 1973 and again in 1992, the Philippines in 1986, and Indonesia in 1998, but in all these cases, the cities were mobilized for the overthrow. In Thailand, in particular, military leaders would obtain legitimacy and democratic credentials for their governments by organizing elections, during which their nominees would obtain overwhelming support from the rural areas. Commentators have remarked on this phenomenon (and the urban reaction) thus: "It is the countryside that makes governments, but it is Bangkok that unmakes them."

The rural electorate's fondness for patronage politics and its occasional association with antidemocratic tendencies have an important consequence. Policies that have actually helped the rural areas have depended on growth rather than redistribution. There is a dearth of policies that systematically redistribute income to the rural poor, whether through a redistribution of assets (such as land reform) or price policies that protect rather than tax agriculture (see Chapter VI). Malaysia; the Republic of Korea; and Taipei,China are the only Asian developing countries that have highly protective policies toward agriculture. Malaysia does so because of its peculiar ethnic mix; the Republic of Korea and Taipei,China began doing so in the early 1970s, when they were already well on their way to being urban and industrial societies.

Bureaucrats

Modern governments are organized into large bureaucracies. The departure of the colonial powers left a cadre of civil servants who were, in some cases, highly capable (although a subset of these might have belonged to the "wrong" ethnic grouping, from the point of the view of the incoming governments). Indonesia, the Lao People's Democratic Republic, and Cambodia were the only countries that were not so endowed at the time of independence, but within a few decades, Indonesia at least seemed to have made up some of the lost ground through heavy human-resource investments. With these exceptions, most Asian systems fit very well Max Weber's classical description of a bureaucracy: fixed jurisdictional areas ordered by rules, hierarchical ordering, and use of written documents; and of the bureaucrat: expert training, full-time work in the position, pursuit of a lifetime career in the bureaucracy, appointment by superiors rather than by election, and enjoyment of social esteem from the governed (Weber [1920]1946). There are many areas, however, in which bureaucrats fall short of the ideal, as measured by the standards of the British or US civil service.

First of all, with very few exceptions, most Asian civil servants remain underpaid. In some countries, their real salaries have fallen relative to those prevailing in colonial times. In others, salaries have lagged well behind those paid in the private sector. Most Asian countries' personnel policies follow the mandarin style, where recruitment is at entry level; a person, once recruited into the Government, is expected to spend his or her lifetime gradually moving up in the civil service (World Bank 1997). Moreover, in adjusting bureaucrats' salaries, many governments have followed a policy of reducing the inequality of incomes by increasing those at the bottom end of the scale relatively more. Salary scales within the public sector are thus considerably narrower than in the private sector. Such a distorted salary structure would be harmless if the Government were the dominant employer in the modern sector's labor market, as it would have been in the early stages of development. In many countries, however, the Government has ceased to be a dominant employer. The distorted scale thus has made it difficult to retain people of high caliber. The public sector has become overstaffed in the lower ranks, but is inadequate, in quality if not always in quantity, at the top.

Two tendencies have emerged within Asian countries. In those where growth has been strong, and where private-sector wages and salaries have risen as a result while government salaries lagged considerably behind, the quality of the civil service has declined. Table II.1 gives the grades of those who passed the civil service entrance examinations in Thailand over the period 1986–1993. This was actually a period when civil service salaries were rapidly adjusted upward, but since they were so far behind private-sector salaries to begin with, the adjustments were insufficient. The figures clearly show that the quality of the entrants has declined noticeably, even though the period over which the comparison is being made is quite short.

Table II.1 Percent of Entrants to the Civil Service Scoring Less Than 2.5 in the Civil Service Entrance Examination in Thailand, 1986–1993

Year	Percent
1986	28.6
1987	25.7
1988	32.0
1990	42.5
1993	49.7

[a] Passing grade is 2.0, and maximum grade is 4.0
Source: unpublished data, Office of the Civil Service Commission, Thailand.

In other countries that did not grow as rapidly economically and therefore have faced severe employment problems, the civil service has been allowed to balloon in size. Bangladesh, for example, increased public-sector employment from 450,000 in 1971 to almost one million in 1992, at a compound rate of 3.6 percent per year, or well in excess of the population growth rate of 2.5 percent. Within just four years (1991–1994), the number of departments and directorates grew from 109 to 221. Partly because of this expansion, the real base pay of the most senior civil service positions declined by as much as 87 percent (World Bank 1997). With such growth in numbers and decline in salaries, it is more than likely that the quality of the average recruit has also declined.

Weber stressed the importance of social esteem as a characteristic of the bureaucrat. In the past, this social esteem was taken for granted. Over the years, as salaries lagged behind, as the quality of the personnel in the civil service declined, and as corruption increased, the status of the civil servant began a decline that has continued unabated. Among the civil service systems that are modeled along British lines, the autonomy of the civil service in matters of recruitment and promotions has come under severe strain, as both the political systems and the bureaucracies have become highly personalized.

The civil service in nearly all countries (except those that became Communist) steadily became more patrimonial in character. Instead of neutral application of impersonal rules, which should normally characterize the bureaucratic ethos, decisions became more and more personalistic, both in terms of the bureaucracy's dealings with its clients and in terms of individual bureaucrats dealing with either their superiors or subordinates. Instead of accountability, loyalty became a more important criterion by which bureaucrats were judged. Instead of using the information at their disposal to perform their tasks of designing rational (i.e., reality-based) measures to implement their political masters' policies, they have conformed to the latter's needs. The lines of division between policies, which are the minister's prerogative, and measures to implement the policies, which are the bureaucrats' business, have become increasingly blurred, as both politicians and bureaucrats are increasingly driven to feed the corrupt political machine.

It is little wonder that governments are becoming less capable of undertaking and implementing rational policies and that people have begun to recognize it. With better education and with longer experience of their own (as distinct from colonial) governments, their perception of government failure is now matching their awareness of market failure. While the Thatcher-Reagan critique of government as applied to the West may carry over to Asia to some extent, particularly through the multilateral lending agencies, what makes it really resonant is the clearly perceived facts of increasing corruption and the decline in the quality of government output. Consequently, various sectors have begun to organize themselves to tackle tasks that would in the past have been left to the central Government.

The Budget Constraint

The fiscal systems incorporated into the constitutions of Asian countries set out the rules to enforce a *pro forma* budget balance for the central Government. In a parliamentary system, the executive branch is in charge of ensuring this balance; the legislators' role is sharply limited by their inability to submit money bills without the express approval of the executive branch.

In a presidential system like that of the Philippines, problems may arise (as has been the case with the US) because the legislature may mandate many expenditure programs without being willing to fund them adequately. But in the Philippines, when the executive branch submits the annual budget to Congress, individual items may be reduced by Congress, but cannot be increased. This ensures that the executive branch, which has a stronger interest in balancing the budget, does not have its objectives deflected by pork-barrel haggling in Congress. It is possible for Congress to mandate programs without budgeting for them. Examples of unfunded mandates will be discussed in Chapter III in connection with the Philippines' devolution program.

Asian governments have a reputation for levying modest taxes (World Bank 1993c). This observation is borne out by Table II.2, which gives data on the shares of central government revenues in GDP. The PRC has an unusually low revenue-to-GDP ratio of only 6.6 percent., but this figure does not include taxes collected and retained by provincial and local governments, which in the PRC are very important. The relatively low figures for Asia suggest that the budget constraint on the governments should not be so binding—they do have some room to expand their resources by levying new

Table II.2
Share of Central Government Current Revenues in GDP (%)

	Asian Countries	Rest of World
Low Income	8.6 (6)	18.9
Excluding PRC	14.3 (5)	
Lower Middle	18.1 (4)	21.3
Upper Middle	24.9 (1)	24.2
High	22.6 (13)	29.1
Total	14.5 (12)	28.2
Excluding PRC	19.1 (12)	

Notes: Figures in parentheses denote the number of countries in the sample. Data availability limits the Asian countries to the following: India, Indonesia, Republic of Korea, Malaysia, Mongolia, Nepal, Pakistan, Papua New Guinea, Philippines, People's Republic of China, Singapore, Sri Lanka, and Thailand.
Source: World Bank (1998 and 1999)

or higher taxes. Many of the issues plaguing Asian governments, for example, poor O&M of infrastructure and the deteriorating quality of the civil service on account of its low pay levels, can be tackled by increasing the tax rates.

Within the constraints imposed by their somewhat modest revenues, most Asian governments (except those running the transitional economies) have had few problems with balancing the annual budget, unless there are special cases, for example, a very high level of military spending. That said, it must also be pointed out that Asian governments have yet to learn the art of multiyear and multicontingency budget balancing.

In the case of multiyear budget balancing, past experience has shown that when faced with resource constraint, governments are tempted to defer—through borrowing—the tax burden necessary to break that constraint. This of course can pyramid until it becomes unsustainable. A few countries went through this cycle in the aftermath of the oil crises of the 1970s. The debt crisis that hit the Philippines with full force in the late 1970s affected some other countries as well. As a consequence, many of these countries began to put in place a number of reforms that increased their capability for public-debt management.

Even a Government that borrows prudently may face a sudden fiscal crisis if it makes contingency commitments to various other actors in the economy. The most common claimants are State enterprises, whose borrowings are usually guaranteed by the central Government. The most spectacular example of such contingency commitments, of course, has been the recent burden placed on the governments of Indonesia, the Republic of Korea, and Thailand by the (sometimes-implicit) guarantee on bank deposits.

The fiscal balance problem is, first and foremost, a macroeconomic problem. This has two important consequences for rural policies. First of all, poor multiyear and multicontingency fiscal management means that the availability of public resources is inherently fitful and that the funding of rural programs is therefore unreliable. Second—and this is the more insidious consequence—fiscal imbalances tend to have an impact on the real exchange rate. Without controls on capital movements, a fiscal deficit tends to produce a deficit in the current account and therefore an offsetting capital inflow. This leads to an increase in the price of nontradables and a real appreciation of the domestic currency. Since the agricultural sector produces mostly tradable goods, this appreciation in the real exchange rate affects it adversely. Besides, if there is little stability in fiscal management, the fluctuations in the real exchange rate add to the already high degree of price instability that characterizes agricultural commodity markets. One of the contributions of the study on agricultural pricing policies by Krueger, Schiff, and Valdes (1988) is to show that this effect is of considerable magnitude and in some cases overshadows the impact of direct taxes and subsidies in the agricultural sector.

Fiscal management problems still remain in the transitional economies. Recall that in the past, being centrally planned, with the means of production owned by the State, these countries did not separate what is known in market economies as the public sector from the productive sectors. Many countries, notably the PRC and Viet Nam, have now effectively separated the two, particularly with respect to the agricultural sector. The Central Asian transitional governments have now, to varying degrees, undergone this process, with Kazakhstan and the Kyrgyz Republic somewhat ahead of the others. In all these countries, however, large shares of the productive sectors outside agriculture still remain with the Government, so the Government is still exposed to their losses.

Local Governments

Rural development by definition has to be dispersed, as both the activities necessary to carry it out and the beneficiaries are dispersed. Yet, from the time when most Asian countries achieved independence, the main motive force and control of rural development have emanated from the central Government. This adds to the discrepancy between the theory and practice of the modern State alluded to already on pp. 37–50 above.

The first alternative candidate to undertake the tasks of rural development is the local government. By this is meant a duly constituted unit of government whose officers are ultimately accountable to the local electorate. This local government unit should not be confused with a local administrative unit of the central Government, whose officers answer to their superiors in the ministries of the central Government. There are many tiers of local government and it is best to start with the lowest level, namely the village.

Villages or Local Communities

Anthropologists consider the village community the most "natural" in a society, although the reader must be warned that the term village covers many sorts of entities. The key distinction for this level of government is that it must be small enough so that its members can have face-to-face interaction on a regular basis. Population sizes of individual villages can vary considerably: in mainland Southeast Asia, village population is typically less than 1,000 (Keyes 1977), while in the uplands of southern India it ranges from 1,000 to 4,000 (Wade 1988). Administrative villages, on the other and, are defined for the convenience of the bureaucracy and may not always correspond to the natural boundaries of rural communities.

Few governments in Asia have personnel other than schoolteachers in villages. In that sense, and in that sense alone, villages are said to be self-governing. In other respects, villages are given very few resources to undertake any serious collective task, despite rhetoric and even sometimes action to devolve power to them (Wade 1988 and Motooka 1976, among many others). Despite the small amount of power explicitly granted by the State to the village, as a community it has in many instances taken collective action upon itself. Wade (1988) and Ostrom (1996a) have given comparative accounts of the village community's role in collective action. They call attention to the forces that work to elicit the community's participation.

Wade, for instance, stresses the demand side of the problem. Examining collective action among various villages along an irrigation system in South India, he suggests that villages with a less assured water supply (usually at the tail end of the system) undertake more collective action to increase that assurance than those whose water supply is naturally more abundant. They would hire more field guards and engage in measures upstream to get more water, including bribing the State's irrigation officers. They would also raise more funds to finance these activities. Similarly, Ostrom (1994) observes, from her examination of school systems in various parts of Nigeria (admittedly an example outside Asia, but suggestive nonetheless), that even though village schools are supposed to be run by the State, parents nonetheless take an active interest in them if they are convinced of the importance of education.

It has often been remarked that rural communities in the relatively small irrigation systems of East Asia tend to display a greater social cohesion than, say, communities in the large-scale, publicly-built and -managed irrigation systems in the great flood plains of South and Southeast Asia. This is because the need to engage in communal activities to build and maintain the irrigation facilities has forced individual farmers to interact with one another and to develop working and cost-sharing rules and other norms to make the systems work. Since irrigation is vital to their livelihoods, the communities have, over the years, been able to build up this system of cooperation, which has come to be known as "social capital" (See pp. 74–78 below). Once it has been accumulated, social capital can be put to effective use in other areas as well, for example in the setting up of cooperatives.

Against the demand-side views from Wade and Ostrom, who argue that the amount of social capital is a function of the amount of collective work that needs to be done, there is another set of arguments that proposes that villages and villagers are guided by some inner impulse. Scott (1976) argues that the precapitalist (and precolonial) peasant communities in Southeast Asia were guided by a subsistence ethic, which stressed a safety-first strategy in the face of risks. This affected not only private decisions on which crops to grow and how much to market, but also social behavior, as people relied on their communities to provide them with insurance against all sorts of risks. Since membership in the villages implied reciprocity and sharing, individualistic behavior that facilitated integration into the market was shunned. Indeed market integration was considered highly risky and incompatible with the subsistence ethic. Scott then claims that the emergence of the market and the arrival of colonial government (the two came in tandem) led to the destruction of this subsistence ethic and of the sense of community that had existed prior to this point. The problem of why peasants turned to the market if it was so disadvantageous for them was obviated by arguing that the State forced them to do so by increasing the tax burden and by collecting taxes in money instead of, say, corvée labor.

Scott's work remains influential despite the strong attack launched on his thesis by Popkin (1979). Popkin's approach is essentially neoclassical, in his analysis of both the individual peasant's behavior and of peasants' collective behavior, which is why he calls his approach "political economy" as distinct from Scott's "moral economy." The reason why Scott's view finds resonance, particularly among the NGO community, is that it purports to explain the lack of social capital as a consequence of the commercialization of agriculture in particular and of rural life in general. It has thus provided a powerful platform for an attack on the market mechanism. The view of this volume is that the thesis of the causal relation between commercialization and the loss of social capital remains unproven. If community and market are not considered as alternatives or as antagonistic, as Scott theorizes, then attempts can be made to build up social capital within a framework of a market economy (Hayami 1989). After all, developed market economies do have social capital that helps communities to undertake collective action (see below).

It needs pointing out that the kind of social capital built up in traditional villages may be incompatible with certain fundamental human rights (admittedly an imported concept). Thus, Kerala used to have a very strong caste system, which was eventually destroyed by an organizational drive among the laborers under the aegis of the Communists. After this successful organizational drive, the Communists (as well as their opponents, who had to imitate the Communists in order to survive politically) went on to implement a series of major reforms, both in the rural and urban areas of Kerala (Heller 1996).

Other Tiers of Local Government

Between the villages and the central Government, there are of course other tiers—district, region, and province. Whereas villages in some areas often possess social capital, the other tiers of government have very little of it to back up their activities. It is no wonder that this intermediate level of local government has played so small an independent role in rural development. It is only recently that the intermediate tiers have, in some countries, been asked to shoulder more of the burden. Since the issues related to this are quite large and complex, detailed discussion has been deferred to Chapter III.

The Budget Constraint on Local Governments

As rural development is by definition spatially dispersed, why do local institutions play such an insignificant role compared to that of the central Government? A large part of the answer can be seen quickly by examining even cursorily the problem of local government financing.[2]

Modern economies have to be integrated nationally, which means that rates of taxation of goods and services have to be uniform, or at least near uniform, across the nation. This implies that the national Government should normally be setting—and collecting—the taxes for the whole country. It is not surprising that the central Government has ended up with the lion's share of the country's resources. With such a command over resources and with such an emphasis on a national development strategy (Chapter I), it follows that the

---

[2] As mentioned in Chapter I and discussed in greater detail in Chapter IV, another part of the answer, at least during the past three decades, has been that the green revolution technology, consisting of a simple, uniform package of inputs and credit, lent itself extremely well to centralized, top-down dissemination.

central Government has used its financial clout to impose its own will through rural policies.

It is ironic that the countries that at present have much the strongest local governments (measured in terms of their financial strength *relative to that of the central Government*) are the PRC and Viet Nam. The reason is that in a centrally-planned economic system, much of the tax base is associated with production units. With the disappearance of central planning, the production units came to be increasingly controlled by local governments at various levels (see the discussion on the PRC in Chapter III). Further, unlike market economies, where the central governments provide grants to local governments either through annual appropriations or through legislation, central governments in the transitional economies have to bargain with the local governments to obtain the tax resources that they need.

One method commonly used throughout the developing countries, and currently being tried in the Philippines and Thailand, is the tax assignment system. In this system, fixed percentages of a number of specified nationally-collected taxes are earmarked for local authorities. In the Philippines, for example, legislation specifies that up to 40 percent of all tax revenues are to be granted to local governments at various levels. The PRC has an essentially similar arrangement; unlike in other countries, however, the solution was arrived at after hard bargaining between the provinces and the central Government. (For a general discussion of tax assignment, see Shah and Qureshi [1994]).

Tax assignment is a useful, almost necessary, first step toward financial devolution. Contentious issues begin to arise, however, particularly during the early stages, over the question of what expenditure items are to be the responsibility of the local governments and whether the expenditure assignment matches the tax assignment. Normally, expenditure items should be assigned first, and from their current levels, the percentages of the taxes to be assigned can then be calculated. In the Philippines and the PRC, this has not taken place with the requisite degree of precision, and arguments have arisen that the amount of taxes assigned has not matched the expenditures required.

In assigning these expenditure items, again the Philippines' situation (see Chapter III) gives a forewarning for others that there are a myriad of issues involved in devolution. Personnel problems are particularly explosive. This is because in transferring personnel from central to local governments, contingent liabilities are transferred regarding pensions, health insurance, and the like. If civil servants are not satisfied that their standard of living is being protected in such transfers, they are liable to put up stiff resistance.

One unfortunate outcome of the tax assignment system may well be that, with such grants from the Center, local governments become "lazy" in their attempts to collect their own taxes. Once specific expenditure items are assigned to the local governments, the *level* at which money is to be spent on each of these should be at the discretion of the locals as much as possible.[3] This is probably best done if local governments can raise a sufficient portion of their own taxes; otherwise there is a temptation for each local government to free-ride on the rest of the country, by first underperforming on its assigned responsibilities and then claiming that its grants were insufficient.

What items can local governments efficiently tax? Clearly, these should be taxes that are residence-based, e.g., sales taxes on consumption goods and excise taxes on certain items (e.g., on liquor, but not on "big ticket" consumer durables such as automobiles, for which the relative size of the tax may justify traveling to other regions where taxes are lower). Above all, taxes on various forms of fixed property have traditionally been the backbone in countries with strong local governments. In this last respect, it is a pity that the land taxes that used to be collected during the colonial period have been almost entirely removed. Even though these taxes were and still are collected by the central Government, they provide an obvious—and often ignored—potential tax base for the local governments.

---

[3] Expenditures about which caution is in order include merit goods like vaccinations, basic health care, and education, which may tend to be underfunded if left entirely to local discretion. See Chapters III and VII.

Finally, one issue that keeps recurring in policy discussions with respect to local governments is their ability to borrow. This is a problematic area. What is the collateral basis of a local government loan? In cases where most local revenues come through tax assignments, how strongly guaranteed is the cash flow from the central Government? In this respect, loans to local governments are similar to local-currency loans to the central Government, except that the central Government can always print the money to service the loan. If a comparison is to be made with central government borrowing, the similarity is with a *foreign-currency* loan.

To the extent that the final guarantor, whether de jure or de facto, is the central Government, the central Government therefore has a deep interest in controlling the local government's ability to service the loan. Hence, there is usually reluctance by ministries of finance all over the world to allow local governments to borrow.

Nongovernment Organizations

Types of NGOs and their Relationships with Government

Nongovernment organizations (NGOs) vary in the scope of their operations. Korten (1990, cited in Romero and Bautista 1995) describes four types:

- Voluntary organizations that pursue a social mission driven by a commitment to shared values;
- Public-service contractors that function as market-oriented nonprofit businesses serving public purposes;
- People's organizations that represent their members' interests, have member-accountable leadership, and are substantially self-reliant; and
- Government NGOs that are creations of the government and serve as instruments of government policy.

All four types have a history in Asia, including the last, which will not be covered further. Of the first three types, most began as charitable organizations, more often than not affiliated with various Christian churches, Buddhist temples, or Islamic orders. This pedigree is important in that it imparts certain biases in the way NGOs function, even though a large number of them no longer function as charitable organizations. In terms of their activities, NGOs now embark on action projects, organize communities, advocate policies, and conduct research and training. There is a second tier consisting of NGOs that raise funds for other NGOs or are networks of NGOs.

Despite the NGOs' long history and the diversity of their activities, there is a surprising uniformity (relative to, say, governments or political parties) in their ideological orientation, particularly among the first of the four types listed above, for whom ideals matter. With their roots as charitable organizations, they are naturally much closer to the poor than the other actors covered in this chapter, hence their proclivity for a relatively radical political stance. Moreover, while it is true that they have had a long history, their growth has been very rapid during the last two decades, fueled by funding from a rather small group of donors, almost entirely Western governments. We shall return to the implications of such funding later.

Because of their ideological orientation, relationships between NGOs and many Asian governments have been prickly. NGOs that advocate policies have a particularly hard time. The hostility does not always stem from the Government. Some NGOs feel that to cooperate with an authoritarian Government means "selling out" (Lewis 1993). With democratization, however, many countries, notably the Philippines, Bangladesh, and Indonesia, have eased restrictions on NGO activities. Some countries even have sections within the key ministries concerned with rural areas (e.g., agriculture or health) to deal specifically with NGO relations, because they perceive that cooperation with NGOs will ease their task in specific areas. For one thing, NGOs are very good at working "in the small." In agricultural research and extension, for example, they can tailor their work to deal with localities much better than a bureaucratic extension system (see Chapter IV). Thus, the Indian Eighth Five-Year Plan envisaged turning over extension functions to NGOs in certain geographical areas.

How does NGO performance measure up against State performance? After surveying the literature on the subject, Edwards and Hulme (1996) conclude that "there is evidence that some large NGOs are able to provide some services more cost-effectively than governments," but "NGOs are not automatically more cost-effective than other sectors." In terms of their ability to target the poor, "there is certainly some evidence that NGOs commonly perform better than government or commercial institutions," but the claim that they reach the poorest of the poor—those totally without assets or skills—is inaccurate (Edwards and Hulme 1996), although even with this latter group, NGOs can help, at least relative to what central governments can or are willing to do.[4]

Financing the NGOs

Very little clear documentation and analysis exists regarding NGO finances. The main source of aggregated information is the statistics collected by donor countries, which the Organisation for Economic Co-operation and Development (OECD) has compiled (cited in Edwards and Hulme [1996]). These data indicate that the proportion of total bilateral aid from OECD countries channeled through NGOs worldwide rose from 0.7 percent in 1975 to 3.6 percent in 1985, and at least 5 percent in 1993–94, when the dollar figure was $2.3 billion. These figures include voluntary contributions as well as official aid, although the share of the latter is increasing. How does this compare with the NGOs' domestic sources of finance? Only one set of data allows such comparison, and this is from India. Robinson,

---

[4] A useful paper prepared recently by Liamzon (2000) summarizes several case studies of NGO efforts to promote land tenure security in Brazil, Cambodia, and India, plus the more standard roles of NGOs and other civil society organizations in mobilizing the poor.

Farrington and Satish (1993) say that Indian NGOs' annual revenue from abroad is 9 billion rupees (US$520 million). The authors do not state to which year the data pertain. The Government of India itself provides a further 500–700 million rupees. When individual and corporate donations are added, annual NGO revenue would total almost 10 billion rupees, which means that foreign sources account for as much as 90 percent of the total revenue—this for a country which tends to be rather averse to foreign aid. It must be borne in mind that these figures tend to exaggerate the role of foreign donors: excluded from them is the value of the work put in by volunteers.

The dependence of advocacy NGOs on foreign funding is likely to be higher than for the other two types. Given the aggressive position that these NGOs have taken on many issues, this dependency can raise questions of authenticity. But raising voluntary contributions locally to lessen reliance on foreign sources is an extremely difficult task. While it is possible for a government to finance service-providing NGOs, it is problematic for it to finance the advocacy NGOs. For want of anything better, NGOs have to depend much more on voluntary contributions. The tradition of voluntary donations in Asia is not entirely absent, for how else can the continual building of temples, mosques and churches be explained? Moreover, some of these contributions also spill over into what can be subsumed under the terms of charitable organizations, such as hospitals and schools.

Donation, whether to religious institutions or to NGOs, does not fit comfortably with the basic assumptions of economics, as it is subject to a different sort of psychology and ideology than the ones that economists are used to. In his analysis of philanthropy in Thailand, Anan (1998) points out that the motivation for donations to temples in Thailand was enveloped in the Buddhist ideology of merit-making, which pushes the contributions in certain directions. NGOs, on the other hand, grew out of Western humanitarian concerns, which are somewhat alien to the version of Buddhism practiced by the Thais. Not surprisingly, the first NGOs in the country were formed by the Christian churches (Amara 1995), and concentrated on education and health facilities for the poor.

NGOs that try to define their role with explicit Thai roots (they are at the moment mostly of the advocacy kind) are having problems raising funds locally.

In general, service-providing NGOs have a broader set of financing options than the advocacy NGOs. Many of the services that they provide are really private goods. This is the case to some extent with health care and even more so with education (see Chapter VII). Thus, it is possible for them to sell their services at different prices and cross-subsidize the poorer beneficiaries, fulfilling their role of assisting the poor. This, in fact, has been the traditional method employed by Christian missionaries in their provision of health and education services. It is not surprising that the best schools for middle-class children in much of Asia are missionary schools. The problem with this approach is, of course, that a single-facility NGO can only operate in this way if it is located in areas with high purchasing power, and that would mean in the cities, not in the rural areas. Of course, a multiple-facility NGO can still engage in cross-subsidization, but the temptation within the NGO to go where the money is will remain strong and somewhat distort its delivery.

For-Profit Private Sector

Although the most important among the actors considered in this chapter, discussion of this sector need not be prolonged, as its motivation is straightforward. It is important to note, however, that the for-profit private sector can function properly only when the legal framework for its existence is firmly established. This has become obvious in recent years as the result of two developments: first, the mismanagement and massive economic collapse that occurred as many former centrally-planned economies privatized their major industries; and second, the "discovery" during the Asian economic crisis of the inadequacies of the laws and regulations governing business and the financial sector. Indeed the complacency of many Asian governments during the years when their economies were growing rapidly is now costing them dearly. The themes that have emerged from this experience are covered below under the rubric of "governance."

While the private sector, per se, and its profit-seeking motivation do not require detailed discussion, the process of privatization is of interest because almost all of Asia's former centrally-planned economies—and even some of the market economies—are grappling with it. As alluded to above, there has been almost universal progress in the privatization of farming, but progress has been slower in industrial activities, including large rurally-based industries. In this regard, the experience of the PRC is noteworthy. As compared to the "crash" approach to privatization taken by the former Soviet Union and Eastern Europe, the PRC appears to have hit upon a transitional form of private-sector development. Although manufacturing units are not privately owned as in the market economies, their behavior nonetheless conforms to the role of a for-profit sector working in a competitive environment. These units were instrumental in rural industrialization, an area in which the PRC has been uniquely successful.

The PRC has a number of distinctive types of enterprise. These include central and local publicly-owned enterprises, as well as private firms, proprietorships or private cooperative firms started by groups of individuals. The share of private firms in the gross value of industrial output in 1986 was 21.3 percent. Their importance varies greatly from province to province, with a larger presence in the more developed and commercialized provinces such as Guangdong. They still lead a somewhat fugitive existence in the PRC, however, despite the extensive reforms and the greater presence of markets. In addition, their ability to expand employment has been limited by regulations and they therefore remain small.

The limitations on private enterprises have led to the spectacular growth of the township and village enterprises (TVEs), which were the successors of the erstwhile commune and brigade enterprises. Unlike publicly-owned enterprises in other countries, the TVEs are essentially for-profit organizations that function in a competitive environment. They have strengthened the position of local governments in relation to the central Government by providing the former with additional tax resources for social investment and rural infrastructure projects. The TVEs provide a major tax base to local governments and extra budgetary funds for social services. They are unevenly distributed, however, tending to cluster in the coastal provinces and in rural areas near cities. Poorer inland provinces with few or no TVEs have generally smaller revenues. TVEs have also become a very important contributor to the increase in rural welfare: in the 1980s, TVEs played a major role in poverty alleviation programs (Wong 1997).

Prior to their post-reform growth, TVEs had a checkered history, which followed the swings in policy during Mao's rule. During the Great Leap Forward, their earlier incarnations expanded greatly, only to decline equally sharply when that effort collapsed. In the more recent period of the Cultural Revolution, the commune and brigade enterprises were again encouraged to expand, particularly into agriculture-related industries such as farm machinery and implements. But this time, they remained and continued to grow throughout the 1970s. Their growth until about 1983 was still based on agriculture, but thereafter became more overtly industrial. Indeed, after 1983 the TVEs in some provinces began to support agriculture rather than the other way round (Byrd and Lin 1990; Du 1990).

The reforms, by allowing households much more leeway in managing their time, had opened up opportunities for the growth of this particular form of enterprise. As noted above, the TVEs benefited from the restrictions on private firms that could have competed with them. In addition, local governments became very willing investors in TVEs. They preferred them to private enterprises, which did not possess clear private property rights over their productive assets (Che and Qian 1998). The TVEs also benefited from the active role played in their management by local officials and cadres, especially in the beginning. This was particularly important in a country without a private sector, as managerial abilities were scarce. In addition, the local officials had extensive networks of contacts at various levels of government.

While obtaining tax revenues from these TVEs, the central Government requires them to retain at least 60 percent of their profits for future development. The local government can also levy various taxes and fees on a TVE under its control. However, the central Government also requires that funds thus acquired have to be spent on rural social programs and infrastructure. It appears that the nominal owners of the enterprises, the local citizens, get relatively few direct benefits in the form of dividends: Che and Qian (1998) report that in 1986, 46 percent of after-tax profits were reinvested and 49 percent used for local public expenditure. In 1992, the figures were 59 and 40 percent, respectively. Nonetheless, local people do benefit from the expansion of employment made possible by the reinvestment of the profits and from the expenditures of the local government.

Because of their many desirable features, the TVEs are often cited as models for other countries to emulate. However, their growth is associated with unique features that are not present elsewhere in Asia (with the possible exception of Viet Nam): the "binding" of individuals to their places of residence, with some limitations on movements into and out of these places, and the lack of a private sector with easy access to capital and managerial inputs.

The TVEs also have some less attractive features. Because they are under the control of the local governments, which still wield considerable regulatory power, there is a tendency for the TVEs to use that power against outside enterprises, in a form of local protectionism (Shirk 1993). In the grain trade in particular, the provincial enterprise can often get its local government to prevent outside traders from procuring grain until it has fulfilled its own needs.

Multilateral Lending Agencies

For most Asian developing countries, two multilateral lending agencies—the Asian Development Bank and the World Bank—are of considerable importance for two main reasons. First and most obviously, they are a source of development finance, but at the same time they are also a source of policy thinking and advice and at times are influential in policy choices. The emphasis here will be on the second set of roles.

These two multilateral agencies are, first and foremost, politically-based institutions. The governing bodies of both agencies consist of representatives of both donor countries (i.e., the developed countries that have contributed major shares of the capital funds) and the developing countries that are the borrowers. In both banks, the developed countries tend to play a dominant role. Their representatives on the boards of directors are accountable to their governments and ultimately to the electorates in their home countries. The electorates in the larger countries (particularly the US) have generally been somewhat averse to the work undertaken by the lending agencies and have required their representatives to reflect their own vested interests and preferences: for example, the soybean lobby in the US has for a long time made it difficult for the World Bank to lend for palm-oil projects.

Aside from lobbying for vested interests, the developed-country board members have been guided by the current economic and development thinking of their capitals. It is certainly no coincidence that support by the two banks for market-oriented reforms and fewer State interventions at the macro and sector levels began to rise significantly during the era of Ronald Reagan and Margaret Thatcher. More recently, these banks have been steered by their boards away from projects that entail great environmental risks, are gender-biased, or involve biotechnology.

The original purpose of the World Bank, it will be recalled from Chapter I, was to finance the reconstruction of Western Europe after World War II. At that time, the belief was that capital accumulation was the key to raising income, a belief that was also widely held by economic planners in the developing countries. For the latter, this meant investments in infrastructure, such as roads, irrigation, and ports. Starting from the late 1970s, there was a perceptible shift among the donors toward programs and projects in which the impact on the poor was more direct. In the 1980s, market-oriented policies came to the fore, but these have been overtaken in recent years by concerns about poverty reduction and a range of crosscutting considerations, including governance. These shifts have been faithfully reflected in the work that the banks' staff do, although in fairness it has to be pointed out that the staff itself has at times initiated these shifts. Throughout the post-World War II period, the World Bank, in particular, has been a fount of new ideas on development, while both banks have made great efforts to find new, innovative approaches in the design of development projects.

The resources that the two banks lend have made a significant difference to the Asian developing countries. As just a single example, even before the 1997 crash, the two banks provided as much as 10 percent of the total government budget of Indonesia. This figure exaggerates the resulting leverage that the banks have, for the Indonesian Government had alternative funding sources. A concern more serious than their leverage has been that the banks' capacity to lend has, at times, run ahead of the absorptive capacity of the borrowing countries. It has been acknowledged by both institutions that the ability of staff to "deliver" loans has mattered too greatly to their careers.

In this context, it is a sad fact that, by and large, agriculture-sector loans have not performed as well as loans to the "harder" sectors. It is recognized, of course, that agriculture projects are inherently more difficult because of the dispersed nature of the beneficiaries and the executing agencies, among many other reasons. Agricultural loans are dominated by irrigation projects, which have many serious problems—so many that it is deemed necessary in this volume to cover the subject in detail (Chapter V). The question also has to be raised whether agriculture is inherently less profitable than other sectors, for otherwise its share would not be shrinking with economic growth.

A final note with regard to this form of financing: if the two banks acted as hard-nosed lenders, strictly on the basis of returns to the loan and nothing else, then the relationship between the banks and the borrowing countries would be somewhat more arm's-length. But the banks sometimes wish to project the preferences of their developed-country sponsors onto the borrowers (whether it is on behalf of the poor or for the private sector). Since the grant element of many loans has been minimal (except for loans from the International Development Association and the Asian Development Fund, the soft windows of the two banks), the taxpayers of the borrowing countries end up paying for these preferences.

INTERACTIONS BETWEEN ACTORS AND ROLES

The first section of this chapter examined the various types of collective action that are required by rural people and thus set out the roles for the actors discussed in the second section. The discussion of the actors showed their evolution without saying much about their roles. This was because the various actors and institutions have their own histories, whose course has run somewhat independently of the roles they have to play or that they are fitted to play. But in this part of the chapter, the actors and their roles are linked through consideration of a number of principles that may be applied in order to slot the actors into the various roles, starting with the principle of comparative advantage.

Comparative Advantage

The central governments of most Asian states have had a dominant role in rural development. This is quite paradoxical. Even a medium-sized country has a very diverse rural sector: its problems are myriad as well as subtle, and certainly of a kind that people who staff the central bureaucracies can barely comprehend. Bureaucrats have a predilection for general rules when it is location-specific measures that are needed. They tend to be insensitive and even antagonistic to the idea of community, when many (though not all) parts of Asia have vibrant local communities. In fact, looked at in the cold light of day, central bureaucrats should not be in the business of rural development at all.

Central governments do, however, have an undeniable comparative advantage in three areas, all ultimately resting on their monopoly of coercive power: in raising resources, in assigning property rights, and in regulating or enforcing the quality of essential goods and services (whether these are provided publicly or privately, or centrally or locally). To the extent that many of the needs of rural societies cannot be met by voluntary action without running into free-rider problems, only central governments can raise the resources to meet these needs. It is this power to raise money that gives them the impetus in the end to take over almost the entire area of rural development. Even for those regimes that are democratic and not predatory or authoritarian, having raised the money coercively through taxation, they remain accountable to their electorate as to how the money is spent and must therefore control the expenditures almost all the way to the end. They have been loath to devolve power and send money to local governments.

Their reluctance can be explained by their assumptions about agency costs. Agency costs arise when a party (the principal), rather than undertaking a task itself, contracts with someone else (an agent) to do it. The principal will then have to supervise and monitor the agent; in case the agent's performance is not in accordance with the contract, the principal will have to enforce the contract or penalize the agent. Governments' reluctance to devolve arises from the assumption that the agency costs of supervision, monitoring, and enforcement that arise from devolution are too high and that it is better that central governments go ahead with what needs to be done. If they were to liberalize and allow the private sector to take over particular functions (say, grain marketing), then it might also be claimed that regulating those functions would be too complex and the regulatory costs too high.

But if central governments undertake the tasks themselves, they do not avoid the agency costs. After all, the individual bureaucrats who help design and implement the policies with which the electorate has entrusted them may shirk just as much as the contractors. It therefore becomes an empirical matter whether devolution or privatization would economize on agency costs. The recent trend towards both is based essentially on the hunch (and at the moment, it is no more than that) that the agency costs associated with devolution or subcontracting are lower than the agency costs of supervising the employees of the central Government.

Given the comparative advantage of central governments in raising revenues and their frequent failure to spend them with optimal effectiveness as far as local rural development is concerned, a distinction has to be drawn between financing on the one hand and provision and delivery on the other. Most public goods and many merit goods cannot or will not be adequately paid for in the same way as private goods and services: voluntarily by the beneficiaries. Although central governments must necessarily be involved in financing these goods, other actors may do the actual provision and delivery (Ortiz and Moser 1996). Chapters IV through VII explore, first, how the provision and delivery of various services that are usually in the domain of central governments can be devolved or privatized and, second, what residual regulatory roles the State might or should retain.

Coproduction

The principle of comparative advantage may partly explain the assigning of roles to the different actors, but it rests on an assumption that the different actors are rival candidates for each role. In some instances, however, this view may prevent consideration of a possibly more attractive alternative: the different actors may cooperate, with better results.

Ostrom (1996b) points out that the provision of services (and most of what the government provides is services) is not like the provision of goods. In many cases, services involve the participation of both the provider and the recipient. The productivity of the former depends very much on the activities of the latter. The modern approach to agricultural extension reflects this concept. Instead of viewing farmers as passive recipients of technological advice and input "packages" from the extension agents, as has been done in the past, it is more useful to bring in the farmers as partners in the exercise from the beginning. The methods of integrated pest management cannot be "disseminated" to farmers by means of traditional, top-down extension, nor can the resource management concepts that need to be applied in rainfed areas. These topics will be discussed further in Chapter IV.

Such interdependence exists in most other areas of service provision, such as irrigation, health care, and education. Ostrom coined the term "coproduction" for this phenomenon. Coproduction implies that the production function in most service industries is determined not only by the inputs under the provider's control, but also by those under the recipients' control. This specification is substantive and not just formal, in that the inputs from the provider and recipient cannot be substituted for each other. This is the basis for the synergy between the two. Consequently, for service provision to be truly effective, it is essential that the intended beneficiaries be brought into the picture from the very beginning, i.e., from the design stage. Beneficiaries here need not be individuals and indeed, in most cases it would be impractical for individuals to participate. It is more efficient if entire communities are brought on board.

Social Capital

The discussion of coproduction leads naturally to the concept of social capital, which is richly discussed but poorly defined in the literature. It was already considered extensively above in the discussion about the interaction and cooperation among individual villagers and villages that have evolved in order to carry out community tasks like the maintenance of irrigation systems. Another way to convey the concept is found in the following description of Kerala, the most densely populated and still one of the poorer states in India:

> Even the most casual observer of Kerala society would be quick to note the sheer density of civil organizations and the vigor of associational life. Keralites of all walks of life, it would seem, have an irresistible inclination to combine, associate and organize, and to do so without the outbreaks of violent disorder... Thus, despite extremely high levels of social mobilization, Kerala has largely been spared the sectarian and casteist violence that has recently been on the upswing throughout most of India.
> Across both the formal and informal sectors of the economy, rates of unionization are high. The state boasts the most extensive network of cooperative societies, as well as numerous nongovernment organizations... Kerala's caste self-help and social upliftment societies have a long history of active civil engagement. Its 'library movement,' literary associations and film industry [have] earned it a reputation as a cultural center rivaled only by Bengal...
> The vigor and dynamism of civil society [are] matched only by the size and activism of the state... Kerala has the most developed social welfare system in India, including the most extensive network of fair-price shops (public food distribution), and rates of social expenditure that continue to be significantly higher than the national average. Through the implementation of the land reforms of 1970, by far the most radical in the subcontinent... the state transformed the agrarian social-property structure, destroying the traditional landlord class and creating a new class of small proprietors. The government-run system of primary health care units has reduced infant mortality to near-First World rates. Moreover, even by Indian standards, the state has been very active in regulating the market, restricting labor-displacing technologies in traditional industries, legislating work conditions and hiring practices in industry as well as in agriculture and aggressively enforcing minimum wages (Heller 1996).

It is the quality of the civil society in Kerala—and the quality of its interactions with public institutions—that explains the ability of the State to perform many tasks that would be considered too ambitious for countries with many times the per capita income of Kerala.[5] That quality of civil society is also called "social capital."

Still another perspective is offered by Putnam (1993), who constructed a theoretical framework based on his research on the comparative functioning of provincial governments in Italy. He points out that collective-action problems are normally shot through with all sorts of "prisoner's dilemma" games. In such games, if individuals choose a selfish and uncooperative strategy, they will end up worse off than if they had cooperated with others. If the game is played only once, it is attractive for individuals to act selfishly and cheat on all the others, which makes noncooperation the expected outcome of the game. If, on the other hand, such games are played repeatedly, over time individuals will gradually learn the art of cooperation in their relationships with one another and also begin to trust one another (Axelrod 1984). If a network of individuals is involved in such transactions, they will also come to trust one another. It is this relationship of trust within the network that we call social capital and that will increase the productivity of a society just as much as physical capital.

Note that social capital is defined for a particular network of individuals. Heller's work on Kerala is at the level of a province in a larger nation-state. Putnam's work compares the provincial governments in Italy. Thus, these authors define social capital for the populations of Kerala and the Italian provinces. As social capital is defined for particular networks of individuals, it can be "large," relative to Kerala, but "small" relative to India, however it is measured. This implies that the relative performance of the different tiers of government will vary depending on how far the networks of trust extend within a society. Clearly, this must be an important consideration in the design of any programs for devolution.

---

[5] Dreze and Sen (1995) mention the role of civil society in their analysis of the uniqueness of Kerala, but stress the role of education as an explanatory factor for the quality of civil society.

In rural Asia, social capital is most developed at the village level. Until the coming of modern means of communications and transport (and with them the emergence of markets), the opportunity to interact with members of the broader society was small and there was no social capital to back up the performance of the larger geographical units. At the national level, on the other hand, much of the social capital that has emerged has been for urban, nonagricultural sectors, because the networks that arise from the functioning of the national economy are mostly concentrated in urban areas. Consequently, the political and cultural language used at the national level has been that of the urban middle class, into which rural-based representatives have to fit uncomfortably. This is one explanation for the dissonance between the political logic driving national governments and the needs of the rural societies that were discussed earlier in the section on central government politicians (pp. 45–47).

A cluster of social capital that is important for rural societies and for national economic performance is the relationship of trust that has developed among the traders and middlemen of agricultural commodities, for example among the Chinese in Southeast Asia, or among the trading castes in India.[6] Interestingly, despite their economic importance as a group, these people are often the target of abuse from the dominant urban middle classes. Government policies are sometimes directed at the destruction of such social capital (see Chapter VI).

The use of the term "social capital" invites comparison with the concept of physical capital. Both are accumulated over time and both can be destroyed; in the case of social capital, the destruction may occur through disuse or deliberate acts of policy, as when the Chinese Communists erased the social capital that had been built up over centuries of Chinese history. But social and physical capital differ in that the accumulation of the former occurs in a relatively time-consuming and unpredictable process. For example, one of Putnam's more depressing conclusions is that Italian provinces that are well governed have been well

---

[6] An interesting parallel can be drawn with families and minorities (Jews and Huguenots) engaged in merchant banking in 19th-century Europe (Landes 1958).

governed for centuries and the same applies to those that are poorly run. In the language of game theory, once players in a society hit upon a noncooperative equilibrium, it may be difficult to pry them loose from that equilibrium.

There is one other important aspect in which social and physical capital differ. Normally, when one considers different subunits of physical capital, say the plant and machinery belonging to the Ford Motor Company and General Motors, one thinks of them as being additive: both sets add to the world's productive capacity. This is not necessarily so with social capital. As already noted, it enhances the productivity of the individuals belonging to a particular network (say, an ethnic group): it can therefore be said to belong to this network. However, in the interaction that any particular network may have with other networks in society, the high level of social capital that any one of them possesses could be detrimental to the proper functioning of society as a whole. For example, the group-specific social-capital embodied in patron-client networks often undermines the functioning of the economy and leads to nepotism and corruption in government. As one political scientist tersely put it, "In factional settings, solidarity is a problem and not a solution" (Holmes 1989).

The concept of social capital provides considerable insight, but applying the concept "in the field" requires the exercise of some skepticism, for social capital is a matter of long-term evolution. It cannot be easily created or manipulated as an instrument of policy. Even its destruction is fraught with difficulties. The social capital embodied in the rules of patron-client relations pervades much of rural Asia and at one time performed a useful function. However, in a democratic nation-state and in the modern globalized economy to which rural societies must adapt, this particular form of social capital is no longer appropriate, as it tends to undermine the new social institutions that are being set up in the name of the nation-state and a competitive global order. Despite the harm that results from their persistence, patron-client relationships have proven resistant to change and still play a very important role in social relationships in much of rural Asia.

Governance

One of the most important goals of collective action is to ensure that whoever undertakes it satisfies—quantitatively, qualitatively, and efficiently—the needs of the intended beneficiaries, as well as of those who finance the action. To attain this objective requires good governance. A good way to come to grips with this somewhat elusive concept is to examine the concepts that have been proposed to define the State's provision of good governance: accountability, transparency, predictability, and participation (ADB 1995).

- *Accountability* means that in all institutions of the State, there is a clear line of responsibility that ultimately ends up with the electorate, from which authority flows. This concept has been developed over the centuries in Western countries and culminated in the modern democratic State. But when the Western countries came to rule over their colonies in Asia, they took an authoritarian line vis-à-vis the people over whom they ruled. Colonial governments quite naturally saw themselves as being accountable to their home countries. When the colonies became independent states, they retained most of the laws, the regulations, and the authoritarian bent. Where social revolutions led to Communist states, there was no transition in their State structures to match that of their economies. Furthermore, the postcolonial societies were in many respects less accustomed to accountability than to loyalty, a concept that has quite different ramifications: loyalty is really a relationship between persons, whereas accountability is a (somewhat more abstract) relationship between offices or groups. Consequently many State systems have over time become quite personalistic.
- *Transparency* is a concept that makes it possible for governments (and other institutions) to be accountable. Because of nepotism and the tradition of patron-client

relationships, as well as the authoritarian bent and the mandarin tradition of the civil service that Asian governments inherited from the colonial powers, transparency in Asian governments is remarkable only for its rarity.
- *Predictability* is yet another concept tied to the more modern form of government and economy. When people decide on, say, investment, or any other activity that links them to the future, they must do so with the belief that there will be no change in the rules of the game that they could not have taken into account at the time of the decision. If there is any such change, then there must be some clear reasons for it.
- While accountability, transparency and predictability are principles of good governance, *participation* is both a principle and the means for achieving it. Clearly, if beneficiaries are brought into a public activity from the beginning, then there will be more transparency and predictability in the way it is carried out. Participation generally leads to increased efficiency as well (see Chapters V and VII). One of the major contributions that NGOs have made in Asia has been to increase people's participation in various aspects of government.

These four criteria carry with them an academic and rather technocratic flavor: the focus is on principles and abstract mechanisms rather than on the institutions and social framework (or what is called above the social capital) that make the principles meaningful. Accountability and transparency are meaningless in societies that have no free press or any other mechanisms whereby those who do not live up to their requirements can be effectively penalized. Moreover, the principles of good governance could, at the extreme, sometimes justify policies directed at the destruction of social capital, even though that capital may be highly productive for the economy as a whole (see Chapter VI).

CONCLUSIONS

The coming chapters will demonstrate that the types of collective action that a society needs to undertake have, if anything, shrunk in scope over time. All developing countries have moved away from the centralized strategic approach to development that received heavy emphasis in the 1950s and 1960s, entailing as it did a planned economy that directed resources into particular sectors. Good examples of the old approach can be found in the first few five-year plans in India. Certainly, the sectoral policies espoused in such plans have all but disappeared from Asia. There remains the dispute as to what role the State has in fostering specific lines of industry and in coordinating investments, but this dispute pertains mostly to the industrial sector and has little relevance for rural Asia.

In place of these broad sectoral policies, what is being demanded of the collective actors is a much more complex and sophisticated task, best summed up in the call for a "people-centered" approach, which implies a much more finely tuned sensitivity to the needs of the beneficiaries. A bureaucratically-run central Government is at a distinct disadvantage in this arena. Consequently, in many countries more actors are becoming involved. These new actors, however, far from relieving the central Government of its tasks, have made the tasks much more difficult, for the Government, in the end, must ride herd over them and provide coherence to the whole exercise. The new roles and actors also put a premium on the principles of good governance. Good governance is desirable in and of itself, but in the new circumstances facing Asian societies today, it is also a key to enhancing productive efficiency and social welfare. These complex tasks require a political and bureaucratic system—and a new generation of civil servants—that are at once sensitive and knowledgeable. Unfortunately, few Asian governments have been able to keep up with the pace of the change that is occurring around them. Indeed, there is evidence that in some countries, the quality of the bureaucracy has declined.

The main generalization that can be drawn from this discussion is that governments will, for better or worse, continue to play a lead role in efforts to promote rural development, but they must learn to be much more nuanced in their approach to policies. This generality precludes a presentation of policy specifics at this stage. With reference to the particular arenas of technology, irrigation, food pricing policies, rural social services, and even the broader issue of devolution to local governments, however, concrete recommendations can be made, and this will be the task of the following chapters.

III Devolution and Decentralization

The ideologies of modern nationalism... arising as they do out of intense concern with massive social reconstruction, show a strong tendency toward neglect, even an outward denial, of important variations in domestic cultural patterns... The vivid memory on the part of the elites of the New States of colonial divide-and-rule policies, as well as a fear of the strong divisive tendencies they quite accurately perceive both within themselves and in the mass of the population, leads them to regard any explicit or frank concern with internal diversity as subversive of the whole nation-building effort and to view, or to try to view, their own society in a much too uniform and global, even stereotypic a manner. With regard to national economic planning this leads to a failure to cast proposals in a form which attempts to take maximum advantage of the peculiarities of various local traditions, to an unwillingness even to consider differentiated plans for different cultural and social groups...

– Clifford Geertz (1963)

"Le roi est mort, vive le roi" (the king is dead, long live the king).

INTRODUCTION: WHY DEVOLVE?

In developing countries, devolution of government services—the handing over of all authority to local governments—or decentralization—the reassignment of some authority for selected functions—has become increasingly common in the past few decades (Cheema and Rondinelli 1983). This trend mirrors the generally successful decentralization that has taken place in a number of industrialized countries, such as New Zealand, Poland, and Hungary. In Asia, it is usually closely associated with the move away from highly centralized systems of government, with reform movements marked by demands for more competitive politics, greater popular participation in government, and perhaps most notably in Indonesia, a demand for a fairer local share of the bounty of natural resources. In countries as disparate in size and political systems as the Philippines and Nepal, there have been recent forceful moves to decentralize government. In others, such as Mongolia, which are setting up democratic government structures for the first time, decentralized government has become the model to follow.

Demands for decentralization are not new in Asian countries. In both Nepal and Indonesia, for instance, greater local autonomy has been under discussion for nearly four decades. In recent years, new factors have emerged that have accelerated the process, however. One is the impact of globalization. Better communications have made people at all levels of society more aware of what is occurring around the world, as well as of what is happening in their own countries. In this rapidly shrinking world, comparisons and informed judgments are much easier to make and more opportunities are available to be involved in governance.

A second factor is the impact of the enormous economic and social changes that have occurred in the last 20 years. Liberalization, privatization, and other market reforms all require a different mode of governance. These changes have also underlined the limited capacity of central governments to handle adequately all the demands placed on them. In the future, a State's activity will have to be limited by its capabilities; if these mean devolving responsibilities, that process must occur.

Allied to both of these factors is the growing demand for participation. Although this varies among countries, many local communities are no longer satisfied to accept the dictates of a central Government. There is a strong, growing voice for participation in governance. Even highly centralized systems in countries such as the Soviet Union have been replaced by much more participatory, localized governments. More generally, in almost all transitional countries, the retreat of Marxist-Leninist ideology was accompanied by rapid decentralization, first of economic power and then of political power.

The perceptions of donors, which reflect the thinking of major sources of development financing in many countries, have also changed. Traditionally dealing only with central governments in their lending operations, believing that central governments alone had both the responsibility and capability to manage development, donors have recently shifted to supporting better governance and with it, greater local participation and autonomy.

Consequently, decentralization of government is now sought in nearly all developing Asia. It encompasses the transfer of both administrative and financial authority, since it is understood that without adequate fiscal resources decentralization will not work. It also involves the participation of local civil society, whether this be citizens' groups or nongovernment organizations (NGOs). Its potential benefits are clear. It will strengthen the overall responsiveness of government in the country, better match the provision of government services to local needs, and more effectively support and utilize the local economy. It will also bring government closer to people; through participation, it will create more accountable, transparent, and, it is hoped, more capable governance.

Yet decentralization is not a panacea that will solve all problems. It requires full political will. Unfortunately, while this will is often expressed in rhetoric, it is not always backed up with full commitment. In Bangladesh, for example, the central Government introduced elected people's councils to please the donors, but power remained firmly in central government hands (Crook and Manor 1994). In addition, decentralized governments do not always adhere to the principles behind their own creation when dealing with other local bodies. Thus, in Pakistan, provincial governments can be found treating municipalities as subordinates, a return to earlier centralized attitudes (World Bank 1997).

Political will is not sufficient by itself. Clear legal and administrative mandates are also highly desirable. The time needed for their establishment, however, may just create excuses for inaction by central authorities. Thus, more fundamentally, decentralization requires intensive interaction among stakeholders. But the process has no universal blueprint, given the varied and usually complex political, administrative, and social systems found in the developing countries.

Decentralization also has dangers. If not well managed, central governments could lose control over the macroeconomy as the result of uncoordinated local decisions. Regional disparities could be exacerbated, leading to economic and social tensions. Local governments could also fall under the sway of particular local interests, thereby undermining State power and accountability.

Thus, decentralization is a double-edged sword. It is clearly the way to go if the people want it, but it is not a simple or quick remedy for all of society's problems. Nor is it a process that is anywhere near complete in Asia. This is well illustrated by the three case studies that follow. In Indonesia, the Government, under strong political pressure in an uncertain new era of reform, moved quickly to formally decentralize its highly centralized political and administrative systems. Political pressure has also provided the impetus for decentralization in the Philippines, which has undergone considerable and fairly successful legal decentralization since 1991 with the active involvement of a vibrant civil society. In contrast, reforms in the PRC have been largely economic rather than political. Nonetheless, despite few formal changes in legislation and a limited civil society, the PRC has achieved considerable decentralization through the sweeping economic reforms that allowed local governments a good many decision-making powers.

COUNTRY EXPERIENCES

Indonesia

Since its independence from colonial rule in 1947, Indonesia has seen a constant dialogue between forces pushing for, and mostly achieving, a centralized State and those seeking greater local autonomy. Set up as a unitary State under the 1945 Constitution, which gave the central Government strong executive powers, Indonesia between 1945 and 1965 undertook a number of experiments to give greater autonomy to its provinces. These included an attempt in 1948 to set up three levels of autonomous regions, consisting of the province, the district, and the village; the plan was never implemented. At different times in the 1950s, fairly extensive powers were delegated to lower levels of government, but regional rebellions and the near disintegration of the country had led by 1959 to a greater concentration of authority than before.[1] This tendency was accelerated with the advent of the New Order (Order Baru) period in 1965, which saw the establishment of a strong centralized Government under President Suharto. During the New Order period, little real decentralization occurred, and even when it did, it was administrative and financial in nature, and not political, since the political system was tightly controlled. This has changed dramatically since Suharto's fall and the collapse of the New Order Government in 1998. With the arrival of the era of *reformasi* (reform), Indonesia has once again swung back to trying to give greater autonomy to its various regions and to decentralize government.

Basic to these swings between centralized and decentralized government in Indonesia has been one dominating theme: the need for national unity. National unity has not

---

[1] Presidential Decree No. 1 of 1959 markedly reduced the powers and autonomy of the provinces that had been provided in earlier legislation. It remained in effect until superseded in 1974 by Law No. 5 on Basic Principles of Regional Administration.

been easily achieved due to Indonesia's size, large population, and island geography, with marked economic and social disparities among its various regions, an unequal distribution of its population, marked ethnic diversity, and religious differences. Indonesia covers a land area of 1.9 million square kilometers, has 13,667 islands, a population of over 200 million, around 300 ethnic groups, and, while predominantly Moslem, has three other officially recognized religions (Christianity, Buddhism, and Hinduism). Some 62 percent of its population lives on the small central island of Java, with the balance spread unequally throughout the outer islands. There is a world of economic, social, and cultural difference between, say, the strongly Muslim, resource-rich province of Aceh in the westernmost part of the country and the predominately Christian and resource-poor province of Nusa Tenggara Timor (NTT) in the east. Even where a province may appear to be rich in resources, such as Irian Jaya, the wealth derived from those resources is usually not distributed within the province. Given these disparities, one can appreciate the constant search for ways of establishing national unity at every stage of Indonesia's postcolonial development.

With the political and macroeconomic stability that was achieved in the early years of Suharto's rule, coupled with large inflows of oil revenues and official development assistance, rapid growth and development followed in nearly all parts of the country. This was achieved, however, by retaining an authoritarian political system that allowed only very controlled participation by the greater part of the population in government and in decision making. The events of May 1998 and the overthrow of Suharto have ushered in the Reformasi Era, in which the restrictions of the New Order period are being swept aside. Today all levels of society are seeking participation.

The New Order Period

The New Order period that began with Suharto's accession to power in 1965 was characterized by a strongly centralized Government committed to national unity;

establishing firm political and administrative control was made the first priority. A strong central government apparatus was built up in the first decade, with powerful central sectoral ministries, centrally appointed governors in the country's 27 provinces, and centrally approved district heads. The state ideology, Pancasila, was widely used to emphasize the importance of national unity.[2] A strong and dominant government political party, GOLKAR (from Golongan Karya, or "functional groups"), was established (Reeve 1985), which received the compulsory support of all civil servants at election time. The educational system was tightly controlled, with bans on student political activities and the use of blacklists to restrict public-sector employment opportunities, particularly in the early 1980s, for students regarded as not fully conformist.

Within this framework, development was given first priority and used as a political tool, first to stabilize and then to develop the country. As a political tool, the considerable inflow of funds[3] devoted to development from the late 1970s onwards helped establish a pervasive patronage system, using project funds to pay additional honoraria to the country's large civil service. Since it is estimated that a middle-ranking civil servant has to augment his or her salary by at least 70 percent in additional earnings in order to make ends meet, access to projects and the honoraria they provided in fact became the criterion of a successful posting in the civil service.

Development budgets increased rapidly in the 1970s; in the latter years of that decade the development budget had grown to be the same size as the routine budget, from half its size in 1969/70 (Booth 1986). Thereafter, this growth slowed and was then reversed: during most of the 1990s, the

---

[2] First put forward by President Sukarno in a 1945 speech, Pancasila was extensively used as the ideological basis of the New Order. The third of its five principles emphasizes the need for national unity. All civil servants from 1979 onward were required to attend periodic Pancasila training courses (Morfit 1986).

[3] These came mainly from oil taxes, which contributed 60 percent of all government revenues by 1980/81, including those from foreign borrowing (Booth 1986).

development budget averaged slightly less than two thirds of the routine budget. A large part of this was dispersed to local governments in the form of bloc grants, providing the major part of the budget available to both provincial and district levels of government: in the early 1990s, for instance, 76 percent of the provincial and 82 percent of the district budgets on average came from central government grants (GTZ 1998).

This system was highly effective in bringing about the development of Indonesia in this period. In all parts of the country there were new roads, clinics, and schools. Major agricultural and food programs such as rice intensification (BIMAS, from the Indonesian acronym for "mass guidance") were introduced that benefited large segments of the population. Economic growth was rapid, supported by a well-planned macroeconomy run by a small group of central civil servants, most notably in the Ministry of Finance and the National Development Planning Agency.

In this system, little attention was given to decentralization and local autonomy. The emphasis of the New Order Government in retaining complete centralized control generally precluded this. Yet various forces were, in fact, working towards this end. The rapid development of the country's communications and educational system led to greater mobility. There was increased urbanization and, in general, greater contact with the outside world. Economic and social development brought new wealth to many provinces and created a new, better educated and more articulate middle class that, within the confines of the centralized system, became increasingly aware of its rights. This, in turn, reawakened the dormant provincial desires for autonomy that had been so strong in the earlier periods of Indonesia's independent history.

Thus, some moves towards decentralization took place at various times throughout the New Order period. On the one hand, there were attempts to formalize (although not to implement effectively) administrative and fiscal decentralization of the government system. At the same time, some decentralization took place in individual sectors such as agriculture, health care, and urban services. In the case of agriculture and health care, this decentralization continued a process that had started in the 1950s, prior to the New Order. In the case of urban services, it occurred in the 1980s, as the limited capacity of the central Government to handle local urban development became clear.

The foundations for administrative decentralization were provided in 1974 with the issuance of Law No. 5 on the Basic Principles of Regional Administration. This established the basis for Center-province relationships. It set out the functions of local government at the provincial and district levels, stating that the district would be the level that might at some stage become autonomous. The law made it clear, however, that any such autonomy would be dependent on the capability of each of the country's more than 300 districts and would not, as envisaged in the 1945 Constitution, be automatic. In this the law marked a significant change from the earlier accepted notion that autonomy was the right of local governments. Now local governments would have to show that they had the capacity to handle their own administrative and financial affairs before they would be considered for any autonomy.[4]

While the Law of 1974 was useful in providing the broad outlines of the division of powers and functions between the central and local governments, nothing was done for a considerable period to implement it. The first necessary backup regulation was not issued until Regulation No. 45 of 1992, passing some of the functions of the central sectoral ministries to the lower levels of local government. This was consistent with Indonesia's practice of first establishing a policy with a broad enactment and then, very gradually, spelling out the details of implementation with government regulations.

---

[4] The 1945 Constitution had provided for "very broad autonomy" (*otonomi seluas-luasnya*). This was now replaced with autonomy that was "real, dynamic, and responsible" (*otonomi yang nyata, dinamis dan bertanggungjawab*). In this definition, "responsible" was equated with a district's capacity. In the 1980s, several attempts were made by the Ministry of Home Affairs (which oversaw local government administration) to classify Indonesia's districts according to their capacity. This classification was then to be used to determine which districts would be eligible for autonomy. See Smoke and Lewis (1998).

Implementation indeed proceeded very slowly; pressure continued to grow within the country for more local autonomy and finally, in 1995, a pilot district program was introduced.

This District Autonomy Pilot Program was an attempt by the Government to introduce some measure in response to growing calls to move the promised decentralization ahead. As with many other programs in Indonesia, it was initially tried out as a pilot project with one district in each of 26 provinces targeted for the decentralization of a wide range of central functions. These came from 16 sectors and, in addition to general government, comprised agriculture, forestry, mining, trade, health, education, fisheries, plantation crops, livestock, transmigration, social affairs, cooperatives, tourism, labor, and industry.

The aim of the project was to achieve better local resource mobilization and improve services, as well as to bring about greater local participation in government and strengthen local initiative. Unfortunately, the pilot project met with little success, due mainly to two factors. First, many of the functions finally given to the districts after intense negotiation with various central ministries were not ones easily taken over by a district government. In addition, the districts lost some functions that they were already carrying out well, which now reverted to the provinces in compensation for ones the latter had lost. One example was the reversion of the profitable issuance of permits to engage in trade from the district to the provincial level. Second, the planned transfer of central government funds to the districts to meet the considerable costs of taking over the new functions did not push through. Thus, many districts were either unable to reorganize their offices to handle the new duties or were severely hampered in doing so.

Fiscal decentralization proceeded even more slowly. Throughout this period the largest part of local government budgets consisted of central government grants; little attempt was made to mobilize local resources. A law passed in 1956 had, in principle, given the provinces between 75 percent and 90 percent of the proceeds from natural resource and export revenues, and it was expected that this tax sharing would cover about two thirds of local government expenditures. This law was never fully implemented, however, and the proposed distribution was replaced by the central Government's Subsidy for the Autonomous Regions.

The 1974 Law on Basic Principles of Regional Administration, which provided only some general stipulations on local taxes and fees, became the only guideline available on the fiscal relationships between the Center and the provinces. This gap in fiscal authority led local governments to introduce a wide variety of local taxes, levies, and fees. None of these provided large revenues, however, and some cost more to collect than they yielded in receipts. Finally, a new central fiscal act was passed in 1997 that established clearly the taxes that could be levied at both the provincial and district levels. This act, Law No. 18 on Regional Taxation, rescinded most of the small and unwieldy taxes that had emerged in many areas, replacing them with three taxes at the provincial level and six at the district level. Thus, the total number of taxes was reduced, while the potential revenues of both provincial and district governments were enhanced.

Yet even with this revised tax base the local governments' dependence on central government grants continued. At the same time, the central Government shared control of very little in the way of the tax revenue that accrued to it: an analysis of 1993 data on shared taxes and sources of revenue showed that 92 percent was controlled at the central level, less than 5 percent went to the provincial level, and just over 3 percent to the district level (Panggabean 1997).

Sectoral Decentralization during the New Order Period

Although administrative and fiscal decentralization proved difficult and generally did not progress far in the New Order period, moves were taking place to decentralize responsibilities in other areas. Provincial and district planning boards (*bappeda*) were created by legislation in the late 1970s and early 1980s; however, it took a decade or more before these boards were adequately staffed and fully functional (MacAndrews 1986). At the sectoral level, some decentralization occurred in the areas of urban services, agriculture, and health. In all three cases this decentralization eventually led to some improvements in the provision of services.

Indonesia's effort to decentralize *urban development* is of relevance to rural Asia because of its rationale and approach. A major factor in the decision to decentralize was the recognition of the inadequate management performance of central government agencies. This inadequacy resulted in long delays in the implementation of urban projects by central ministries and a decline in the quality of many projects. It also resulted in a lack of flexibility in design so that urban projects often did not fit local conditions. To deal with these problems, the Indonesian Government initiated a process by which central agencies were to support local agencies until adequate local capacity was built up. This approach potentially provides a model for decentralized, integrated rural services (e.g., for irrigated agriculture).

In 1985, the Ministry of Public Works launched one of the most successful efforts to decentralize urban development, the Integrated Urban Infrastructure Development Program (IUIDP). Aimed at introducing an integrated approach to replace sector-specific infrastructure development (e.g., roads versus water supply), the IUIDP empowered local governments to determine, plan, and implement projects in accord with local priorities. Of critical importance, local governments were given assistance to prepare and implement five-year comprehensive investment plans, to raise additional revenues, and to strengthen their technical and administrative capabilities. The principles underlying the IUIDP were formalized in the 1987 Statement on Urban Development Policies and subsequently reiterated in the Five-Year National Development Plan.

The second major initiative was the setting up of the Urban Development Coordination Team in 1987. This involved the National Development Planning Agency and the Ministries of Home Affairs, Finance, and Public Works and aimed to coordinate the formulation of integrated urban development policies. This quickly became the channel for donor funding, including that of ADB, with most ensuing projects being decentralized to local governments. New financing for urban development was provided in 1985 by enacting a land and building tax and by setting up an urban loan facility through a new Regional Development Account, which was also used to coordinate donor loans for urban infrastructure and services.

In the *agriculture sector*, decentralization began very early, as far back as the 1950s. At that time, most of the services provided to small-scale farmers, including extension, seeds and planting materials, plant protection, post-harvest processing, and soil and water conservation, were moved first to the provincial level and then later to the district level (plantations remained at the central level, however). At both levels, four separate offices were established for food crops and horticulture, smallholder estate crops, livestock, and fisheries. These offices, following the usual Indonesian practice, reported to the local head (whether the governor or the district head), but received technical direction and guidance from their respective directors general in the central Ministry of Agriculture (MOA) in Jakarta. Although common in the Indonesian local government system, this double supervision and reporting caused confusion at times, but the local offices at both levels were generally free to carry out their duties on a day-to-day basis.

It is noteworthy, however, that little donor support was ever provided to help build up the capacity of these local offices. Donor loans, particularly those of the World Bank, always seemed to be given to MOA for national programs. In fact, the extensive World Bank support led to a considerable duplication of agricultural extension services. The World Bank funded the setting up of large-scale agricultural extension services to support the national BIMAS rice campaign; these duplicated services already provided at the district level. Later it funded new Rural Extension Centers at the district level that remained under central control and often did not cooperate with the other district-level agricultural offices. It was only in 1994 that a new institution, the Agricultural Information and Extension Center, was set up in each district specifically to integrate extension services.

Indonesia has been experimenting with a decentralized agricultural research system since 1992, when there was a major reorganization of MOA's Agency for Agricultural Research and Development (AARD). A 1994 ministerial decree established 17 Assessment Institutes for Agricultural Technology (AIATs) in the provinces to regionalize research and promote development of farm technologies suited to individual agroecological zones. This reorganization is currently being evaluated (Manwan et al. 1998) and there are still many problems to be threshed out. The role of the central organization is not yet clear, and some of its assets (e.g., the gene banks), which should have remained centralized, were given to the newly-formed provincial institutions. Both ADB and the World Bank have provided funding to support this decentralization. However, the general management of the AIATs remained under AARD, while the decentralization process suffered from a chronic lack of resources. The share of the national development budget for agriculture, forestry, and irrigation declined from 30 percent to 10 percent during the 25 years prior to 1998. Furthermore, in the Five-Year Development Plan in effect through 1999, more than 60 percent of this combined budget was earmarked for irrigation.

Moreover, there was continuous conflict between MOA and its agencies and the local governments as to what financial resources should be delegated. If Indonesia's laws dictated that funds must be appropriated to support decentralization, central officials read this to refer only to the routine budget and not to the development budget, whereas local government officials naturally felt they should also get a share of the development budget. The lack of funding affected not only the implementation activities of the local offices but also their personnel policies. Without a share of the development budget for projects and project honoraria, as noted above, these local offices could not provide the added financial incentives necessary to attract and keep competent staff.

If agriculture experienced some attempts to decentralize, albeit undermined by the lack of funding and central support, a better picture can be seen in the *health sector*. As in agriculture, partial decentralization efforts took place as far back as the 1950s, when health affairs were transferred to the provinces in Java, Sumatra, and Kalimantan. This pattern was followed in 1969 when Irian Jaya became a province and again in 1976 in when the province of East Timor was created. No services were transferred to the four provinces comprising Sulawesi or to the provinces of Maluku, Bali, and NTT. It was not until 1987 that these initial steps were consolidated under a new regulation, No. 7, for the nationwide decentralization of health affairs. This, like so many attempts to standardize decentralization in Indonesia, was difficult to implement in all provinces, due to their considerable differences in size, budgets, and local resources. The regulation also failed to spell out clearly which functions should be handled at the provincial level and which at the district level. In practice, the districts, through the local health offices, carried out nearly all implementation. At the subdistrict level, the community health centers (*puskesmas*) reported to the district office.

Health services in Indonesia have benefited from a pilot integrated budget system introduced in 1993/94 that brought together the routine and development budgets. This allowed a greater share of the development budget to be used at the district level and, in turn, provided projects and project honoraria that greatly assisted the local health offices in attracting more qualified staff.

The Reformasi Era

With the collapse of the New Order regime in May 1998 and its replacement by the Reformasi Era, the decentralization of authority became an urgent political preoccupation. After the centralized system of the Suharto regime, the pent-up desire for more autonomy led to strident demands for the almost immediate decentralization of government authority and the opening up of the rigidly controlled political system. The aim was to pass the necessary laws, political, administrative and financial, by the time of the first general elections of this era in June 1999. Some of the major legislation had been passed by late 1999, but an enormous task remained of preparing implementing guidelines and revising related regulations in order to eliminate conflicts with the new political and administrative reforms.

Three electoral laws were the first to be processed. These allowed for the free establishment of political parties, as well as more representative, and responsible, assemblies at the local level. They also laid out the rules for the June 1999 elections, as well as for local elections to be held a year later. Together, these laws opened up the political system at all levels. They also provided the political changes necessary to back up the administrative and financial measures for decentralization.

A further landmark development was the preparation of the new Law on Regional Government. Its drafting, and the heated debates in the National Assembly before it was finally passed, showed how difficult it was going to be to implement decentralization in so large and diverse a country. It was drafted by a special committee comprising government and university representatives that was set up by the Ministry of Home Affairs in June 1998, almost immediately after the fall of the Suharto regime. Intense discussions ensued, with no fewer than seven drafts of the law being processed before a final draft was sent in February 1999 to the National Assembly to be ratified. Unfortunately, the very limited time allowed to prepare the legislation precluded any extensive consultation, within or outside government, on the law's makeup.[5]

The drafters faced a number of major issues. One was whether both the provinces and the districts were to be given autonomy. After considerable debate it was decided that the provinces would be given limited autonomy, but full

---

[5] Only one meeting was held with local government representatives. This occurred in late October 1998, when 40 district heads were called into Jakarta to be briefed. In general, few people in either the public service or civil society in Jakarta knew what was being proposed.

autonomy would be given to the country's districts and municipalities. The districts will now be responsible for all local affairs, including finance and the recruitment and administration of staff, with the central Government retaining responsibility only for external affairs, defense and security, justice, fiscal affairs, religious affairs, and strategic matters.

A second issue was how to ensure autonomy and local accountability in the autonomous districts. This was achieved by making the district heads entirely responsible to an elected local assembly, which would also appoint them; they would no longer have to answer to the central Government for any of their actions. Prior to this, both the provincial governor and the central Government had to approve the appointments of district heads, who were accountable to the provincial governor. In addition, to ensure full community participation at the village level, a new village institution was to be set up. Called the Village Representative Body (Badan Perwakilan Desa), it would replace the present Village Consultative Body and would consist of freely elected community members.

A third issue was how to ensure adequate financing for this decentralization. This was to be done by providing a central government bloc grant to fund the newly autonomous districts: up to 55 percent of central government revenues, large enough to meet all devolved costs. It was to be distributed based on a formula that would take into account the diversity of the different districts in population, size, and levels of development.

To back up the administrative and political reforms, a Fiscal Law[6] was drafted by the Ministry of Finance and passed in April 1999. It governs the financing relationships between the central and local governments. It retains some central control over national finances, but delegates considerable powers to the local districts for budgetary affairs. The large

---

[6] Although popularly referred to as the Fiscal Law, its formal title is the Law on the Balance of Funding between the Central and Local Governments.

bloc grant to fund the autonomous districts will be based on a proposed formula to counterbalance the existing inequalities among districts.

Little thought was given to the process of implementation. In this there will be numerous potential problems to solve. One is the extent to which, given the strongly vested interests left over from the New Order period, the new Reformasi Era Government will fully devolve functions to the districts and municipalities. It may well be that in the process it will try to retain its previous central authority by delegating only limited responsibilities.

A second issue is the time required for implementation. Initially, a year's transition was envisaged, but this was later increased to five years. Even though political necessity probably dictates quick implementation, the proposed transition period is clearly too short. Given the diversity and size of Indonesia, the process is more likely to take a decade or even longer.

A third problem is that of reallocating central government staff. It is expected that as many as 22 of the present 39 existing central ministries/agencies will no longer be needed, with the remainder becoming greatly reduced in staff. This will entail the relocation of tens of thousands of central civil servants to the district level and require considerable planning for their deployment, as well as for their salaries and conditions of service.

Fourth, there is the question of the adjustment costs, which will be sizable in terms of infrastructure and transfer of personnel. Additional offices will have to be built to accommodate the expanded district-level governments. No estimates as yet exist, but given the considerable constraint on Indonesia's national budget due to the effects of the economic crisis, funding to support the proposed decentralization may continue to be very difficult.

Finally, assuring that district officials can handle their expanded roles will take time and require a massive capacity-building effort. Yet few steps have been taken so far to introduce training programs to upgrade skills at the district level. Given the large number of districts in Indonesia, it may again take a decade or more to build up an efficient district-level civil service.

With the formation of the first Reformasi Government in late October 1999, headed by the new President Abdurrahman Wahid, concrete moves to decentralize were quickly initiated. Some ministries were abolished and new ones were created, including a Ministry for Regional Autonomy. In the remaining months of 1999 and in early 2000, the process of moving authority and decision making to the district level began in earnest. Large and formerly powerful ministries such as Public Works were reorganized, cutting back both on their central functions and staff. Central ministry budgets that had formerly been predominantly allocated and spent from the Center were now moved down to the local level. The Ministry of Health, for example, proposed to move 86 percent of its annual budget in 2000 to the regional administrations, as against 41 percent in 1999. Yet many local areas, particularly resource-rich provinces such as Aceh and Riau, wanted a far quicker process.

Notwithstanding all the potential problems that will have to be faced, Indonesia is under strong political pressure to decentralize rapidly. This departs sharply from Indonesia's previous history of revising its institutional arrangements slowly by adopting broad legislation and then, over a long period, allocating the necessary resources to bring about full implementation. The pace of the new decentralization policy carries dangers. If not well implemented and funded it could fragment the country's present fragile unity. It also needs time so that clear relationships can be established between the various levels of government, with ways worked out to deal with the significant economic, social, and political differences among regions. However, whether Indonesia's old vested interests and power groups will allow decentralization to proceed fully remains an open question at this time.

The Philippines

The Philippines initially saw some progress in decentralization between 1946 and 1972,[7] but this ended with the advent of the dictatorship of President Ferdinand Marcos in 1972 and the introduction of a more highly centralized Government. It was only with the fall of Marcos in 1986, and with it the restoration of democracy and formal democratic structures, that rapid moves took place to decentralize a number of central government functions to local government units (LGUs). The 1987 Constitution provided for autonomy in local areas. This was followed by a cabinet-developed strategy in 1990 laying out a four-pronged program for decentralization, including a legislative foundation, pilot projects in 14 provinces to improve the capacity of LGUs, and bloc grants to support implementation (UNDP 1993). Then in 1991, a Local Government Code was introduced that moved a number of central government functions down to the Philippines' more than 43,000 LGUs (78 provinces, 83 cities, 1,527 municipalities, and 41,351 *barangays* [villages or local administrative units]) so that they could better respond to the particular needs of their areas.

The 1991 Local Government Code

The 1991 Local Government Code (the Code) was based on the 1987 constitutional provision that ensured the autonomy of local governments. It had five main features:

- It moved to LGUs the responsibility for various services that were earlier managed by the national government.

---

[7] Moves in this direction included the granting of expanded fiscal and regulatory powers in 1950 to municipal and city governments, the granting of legal status to the *barangays* (villages) under an elective council, and the passing in 1967 of a Decentralization Act increasing the financial resources and powers of the local governments. The second Presidential Decree of martial law, PD2, in 1972, also set up a system of regional offices for national government agencies.

These included health; social welfare services; environment (partially devolved: forest management, protected areas and wildlife, environmental management, mines and geosciences, land management, and community-based forestry); agriculture (extension, on-site research, and community irrigation); locally-funded public works; education (the school building program); tourism; telecommunications and housing projects for the provinces and cities; and other services, such as investment support.
- It moved to the LGUs the responsibility for the enforcement of certain regulatory powers, such as the reclassification of agricultural lands, environmental laws, the inspection of food products and quarantine, the national building code, and the processing and approval of subdivision plans.
- It provided for the participation of civil society in local governance by allocating seats to NGOs and people's organizations in key local bodies.
- It increased the financial resources available to LGUs by broadening their powers of taxation, providing them with a specific share of the revenues generated in their area from natural resources (e.g., mining, fisheries, and forestry) and increasing their share of national taxes (the Internal Revenue Allotments, or IRAs) from 11 percent to as much as 40 percent. The Code also enhanced the ability of local governments to generate revenues from local fees and charges.
- Finally, it laid a foundation for the development of more entrepreneurship by local governments. To encourage more businesslike and competitive behavior, it allowed local governments to enter into build-operate-transfer arrangements with the private sector, to float bonds, and to obtain loans from local private institutions.

To implement the Code, an interagency Oversight Committee was set up. This included the LGUs, through their respective leagues (the Leagues of Provinces, Cities, and Municipalities); national government agencies, such as the Bureau of Local Government Finance of the Department of Finance, the Department of Budget and Management (DBM), and the Department of Interior and Local Government (DILG); and members of Congress. Finding that too many trivial issues were coming to it for adjudication, the Oversight Committee set up Transition Action Teams in May 1995 at the regional and provincial level to facilitate settlement of the less complex issues.

As implementation got under way, a Master Plan (1993–1998) for the Sustained Implementation of the Local Government Code of 1991 was prepared. Approved by President Fidel Ramos in October 1994, it served as the framework for the Code's implementation. The Plan identified three major phases of the implementation. Phase One (1992–1993) would be a changeover phase that involved the transfer to local governments of devolved functions with funding and personnel. Phase Two (1994–1996) would be a transition phase during which the national government agencies and local governments would institutionalize their adjustments to the decentralized arrangements. Phase Three (1997 onwards) would be a stabilization phase, when it is was assumed that the local governments would have built up adequate capacity to manage local affairs and the national government agencies would provide support and technical assistance. Unfortunately, the complexities of implementing the Code, along with national elections in 1995 and 1998, delayed this timetable and it is now likely that the stabilization phase will start only in 2000.

Sectoral Progress in Implementing the Local Government Code

In the **health sector**, the Department of Health (DOH), having the largest number of central personnel (some 46,000) to be moved to the LGUs, perhaps inevitably met a number of problems in relocating staff. These included working out satisfactory career paths for the devolved personnel, their nonabsorption by the LGUs, and lower salaries. At one stage, these issues became so contentious that massive rallies and demonstrations by devolved health staff took place, resulting in a bill being passed by both houses of Congress in 1995 to recentralize the delivery of health services. President Ramos vetoed this bill and the devolution of health services continued.[8] Nonetheless, local governments have been required to pay the upgraded salaries of devolved health workers according to a pay scale prescribed by the Magna Carta for Health Workers and passed by Congress, about which more below.

On a more positive note, health boards were set up at the local level to develop strategic health plans responding to the special needs of the local areas. These boards also encouraged participation of the various actors, including civil society organizations. While these boards are active, with a recent survey showing that over two thirds meet regularly (Perez 1998), DOH reports that they still are not run fully by the local governments and receive most of their funding from DOH.

In general, it appears that both the financing and delivery of local health services have been sustained or even improved since devolution. A 1994 World Bank study showed that financing provided for health services had either remained unchanged or improved in more than 90 percent of the Philippines' municipalities during the initial years of devolution (World Bank 1994). A DOH report describes the initial six years of devolution of the health sector as a period with a "marked improvement in the overall health and nutrition of the population" (Philippines Department of Health, 1998). A comparison of health statistics between 1992, when devolution had not fully taken place, and 1997, when it had been implemented for nearly five years, shows a marked increase

---

[8] On the other hand, in January 1998, President Ramos indicated that he would support the retraction of devolution in the case of the Department of Social Welfare and Development. While he never signed the executive order, this idea still has some support in the Philippines today (Porio 1998).

in the number of pregnant women making at least three visits to a health center, as well as in the numbers of users of family planning and dental care (Perez 1998).

Although encouraging, these indicators should not be accepted uncritically. On the one hand, it is difficult to disentangle the effects of devolution from exogenous factors—including trend effects and other changes in public and private programs—that would influence the demand for, and provision of, prenatal care, family planning, and other health services. Moreover, Heaver and Hunt (1995) expressed the concern that devolution could maintain or even exacerbate the pre-devolution inequities in the provision of social services. In part, this could arise because local administrations in relatively poor regions have weak capacity for revenue generation. Devolution brings little benefit if health financing simply remains unchanged at an unacceptably low level.[9] At the same time, devolution has left many decisions on the levels and types of social service provision to the often politically inspired whims of mayors and local councils. The anecdotal evidence of Heaver and Hunt indicates that there had been significant regional variability in the relative prioritization of social services vis-à-vis roads and other physical infrastructure. Within the health sector, priority has often been given to building new facilities rather than improving the quality of existing facilities. Since poor communities are likely to have the greatest need for social services, a central government role will continue to be appropriate to ensure minimal provision of essential services until such time as local governments can take on more of the financing burden.

In *agriculture* a number of problems were met in the first few years of devolution. In the case of personnel, the LGUs rejected a small number of the relocated central staff when it was thought that their transfer would lead to a duplication of personnel at the local level. Many of the devolved personnel also felt that their move to the LGUs meant the end of their

---

[9] The point will be made again in Chapter VII in regard to the impact of decentralization on education in the Philippines and PRC.

careers, particularly as far as promotion was concerned.[10] There is also a general shortage of funds for training, which was particularly dismaying to devolved personnel used to more plentiful funds at the central level.

On the program side, the unequal distribution of extension workers is a long-standing problem that has not been solved by devolution. In 1997, the National Capital Region accounted for 25 percent of all agricultural extension workers compared to just 9 percent in Region VI, which has the highest percentage of farmers and fishing communities in the Philippines (CCAMD 1997). The LGUs handle implementation but do not have any inputs into the agricultural planning and policy formulation process, which has been retained at the central level, often resulting in badly coordinated programs. Because a clear division of responsibilities has not been worked out, there is still overlap in the extension services provided by the central Department of Agriculture and the LGUs. The LGUs also receive inadequate technical support from the regional offices. This is due mainly to the very low budget allocation that the regional offices receive—just 6 percent of the total Department of Agriculture budget in 1997 (Razon-Abad 1998).

In the area of irrigation, the devolution of locally-funded communal irrigation projects also created problems, for it was found, after their transfer in 1992, that a number of them could not be completed. Even after the transfer of functions took place, some local governments and farmer groups continued to ask for central financial assistance (NIA 1995). This highlighted the fact that the respective roles of the central irrigation agency and the LGUs had neither been clearly defined nor adequately explained to farm communities (see Chapter V).

As *social affairs*—covering the welfare of children, youth, the elderly, and women; nutrition; and family

---

[10] This applies to all devolved personnel irrespective of their department. While there are many opportunities for promotion at the central level, these are very limited in the LGUs, where the highest appointed positions are as municipal, city, or provincial administrators.

planning—had always been implemented at the community level, the devolution of the functions of the Department of Social Welfare and Development went fairly smoothly. However, there have been marked differences in the handling of these functions by different LGUs. Many of the revenue-poor LGUs were unable to create special service units and simply integrated social affairs into other existing agencies. For example, in Caloocan City, Metro Manila, social services were merged with agriculture and urban-industrial services. With no independent budget, social services suffered badly. Local budgets are also generally very limited, with the central offices retaining a disproportionate share of the overall resources (Porio 1998). On the positive side, some LGU social service units have established effective working relationships with community organizations and private business groups, providing them with additional resources. Some LGUs have also created programs that are very responsive to local needs, such as the Program for Preventing/Eliminating Child Labor in Lapu-Lapu City, Cebu.

Interactions between Government and Civil Society

The 1991 Local Government Code provided a prominent role for civil society. In this it had support from the 1987 Constitution, which stipulates that the State should encourage NGOs and community-based organizations that promote the welfare of the nation. The Constitution also stipulates that the State should respect the role of independent people's organizations (POs) in order to enable the people to pursue and protect their legitimate and collective interests. To do this, the State committed itself to the establishment of adequate consultative mechanisms.

To this end the Code specifically provided for NGO representation in various local bodies, including the local Development Councils, School and Health Boards, Peace and Order Councils, and Prequalification Bids and Awards Committees. The Code also provides an opening for NGOs to participate directly in local legislative bodies (*sangguniang bayan*) by providing them the opportunity to determine the various sectoral groupings in such bodies. By 1998, more than 16,000 NGOs and POs throughout the country had been accredited for possible membership in these local bodies.

Many NGOs and POs have also come together through various formations and national coalitions to examine the provisions offered by the Code and to develop strategies to respond to them. One example is the National Coordinating Council on Local Governance that operated from 1993 to 1996. This served as an umbrella network for NGOs that developed, inter alia, advocacy strategies to implement fully the Code's provisions for NGO participation in local governance. In 1996, the Institute of Politics and Governance also served as the focal point for a number of NGOs in disseminating information and advocating NGO and PO interests, as well as heading the NGO/PO working group to review the Code.

Progress, Lingering Problems, and Prospects

The Local Government Code has now been in force for several years. It has been marked by many instances of success, but there have been problems as the Code was implemented. Some of these problems have been solved, but others still remain and present definite hindrances to full devolution. In aspects such as coordination and participation, good progress has been made. In the decentralization of finances and capacity building, progress is more mixed.

Intergovernmental cooperation. Vertical collaboration and cooperation has improved between the different levels of government—the provinces, cities, municipalities, and barangays. There has also been an increase in horizontal cooperation among local governments at the same level. Local officials have organized themselves into the Leagues of Vice Governors, Vice Mayors, Philippine Councilors, and the National Movement of Young Legislators, among others. Of late, they have consolidated their forces into the League of Leagues.

Local governments have also begun to take ownership of national programs, whereas before these programs were often seen as impositions by the national Government. Nonetheless, central government departments, including the DBM, DILG, and the Department of Justice (DOJ), continue to issue instructions that conflict with the autonomy intended by the Code. For example, although the Code authorizes local governments to issue licenses and permits to regulate legitimate activities, DOJ and DILG have in some instances issued contradictory instructions exempting activities from the need to secure local permits. For another, participation in seminars by local governments, even if funded locally, continues to be regulated by central authorities.

The Code has also led to positive steps in the areas of *participation and local governance*. Over the past five years, various consultations have been undertaken by the NGO community to propose amendments to the Code and to study pending legislation on popular participation and electoral reform. Participation in local governance may have reached a plateau, however, considering that many local special bodies have not convened regularly, while elections for sectoral representatives have at times not been held. Slow progress in these and other areas has led to frustration among certain sectors of the NGO/PO community, leading to reexamination of the strategy for participating in local governance and to advocacy of further reforms at the local level to ensure that participation is meaningful. The NGO/PO community has entered into tactical alliances with other actors, such as the leagues of local governments, to advocate common causes.

LGUs were at the forefront of the push for decentralization well before the adoption of the Local Government Code. In the late 1980s, the LGUs began to organize themselves into strong advocacy groups that pressed for the enactment of a Code as mandated in the 1987 Constitution. More recently, various leagues of LGUs have emerged at the province, city, municipality, and barangay level, proposing major amendments to the Code, including reforms in the allocation of the IRA funds that would address the inequitable distribution and allocation of financial resources. As provided for in the Code, these leagues have become a potent force in advocating the cause of local autonomy at the national level.

The leagues have resisted unfunded mandates (discussed below) that distort local planning and budgeting processes. They have also entered into strategic alliances with like-minded sectors of society, including the NGO/PO community. Some of the leagues are now able to fund and sustain secretariats that provide professional support and assistance to league members.

Budgeting and finance. In contrast to the encouraging, albeit incomplete, movement toward participation and local governance, progress in financial devolution has been slower. To back up decentralization, the Code had promised adequate financial resources, which in practice were not fully provided. Initially, there was certainly a significant increase in the local share of the Internal Revenue Allotment. This grew every year, rising from 9.4 billion pesos in 1991 to more than 71 billion pesos in 1997. Given this increased share, it was not unusual to see local government budgets triple and even quadruple. But this sum was still inadequate to cover the LGUs' costs of administering the newly decentralized functions as well as the costs of national government personnel devolved to them. A recent estimate of the deficit between LGU revenues and expenditures shows an annual gap of between 5 billion and 6 billion pesos (DILG 1998). Although increased funding is always desirable, it is not always feasible; the gap might also be reduced if there were a better allocation of funds by the individual LGUs.

While the IRA still constitutes the main source of the budgets of most lower-income municipalities, many local governments, especially at the provincial and municipal levels, find it inadequate to cover the costs of devolution. To address this, a recent effort was mounted by the interagency Oversight Committee to create a devolution adjustment fund. This fund would be carved out of the IRA allocations of local governments for possible redistribution to local governments based on their needs (Manila Bulletin 1998).

Hopefully, this initiative will begin to redress the problem of "unfunded mandates," whereby central government agencies have continued to formulate and develop programs and projects at the national level, then instructed local governments to implement them—without financial support. Indeed, the countryside development funds and budgetary initiatives and insertions of many individual members of Congress are often larger than the budgets of entire provinces! In addition, many local governments have been unable to afford the salaries of national government personnel devolved to them. This has been particularly true in the health sector, where, as noted above, the local governments have been required to pay the upgraded salaries of devolved health workers according to a pay scale passed by Congress and considered by many local governments as yet another of the unfunded mandates that put local government budgets under considerable pressure.

National government institutions (executive and legislative) continue to dominate the allocation of financial resources in the politico-administrative system. Despite the devolution of responsibilities to local governments, budget allocations to national departments of health, agriculture, social services, and environment have actually grown over the past five years. The IRA, while indeed increasing the budgets of LGUs, constitutes only 14 percent of the national budget, the bulk of which is controlled by the national Government.

Fortunately, the Code encouraged the LGUs to go into business with the private sector and, where appropriate, to adapt private-sector strategies to generate resources, which began to occur in some LGUs after a few years. The LGUs also launched more vigorous tax collection campaigns to supplement locally generated resources. They have begun to explore borrowing from banks, both government and private, to finance local development efforts.[11] In addition, local governments have stepped up efforts to access funds from external sources, including Official Development Assistance, and to get their

---

[11] In practice, loans are usually obtained from the government banks, because this is where the LGUs deposit their funds. Private banks are reluctant to make loans to LGUs since they are forbidden to place a lien on local government deposits under the Local Government Code. In contrast, the public banks have an informal arrangement with the LGUs to take loan payments out of their accounts.

full share of revenue from natural resources located within their jurisdiction. They have also become more innovative in mobilizing local resources, including build-operate-transfer arrangements, joint ventures, and bond flotation.

Local capacity building. There is a still great deal to be done to build up the capacities of the LGUs. One of the major sources of concern before the implementation of decentralization was the perceived lack of capabilities among local government personnel. Efforts have been made to develop and implement various training and capacity-building programs to enhance the skills of individual local officials, ranging from general financial management to presiding over meetings and on to general techniques for preparing local legislation. While such individual skills are needed, "capacity building" should also enhance more broadly the capacities of local government institutions, structures, and processes. Moreover, specific assistance is desirable to encourage and enable local government to develop partnerships with the private sector, civil society, and international organizations. Enhancing their entrepreneurial abilities and developing their corporate powers as envisioned in the Code should be a key part of the capacity-building process.

National Support and Monitoring. Better support for decentralization is also needed at the central government level. The interagency Oversight Committee that should play a lead role in the process is severely hampered in its work by the lack of a secretariat with full-time staff. In addition, the legislated five-year review of decentralization has yet to take place; NGOs and the League of Local Governments are undertaking the main ongoing reviews of the decentralization. At one stage in 1996/97, the DILG did initiate a process of consultations on needed amendments to the Local Government Code. These amendments were proposed to the President in October 1997, but no action ensued.

Overall, the Local Government Code of 1991 provided the framework for the Philippines to decentralize selected central government functions to the local level. It transferred considerable powers to local communities in general, and to local governments in particular, to enable them to respond to the unique needs and demands of their localities. As in Indonesia, the move has been crucial for the archipelagic Philippines, which is characterized by geographical, cultural, and economic diversity at various levels. There are still a number of problem areas to be dealt with, but given that the political impetus for devolution remains, devolution should eventually be fully implemented.

The PRC

The PRC represents quite a different example of decentralization from that seen in either Indonesia or the Philippines. Instead of the more formal and legalistic transfer of authority that has occurred in the Philippines and is underway in Indonesia, the PRC has undergone a process of de facto decentralization in the last two decades. In this process, there has been no national decentralization legislation such as Indonesia's Law on Regional Government or the Philippines' Local Government Code, but rather a series of decisions, relating primarily to the financial system, that have constituted a considerable transfer of power to local governments. Moreover, in taking steps to decentralize government revenues and expenditures first, with the responsibility for delivering public services following later, the PRC avoided some of the problems occurring in other countries where central governments have delegated the responsibility, but not the wherewithal, to local administrations.

In this process the PRC authorities appear to have taken an innovative experimental approach to implementing changes. Policies were tried out, sometimes on a large scale and making use of the vast size and diversity of the country; if not successful, such experiments were discarded. Thus, the PRC Government, after allowing local authorities to undertake social experiments, learned the appropriate lessons and then generalized from them.[12]

---

[12] The correct lessons were not always learned. Thus, collectivization in the 1950s, which in the beginning did lead to productivity growth, was quickly and wrongly generalized to the rest of the PRC during the Great Leap Forward, with disastrous results (J. Y. Lin 1990).

Decentralization from the 1950s Onward

Chapter II recounted how the frequent upheavals caused by the internal dissension in the top echelon of the PRC Communist Party had led by the late 1970s, on the eve of the Deng Xiaoping reforms, to the weakening of the central government organs. The PRC's organs of local government, however, had been increasing in strength. Despite these changes, the formal fiscal arrangements remained highly centralized, with the Center enjoying almost total control over the expenditures of local and provincial governments. Revenue-sharing contracts, under which the Center and local governments bargained over the share of revenues that were to be kept by the parties, were used by the Center to equalize income between rich and poor provinces, rather than to allow the local governments any decision making.

There had been various moves in the 1950s to reallocate revenues to the local governments. Decentralization measures in 1951, 1954, 1956, and 1958 all foreshadowed the later reforms of the 1970s and 1980s (Lardy 1975). After these moves, centralization was subsequently tightened again at two points, the first in 1961, due partially to the huge recession caused by the Great Leap Forward, and the second in the mid-1970s, when the Center regained control of the financial system after the upheavals of the 1966–76 Cultural Revolution. Thus, the financial reforms that began in the late 1970s need to be seen against the background of a highly centralized, if not overcentralized, system.

The first change came in 1977 with the introduction on a trial basis of a fiscal devolution program. This was based on contractual arrangements between the Center and the provinces and took place initially in two provinces, Jiangsu and Sichuan. In Jiangsu, for instance, a contractual arrangement was set up whereby it could retain 42 percent of all revenues, with total control over their disbursement. The main benefit of these contractual arrangements was that there was a clear division of responsibilities as well as of finances; from the central Government's point of view, its revenues were guaranteed. From the perspective of provincial leaders, little was sacrificed in exchange for the financial autonomy they received; thus they wanted greater autonomy (Shirk 1993). The arrangements were also aimed at giving the provincial government incentives for local revenue generation and collection.

Also in 1977, ten provinces and municipalities directly administered by the State Council were selected for another experiment linking expenditure with revenue: local governments would retain a part of above-target revenue. This initially left the selected provinces with more revenues, but a large central budget deficit in 1979 led to cancellation of the arrangement.

The demand for reforming the financial system, however, remained strong. The top leaders saw that the delegation of powers (*fen zao chifan*, or eating out of separate kitchens) provided effective local incentives for collecting revenue and also stimulated economic growth.

Consequently, in 1980, additional changes were introduced that set up revenue-sharing formulas between the central and local governments. These differed from province to province, but with few exceptions had a five-year time span (Beijing's, Tianjin's, and Shanghai's formulas were on a year-to-year basis [Shirk 1993]). Under them, the central Government was responsible for major investment projects and the local governments were responsible for day day-to-day economic activities and the operation of the local administration. In the early 1980s, the formulas were adjusted to reflect the rapid economic and policy changes taking place. Finally, in 1983, most local governments, with the exception of a few large cities and the provinces of Guangdong and Fujian (Shirk 1993), changed to a uniform system whereby all local revenues were divided between the province and the Center.

A further change occurred in 1985, when tax reform took place. The effect of this was to make revenues shared between the central and local governments the main part of the budget. This, in turn, ensured that local governments had a strong incentive to vigorously collect shared revenues.

Impacts of the Recent Decentralization

Most of these adjustments, it appears, were at the expense of the Center, leaving it in a severely constrained financial position. Among many steps taken to deal with the situation, the Center handed over more and more responsibility to the provinces. These included price subsidies, housing and urban infrastructure construction, education, health, and many other budget items (Shirk 1993). Below the province level, counties became responsible for social services, particularly education, and for administration. Townships and villages became responsible for community-run schools (Wong 1997; West 1997). In health care, a county would run the general hospital(s), an epidemic prevention station, and a maternal and child health station, while the township or village would look after the small health center or health station.

The reforms induced provincial and local governments to use their enhanced financial resources to invest in development activities. They also provided local governments and State enterprises with economic incentives to improve efficiency and productivity. The success of the township and village enterprises (TVEs), described in Chapter II, was merely a spectacular example. Revenues raised from these investment activities, particularly the profits from TVEs, did not have to be shared with the central Government. Overall, fiscal decentralization thus became a major feature of the PRC's industrial as well as countryside reform.

While the high degree of fiscal decentralization appears attractive, there is no question that a price has been paid in terms of equality. Despite mechanisms at all levels of government to equalize fiscal burdens—e.g., higher revenue shares to be paid to the central Government in richer provinces and lower or even negative shares in poorer ones—considerable inequality has remained. In fields where quantitative measures of the output of public services are available, wide disparities exist. Thus, in Shandong in 1993, 83 percent of primary school graduates continued on to junior high schools, compared with only 42 percent in poorer Guizhou province. Similar contrasts can be drawn using other measures such as teachers' academic credentials and school facilities (West 1997).

It also appears that as a result of fiscal decentralization, there was an overall decline in infrastructure investments, a lack of funds for agricultural research, and a drop in student enrollment in rural schools, particularly in senior high schools (Lin and Zhong 1996). In the case of infrastructure, a development indirectly related to decentralization—the decline of the communes—caused local governments to lose their power to mobilize rural labor without wage payment. With projects now requiring a local budget for materials and wages, local governments were able to undertake fewer projects and infrastructure deteriorated. Telecommunications services, for example, had seen rapid increases in the rural areas from the 1950s through 1978, after which investment declined considerably (Lin and Zhong 1996). The agricultural research and extension network built up in the 1950s and 1960s had worked well, but was seriously affected by the reduction in budgets above the county level, where local governments had to force the agricultural research institutes to become more self-supporting. In education, with funding now provided at the local level, there was less money for school construction and operating costs, and enrollments declined.

Overall, the central Government in the PRC has considerably reduced its role in local affairs, to the benefit of local governments. In addition to decentralizing government finances, it accomplished this by reorganizing the agricultural production system, lifting the mandatory quotas that farmers were expected to deliver to the State, and devolving power to local authorities. In many of these instances, the approach was experimental. When the agricultural production system was reorganized, the initial decision was taken almost surreptitiously by a few local authorities, who allowed the production teams to experiment with the new household responsibility system. In other cases, for example in the devolution of power to the local governments, the change resulted from bargaining in an explicit, and at times formally contracted, give-and-take manner.

That the local authorities (at various levels from provinces downward) were able to take such initiatives indicates that political power in the PRC was much more dispersed than generally thought. In its various policy initiatives, whether fiscal devolution, agricultural reform, or rules regarding the retention of profits by TVEs, the central Government had to negotiate constantly with other loci of power.

LESSONS LEARNED

The experiences with decentralization in these three countries and elsewhere in Asia provide interesting lessons that will apply in some degree to nearly any country undertaking the process:

- Full and continuous *political support* must be mobilized at all levels if decentralization is to be successful. In Indonesia, the early attempts to decentralize did not reflect such a commitment and the highly centralized Suharto Government took 18 years to begin implementing the 1974 decentralization legislation. In the Philippines, commitment has been firmer and decentralization is moving ahead.
- Once the decision is made to decentralize, governments should *move quickly*. In most countries, there is a momentum that needs to be capitalized on, as seen in the Philippines and Indonesia. While this may reduce detailed preparatory planning, experience has shown that teething problems can usually be resolved, perhaps with even better solutions, during the process of implementation. The dilemma of the simultaneous needs for urgency and caution in decentralization underscores the need for full political will and commitment to the long time frame required for it to succeed.
- *Clarity and precision* are needed in all enactments and in the devolution of responsibilities. The

differing interpretations in Indonesia on the sharing of development budget resources illustrate what can happen when the details are not carefully spelled out.
- Full *participation* of local governments, political leaders, and civil society is needed at all stages in carrying out decentralization policies. Local representatives know best the potentials and problems of their areas. A capable and well-functioning local government will only result from a fully participatory process that involves all stakeholders. This includes the public and private sectors, civic organizations, and NGOs. Democratization will obviously be complementary to decentralization by contributing to greater participation, accountability, and transparency by all concerned.
- The PRC presents the principal exception to the rule that decentralization involves *political as well as administrative and financial transfer of functions.* In general, if any one of these is left out, the process is constrained. In Indonesia, the lack of political decentralization in the Suharto era would certainly have hampered any decentralization that might otherwise have occurred. In the Reformasi Era, the political element is strong and its continuation will be critical to ensuring full local participation in and support for decentralized local governments.
- Adequate *financial resources* are needed. The decentralization experience in both the Philippines and Indonesia shows the process being undermined by lack of funding. But central governments simply do not have the funds or capacity to satisfy all needs. To raise additional resources, local governments must have the autonomy to tax and to mobilize the involvement of the private sector. They will also need freedom to borrow and to privatize, as in the Philippines and to a limited extent in Indonesia. Creative approaches must be sought to develop local

public-private partnerships and to exploit opportunities for coproduction between concerned stakeholders.
- Adequate *capacity* must be built up, and this takes time. While more capacity often exists at the local government level than is given credence by donors, local governments and institutions still need extensive support as they learn how to take on devolved functions. For this, the provision of appropriate training for relocated and existing local government staff is essential. Capacity will vary among local governments, so tailored approaches are also needed.
- Decentralization is *not an alternative to central authority*. A measure of each is needed. As noted in Chapter II, in any society, some functions—macroeconomic management, national finances, and the judiciary system (rules and many property rights)—need to be controlled at the central level, while others can be better performed locally. Although little comprehensive evidence exists, the scattered examples presented above suggest that decentralization may be associated with a decline in the quality, accessibility, and—among regions—the equity of rural services for agricultural research, irrigation, education, and health care. Inasmuch as the central Government will still be collecting most of the taxes in the country, it should pay close attention to this issue and design the revenue share-out to correct the inequality that would otherwise occur. In addition, the regulation of essential goods and services (regardless of how they are financed and provisioned) constitutes one of the comparative advantages of central Government, a point that will be returned to in the next four chapters.
- The difficulty of ensuring *accountability* also constitutes an important caveat about devolution. Devolution may appear to bring government "closer to the people," but it does not automatically follow

that it will be more responsive. As is widely realized now, for governments to function well from the point of view of the people being ruled, there must be a vibrant civil society. And this must be mobilized not just to push through the devolution program, but also to keep an eye on the local government units when they are up and running. There are too many local governments (and not only in developing countries) that are venal and corrupt.
- Finally, greater *intergovernmental coordination* is desirable. Local governments are likely to experience many common problems in adjusting to decentralization. In the Philippines the various leagues of LGUs and local government officials are providing useful forums to review and articulate responses to the shared problems.

To conclude, some degree of decentralization is now an almost inevitable process in most developing countries as a result of the economic and social changes of the last two decades. The growing complexity of rural development dictates the need for more participatory governance. Nonetheless, the dangers of uncontrolled decentralization are real. Too many local governments borrowing funds indiscriminately or coming under the sway of particular groups can easily destabilize a national Government in any country. Thus, decentralization needs to move forward with caution.

IV THE CHANGING CHARACTER OF TECHNOLOGY AND ITS IMPACT ON RESEARCH AND EXTENSION

> The "technology" of farming means "the way it is done." It includes the methods by which farmers sow, cultivate and harvest crops and care for livestock. It includes the seeds, fertilizers, the pesticides, the medicines and the feeds they use, the tools, the implements and the sources of power. It includes enterprise combinations by which farmers seek to make the best use of their labor and land. For agricultural development to proceed, these must be constantly changing. When they stop changing, agriculture becomes stagnant. Production stops increasing and it may even decline due to decreasing soil fertility or to increasing damage by multiplying pests and diseases.
>
> – Arthur T. Mosher (1966).

PATTERNS AND TRENDS IN TECHNOLOGY DEVELOPMENT

The central breakthrough of the green revolution, which had such enormous impact on rural Asia, was the successful breeding of the rice variety IR-8. After this event, the attitude of Asian governments toward agricultural development went through a major change. The profitability of agricultural research was dramatically demonstrated. Investments in research, irrigation, fertilizer production, and a host of other modern inputs were more willingly made, particularly by the public sector. At the same time, it is important to bear in mind that in very large areas of rural Asia, there was no green revolution. For these areas, research has in general borne very little fruit, because their natural resource base has proven to be insufficient to support the green revolution's extremely intensive form of agriculture. These less-favored areas will be discussed further below.

Among the case studies of collective action that are analyzed in depth in this and the next three chapters, agricultural research is unique because of its large international dimension. First of all, the fruits of agricultural research undertaken in one country may find widespread applications in and therefore reap benefits for other countries. In other words, the fruits of research are often *international public goods*. Consequently, there are international actors in addition to those discussed in Chapter II: within the nonprofit sector alone, the international agricultural research centers (IARCs) belonging to the Consultative Group on International Agricultural Research (CGIAR) have contributed mightily to the advancement of agricultural technology in Asia. Within the for-profit sector, multinational firms have always been suppliers of chemicals and are emerging as suppliers of seeds and of the technology embodied in the chemicals and seeds. Furthermore, developed-country governments also have also played a role, at the very least in providing funds to the IARCs. In addition, in various international forums, particularly the World Trade Organization, these governments exert considerable pressure on Asian countries to provide intellectual property protection, a subject intimately connected to agricultural research, and to be discussed below.

A Typology of Factors that Shape Agricultural Technology

In analyzing agricultural technology and the contribution of research to enhancing it, it is convenient to divide the factors influencing technology into the following three categories:

- *Genetic base.* This is what gives the plant its basic biological characteristics and yield potential. Much agricultural research is devoted to enhancing the quality of the genetic base, so that the plant is better adapted, not only to its natural environment, but to any other input that the farmer may introduce.
- *Resource base and environment.* These comprise the soil, water, temperature, and other external factors that provide what the plant requires for its sustenance (and also provide the plant's natural enemies). Agricultural research is devoted to understanding the nature of the relationships between the plant and its resource base in order to enhance that resource base and correct any imbalances that may exist, thereby increasing productivity.
- *Support and post-harvest inputs.* Besides the two basic factors that affect the plant, agriculture involves inputs that may modify the resource base and environment, such as fertilizers or pesticides, or help the farmer use his land more effectively, such as agricultural machinery. Each input has its own technology of production and use. In addition, once the crop is harvested and leaves the farm, its storage, transport, and processing have their own technologies. Such technologies may change because of agricultural research, or sometimes fortuitously through more general scientific and technological developments.

The above classification pertains to crop production. The classification of technologies in livestock production is somewhat different. There is also a genetic base to livestock technology, which will be touched on below; the fields of animal nutrition and health are subject to extensive research, but will be considered only briefly in this chapter.

A key feature of much agricultural research is its interdisciplinary nature; hence the above classification should not be construed as compartmentalizing the work done at agricultural research stations. When technologies are applied in a farmer's field, they come together and interact with one another, and it would be an incompetent researcher who ignores the interactions. Even in the case of the green revolution, where the central thrust of the work was genetic improvement, plant breeders were successful only because they enlisted the help of plant physiologists, soil scientists, and agronomists. Later on, when pest buildup became a problem, entomologists had to be brought on board. Moreover, a major goal in developing IR-8 was to find a rice variety that was responsive to nitrogen. This objective would not have been selected if the previous decades had not seen a sharp fall in nitrogen prices because of developments in the chemical industry (Hayami and Ruttan 1985).

Within each category in the above classification, the roles of the various actors in research have changed in response to developments in the concerned scientific disciplines. The remaining part of this section will trace these changes.

Genetic Improvement before Biotechnology

For as long as agriculture has existed, farmers have striven to improve the genetic base of their crops and livestock. The traditional method has been simple selection of seeds or stock from plants or animals with desirable traits. The selection would vary with growing conditions, which, in turn, vary with geography. The selections made by farmers in various growing environments gave birth to the diversity of plants from a given species. Crossing of plants of different varieties and breeding of animals from different stocks were also widely practiced on a trial-and-error basis. There was also the purposive movement of plant species across regions and continents during the colonial period and even earlier, when new plants were introduced from one region or continent to another. The most famous example, of course, was the bringing of the rubber tree from Brazil to Southeast Asia by the British (Plucknett et al. 1987).

The birth of Mendelian genetics allowed the exercise to become more systematic; the organization of research also became more formal. The classical process involves a crossing of two individuals from a given species in order to obtain progeny with the combined characteristics, followed by replication from which selection is made for further crossing. Once the desired traits are derived, the individuals are planted and replanted until the seeds obtained from the plants are genetically uniform and ready for distribution.

From the beginning, the organization of scientific work in genetic improvement has been carried out in publicly owned and operated experiment stations, both in market and centrally planned economies. Even the research into hybrid maize in the US, later to be carried forward by private firms, was initially conducted at public experiment stations, where the first inbred lines used in the hybrids originated.[1] This pattern has been more pronounced in crop genetic improvement work than in animal improvement (and there are variations also among types of crops, as will be discussed below). There are two reasons for the public sector to undertake this role: economies of scale and the public-goods nature of the outputs of much agricultural research.

For plant breeders to do their work effectively, they need access to as much genetic material as possible, so as to obtain the right kind of plant for the particular breeding objective desired. For them to be able to cast their nets widely, there must be a gene bank. This is a storehouse of seeds (or other forms of germplasm) of the vast varieties within a given plant species

---

[1] With cross-pollinating plants, the chromosomes are heterozygous, that is, the genes on them that come from different parents are not necessarily the same. By interbreeding a particular variety within itself and selecting, the population can be made more and more homozygous (i.e., the genes from the different parents become more nearly the same). Inbred lines consist of plants that are made homozygous by such interbreeding. These plants are usually weak and unproductive, but the progeny obtained from crossing two different inbred lines are usually much more productive—the technical expression is that they have "hybrid vigor." This phenomenon is the basis of the hybrid seed industry.

that can be reproduced for breeders to use in their work. It is clearly more convenient to have all the varieties in one place, with appropriate documentation of their characteristics. Hence, the economies of scale in a gene bank are such that it is more efficient for the public sector to operate it—although the use of information technology by now may have reduced the importance of this factor considerably.

In any case, the economies of scale in a gene bank are not by themselves sufficient to give the public sector the advantage in conducting genetic improvement work, for the public sector could easily run a gene bank (much as it does a library) and allow plant breeders access to it. Rather, the differing roles for the public and private sectors in research depend on how easy it is to capture the benefits of any new technology arising out of the research. Plant and animal breeders can capture the benefits arising out of their innovation in two ways: the first is when their "intellectual property" is naturally protected and the second is when it is legally protected. The use of the term "intellectual property" may be deemed to presuppose a legal protection of some sort. Here no such presupposition is being made, and the text will make clear what is meant by natural protection independent of the law.

The natural way to capture these benefits can be shown by dividing crops and animals into three categories:[2]

- self-pollinating crops and vegetatively propagating crops;
- cross-pollinating crops and small animals;
- tree crops and large animals.

Self-Pollinating Field Crops and Vegetatively Propagating Crops

If the plant is self-pollinating, the seeds will breed true; that is, they will reproduce exactly, or almost exactly, the

---

[2] An alternative classification is to divide crops into food crops and export (or plantation) crops (Pray 1991). This alternative classification is discussed further below.

same genes as their parents, because both the male and female parents are from the same plant and the two sets of chromosomes will tend over time to be identical, or nearly so (homozygous). Their offspring will then have the same set of genes. Vegetatively propagating plants also reproduce the same set of chromosomes as their mothers, although the chromosomes will not be homozygous. In both these classes of plants, once the farmers obtain the improved germplasm, either in the form of seeds or of stock, they can obtain the next generation of plants quite easily. Consequently, the research organization responsible for the improved germplasm cannot easily recover the costs of its research and development from the farmers unless it charges a very high price for the first generation of material. In that case, farmers would simply wait to free-ride on other farmers' investments.

These two classes cover some very important crops of Asia. Rice, wheat, cotton, and soybeans are all self-pollinating crops, while cassava, sugarcane, and many fruit trees propagate vegetatively. For rice and wheat there is ample documentation of what has happened in Asia during the last three decades.

The first technological breakthroughs arose for rice and wheat, two of Asia's major food crops. The institution credited with the main breakthrough in rice is the International Rice Research Institute (IRRI), an internationally funded organization, originally supported by the Rockefeller and Ford Foundations. The same two foundations also supported the International Maize and Wheat Improvement Center in Mexico (abbreviated as CIMMYT from its Spanish name), which developed the new wheat varieties at about the same time that IR-8 appeared. The foundations were moved to act in Asia because of their concern over the impact of population growth on per capita food supply; it was also believed that improving agricultural productivity would have the political impact of arresting rural instability and hence the spread of communism (Anderson, Levy, and Morrison 1991).

Lest it be inferred that the CGIAR institutions were the sole originators of the green revolution, a bit of further history is in order. Actually, the PRC's research system produced a fertilizer-responsive dwarf variety of rice in 1964, two years before IR-8 (Lin 1991). Even before that, in the 1920s and 1930s, Japanese researchers pioneered the kind of work that was later done at IRRI (Ishikawa 1967). The Japanese also distributed the seeds to their then-colonies, Korea and Taiwan. Some of the genetic material in IR-8 had its origins in this early Japanese research. Of course, all this work was done within public institutions.

After the initial success of the IR-8 and its adoption by farmers, national governments were moved to support similar research in the publicly funded national research systems. This work still relied a great deal on materials developed by IRRI and on IRRI's large germplasm collection that circulates the material it develops, as well as on the "landraces," or cultivars used in indigenous farming prior to formal breeding work, that IRRI had collected. In the beginning, much of this work involved adapting the parent material supplied by IRRI to local conditions: the most frequently observed breeding strategy was "one parent from IRRI and one from the national system." Over time, the landrace content in the varieties released by the national systems has increased, but these landraces were brought into the genealogies through an IRRI ancestor (Evenson 1998).

Cross-Pollinating Field Crops and Small Animals

Once the seed of a self-pollinating crop like rice leaves the experiment station, it is replicated for distribution to farmers and grown in farmers' fields. The harvested grain can be used as seed for future crops, with only a small loss in quality due to inadvertent outcrossing. Crops that propagate themselves by cross-pollination, however, have quite a high rate of outcrossing. Thus, the seed from an experiment station will lose its quality more rapidly during succeeding generations. This simple fact makes the history of improvement in these crops quite different from that of crops like rice or wheat.

Maize is one important food crop that propagates by cross-pollination. Normally, the pollen from a maize plant fertilizes the ear of some other plant a few meters away. But with strong winds, the seeds can and do travel longer distances; therefore considerable intermixing occurs. The improved varieties of maize that were released initially from the experiment stations are known as open-pollinated varieties. The production of seeds for such varieties is carried out under conditions that protect against contamination, in order to produce seeds that are "true to type," that is, they do not vary significantly in their genetic makeup. But once the seeds are used to grow crops in farmers' fields, outcrossing and contamination naturally occur. Unless farmers take precautions to prevent such outcrossing, they are well advised to obtain their seeds for each crop from specialized seed producers in order to continue to obtain good yields on their crops (CIMMYT 1987).

Because of this particular characteristic of the maize plant, maize was among the first commodities where a commercial seed industry arose to supply farmers' needs, at least in market-oriented economies. In Thailand, for example, commercial maize seed production emerged in the late 1970s (the development of the vegetable seed industry had come earlier). Interestingly, the maize industry came into being after a public university developed a new variety, Suwan, which was successful in resisting downy mildew, a fungus that had earlier plagued Thai maize production (Suthad, Saran, and Banlu 1991).

The existence, or potential existence, of a commercial seed industry is a precondition for greater involvement of the for-profit sector in research. Companies are drawn into research because the sale of seeds permits their capture of the benefits of that research. This is indeed what has happened in many Asian countries. As early as the mid-1980s, private national and multinational firms were investing tens of millions of dollars annually in agricultural research and development in Asia, mostly on maize, sorghum, and sunflowers, and largely in countries like India and Malaysia that had large commercial demand (Pray and Echeverria 1991).

While cross-pollinating crops are most amenable to private-sector involvement, it does not mean that only the private sector can do research in this area. As noted, the Thai hybrid industry came into being on the back of a variety developed by a State university. Even the US hybrid industry, in its earlier days, obtained its inbred lines from the public research system.

For private firms to be able to do their research competently, they must have access to inbred lines. Initially, the private sector would rely on the public system for the genetic materials, but, over time, successful firms have found it profitable to build up their own private collections of inbred lines. As with gene banks, there are economies of scale in such collections. It is not surprising that firms in the seed industry are usually very large and multinational. Moreover, concentration in the industry has increased with the advent of biotechnology (Grossman, Linnemann, and Wierema 1991).

There is a close parallel between cross-pollinating plants and small animals, since animals naturally crossbreed. Thus, the poultry breeding industry is organized somewhat similarly to the hybrid maize seed industry, i.e., with a few large, multinational firms dominating the field. Indeed, the spread of modern hybrid poultry has been far more rapid than even the hybrid maize sector, and now dominates the scene in countries such as the PRC, the Philippines, and Thailand. As will be considered further below, part of the reason for the more rapid advance in this sector is the fact that the modern poultry-raising process is essentially industrial rather than agricultural (i.e., more independent of the environment) and, therefore, has fewer location-specific demands.

Tree Crops and Large Animals

Tree crops and, to some extent, large animals do not lend themselves as easily as field crops to traditional methods of genetic improvement. The traditional method of crossbreeding and then selecting from among the progeny for further crossing and selection is already quite time-consuming for field crops, whose generation length is on the order of three to six months. For crops or animals whose generation length is counted in years rather than months, it is much more costly to crossbreed on a trial-and-error basis, which has tended to keep the private sector from becoming involved. However, the private sector's role promises to grow with the advent of modern cloning technology, which can accelerate the breeding process, particularly for animals.

Farmers have done some of the work in this area, playing a dominant role in fruit improvement in particular. But this kind of improvement in a given species is normally done within the center of diversity for that species,[3] where farmers have access to a large number of varieties in a natural gene bank. Thus, with most native fruit trees, farmers have been constantly and successfully developing new lines. With introduced or exotic species of tree crops, such as rubber, coffee, or cocoa, however, this option is not practical, as farmers would have to explore worldwide for the right kind of germplasm. The public research system would have to be enlisted in order to command the resources for producing any improvement.

Even where the farmers have themselves been at the forefront of genetic improvement, there is a role for the public research system. If farmers are successful, i.e., if the varieties they create are superior to existing varieties, then older varieties will gradually be replaced. If over time the innovation process stabilizes so that fewer new varieties are introduced, the well-known phenomenon of genetic erosion will be observed. Because fruit trees are vegetatively propagated, genetic erosion is apt to be more rapid than with seed-propagated species. Without a publicly-funded gene bank, there is a real danger that farmers' improvement would cease as new, locally available genetic materials are exhausted.

---

[3] Vavilov, a famed Russian botanist, traced the origin and spread of each cultivated plant species by measuring its diversity. He reasoned that only a few varieties of the species would migrate from the place where they originated, so that the further away the species is, the less the diversity. Conversely, the place of origin of cultivation would be expected to have the greatest diversity in that species. This point is known as the center of origin or center of diversity.

Summary

The organization of research to improve each type of crop and animal will necessarily differ depending upon the natural protection offered to innovators, which in turn depends on each plant's or animal's genetic makeup and reproductive characteristics. For self-pollinating crops, no such protection is afforded: public-sector research is not only the preferred mode, it is absolutely essential. For cross-pollinating crops and for small animals, private-sector research is more of a possibility, although even here (at least for crops), some pioneering work by the public sector would facilitate work by the private sector. For tree crops and large animals, farmers themselves should ultimately be credited with the improvements, even well into the modern era. In the future, though, the public system will have to be involved more aggressively, both with respect to introduced species, mostly of commercial crops, and also to the preservation of germplasm of the native species.

Biotechnology

The Promise of Biotechnology

The revolution in molecular biology during the last two decades has blurred the relevance of the distinctions based on natural protection of the intellectual property discussed above; it has also broken down many constraints on genetic manipulation that exist in classical plant breeding. The first constraint is the knowledge base of the scientists themselves. In the past, detecting the location of a gene that expresses a particular trait was a hit-or-miss affair and normally very time-consuming. With new biotechnology tools, this knowledge is increasingly easy to acquire.

But biotechnology is not only increasing the productivity of the scientists, it is also breaking the previous limits as to how "wide" a cross can be made. When Taipei,China in the 1950s and, later, IRRI succeeded in crossing the Japonica and

Indica races of rice, this was considered a great achievement. Now, thanks to the new techniques, interspecific crosses within the same genus can be more easily carried out. This means that plant breeders have at their disposal a wider pool of traits to be drawn upon and put into the particular plant. In addition, the improvement of vegetatively propagated crops has been made simpler by biotechnology.

Equally significant, the molecular biologist can introduce genes from a totally unrelated species that code for specific traits, producing what is known as a transgenic variety. A well-known case is the introduction of a gene from the bacterium, *Bacillus thuringiensis* (Bt), into many plant species. This gene controls the production of a protein that is lethal to certain insect pests. In this way, the plant with the gene can be made resistant to the insects. Resistance viruses and fungi can be similarly incorporated. In general, the introduction of host-plant resistance, particularly toward insects, would tend to reduce the use of chemicals in agriculture. On the other hand, research is also leading to varieties that are herbicide-tolerant, so that herbicides can be applied without harming the crops themselves. This can lead to significant savings on cultivation costs, although of course, it entails increased use of chemical herbicides.

In livestock production, biotechnology has the potential to assist in tackling some serious animal diseases, such as foot-and-mouth disease, which is endemic throughout Asia. There currently exist vaccines to immunize animals, but there are two basic problems with the current methods. First, there are many strains of the virus causing the disease; to be effective, the vaccine has to be specific to each strain. Second, the vaccines must be stored under refrigeration to retain their potency, which presents a particularly serious problem in tropical Asia. Biotechnology research is uncovering the nature of the virus and is also advancing toward developing a vaccine that does not require refrigeration (Sasson 1988).

Biotechnology is no longer merely the promise that it had been over the last few decades; during the 1990s it proceeded well beyond laboratory work to widespread field trials and to the planting of transgenic crops in farmers' fields. The pattern of recent field trials gives an indication of the direction of agriculture in next decade. James and Krattiger (1996) compiled data on officially approved field trials across the world from 1986 to 1995. The data show that nearly all (92 percent) of the field trials were done in the developed countries, with the US alone accounting for more than half of the world total (here, the category of "developed countries" excludes the transitional economies of the former Soviet Union and Eastern Europe). Within Asia, almost all the field trials (97 percent) were in the PRC, with the remainder in Thailand. More recently, India entered the field in 1997 with trials of Bt cotton and herbicide-tolerant Indian mustard, while Malaysia tested transgenic rubber.

Table IV.1 shows the distribution by crop of field trials for biotechnology applications that are close to commercialization. (Transgenic crops are considered commercialized or near commercialization when more than 150 field trials have been conducted.) The table also shows the distribution of the area now planted to commercial transgenic crops This area totaled 12.8 million ha in 1997, having grown from 2.8 million ha in 1996. With such rapid expansion, big year-to-year jumps in the distribution among crops are to be expected. Thus, transgenic soybeans became the dominant crop only during 1997, overtaking tobacco, which had 35 percent of the area share in 1996.

Just as interesting are the traits that are being tested for in the field trials and that are being successfully commercialized. Table IV.2 has the same format as Table IV.1, but presents data on traits instead of crops. The predominance of herbicide tolerance as an objective of research and commercialization is striking, and reflects the dominance of the developed countries in biotechnology. Because of the prevalence of high wages in agriculture in these countries, there is a preference for chemical over mechanical methods of weed control. By contrast, the PRC has no field trials in this area at all, although the proportion of trials for herbicide tolerance in land-surplus Latin America is at least as high as in the developed countries. Furthermore, the fact

Table IV.1 Distribution of Potential and Actual Application of Biotechnology by Crops Worldwide

Crops	Percentage of Total Field Trials 1986–1995	Percentage of Area Planted to Transgenic Crops 1997
Maize	33	25
Rapeseed	21	10
Potato	11	<1
Tomato	11	1
Soybean	9	40
Cotton	7	11
Tobacco	5	13
Squash	3	n.a.
Total	100	100

Sources: Field trials, James and Krattiger (1996); area planted, James (1997).

Table IV.2 Distribution of Potential and Actual Application of Biotechnology by Traits Worldwide

Traits	Percentage of Total Field Trials 1986–1995	Percentage of Area Planted to Transgenic Crops 1997
Herbicide Tolerance	35	54
Insect Resistance	18	31
Virus Resistance	11	14
Fungal Resistance	3	<1
Product Quality	20	<1
Others	13	<1
Totals	100	100

Sources: Field trials, James and Krattiger (1996); area planted, James (1997).

that private firms, many of which have interests in agrochemicals, do most of the biotechnology research no doubt contributes to the dominance of herbicide tolerance as a desired trait.

Genetic manipulation has not been confined to the species of plants and animals that are directly used by man, but is now being contemplated for other species that affect the productivity of the crop and livestock operations. Insects in particular have become the focus of attention, as they inflict considerable crop damage. One common technique, predating the advent of biotechnology, involves inundating the pest population with sterile members, so that the majority of the matings become ineffectual.

This technique has been effective already against the screwworm, a pest that attacks livestock, and against the Mediterranean fruit fly in California. In these cases, sterile insects were obtained by conventional breeding plus radiation treatment, but this method is laborious. Transgenic technology promises a more efficient approach, involving the introduction of "piggybacking" genes onto "jumping genes," which have the capability of moving from one locus to another in the set of chromosomes. The technique allows a much faster replacement of the existing population with the modified population and with less effort. Similarly, an insecticide-resistant predatory species could be developed that preys upon the target pests. Such techniques can lead to a decrease in pest populations using considerably smaller amounts of chemical pesticides (O'Brochta and Atkinson 1998).

The Risks of Biotechnology

Biotechnology is new and naturally carries risks, as well as possible adverse effects on developing countries. The risk issues may be classified into three stages: first, the risks generated by work done in the laboratories or in the experiment stations; second, those that arise when the bioengineered products are in the fields; and third, those that arise when those products are ingested as food.

The first and third stages of risks are, or can be, subject to safety regulations, which are in place in many advanced countries and are being implemented in developing countries. In the research laboratories, the major risk is that some of the waste material may contain transformed microorganisms that could reproduce out of control, becoming a health hazard. The solution is to build containment facilities. The task of the Government is to ensure that such facilities are indeed up to standard, both in its own laboratories and in those belonging to private firms. In the case of food safety, similar considerations apply, although here public opinion in developed countries is considerably more cautious than the views of regulators, scientists, or companies promoting bioengineered products. Thus, the market introduction of bovine somatotropin (BST), a bioengineered hormone used in dairy production, has been held up in the European Union because of popular fears of its impact on human health. Similarly, the Flavr-Savr tomato, designed for a longer shelf-life, has run into considerable consumer resistance in the US.

It is in the second stage, the field application of biotechnology, that the risks are probably greatest and most complicated. The fear is that the introduced genes will run rampant. The potential environmental risks of genetically engineered organisms are summarized succinctly by Wyke (1988): "Their presence might disturb the balance of the environment in unintended ways; they might multiply uncontrollably and therefore become pests or weeds; they might be dispersed to areas far from their intended sites... they might transfer the new bits of DNA to other organisms." Even before biotechnology, there were examples of weeds, or microbes, introduced into a particular location from elsewhere and thriving all too well. The history of disease migration (say, from the Old World to the New or vice versa) is replete with such catastrophes. Such episodes fuel the fears of many who oppose the application of biotechnology in the field.

It is possible, however, to take a reasoned attitude toward this problem. A distinction should be made between the release of bioengineered genes belonging to a domesticated species and those belonging to a wild species such as insects or nematodes. The reason for the distinction is that domesticated plants or animals generally cannot survive without human intervention.[4] Consequently, the probability that genes attached to these organisms will unintentionally run rampant is low. However, with wild or semi-wild species (those only recently domesticated, such as pasture grasses and fishes), the risks are necessarily larger and more caution is required.

A concern raised by other authors is that commercial biotechnology developers, seeking "magic bullets" to deal with

---

[4] There are exceptions, of course: domesticated cats and dogs have turned wild in Australia and are threatening the survival of native animals. To the authors' knowledge, however, no similar example can be found for plants.

specific crop problems, have focused narrowly on genetically uniform biological agents. Bt has been prominent among these. As of 1989, Bt was the genetic source of pest resistance in almost two fifths of all biotechnology research and was the active ingredient in 95 percent of all commercial biopesticides. If pest populations evolve rapidly to adapt to such a specific stress, the risk is that a generation of commercial biopesticide agents could become impotent over a period as short as three to five years, thus necessitating a return to the conventional chemical pesticides that the biotechnology was designed to replace. This danger exists, of course, whether the new varieties are obtained through biotechnology techniques or through classical plant breeding.

Possible Adverse Effects of Biotechnology

The risk aspect discussed above refers to the unintended and unexpected side effects of biotechnology. But biotechnology may also have adverse consequences for Asian agriculture that are inherent in the way it is currently being developed. Two salient facts should be noted. First, biotechnology research is carried out by private firms, which are investing enormous sums in the field. Thus, just one large company, Monsanto, has during the past few years been investing more than $1 billion annually in agricultural biotechnology (both directly in research and in the acquisition of other biotechnology firms), or more than three times what the entire CGIAR spends each year on all agricultural research in developing countries (somewhat more than $300 million). Second, the overwhelming preponderance of biotechnology research is carried out in developed countries (particularly the US), with developing countries making only a minor contribution so far. In fact, the carrying out of biotechnology research by private firms is the result of a conscious policy decision on the part of the US government, the pacesetter among the developed countries. Until a few decades ago, agricultural research there was conducted mostly within the public sector, but US policies have generally now shifted toward letting the private sector undertake more research. This shift can be detected in the strengthening of laws on intellectual property undertaken both by the legislative and the judicial branches, which will be discussed in the following subsection (Fuglie et al. 1996).

The combination of these developments with the expansion of chemical companies into the seed industry (Grossman, Linnemann, and Wierema 1991) produces the scenario of a bias in research toward a more chemical-intensive agriculture, e.g., the explosion of herbicide-tolerant varieties being released by companies involved in biotechnology research. For Asian developing countries to import the crop varieties resulting from this research would also mean an increased use of chemicals in their agriculture.

The second fundamental fact of biotechnology is that most of the research is being done in advanced countries by companies interested in commercializing the fruits of their research by selling both more seeds and more chemicals. As the purchasing power of Asian farmers is considerably less than that of developed-country farmers, the research from these companies will be biased towards the needs of the latter. Where developed-country biotechnology finds direct application in Asia—e.g., in commercial crops like cotton and tobacco—it is likely to be biased toward the region's commercial farming regions that have better endowments of soils, rainfall (or irrigation), capital, and technical skills. There may be adverse distributional impacts both among and within regions as wealthier, better-educated farmers innovate more rapidly. The cash costs of proprietary seeds and other inputs may be beyond the means of resource-scarce, subsistence-oriented farmers. There will be implications, both positive and negative, for farm-labor use. For example, herbicide-tolerant varieties should produce higher yields, thus tending to increase labor use, but could also lead to the substitution of chemicals for the labor, typically female, used in weeding. That said, these potential adverse effects of biotechnology are no different from those arising from the green revolution.

Commercially oriented research in developed countries will tend to overlook the need for research on certain tropical crops grown extensively in Asia, such as cassava, coconuts, and specialty crops such as spices and tropical fruits. Even for crops such as rice, the labor-saving technologies likely to be investigated by the multinational corporations will shift the comparative advantage away from Asia, not only vis-à-vis the developed countries, but also vis-à-vis land-surplus regions like South America and Africa. For example, during the past two decades there has been a major, technology-induced shift of developed-country demand in the international sweetener market away from the sugarcane-based products of the tropics to locally-produced high-fructose corn syrup (Hobbelink 1991). Similar transformations are possible in markets for vegetable oils and crops such as cocoa because of biotechnology research on, respectively, rapeseed and cocoa-butter substitutes. Technologies like BST, if widely adopted in the milk-surplus developed countries, could greatly restrict the future potential for economically competitive dairy production in the tropics. Persley (1990) and others argue that the developing countries, with support from the IARCs, should focus public resources on the so-called "orphan commodities" for which there is likely to be little private investment in the developed countries, either because the commodities are not important in temperate areas or because the expected returns are too small or too uncertain.

Assessment of Biotechnology

With the advent of biotechnology, genetic improvement has changed a great deal and will continue to change even more radically. For better or worse, Asia will have to live with the consequences. Of course, biotechnology has its risks, but many of the risks can be averted if proper regulations are in place. Biotechnology also has potentially adverse social and environmental effects, but those will affect Asia only if Asian governments let multinational corporations monopolize the research. For Asian countries, particularly the small and medium-sized ones, to be able to further their own social agendas, their public research systems must be engaged directly in biotechnology research. Since there is much research already going on in the world, they must be highly selective in their approach and prioritize their activities carefully. For major cereals, such as wheat, rice, and maize, they may cooperate closely with, finance, and participate in the strategies adopted by the IARCs, as a way of pooling resources regionally. For tropical commodities, they may have to set up regional arrangements whereby they can economize on their meager resources and scarce scientific talent.

But biotechnology *research* should not be the only focus. Even if a given country has to forego this activity, it still has to perform regulatory functions necessary to protect its population from the various risks of biotechnology. This means investing in human resources to develop biotechnology *capability* in a broader sense than just the ability to conduct research. Again, pooling of resources across countries should be seriously explored.

Should any Asian government encourage its domestic private sector to conduct biotechnology research? A necessary (although not sufficient) condition for entry of the domestic private sector into this arena is that there must be adequate intellectual property protection (IPP). To anticipate the discussion of this issue in the next section, Asian countries are ill-equipped to provide such protection effectively. Unless this changes, the private sector will have a relatively weak incentive to invest in biotechnology, which further emphasizes the need for capacity building within the public sector.

Intellectual-Property Protection

The discussion of biotechnology highlights the increased importance of the private sector in research. The private sector needs the expectation of profit if it is to engage in research, which requires, as described in Chapter II, that there be excludability in the consumption of the product that the research yields. In the case of agriculture, this assurance can be provided by what has been called above "natural protection" of intellectual property, for example in the cases of hybrid maize and poultry. The other means of protection is legal, followed by enforcement mechanisms to ensure that those who have succeeded in expanding the frontiers of technology can recapture part or all of their costs of research. Thus, where natural protection is not available, legal rights have to be established. But even if legal rights are provided, institutional and human resources must be devoted to enforcing those rights in order to give sufficient confidence to the private sector to invest in research. Enforcement is a far more difficult task for the developing countries, yet it is what must be accomplished if property rights are to be meaningful.

The laws on intellectual property are at present in a state of flux, not least in the United States, which has embraced this particular notion with enthusiasm and is now pushing other countries to follow suit. Asian countries are doing so, albeit not as enthusiastically. Since up-to-date information is not as yet available on the legislation in individual countries, the better strategy is to spell out the broad implications of the various forms of intellectual-property rights, as currently legislated in the US.

Trade Secrecy

The simplest and oldest form of IPP is trade secrecy. This is what US hybrid seed companies used and still use to protect their inbred lines from being stolen and used by others. Not all Asian countries have laws that protect trade secrecy, and hybrid seed companies have been seeking such protection, either from a version of the American trade secrecy laws, or from a plant-variety protection law.

Plant Variety Protection, or Plant Breeders' Rights

A plant variety law would, as the name suggests, provide protection to the plant breeders for coming up with a new variety of plants. It is also known as plant breeders' rights. To be protected under the law, a variety has to be

- stable (succeeding generations will be homozygous, or capable of reproducing the traits of the original);
- homogeneous (each generation will have a uniform set of traits);
- distinctive (it will be clearly distinguishable from any other variety "whose existence is a matter of common knowledge"[5]); and
- "novel" (to establish novelty, a variety may not have been offered for sale or marketed in the country of application for longer than four years, or in the case of the US, only one year).

At the global level, this form of protection is covered by an International Convention for the Protection of New Varieties of Plants, or UPOV after its French initials. First adopted in 1961, UPOV has been revised three times, the latest revision occurring in 1991. As of December 1999, however, UPOV had only 44 signatories, predominantly from the developed countries of the West, the former Soviet bloc, and most of South America, with the PRC being the sole member from Asia (UPOV 1999). Members of UPOV agree to provide each other with protection, the minimum duration being 15 years for annual crops and 18 years for perennials, although members may opt for more.

Because of the requirements for stability and homogeneity, this form of IPP applies to vegetatively propagating plants (before 1970, US law applied *only* to them), and to inbred lines of the sexually reproducing plants. It provides only a "mild" form of protection, because its novelty requirement is not as rigorous as that for patent protection (see below). Competitors can thus come up with very similar products and still obtain protection. Plant variety protection is essentially the equivalent of a trademark, and is used extensively to protect breeders of ornamentals. Plant variety protection laws always have a farmers' exemption clause. This

---

[5] The wording is from the International Convention for the Protection of New Varieties of Plants (UPOV), as cited by Lesser (1991).

allows farmers to use their own seeds or stock to raise the next crop, but they may not resell the seeds to others.

Because plant variety protection has specifically been designed for innovations in plant breeding, it has some attractive features, at least relative to patent protection. Innovators obtain the protection only for the trait or traits they have added to a particular variety. Inasmuch as this allows them to build on the work of others, it reflects better than patents what plant-breeders (and to some extent, biotechnicians) do and for what achievements they should be rewarded.

Patents

For a long time, patents were not given for living organisms, because no living organism had been "invented" by man. But living organisms became patentable, at least in the US., after a landmark 1980 decision in the Diamond vs. Chakrabarty case in the US, where the inventor patented strains of bacteria that the defendant had engineered to decompose crude oil. Like plant variety protection, there are a number of requirements that have to be met before a patent is issued.

First, the patents apply to embodiments of ideas, not to the ideas themselves (Lesser 1991). Second, the patented item has to be useful. Third, it has to be novel. Finally it has to be nonobvious. The formula in US law used to define this last requirement is that the item must be nonobvious "to a person skilled in the art." This last requirement is what really gives a patent its power. By requiring the "inventive step" to be a major one, the law makes it difficult for competing claims to match closely the claims made in existing patents. And by making it thus difficult for competitors to enter the business, the resulting monopoly power serves as an incentive for the researcher or inventor to become a patent holder. This, at any rate is the theory behind the requirement.

Clearly, what constitutes a nonobvious inventive step is sufficiently judgmental to keep many patent lawyers happily in business. It also provides room for policymakers to manipulate the inventive step requirement. Making the requirement very strict means that competing patent applicants have a bigger hurdle to overcome and provides strong incentives to the researcher or inventor. A lax requirement, on the other hand, would encourage creative copying of inventions. At certain stages of development, countries may find it advantageous to have patent protection, but keeping relatively lax the "inventive step" requirement, so as to encourage imitative innovation. This is what Japan did, for example, before it became a technology exporter around the 1960s.

Unlike plant-variety protection laws, patent laws do not have a farmers' exemption clause. This would obviously be onerous—as well as unenforceable—for farmers who wish to retain patented seed for future use.

The opening up of US law to allow patenting of biological products has created concern among developing countries about whether the patent laws can be used to undermine their natural comparative advantage in tropical products. Thus, while it is clear that patent law is useful mostly for bioengineered products, the scope with which the law will be applied is an unresolved question. As examples of potential problems, here are three cases of patent suits in US courts involving India.

The first involves the medicinal properties of turmeric. Two expatriate Indians obtained a patent in the US for turmeric to be used to heal wounds. This prompted the Indian government to undertake a countersuit to have the patent withdrawn. It had to show that the use of turmeric to heal wounds had been known in India for millennia. Eventually, the Indian government succeeded in its suit, but only after considerable effort merely to defeat a frivolous claim.

The second case involves the use of neem, a plant that has many uses, one of which is as a pesticide. The W. R. Grace Company obtained two patents for improvements in the storage stability of neem-seed extracts that contain the key active ingredient (azadirachtin) from the tree. The Indian government again filed a countersuit because of the domestic outcry, but withdrew after it realized that the processes for which the patents were obtained were indeed patentable.

The third involves basmati rice, for which the Rice-Tec Company obtained a patent in the US. This case has certain features that deserve further examination. The patent document (US Patent Office 1997) first shows that basmati rice has certain desirable characteristics (and the document lays out the means to measure these traits), and then that its plant has certain traits that make it difficult and unprofitable to grow outside its normal habitat in India and Pakistan. It then proceeds to show that combining these characteristics and traits with those in a plant that is of short stature, not photoperiod-sensitive and high-yielding in temperate latitudes (all of which would make it possible to grow a plant producing rice with basmati-like characteristics in, say, the rice-growing areas of the United States) would involve a genetic manipulation of some complexity. These preliminaries (which are hardly original) are meant to show that a novelty would be created if the combination could be made. The heart of the innovation for which the patent was sought (and granted) is the use of classical methods of plant breeding to come up with a plant type that has the desirable traits and that can produce rice grain with basmati-like characteristics.

The legal basis of the patent lies in a number of specific claims, some of which are so worded as to enable the patent holders to have rights over a much larger domain than can be justified by their work. For what Rice-Tec is claiming is not a patent on the specific lines that it has obtained from its breeding work, but rather on *any* rice which that meets the following description (contained in claim 1):

> A rice plant, which plant when cultivated in North, Central or South America, or Caribbean Islands
> a) has a mature height of about 80 cm. to about 140 cm.
> b) is substantially photoperiod insensitive;
> c) produces rice grains having
>   i) an average starch index of about 27 to about 35
>   ii) an average 2-acetyl-1-pyrroline [the chemical that gives the aroma of basmati] content of about 150 to about 2,000 ppb [parts per billion]
>   iii) an average length of about 6.2 mm. to about 8.0 mm., an average width of about 1.6 mm. to about 1.9 mm. and average length to width ratio of about 3.5 to 4.5

iv) an average of about 41% to about 67% whole grains, and
v) an average lengthwise increase of about 67%

Other claims (except three, which refer specifically to three particular lines developed by Rice-Tec and their progeny) cover a somewhat narrower range of characteristics of the plant and grain, but a worldwide geographical range, instead of being confined to the Americas as in claim 1.

Observe what is being established under claim 1. Its key feature is the combination of grain characteristics and plant traits, that constitute a high-yielding basmati rice plant. These are *ideas* that are certainly not novel; any person "skilled in the art," such as plant breeders, could come up with the listing shown in the citation above. The basmati characteristics are well known and what it takes to produce a high-yielding plant is also well known. Even if original, what is in claim 1 is more in the nature of ideas rather than embodiments of the ideas. Rice-Tec is making a claim for certain plant and grain characteristics, even though these are well known.

Rice-Tec's achievements presumably arise from the successful breeding of particular lines that have the characteristics listed above. But because of claim 1 and the other three claims, other plant breeders cannot use the original or related varieties of basmati to cross with other parents (other than those used by Rice-Tec) to produce plants and grains that match with the traits and characteristics of those stated in the patent. If these stipulations apply to all patents, it is clear that this form of intellectual property confers a much broader protection to the holders than, say, plant variety protection. From the point of view of Asian countries, the granting of such patents by a foreign government (in this case the US) effectively lowers the value embodied in their genetic resources (in this case the basmati variety).

Benefits of Intellectual Intellectual-Property Protection

Consistently, across commodities and across countries, agricultural research has been shown to have a high payoff.

Evenson, Herdt, and Hossain (1996) summarize the incremental rates of return to rice research in different countries as estimated by various authors, showing figures that range from 30 to 165 percent. And these figures are by no means atypical. The consistency of the results suggests strongly that there is underinvestment in research. As the public sector has heretofore done most of the investment in research, and as the returns to this investment accrue only in the long run—longer at any rate than the time horizon of most politicians—such a misallocation should not occasion any surprise.

It was pointed out above that in the absence of any IPP, be it natural or legal, private companies would have little incentive to invest in agricultural research. Has the conferring of IPP in fact encouraged greater participation by the private sector in research, and has agricultural technology thereby been improved? There are two ways by which such improvement may occur.

The first would be through an in increase in private inventive activity in the developing countries. For patents, there is as yet little evidence one way or the other, as the history of patenting to cover agriculture has been very short. Even for the more general impact of patents in areas outside agriculture, the evidence is at best mixed (Lesser 1991). In the very few developing countries that have been studied (all in Latin America), protection of plant varieties has increased private-sector participation modestly. This could lead to some substitution between private and public financing for research, for which there is some evidence—again for Latin America—although the degree of substitution is modest (Lesser 1991).

The second way would be through an increase in the transfer of technology from developed to developing countries as the result of IPP. Two quite contrasting perspectives are possible on this matter. On the one hand, with IPP, international seed companies should be comfortable about bringing in their products without fear of being imitated. On the other hand, IPP lets seed importers acquire monopoly rights over their products, leading to a distorted market structure. Unfortunately, the question of which influence is the stronger is much more easily stated than answered. At this time, no empirical evidence can be brought to bear either way.

International Undertaking on Plant Genetic Resources and the Convention on Biodiversity

The expansion of the role of IPP, pushed vigorously by developed countries, particularly the US, has led to a sharp reaction in the developing countries. If IPP is to be granted to seeds emanating from developed-country laboratories and experiment stations, it is felt by the developing countries that their farmers should be entitled to claim some rights to the genetic resources that originate from them. These rights are sometimes called farmers' rights. However, there are legal, economic, and practical complications in establishing such claims.

A first step toward overcoming the legal complications is to be found in Article 15 of the Convention on Biodiversity (CBD),[6] in which the parties affirm that access to the genetic resources of a country is considered part of its sovereign rights. A country's Government now has a right to control access to these resources—possibly even if the genetic material itself has already been transported out of the country and deposited, say, in a gene bank. This confirms the evolution of the positions taken in the Food and Agriculture Organization's International Undertaking on Plant Genetic Resources (IUPGR), which was adopted in 1983 but subsequently qualified until the sovereign-rights principle was agreed to in 1991 (see Box IV.1). The CBD thus officially brings to a close the era of open exchange of

---

[6] The Convention on Biodiversity (CBD) was signed at the Earth Summit in Rio de Janeiro in 1992. Its objective is to ensure the conservation of biodiversity, the sustainable use of its components, and the fair and equitable sharing of the benefits from their use (Article 1). The components of biodiversity are to include diversity within species, among species, and among ecosystems. The bulk of the Convention deals with various measures to promote biodiversity that are to be undertaken by the signatories. Developed countries are asked to provide financial resources for the implementation of the Convention by developing countries (Article 20), through some mechanism to be decided later (Article 21).

Box IV.1: The Flow of Genetic Resources across Borders: A Legal History

The 22nd Session of the Food and Agriculture Organization (FAO) Conference in 1983 adopted a legally nonbinding International Undertaking on Plant Genetic Resources (IUPGR), which based itself on the "universally accepted principle that plant genetic resources are a heritage of mankind and consequently should be available without restriction." This ringing endorsement of the free flow of genetic resources did not, however, command support among countries that protected plant breeders' rights. It was feared that the IUPGR might be incompatible with the protection of such rights. In 1989, therefore, the FAO qualified the free-exchange principle by an "agreed interpretation" that the plant breeders' rights provided for under UPOV are "not incompatible" with the IUPGR. This qualification was balanced by the recognition of a farmers' rights concept. In 1991, the free-exchange principle was further qualified by the endorsement that nations have sovereign rights over their plant genetic resources.

Parallel to these changes was the regularization of the gene banks run by the CGIAR centers, which is of great importance for developing countries. In the past, the control and ultimate ownership of these collections were a matter of agreement between the centers and their host governments. In 1994, the FAO signed agreements with all the centers holding plant genetic resources, stating that the centers hold their collections in trust for the benefit of the international community and shall not claim legal ownership over the germplasm or apply any form of intellectual-property rights to the material itself or related information.

Source: Leskien and Flitner (1997).

genetic material across borders, which has been the rule, particularly for staple food crops, ever since Mendelian genetics became the driving force behind technical change in agriculture. It was unfortunate that the CBD was negotiated during the same period as the Uruguay Round of trade negotiations, as developed countries pushed very strongly to include intellectual property as an item on the agenda during the negotiations on the CBD. Developing countries responded by using the CBD to attempt to protect their rights, but in the end, the attempt did not lead to a very strong Convention.

The retreat from the free-exchange principle toward the national-sovereignty principle embodied in the qualifications to the IUPGR and in the CBD has the following novel features. First, the exchange of genetic resources must be based on mutually agreed terms and subject to prior informed consent of the concerned parties, i.e., the governments of the countries in the transaction, and particularly the exporting country. Second, the CBD requires that parties to the transaction obtain the approval of and share benefits with the holders of knowledge, innovations, and practices, i.e., the farmers practicing traditional agriculture and using traditional seeds. This sharing of benefits is in line with the idea of farmers' rights endorsed by the IUPGR (note that in the IUPGR the notion of farmers rights differs from, and is less legally precise than, the concept of farmers' exemption discussed above on pp. 145–146).

What are the economic benefits of this change in regime? A simple answer would be that genetic resources are of value and the countries in which they are to be found should have some ownership claim over them and presumably obtain some revenues from those who make use of them. A more complex answer would be that to preserve these genetic resources over the long term requires resources and therefore those who make use of them should be made to pay for the "upkeep." This in turn will provide the incentive for those who possess the resources to conserve them.

How valuable actually are these resources? Here empirical evidence is rather hard to come by, particularly with reference to genetic resources that are useful for agriculture. For want of precise evidence, it is necessary to look into a related kind of genetic resource, for which some work has been done. A much-discussed use of biodiversity is "bioprospecting" in order to derive new products, in particular, new medicines. Examples of profitable uses of tropical plants and microorganisms abound. A few countries and companies hoped to profit from entering this arena: Costa Rica, for one, entered into long-term contractual arrangements with Merck, while Shaman Laboratories wanted to conduct bioprospecting in many countries and share the benefits with local communities that helped them in their work. These examples are often cited because other examples are hard to find, leading one to suspect that bioprospecting will not yield as much value as has often been touted. Extrapolating from successful hits is hardly an appropriate means of assessing the profitability of search.

Even multiplying the probability of discovering a commercially valuable substance by the value of a discovery is not adequate for the task at hand. As Simpson, Sedjo, and Reid (1996) put it: "By multiplying the probability with which an organism sampled at random contains *some* chemical compound of commercial value—whether unique to that organism or not—by the expected value of a successful commercial product, earlier researchers have failed to recognize the *possibility* of redundancy among natural products [italics in the original]." Incorporating these considerations into their exercise and assuming plausible values for some of the key parameters, the authors estimated an upper limit for the economic value of biodiversity for pharmaceutical research and found it to be quite modest.

The genetic resources used for bioprospecting by the pharmaceutical industry are mostly located *in situ* (i.e., in their original environments). In contrast, the genetic resources used for agriculture are cultivated all over the world. Furthermore, for most major agricultural crops, there are already in existence many *ex situ* collections that could provide resources for plant breeders. These collections already have within them a very large proportion of the genes for these crops. The marginal benefits of *in situ* sources of genes for these crops cannot be very large. Considerable skepticism must therefore be expressed about the value of the protection for indigenous sources of genes that could be used in agriculture.

Aside from the law and the economics of farmers' rights, the practical problems of enforcing such rights should not be overlooked. In cases where the genetic resources have been in use for some time and spread far and wide, how is their ownership to be established? And having established it, how are the presumed owners to collect on their rights? And if the Government is to collect on their behalf, how are the farmers who are the purported owners of the rights to be provided with the right incentives to maintain the resources?

Assessment

It is not clear what Asian governments stand to gain in return for providing IPP if the only impact considered is the incentive for research by the domestic private sector. With plant-variety protection, the gains are at best modest. Patent protection is usually provided for biotechnology research, but for the foreseeable future in Asia, domestic private involvement in biotechnology will remain small because of the field's high-tech, capital-intensive nature, which is extremely demanding of highly trained human resources.

Gains from IPP through technology transfer from developed countries and multinationals would take the form of imports of protected varieties or inbred lines. It is sometimes claimed that hybrid maize producers in Asia's developing countries—often exclusive local distributors of seed developed by multinational companies—are reluctant to import inbred lines, for fear of their being stolen by competitors. There is no doubt that the provision of even a mild form of protection, such as plant variety protection, would be sufficient to make hybrid producers sleep more soundly; to that extent, they would prefer such protection to having none. However, even without benefit of such protection, local hybrid producers in numerous Asian countries have already imported inbred lines in order to cross them. Pray and Echeverria (1991) assess the determinants of the location of the research and development units of these multinational companies. They identify three main factors that encourage location in a specific country: (i) the existence of a profitable affiliate, (ii) a growing and sophisticated market, and (iii) an adequate scientific and technical infrastructure for research. They also list as obstacles the scale economies of centralized research at headquarters and the difficulties of assembling adequate research staff in developing countries. Conspicuously absent is any mention of IPP.

Note also that the above discussion pertains to the location of research and development facilities, and perhaps of seed production. Where the nature of the crop permits (e.g., with cross-pollinating crops), developed countries can and do export hybrid seeds directly. Echeverria (1991) reports a lively trade in hybrid maize seed, although most is between sellers and buyers in developed countries.

With respect to biotechnology research, the key problem is the farmers' exemption. With a very large number of small farmers, firms in Asia, whether domestic or foreign-owned, will find it very difficult to ensure that farmers do not reuse the seeds from their crops. This will certainly wipe out the incentive to do research or even to import ready-made seed for self-pollinating crops. For example, Monsanto is finding it difficult to introduce its Bt cotton into Asian countries containing many small farmers, such as Thailand (TDRI 1996). It is difficult to envision Asian developing countries enacting laws on seed that would not have a farmers' exemption clause; even if they did, it is difficult to envision them enforcing such laws. For cross-pollinating crops, on the other hand, firms are in any case naturally protected against imitation or farmers' reuse, so that there is little net gain from providing patents or other forms of legal protection.

Overall, it must be concluded that the issue of IPP in agriculture is overblown. The benefits to developing countries of adopting IPP are at best minor. The nuisance from frivolous filing of patents (as in the turmeric case) in developed countries, and the need to be vigilant against such dubious claims, would be costly. Indeed, the cynical view that IPP is designed to protect the intellectual property of patent lawyers in developed countries is not altogether flippant.

Nevertheless, developing countries will be subject to unrelenting pressure from developed countries to enact legislation to protect intellectual property, and they will probably end up doing so. It is important, therefore, that they prepare themselves for a world in which multinational companies will dominate advanced agricultural technologies. They may have to buy these technologies, but they can have some choice about the terms on which they will have to pay. Their negotiations have to be based on a thorough understanding of the benefits and risks of the new technologies. This understanding will not be there unless the public sector has the capability that is built on a well-functioning research system. This reinforces the important point that a good research system, one with active public and private participation, would yield very high returns, as has been repeatedly shown in evaluation studies.

If the benefit of the existing forms of IPP to developing countries is small, the same could be said of the various defensive measures attempted by them, embodied in instruments such as the CBD or in concepts such as farmers' rights. While the controversy over intellectual property has mainly concerned its impact on investment, the problem with these new concepts is more fundamental, namely the possibility of implementing them at all. Not surprisingly, evidence concerning their impact has thus been hard to come by.

Sadly, the push by developed countries in favor of wider IPP application on the one hand and the pursuit by developing countries of the dubious benefits of farmers' rights on the other may well end the present era of open science in agriculture. Central to the conduct of open science is the free exchange of genetic resources among nonprofit (mostly tax-financed) institutions. Altogether, the regime of open science has brought enormous benefits to Asian farmers. Some Asians may regard the coming changes as retrogressive, but they cannot be ignored. Asian governments will have to adapt to the new regime, at the very least to minimize any adverse impacts of the rapidly changing environment of international agricultural research.

Research to Improve Resource Management

Up to now, discussion has centered exclusively on genetic improvement as a central strategy in enhancing agricultural technology. The priority and length of that discussion reflects the greater emphasis and financing given to genetic improvement than to other types of research, an imbalance rooted in the reality of agricultural research in Asia over the last two decades. Ultimately, this imbalance is due to the simple fact that genetic improvement is in some cases "closer" to productivity enhancement than is improvement in resource management. The objective of research on resource management would be, for a given genetic technology and natural resource base, to maximize productivity on a sustained basis. This involves much more extensive changes in farm-management practices, which may take a longer time to show results. Furthermore, in many areas, the basic science is less developed than that of molecular genetics. For example, the following is an observation on soils, which would be a central component of any research resource management program:

> Soil structure is still not well understood at a fundamental level, and much of the science is largely empirical... This rather weak theoretical basis means that much of the work on these subjects must be empirical, applied and adaptive, *as opposed to theoretical and revolutionary* [italics added], though absolutely essential. (TAC/CGIAR 1996).

Consequently, much of the work done in natural resources management is necessarily location-specific. Dramatic results equivalent to the breeding of IR-8 are, therefore, rather rare, although successful cases do exist. An example of the kind of work that leads to success illustrates the contrast between the work done in this area and work on genetic improvement. In 1991, the state of Rajasthan in India created a multidisciplinary Department of Watershed Development and Soil Conservation, which began to carry out conservation and development work on more than 100,000 ha spread among more than 250 locations. The Department's goals were to develop environmentally sound, socially acceptable farming system technologies. Organizationally, its approach emphasized local participation and the working out of rules and procedures for sharing costs and benefits among local residents and the Government. The work was done in a very decentralized fashion, with a team assigned to each subwatershed, whose average size was only 4,000 ha, and with the staff encouraged to experiment and innovate (TAC/CGIAR 1996). The difference between this sort of interactive, location-specific work and the work done by plant breeders is obvious, but it also has to be noted that the approach adopted in Rajasthan is distinguished by its rarity.

Broadly, it can be stated that the stress on genetic improvement has favored the areas where water supply is assured. Areas that are not so well endowed have tended to lag considerably behind (David and Otsuka 1994). Within the irrigated areas, the intensification of production (particularly for rice and wheat) has been profound—many farmers have moved from growing as little as two tons per hectare and one crop per year to growing 4–5 tons per hectare and three crops per year—and cannot but put considerable stress on the natural resources that sustain the production. The problem in the less favored areas is somewhat different. Not having benefited as much from genetic improvements, farmers in these areas have to manage their meager resources better in order to increase productivity. Since very different sets of problems face these two areas, the following discussion is divided between them.

Irrigated Areas

In irrigated areas, intensification has given rise to two sets of problems. The first is a very long-term one, namely that the genetic-based strategy has run into what appears to be a limit. As noted in Chapter I, the differences between experimental yields and yields on Asia's best farms have gradually narrowed during the past decade. The other problem, more short-term and more visible, is the increased infestation of pests and diseases, which appears to be a direct outcome of the intensification.

As to the first set of problems, long-term studies of rice yields in experiment stations and in farmers' fields in areas that switched over earlier to modern technology indicate that yields—for a given level of technology and input use—have actually been declining (Pingali, Hossein and Gerpacio 1997). The cause or causes of this worrying trend are still not fully understood and work is proceeding at IRRI on this important issue. This problem, at the moment, remains one of high science, which the science-based centers are best equipped to study. However, if the causes of declining productivity can be identified, it does not necessarily follow that these centers can or must formulate the solutions.

As to the second set of problems, a number of actors other than the research centers are involved. The increased infestation of pests and diseases following upon intensification should occasion little surprise and is certainly one of the reasons for the decline in yields cited above. There are two main approaches now used to combat the problem, plus another one that is emerging as an important addition to the pool of pest-control strategies.

The first approach is the use of chemicals. Unsurprisingly, chemical companies have almost exclusively carried out the research in this area. Not only do they conduct research, they also have marketing networks that reach down to the farmers; indeed in some countries, they have developed excellent connections with the departments of extension as well, not always with the public interest in mind.

Agricultural chemicals, if properly used, can prevent crop losses, and, in the case of herbicides, save labor. The problem is that there has been a lopsided dependence on their use and in many cases this has proved, at the very least, unnecessarily expensive. In some cases, they have even been counterproductive. That the farmers have gone along with such a counterproductive method of plant protection could be attributed to ignorance—but government officials have also not shown themselves any wiser. Intensification of agricultural production has been especially rapid over the last two decades; is not surprising that adaptation to the new technologies has reflected, at least initially, elements of irrationality and ignorance. This problem will be further discussed below in the section on extension and again in Chapter VI in the context of fertilizer subsidies.

The second approach to coping with increased infestation of pests and diseases is to go back to the plant breeders and get them to introduce resistance into the host plants. This approach is, of course, environmentally friendlier and to be preferred over the use of chemicals.

Both of these approaches, sometimes called collectively "kill or be killed," suffer from a fundamental flaw, however. Insects and other enemies of the plants have very short life cycles. It does not take a very long time for them to develop tolerance to the chemicals or to the built-in resistance of the host plants. The classic example in this respect is Indonesia in the mid-1970s. Following a heavy attack of the brown plant-hopper on rice farms, scientists came up with a new variety of rice that was resistant to it. Within a few years, the insect was found to have evolved into a new biotype that infested the new variety just as nonchalantly and thoroughly as the old one. A third variety was introduced, and a third biotype just as surely followed.

Because of these problems, a radically different approach is now being advocated widely and adopted in some countries: integrated pest management (IPM). Briefly, this involves an ecological approach to pest control: the cultivated plants, their enemies, the pests (including weeds), and *their* enemies, i.e., their predators and competitors, are viewed as sharing a habitat. An imbalance in one component, caused, say, by increasing the biomass of the plants, sets off other changes. Completely eliminating one of the plants' enemies would also introduce an imbalance in other components. In the case of pests, in particular, their elimination would open up an ecological niche that would be quickly filled in. In the Indonesian example above, for instance, it is the new biotype of the brown plant-hopper that stepped into the niche.

The correct strategy, according to advocates of IPM, is to replace the older "kill or be killed" strategy with a "live and let live" approach. Of course, the primary objective of agriculture remains the sustainable yield of usable crops from the land, but instead of eliminating the pests at first sight, a more careful look has to be taken at the other organisms on the farm. These include the pests' predators and competitors. In that way, some control is kept on the pest population without necessarily eliminating the pests altogether. The use of chemicals is particularly to be faulted, as they tend to kill the pests and their predators and competitors indiscriminately.

While IPM relies much more heavily on farmers' management skills, the central Government also plays a crucial role in setting the policy framework. One case where IPM has been successfully applied is Indonesia. Indonesia's IPM areas have achieved lower pesticide use while avoiding, by and large, major pest outbreaks (although it must be acknowledged that the 300,000 farmers who have been trained in IPM field schools constitute only a small proportion of the country's 16 million farm households [Untung 1995]). Probably just as effective was the elimination in 1988 of pesticide subsidies, which at one time amounted to 80 percent of their cost. Additionally, there was a ban on the "extremely" and "most" hazardous pesticides, as defined by the World Health Organization. In contrast, the policies pursued in Thailand have been somewhat lax. While there has been no direct subsidy to pesticides, tariff barriers do not tax farmers and there is also an emergency outbreak budget that allows the Department of Agricultural Extension to spray infested areas. Consequently, growth in the use of pesticides has continued unabated, as has the frequency of pest outbreaks, not only in rice, but in other crops as well (Jungbluth 1996).

It is clear that IPM involves a far more sophisticated approach by the Government and farmers than was practiced at the time when the modern varieties arrived in Asia. At that time, the Government aimed to ensure that farmers obtained a bundle of inputs: seeds, fertilizers, water, and perhaps pesticides, with credit as a facilitating mechanism. Under IPM, the farmer is supposed to understand the process of pest buildup, perhaps after being trained and assisted by pest ecologists. Byerlee (1998) called the earlier, more arm's-length type of knowledge *embodied*: what enhances productivity is the inputs. Technology transfer is easier with embodied knowledge, because all that the farmers need to obtain are the inputs themselves. The knowledge of IPM, on the other hand, is *disembodied*: farmers have to learn how to manage the various inputs in different circumstances, and this requires greater knowledge and judgment.

Fertilizer application is another area where disembodied knowledge is required. Byerlee (1998) cites research showing that the fertilizer response function in Asia has been shifting downward over the years as a result of deterioration in the soil resource base. This is yet another aspect of the yield decline story mentioned earlier. In Indonesia, which contains some of Asia's most intensive rice-growing areas, the farmer's response has been to increase the use of nitrogen (N) and phosphorous to levels that significantly exceed agronomic and economic recommendations (Roche 1994). Furthermore, the efficiency of N use—i.e., the percentage of applied N that is actually taken up in grain and straw—is also quite low among Asian rice farmers. The way to enhance that efficiency is to precisely time the application of N during the growing cycle to match the nutrient demand and root absorptive capacity of the plant. This, however, is a highly sophisticated approach, requiring, at the very least, soil and tissue testing, but possibly also the application of crop models, use of fertilizers other than prilled urea, and so on. Most problematic is that the technique is not generic, but highly location-specific, indeed, almost farm-specific.

Such an evolution implies that the older top-down model of research has to be substantially changed. Even more affected will be the extension system, which is discussed below. The earlier separation of research and extension or, more accurately, the one-directional relationship between them (with research supplying technology for the extension system to transfer to farmers) will have to end. Farmers will have to be brought directly into the process of technology development (see pp. 72–73). They will also have to become more sophisticated and critical, giving priority to getting the right kind of technical information for their specific circumstances.

Less Favored Areas

Intensification of the irrigated areas, aided by genetic improvement, has brought yields to the point where, in some regions, they are touching the ceiling imposed by resource constraints (including the downward pressure on the yield ceiling imposed by increasing pests, diseases, and other factors). In contrast, the resource constraints in less favored areas have been more binding from the beginning.

The elite agricultural research organizations, both the IARCs and the national systems, have always emphasized genetic improvement. At the same time, they have, over the years, been pressured to pay attention to the resource-constrained areas because of concerns about equity. Because of donor influence, this pressure has been probably been stronger on the IARCs than on national systems. But it is fair to say that all these research organizations have failed to deliver, or at least to have had as dramatic an impact, as they had in irrigated areas in the 1960s and 1970s. The fundamental problem is that the resource-constrained areas do not lend themselves to easy solutions; if there is any solution, it is unlikely to be delivered solely by the high science characteristic of these elite institutions. For if resources are the constraint, the solution will have be one of two kinds: either the constraint has to be lifted, or farmers will have to better manage their farming within the constraint.

The lifting of the resource constraint requires investment. Usually, but not always, the most limiting constraint is water. Irrigation moves land out of the unfavorable category and makes it amenable to the modern genetically-based technology. Thus, Asian governments have invested heavily in irrigation, particularly in the 1970s, but that investment has fallen off since the mid-1980s (see Chapter V).

Unirrigated land includes a vast category ranging from semiarid zones to fairly humid, even flood-prone regions. The already difficult problems of farming with severe resource constraints are compounded by the fact that the variations within these areas make it very difficult for scientists to devise new technologies that would be widely applicable. Agricultural scientists also point out that there is no research paradigm for resource management equivalent to Mendelian biology for genetic improvement. It is partly for this reason that elite scientific research has failed.

Two ways out of this impasse suggest themselves. One is to redirect the research system away from the genetics-driven commodity focus and toward a more interdisciplinary farming-systems approach. This approach has been advocated for many years, but unfortunately, despite the strong support it has received from the donor community, results on the ground are hard to come by, much less to generalize about (the Indonesian experience is presented in Manwan et al. [1998]).

The second way out, sometimes called diversification, is more promising, but actually requires much more than research. The term "diversification" is misleading, for it suggests that each farmer should grow a wide variety of crops to minimize risk. While that may itself be a wise course (particularly if farmers choose crops whose yields are negatively correlated with one another), it does not necessarily follow that farmers should move away from the basic food crops. People living in less favored areas tend to concentrate on the production of food crops because less favored areas also tend to have poor transport. For them to grow something other than food crops is to incur a double penalty: the cash crops will have to be transported out and the food will have to be transported in, both at high cost, while the farmer is exposed to the new risk that market prices may move adversely. Consequently, the choice facing these farmers is often limited to food crops, e.g., upland rice, even though the land is far from ideal for such crops.

If their choices could be broadened to include other crops, the resource constraint might not be as limiting as that for food crops. Which crops are appropriate for the resource conditions and which crops may find an adequate market are clearly far more subtle questions than can be handled by elite scientific research institutions with a mandate for just one commodity or only a few. In fact, the shift to new cropping patterns can often be induced without any new research. The key example is a good road that facilitates the shift by reducing transport costs, as illustrated by the experience of northeast Thailand in moving away from rainfed rice to cassava. Building better transport infrastructure also reduces consumption risks for households, as they can draw on a larger supply pool for food.

The role of the central Government is critical in formulating a correct development strategy for remote, resource-poor areas. Investments in infrastructure are essential to encourage the expansion of commercial markets and the involvement of the private sector. At the same time, the skill of the farmers is itself an asset that should not be overlooked. Technology in these areas will have to be highly location-specific. Consequently, the top-down approach from research to extension to farmers, which was appropriate for a program of genetic improvements in irrigated areas, cannot work here. Indeed, even in irrigated areas, as resource constraints are making themselves felt (at a much higher level of production), the old centrally-directed research system will have to deal with farmers less as passive recipients of technology and more as active interlocutors and partners.

Nongovernment organizations (NGOs), about which more below, can fill a particularly important role in applied research and extension in less favored areas. Throughout Asia, NGOs have conducted "action research," which involves the participation of local communities. Two features distinguish these NGO efforts from the approach adopted by the conventional research and experiment stations. The first is the generally small-scale nature of their activities, which is altogether appropriate, given the location specificity of the task. Second, there is a much closer interaction between the biophysical and social science aspects of the research. The communities are asked to participate from the stage of designing the research, instead of being brought in after there is a finding to be adopted by the individual farmers.

Mechanization

As productivity in irrigated areas has grown, so has mechanization. In rice areas, there is a typical sequence. First, land preparation is mechanized, with small power tillers whose engines can also be used for pump irrigation. Next, as the timeliness peak at harvest becomes accentuated, threshers are introduced. The peak during transplanting does not lend itself readily to mechanization, however, so farmers have resorted to broadcasting pre-germinated seeds instead (substituting herbicides for labor). Finally, harvesters begin to come in. Parallel to these farm developments is the introduction of power milling. Within areas where rice is commercially grown, power milling is a feature antedating World War II. The main development in more recent times has been the expansion of small power mills in areas where most of the rice is locally consumed. A key factor that facilitates mechanization is obviously the level of wages (Pingali, Hossein and Gerpacio 1997).

Asian governments and international research institutions such as IRRI have had an ambivalent attitude toward mechanization. On the one hand, it is feared that mechanization would lead to considerable labor displacement, as well as an enhanced competitiveness and power of the larger landholders relative to the smallholders. On the other hand, if market prices reflect social scarcity values, mechanization undoubtedly increases economic efficiency (Pingali, Hossein, and Gerpacio 1997). Sometimes, for example, by breaking the bottlenecks in labor availability during the peak seasons, it helps small farmers as much as larger ones. Indeed, in some cases, breaking such peaks is a necessary step to increasing cropping intensity, which significantly increases labor demand. In accordance with this ambivalent attitude, policies toward mechanization have also been somewhat confused. While research by international institutions has been intentionally cautious, certainly in organizations such as IRRI, public policies in other areas, such as the setting of low interest rates for agricultural loans, inadvertently promote mechanization.

Most public research systems in Asia have modest programs in mechanization research. However, in most instances where new machinery has been successfully introduced, as in Thailand, it was done first through imports from the more advanced countries in Asia, then through the imitation of such design imports by local producers, followed by adaptation to fit local conditions. Therefore, probably more important than research for the growth of mechanization is an active machine-producing sector, often small-scale and rurally based, which can adapt and invent new machinery that is appropriate for the local environment. A dynamic agriculture sector with growing demand for labor-saving inputs is obviously the key to jump-starting this process.

Who Will Undertake and Who Will Pay for the Research?

In the above discussion, the research tasks were broken down into many categories and the roles of different actors were shown to have evolved over time in response to the changing science and environment. Table IV.3 summarizes the comparative advantages of the different actors. Where no distinction between local and central research institutions is made, the reader should assume that central institutes would take primary responsibility for basic research, while local institutes would be largely involved in adaptive research.

Pray (1991), in a survey of Asian research institutions, describes many different systems of research that exist, sometimes coexisting within the same country. Most of the research systems are publicly funded, but they vary according to how much autonomy the system has in the allocation of research funds. Further, during colonial times, for political and economic reasons, export and plantation crops received a disproportionately large share of total research funding relative to the value of their production. Investments in research on foodgrains became higher only during the 1970s.

Table IV.3 Comparative Advantage of Different Actors in Agricultural Research

Research Tasks	Products	Current Situation	Future Comparative Advantage
1. Genetic improvement	Self-pollinating crops	Public research system	Public research system
2. Genetic improvement	Cross-pollinating crops and small animals	Public research system plus private firms	Private firms
3. Genetic improvement	Local fruit trees and large animals	Farmers	Public system or private firms (with biotechnology)
4. Genetic Improvement	Introduced species	Public research system	Public system or private firms (with biotechnology)
5. Crop protection by chemicals	All crops	Private firms, public extension system, and farmers	Same, with greater regulation by public agencies
6. Crop protection by host-plant resistance	All crops	Same as 1–4 (depending on type of crop)	Same as 1–4
7. Crop protection by IPM	All crops	Public extension system, farmers, and NGOs	Same
8. Resource management (soils, cropping patterns)	All crops in unfavorable areas	Local public research, farmers, and NGOs	Local public research and extension system, farmers, and NGOs
9. Mechanization	All crops	Private firms	Private firms

Part of the reason for this was that during the colonial period, research on export crops was funded by the producers themselves. Since the benefits of research on export crops accrue mostly to the producers *as a group*, it is possible for the Government to ensure that they finance the activity, by levying a tax on the commodity. Of course, individual producers have no incentive to pay for research because of the public-goods nature of its outputs. But conveniently, export taxes are easy to collect. Where the entire production is exported, the incidence of the tax falls exactly on producers. If any amount is consumed domestically, then an export tax acts as a subsidy to domestic consumers. If the country is also a significant player in the world commodity market, part of the tax incidence will be shifted to foreign consumers. Thus, many countries finance research on export crops by means of such a tax. Table IV.4 shows the use of specific funding schemes for research in Asian countries.

An export tax earmarked for research can be turned into something more than just a financing mechanism. Since the industry—and by this is meant not just the growers of the commodity, but the processors and exporters as well—will be asked to pay for the research, its political support for such a mechanism will be more wholehearted if its members can contribute to determining the research priorities and strategies. Besides, their participation cannot but add value to the exercise. Therefore, a common feature in developed countries that use earmarked taxation is to set up a council consisting of representatives of the industry to direct the research agency involved.

Theoretically, as foodgrains are tradable, any cost reduction brought about by research should primarily benefit the producers. Most countries intervene heavily in the import and export of foodgrains, however (see Chapter VI), often making them effectively nontraded. Under such circumstances, the benefits of research accrue largely to consumers. As direct consumer taxes on foodgrains would be politically unacceptable as well as economically regressive, financing the research out of general tax revenues can be justified.

It has been conventionally assumed that agricultural research can and should be financed out of general tax revenue. But actual practice in Asia in the past has shown much more variety and, it must be said, more imagination in regard to how governments have tackled this problem. The following principles should guide the response to the question of who pays for the research:

- Beneficiaries of the research should pay for it;
- The number of collection points for taxes should be as small as possible;
- The allocation of resources should be distorted as little as possible; and

Table IV.4 Commodities with Producer-Funded Research

	Bangladesh	India	Indonesia	Malaysia	Pakistan	Philippines	Sri Lanka	Taipei,China	Thailand
Areca nut		1966							
Cashew							X		
Cocoa			X	X					
Coconut		1966			1981	X			
Coffee		X	X						
Cotton		1966			X				
Jute	1973	1966							
Lac		1966			1981				
Oilseeds		1966			1981				
Palm Oil			X	X					
Rubber		X	X	X			X		X
Silk	X	X							
Sugar	X	1969	X			X	X	X	X
Tea	X	X	X				X		
Timber						X			
Tobacco		1966	X		X	X		X	X
Agricultural Produce		X			1981				

Notes: An X indicates that an industry funding scheme is currently in operation (except for cocoa in Malaysia, for which there is legislation that has not been implemented). Cells with dates indicate that the schemes are no longer in operation; the figures indicate the year of cessation.

Source: Pardey, Rosenbloom, and Fan (1998).

- If the number of collection points or the distortion cannot be kept reasonably small, then general tax revenues should be used.

With these principles as background, the following observations may be made. First, the production, processing, and consumption of food crops and perishables like horticulture crops tend to be quite dispersed. Second, cash crops are mostly exported, or else tend to have only a few processing points through which most of the production flows. Third, economic distortions caused by any of the levies earmarked for research can be ignored, because the required tax rates are usually small, typically less than 5 percent of the value of the crops.

Given these observations, commodities may be subject to a two-way classification: first, they may be classified into food crops and cash crops, and second, they may be classified into export crops on the one hand and import-competing and nontraded crops on the other. Table IV.5 proposes effective research funding sources for the various types of commodities thus classified:

Table IV.5
Proposed Funding Sources Classified by Commodity Type

	Import-Competing and Nontraded	Export
Food Crops and Perishables	General Tax Revenues	Export Levy
Cash Crops	Processing Levy	Export Levy

In general, specific levies and other earmarked funding should be used wherever possible, as it is politically easier to devolve decisions on the direction of research to an industry group. (When the funding is obtained from general tax revenues, accountability would require central government supervision.) Clearly, devolution to the industry, which is aware of the problems it faces, will increase the efficiency and relevance of the research.

A final and very important caveat must be noted. The above breakdown implies that research will be organized along commodity lines, but as indicated earlier, this is appropriate only for genetic improvement research and perhaps for mechanization. Research to improve natural resource management requires a much broader, multidisciplinary type of organization, funding for which is probably best obtained from general tax revenues. Where local governments can raise adequate taxes, they may provide useful supplements to central government resources.

EXTENSION

Traditional Extension

Compared to the voluminous literature on the profitability of research, literature on the profitability of extension is meager. Hayami and Ruttan (1985) summarized a limited number of studies that examine returns to extension studies, of which four are from Asia (two in India and one each in the Philippines and Nepal). In the Nepal study, the returns were not significant, but the two Indian studies showed significant rates of return in the range of 15–20 percent. The study from the Philippines also showed a significant and "relatively high rate of return to extension contact" (Hayami and Ruttan 1985).

Evenson (1991) analyzed data on food crops in Africa, Asia, and Latin America, and concluded that extension services are generally productive, although their impacts are much more variable than the productivity of research (the rate of return on extension systems is, however, high—in excess of 80 percent). To explain the variability, Evenson hypothesized that many extension services are not well organized to disseminate the findings of research directly to farmers.

These findings are broadly representative of Asian countries, but are also rooted in a particular model of the extension system. Most of the studies examined data from the green revolution period, when the sequence of technological change was top-down. Scientists came up with better seeds, which were then produced at the seed stations (sometimes belonging to the extension departments) and distributed to farmers, usually with other inputs, i.e., fertilizers, pesticides, and credit. As already discussed, "packaged" extension was warranted during the green revolution, but that era is now drawing to a close. Farmers have absorbed most of the available technology; indeed, in some countries the extension goal should now be to decrease the use of pesticides (and even fertilizers in a few cases), as exemplified above in the case of Indonesia. Subsidized credit, if it was ever needed, is no longer necessary to induce farmers to adopt the technology. (Meyer and Nagarajan [1999] provide a detailed discussion of the adverse impacts of subsidized public credit on rural financial markets).

It would be wrong, however, to associate the top-down approach to extension exclusively with the period of the green revolution. This approach preceded the green revolution (Hayami and Ruttan 1985), and has remained alive and well since. Despite the intellectual influence of economists like Theodore Schultz (1964), most agricultural ministries remain steeped in the tradition of looking at farmers as backward and ignorant and assuming that technologies already exist on the shelf that can be distributed to farmers for their benefit. To counteract this image, extension agents have sometimes been referred to euphemistically as "change agents," but the behavior of the extension system has usually changed little as a result.

The evaluative studies cited above started from the perspective of the government extension system and asked how well it performs its mission. An alternative approach is to take the farmer's perspective and ask which of the various sources of information are most important in influencing the farmer's knowledge, practices, and performance. In a study of Northern Thai farmers, Mingsarn, Kanok, and Chaiwat (1989) found that they have a rich variety of information sources, including the local commodity trader, other farmers (particularly the more adventurous farmers who are always experimenting with new crops and new technologies), the mass media, and of course the extension agent. Information is conveyed in ways that are at times quite complex. The commodity trader in the Thai study was more than just a trader; his trading business was closely interlinked with credit provision. He was therefore instrumental in the farmers' choice of crops and even varieties, soybeans in this case. The trader took charge of distributing a new variety of soybeans, which was originally stolen from an experiment station.

The picture painted by this study shows farmers as active agents in their own behalf, rather than as passive recipients of information handed down to them. By and large, the private sources of information were reaching farmers somewhat faster than the public sources, particularly in regard to market demand and prices. It appears that in one respect both sources of information failed badly: that is in the use of agricultural chemicals. In the Thai study, farmers were experimenting mostly on their own, occasionally in consultation with extension officers. It is tragic that in many cases, despite their hunger for it, farmers appear unable to obtain information about pesticides from a disinterested source.

Private Contract Farming as a Means of Extension[7]

Technology transfer can also be achieved by the private sector through the system of contract farming. The Thai case depicting the soybean trader sitting astride the commodity, input, and credit markets is an example of informal contract farming. More formal systems of contract farming exist: a well-known example in the case of poultry farming was first pioneered in Thailand by the Charoen Pokphand company (CP), a firm that later became a large conglomerate, extending its reach to other Asian countries. Sompop and Suebskun (1992) studied this experience.

Farmers traditionally raised poultry on a very small scale, most often as a sideline. CP brought in a hybrid breed from the Arbor Acres Company in the US. They also set up large automated feedmills, which remain the core of their operations. The arrangements between the farmers and CP range from a guaranteed wage contract to a guaranteed price contract.

---

[7] Another form of contract farming, not covered in this chapter, is the contract farming associated with public resettlement schemes. See the papers on Malaysia and Indonesia in Glover and Lim (1992).

Under both, the sheds in which the chickens are raised are owned and operated by the farmers, although their construction may be financed with loans from the contracting company. With a guaranteed wage contract, the firm bears both the production and price risks. Clearly, CP would prefer to avoid the production risk, but a guaranteed wage contract is offered as an opening inducement to farmers to join the firm, from which they may "graduate" as they acquire more expertise. With a guaranteed price contract, prices of inputs and output are fixed in advance, with CP bearing all the price risk, while farmers take on the production risk in return for the expectation of higher net income.

The intensity and quality of CP's performance in providing extension services is remarkable. The firm's extension staff, all of whom have veterinary degrees, visit the farms every two or three days to provide technical information, check on the animals' health, and ensure that the farmers follow the firm's regulations. It might appear then that these farmers are little more than wage laborers for the company. But in fact, they are relatively well off, particularly when operating on guaranteed price contracts. Many of them eventually graduate to fully independent status as contractors, although links to CP are usually maintained through purchases of the company's feed. Sompop and Suebskun (1992) also note that when agricultural cooperatives tried to enter the business, they failed, because they were unable to maintain the timeliness and precision required in the operation.

Poultry raising in Thailand has grown within two decades to a major export industry. CP's success has turned the firm not only into a major player in Asia outside Thailand, but also into a major voice advising the Thai Government in agricultural development. The Government has observed the successful technological transfer implemented by CP and believes that it provides a model that can be replicated elsewhere. CP also appears to believe its own propaganda and has tried to initiate similar arrangements in rice and maize. By and large, however, these schemes, along with similar ones initiated by the Government, have failed, except for hybrid seed production. Maize and rice are traditional crops; all inputs used in their production can be procured in arm's-length markets and the technology is fairly standard. These characteristics combine to make farmers of these crops more self-reliant compared to the knowledge-intensive poultry industry.

Private contract farming is not a panacea. Indeed, it has only a very limited role to play. Where it has been most successful, there is usually a relatively rigid package of technical inputs and a high ratio of purchased inputs in total costs. In addition, because of economies of scale, companies like CP tend to work with the larger farms, and also to push small farmers into undertaking larger operations. The main lesson that it demonstrates, which has a wider applicability but which is not generally recognized, is that a very input-intensive agriculture such as poultry raising also requires very intensive input from a labor force that is suitably educated (in this case the extension staff of the contracting company and, over time, contract farmers who have acquired skills).

The Role of NGOs in Extension

The direct role of NGOs in research, particularly in resource-constrained areas, has already been touched on. Since there is a continuum between research and extension and also between work in the biophysical sciences and that in the social sciences, it is not surprising to see NGOs becoming quite active in these areas. The range of their activities is enormous: agroforestry in Nepal, tea production and vaccine research on cattle diseases in India, soil and water conservation techniques in the Philippines, to name just a few gleaned from the case studies cited in Farrington and Lewis (1993). The range of NGO inputs in the research-to-extension continuum is also quite wide, as is the range of their organizational frameworks.

In most countries, NGO activities are completely separate from those of the Government. Often the relationship between NGOs and the governments has been more adversarial than cooperative. Where the two actors have cooperated closely, as in Bangladesh, India, and the Philippines, the results have been extremely fruitful. In India and the Philippines, the Government has taken the initiative to establish close ties with NGOs. The Indian Council for Agricultural Research has set up farm science centers (known by their Hindi initials as KVKs) to serve as centers for demonstration and training in "scientific farming" (Farrington and Lewis 1993). While the structure is no different from a conventional extension system, the aim is to use this structure to open up NGOs' access to the public research system. Similarly, the Philippine Department of Agriculture has set up an NGO Outreach Desk (Farrington and Lewis 1993).

Devolution of Extension Services: a Wave of the Future?

As argued above, agricultural extension must evolve into a more localized, bidirectional system that answers technological questions posed by actual farming practices and that is more responsive to the farmers' needs. Two possible avenues have been explored, one involving contract farming with private corporations taking over many of the functions of the extension system, and the other involving closer cooperation with NGOs. The first has limited applicability outside specific sectors such as poultry, while the second holds more promise but has to be more widely applied before clear conclusions can be drawn.

A third avenue lies in the devolution or decentralization of extension services, a realm in which many countries are at present experimenting, although it cannot yet be said that a magic formula has been found. As was discussed in Chapter III, Indonesia's efforts to decentralize agricultural research and extension have been hampered by financial wrangling between the Center and the periphery, as well as inconsistent donor support. From the perspective of this chapter, the main problem with Indonesian extension remains its lack of responsiveness to the needs of the farmer, or even to the demands of local governments, because it still takes its orders from the central Government. Inadequate funding of devolved extension has also occurred in the Philippines, where the extension system is now managed largely at the local level. Although judgments vary on the effectiveness of the Philippines' reform, the experience so far suggests that there has been a trade-off between the effectiveness of technology transfer, which seems to have suffered, and the accountability of the system to its clients, which seems to have improved. Indonesia and the Philippines must both grapple with the overlap in central and local services that has arisen in the absence of a clear division of responsibilities. Despite these difficulties, the widespread popular support for decentralization leads to the prospect that these teething problems may eventually be overcome.

Another possible option is for the central Government to pay for (or subsidize) the extension services, but to make the agent accountable—ideally to farmers, but as a compromise, to a local unit of government. In this area, it is the former socialist countries that have gone furthest. Thus, in Viet Nam, the extension agent is hired, fired, and paid by the District People's Committee. Alternatively, a government could contract for, or subsidize, the activities of the NGOs, provided that the NGOs are demonstrably delivering a service that farmers in a given locality demand and use.

A final alternative is to have the provision of extension services completely privatized, as has been done in Chile. In such a situation, the extension agent becomes a professional or a consultant, selling his or her services to farmers for a fee, much as a doctor does. No Asian country has gone this far and it is not expected that many will follow the Chilean example.

CONCLUSIONS

There is clear evidence that investment in agricultural research is highly profitable for society, so much so that one must conclude that there is underinvestment in it. Since much of the knowledge it produces is essentially a public good, the Government has to be centrally involved. Yet, with the exception of the period surrounding the green revolution, political support for agricultural research has been tenuous, and much of the pressure for putting in greater resources has actually come from foreign donor institutions. Before more investment in agricultural research is once again advocated, the question of what is wrong with agricultural research as actually practiced must be addressed.

The World Bank, which has funded a good part of the agricultural research investments in developing countries, has conducted an evaluation of this support (World Bank 1996a) that is useful in summarizing many of the points raised in this chapter. It found that apart from a lack of sustained funding, there is, firstly, inadequate research planning and prioritization, which is attributed to inadequate economic and social analysis by the research agencies. Secondly, there is no clear attempt to make the research more relevant to the farmers' needs. Underlying these two shortcomings is a lack of clear articulation of what it is that scientists in the research institutions are doing and why they are doing it. It is small wonder then that research institutions are finding it difficult to convince their own governments to finance their activities, even though, quantitatively, research in most countries takes up only a small proportion of the total agricultural budget, easily overshadowed by irrigation or extension.

These shortcomings are those of traditional commodity-focused research, with a top-down approach to extension. This chapter has described how technology has been changing and making this approach increasingly irrelevant except in the area of biotechnology. In both irrigated and rainfed areas, resource-management issues are becoming the dominant themes, leading to a much more knowledge-intensive agriculture than before. Whether it is in the area of crop protection or nutrient management, the research that needs to be done will be much more location-specific and the interaction with farmers much closer than it has been. This implies a total restructuring of both the research and extension systems. The key elements of such restructuring will be a decentralization of research activities and a much greater responsiveness to the needs of the farmers, whose participation will have to be much more actively solicited.

Change has to be in the direction of increasing the system's accountability to the farmers who are meant to be its beneficiaries. One approach is to decentralize the authority over extension agents to local governments. This approach is being tried in the Philippines and Indonesia. Unfortunately, in both cases the transfer of functions is being bogged down by strictly bureaucratic issues of personnel policy and resource control, but it is hoped that the basic soundness of the concept will not be undermined by what surely is a transitional administrative problem.

Asian governments need to increase their investment in biotechnology research, at the very least to overcome some of the inherent biases in an area where multinational corporations are dominant. Aside from the benefits of the research itself, the public sector needs to have a trained cadre in this area for the tasks of regulation and risk assessment; such a cadre would be necessary, regardless of whether the research task is to be done by the multinational corporations or by the Government.

On the vexing issue of intellectual property protection, pressure is likely to be exerted on Asian developing countries by developed countries, particularly the US, to extend such protection to the fruits of agricultural research. The benefits to Asia are likely to be rather small. If, however, some sort of protection is deemed necessary to placate the developed countries, then plant variety protection should be the form provided, for two reasons. First, it gives the reward exactly for the value added by the scientists. Second, it is a form of damage control, for the alternative (patent protection) is liable to be much more costly.

V Irrigation Management Under Resource Scarcity

> Even thinking about water is difficult; keeping track of it can be impossible. It flows, drips, seeps and percolates, evaporates, condenses, freezes and transpires. It combines in compounds; it forms part of living things; it is in the soil, in plants and in the air. It is brought unpredictably in and out of environments by the weather, falling in rain or hail or snow, or settling as dew. Nothing is constant. Flows change. Movements from one place or medium to another are hard to put numbers on. Water for irrigation is difficult to handle: it has to be captured, stored, transported and delivered to a myriad of small fields and applied for crops to grow. Water is at once ubiquitous and elusive, a maddening compound which mocks measurement.
>
> – Robert Chambers (1988)

INTRODUCTION

The control of water has been central to Asian agricultural development. Irrigation accounts for 70–80 percent of Asian water diversion. Heavily subsidized irrigation investment claimed by far the largest share of public investment in agriculture during the green revolution. But water is also a basic human need, an essential input in most industrial processes, a resource for the provision of electricity, and an essential element in the conservation of desirable natural environments. The past decade has seen increasing concerns about the sustainability of the costly physical infrastructure for water's control and about the emerging scarcity of water due to growing demand for its competing uses. These concerns have led in turn to the rethinking and retooling of the roles of the State in irrigation development and management.

Two somewhat contrary thrusts have emerged. On the one hand, the sustainability issue, bolstered by recent constraints on State financing capacity, has prompted a variety of approaches to devolve or privatize the development, or at least the management, of individual schemes. On the other hand, at the "macro" level of the water basin, the increasing scarcity of water is likely to require enhanced State regulatory roles in allocating and ensuring the quality of water allocation and in resolving conflicts over its use. Irrigated agriculture will tend increasingly to be a residual claimant of water and so will come under increasing pressure to economize.

This chapter concentrates on irrigation because of the enormous scale of past investment and because of its importance to agricultural growth in most of Asia during the past two decades.[1] The first section deals with the sustainable development of the relatively small-scale irrigation systems located primarily in Asia's upper watersheds. The second section covers the more complicated development and management of large-scale irrigation in the lowlands, dealing also with groundwater irrigation in light of its dramatic recent growth. The third section deals with water management issues in the water basin as a whole, examining alternative responses to scarcity, the problems of water-use efficiency and watershed management, and irrigation's role in the context of broader water resources policy. The final section sums up by synthesizing the medium-term issues for public policy.

---

[1] Rural nonagricultural water use is covered in the discussion of rural social services in Chapter VII. Water surfeits requiring flood-control infrastructure are considered only in passing in the present discussion, as such large works have traditionally fallen entirely within the domain of the State in Asia and will largely remain so during the medium term.

THE LANDSCAPES OF IRRIGATION MANAGEMENT

The water basin provides the macro perspective on water-management issues. A water basin can be regarded as an integrated unit because of the interdependence of water supply at its different points. The basin also usually forms a more or less distinct unit because the transfer of water between basins is expensive. Among the different basins, and within a basin, there can exist different types of irrigation systems and institutions. Taking a broad historical perspective, Wade (1995) hypothesizes that these systems and institutions depend on four ecological factors: population density, irrigation requirements, temperature constraints on crop-growing periods, and topography. For the present purposes, topography is the primary factor determining the scale of the infrastructure, which in turn determines the relative scope for public- and private-sector involvement in irrigation development.

There are generally two broad types of landscape within each water basin. The first is the upper basin, where small-scale gravity irrigation systems are normally designed and built, usually, at least initially, by communities of farmers themselves. Included in this category are the lower reaches of the small water basins, where the communities sometimes operate irrigation as well. The second type of landscape encompasses the lower floodplains of large river systems,[2] where large-scale irrigation systems are invariably designed and built by the State. Groundwater constitutes an alternative source of water supply in the lower reaches of the water basins, so it will be considered along with the lower floodplains.

---

[2] Trung (1978) suggests a different taxonomy, distinguishing the river systems of mainland Asia from those of Asia's islands. Many water basins in island Asia are small and therefore correspond to the first type discussed in this chapter. However, most of the larger water basins in mainland Asia also contain the first type of landscape, e.g., in the upper reaches of the Mekong basin in the southern PRC, Lao PDR, Myanmar, and Thailand.

Upper- Basin and Small-Floodplain Irrigation

Evolution and Organizational Characteristics of Small-Scale Schemes

Traditional societies in Asia, both on the mainland and on islands, have practiced small-scale irrigation for millennia, well before their modernization. Because of this historical origin, communities played a major role in design and construction and, in some cases, still play a very active role in the operations and maintenance (O&M) of the infrastructure. In many cases, however, their role has been progressively reduced, with the State taking over many of the traditional functions of these communities. The first stage of the State's intrusion into these irrigation systems has been upgrading the facilities.

The food and energy crises of 1972–74 provided the impetus to intensify agriculture, while the green revolution provided a technology that was highly complementary to water. On a massive scale from the early 1970s onward, governments initiated irrigation projects to upgrade and often to take over existing community-based systems. This intrusion by the State was not necessarily unwelcome in the communities. In most cases, the traditional systems required labor-intensive O&M. By building more permanent structures for free (from the communities' point of view), the government reduced the farmers' burden. But bureaucracies all over the world have tended to be insensitive to local customs and institutions. Consequently, many stories of wasted investment can be recounted.

In many cases where projects were to overlay existing systems, the State or foreign donors' engineers would redesign the infrastructure, substantially ignoring the old system and canal networks. This top-down approach rested on the assumption that the design of the physical infrastructure was the most important determinant of a system's efficiency, to which the management and the social arrangements would naturally adapt (Siy 1987). Where the older system had already fixed the social arrangements, the intrusion of the new system led to conflict, and in many cases, to the disuse, modification, or even intentional destruction of the new structures. The inefficiency of insensitive State intrusion has been demonstrated in case after case, as compared to irrigation systems in which a participatory approach was adopted from the beginning (see, for example, the Philippine studies by Siy [1987] and De los Reyes and Jopillo [1987]).

Even in cases where irrigation was introduced into areas that previously had none, the performance of the systems has tended to be superior when the irrigation agencies has effectively solicited participation from farmers. This is because the social relations that underpin a cooperative venture like community-run irrigation were there prior to the coming of the "hardware" and should therefore shape the design of the hardware to a considerable extent.

Only a few East Asian countries present exceptions to the rule that the central Government has been the driving force in the development of "modern" irrigation systems. Japan's history of relatively large-scale, farmer-managed irrigation extends back to the 17th century (Nagata 1994). During their period as Japan's colonies, the Republic of Korea and Taipei,China in turn acquired an organizational framework in which irrigation associations were established to develop irrigation by collecting fees to finance investment and O&M. In the beginning, it was expected that these associations would cover the entire cost—both investment and O&M—but over the years the subsidy element progressively increased and with it the central Government's role in designing the systems. Nonetheless, the associations still share significantly in the cost (recently about 30 per cent of the total) through long-term, low-interest loans: it is likely that the associations scrutinize the designs more closely if they have to foot part of the bill rather than the Government financing the entire investment, as is standard practice in South and Southeast Asia (Small and Carruthers 1991).

Once the hardware is in place, the O&M of the irrigation scheme has to be considered. There are a large number of ethnographic studies that examine the operation of traditional community-based irrigation systems. Coward (1980) usefully compared a sample of community-based and bureaucratically run systems. Three themes can be discerned. First, community-based systems have rules of accountability: irrigation leaders serve small groups of water users; are selected by members; are subject to review and replacement; and receive some compensation from the members, mostly in kind. Second, even when the irrigation areas are small, they are often multitiered, with even smaller subunits in charge of mobilizing labor and organizing work groups. Third, irrigation command areas are seldom coterminous with village boundaries, complicating interaction between the community and the State, e.g., in the administration of O&M financing and agricultural support services (Coward 1980).

When these systems are examined in equilibrium, they appear attractive. But they are subject to various stresses. Besides State intrusion, two others may be identified. First, since O&M is labor-intensive, if real wages throughout the economy edge upward with development, difficulties may develop in procuring enough labor to maintain the systems (Coward and Levine 1987). Second, as population pressure builds, the system may be stressed internally by increasing water demand and externally by declining water availability because of developments upstream.

Ostrom and her colleagues have developed an analytical approach based on extensive empirical study of a large number of systems (Ostrom 1992, 1993, and 1994; and Ostrom, Gardner, and Walker 1996). These analyses indicate that the open access that characterizes water distribution within most developing Asian countries requires a form of social capital that can be (and indeed has been) developed by communities. The working of this social capital has its own logic, which explains the success and failure of different systems and also the success and failure of government interventions (see the discussion of social capital in Chapter II). In particular, an open-access system need not lead inevitably to overexploitation, as is commonly believed by economists. At the same time, a communally-managed system may not always survive, particularly in the face of misguided intervention by the State.

Ostrom (1996a) spells out the detailed considerations needed to predict whether a rule for allocating water will "work," i.e., whether it will be followed by the individual farmers. An example that she provides is one where the physical layout allows the benefits to be symmetrically distributed, versus the situation that favors one subgroup over another. The most obvious case of the latter is the perennial conflict between farmers near the source of the water (the head-enders) and those far removed (the tail-enders). She demonstrates that in situations where the costs of O&M are large relative to the benefits of the water, the tail-enders may end up with better bargaining power for a more equitable water share, as the head-enders will have to depend on their contribution towards the costs of maintenance. In fact, the higher the costs of O&M, the more bargaining advantage the tail-enders have. Thus, when the government or donor agency makes, say, a bamboo weir more permanent or lines the canals with cement, it may so unbalance the relationships within what had been a working traditional arrangement that the irrigation system ends by being less productive and less equitable than before.

Ostrom (1993) identified the following attributes of the governance structure of a communal irrigation system that has survived for a long time:

- It limits access to a clearly defined group and excludes others;
- It has clearly defined rules that set out who gets how much water, and when;
- Users' behavior is well monitored;
- Violation of rules is penalized;
- Each user is well informed about water availability and other users' withdrawals;
- There is a conflict-resolution mechanism; and
- The rules are situation-dependent and can vary according to external supply conditions.

Thus, one of the key lessons learned during the past 20 years is that a small-scale irrigation system is delicately poised. The capital invested in it is both physical and social.

Improvements to the physical capital may end up being harmful if they undermine the preexisting social capital, which is no less important than the hardware itself.

Devolution of Management in Small-Scale Schemes

Small-scale irrigation provides one of rural Asia's clearest examples of the opportunities for effective "coproduction" by public agencies and participating communities (see Chapter II and Ostrom [1996b]). Having learned the benefits of participation, donors and, increasingly, governments have looked during the past decade to opportunities for transferring some or all responsibility for irrigation management back to the farm communities. Equally, this trend reflects the recognition that fiscal constraints prevent continued subsidization of irrigation in an era of emerging resource scarcity and shifting sectoral priorities. The objectives of transfer or turnover programs generally include some combination of (i) reduced public cost; (ii) improved O&M; and (iii) improved efficiency, accountability, and equity in water use, leading to higher productivity. The extent of turnover has varied depending upon the nature of the scheme, the community, and other sociopolitical circumstances. It has ranged from the reallocation of some or all O&M responsibilities to, occasionally, the complete transfer of ownership back to the local communities. Because of their relatively small size and generally higher level of traditional community involvement, irrigation turnover has naturally gone furthest in the upper- and small-basin environment.

The experience with turnover in a sample of 29 schemes (18 in ADB member countries) was reviewed by the International Irrigation Management Institute[3] (IIMI 1987, cited in Vermillion 1997), focusing primarily on financial performance, the quality of O&M, and the impact on agricultural productivity. The evidence on achievement of

---
[3] IIMI's name has recently been changed to IWMI (International Water Management Institute).

these objectives of turnover, although positive overall, is somewhat mixed. Where State subsidies had been significant prior to transfer, they have generally been reduced, including public costs for irrigation personnel. Where the studies provided information on service fees, substantial increases in payment rates were reported. However, there is as yet no conclusive evidence about the long-run financial sustainability of the water-user associations (WUAs), in particular their capacity to raise capital for major repairs and periodic rehabilitation. Similarly, there is little evidence that O&M quality has improved or that turnover has led to higher agricultural productivity.

Overall, the IIMI review was complicated by the wide variety of methodological approaches taken in the different country studies. It underlined the need for more systematic collection of primary data using standardized indicators and longer time series. Because of the wide variety of methodologies, it has not yet been possible to assess the reasons for success or failure or, more importantly, the requisite community and public-sector inputs needed for success.

Thus, until a body of more systematic analyses is available, the prospects for turnover must be viewed with cautious optimism. It is unlikely that turnover programs will prove to be a panacea for the problems of cost recovery and sustainability in Asia's smaller irrigation schemes. Indeed, if the preexisting social capital was damaged during the course of upgrading the systems, it is dangerous to assume that this capital can readily be recreated when the systems are privatized. Turnover programs must therefore be carefully planned and implemented based upon a clear, realistic vision of the objectives, resources, and time frames involved. A cautious, step-by-step approach is required, as is well documented in FAO's recently released guidelines on irrigation management transfer (FAO, 1998). A fundamental, yet difficult, requirement is that the public agencies involved in turnover need to adopt a new orientation and skills mix, focusing much less on engineering and construction and much more on community mobilization and support.

Large Floodplains

Surface Irrigation

While relatively small-scale communal irrigation has been practiced in upper valleys and small river systems for centuries, the scale of water management in the lower floodplains requires a degree of engineering (both physical and social) that only the central Government can provide. It is not surprising, therefore, that the irrigation systems in the lower floodplains in Asia have been constructed by central governments. Because they built and control the structures, they have also played the dominant role in their management.

Generalization across systems here is even more difficult than in the case of small-scale upstream systems, because in addition to the topographical specificity, it is necessary to contend with political and administrative specificity as well. Nonetheless, one broad conclusion is that the benefits actually derived from the larger systems have often fallen short of what was expected when the feasibility studies were conducted (Chambers 1988; Ostrom 1992).

Of the many reasons why the systems fail to meet expectations (see the discussion on donor evaluations below, characterizing both large- and small-scale irrigation) is that project planners have tended to be (or have been pressured to be) overoptimistic and go for a command area much larger than that for which water is available. The result has been that the amount of water must be strictly rationed. It has proven very difficult to ensure that the rationing at least minimizes the farmers' uncertainty about the amount of water that will be made available to them. Given the vast resources invested, this is tragic, if one considers that the whole point of irrigation is to reduce the uncertainty inherent in rainfed agriculture (Reidinger 1980).

Compounding the design failure is the management failure. Large-scale systems inherently require a governing entity that encompasses the entire water basin, which has often led to an inefficient, hierarchically organized, bureaucratic style of management. One excellent example is provided by Wade (1982), in an unusually detailed study of the operations of water distribution in a large irrigation system of Andhra Pradesh, India. He shows quite clearly that the system did not display the rationality that social scientists since Max Weber have often associated with bureaucracies (see Chapter II). To operate the system efficiently, information flows had to be fast and smooth in both directions. This was clearly not the case in the system investigated by Wade. The structure of incentives and penalties exerted by the organization was such as to ensure a wholesale obfuscation of the information at various levels. Field staff had little incentive to report fully or truthfully to their higher-ups about field conditions. No one, not least the field staff, obtained much reward for reporting the requirements of the farmers whom they were supposed to serve.

With such a structure as the starting point, the challenge is to devise mechanisms whereby an irrigation authority and its personnel are responsive and accountable to the water users, whether agricultural or nonagricultural. It does not matter whether the controlling authority is the central government, as in many medium-sized countries; the state government, as in India; or the water-basin authority, as in the PRC.

Maintaining the Performance of Large-Scale Irrigation Systems

The scale and technical complexity of the large floodplain systems make them unlikely candidates for turnover during the medium term in most of Asia. Management transfer will probably be limited, at most, to subsections of the infrastructure that define logical local management units (e.g., secondary canals). The O&M of major weirs and dams is normally beyond the capacity of WUAs in their present state of development and has therefore been retained by the public sector. At the same time, it is both fair and fiscally expedient to hope that farmer-beneficiaries and other water users will contribute at least some of the costs of the infrastructure. User fees for irrigation and drainage have been introduced in a number of countries, with varying but often disappointing rates of success.

The challenge is to establish effective and transparent mechanisms that firmly link user fees to the cost and quality of the services provided. An essential prerequisite is that the revenues from the fees must be kept as close as possible to their local source in order to ensure that the money is actually used for O&M. In many public administrations, unfortunately, the user fees disappear into the bureaucracy. The amounts the farmers pay in and the O&M provided seldom bear a visible relationship to each other. In Thailand, for example, the water fees collected by the Royal Irrigation Department are transferred to the central treasury, with the result that farmers have little incentive to pay and the department has little incentive to collect. In Indonesia, the irrigation service fee has, after ten years, largely collapsed in a downward spiral of poor O&M, farmer skepticism leading to low payment rates, and still poorer O&M that reinforces the disincentive to pay.

Groundwater Irrigation

The growth of groundwater irrigation has been the second most dramatic episode in Asian agriculture of the last two decades, after the spread of green-revolution technology. Although sparked in many cases by government intervention, the development of groundwater has been a harbinger of the growth of private investment relative to the public capital that has hitherto reigned supreme in the agriculture sector. Groundwater development has been most extensive in Bangladesh, Pakistan, India, and Indonesia. In some cases, it involved conjunctive use of ground and surface water, but, more typically, groundwater is used as a substitute for surface water. In general, it can be concluded that groundwater development has been most successful where it has been driven primarily by the local initiatives of farmers, as can be best documented by the cases of Bangladesh and Indonesia.

Groundwater technology was introduced in Bangladesh in the 1960s by a government agency, later called the Bangladesh Agricultural Development Corporation (BADC). BADC ran a heavily subsidized deep-tubewell program, installing and renting wells to cooperatives, which contributed nominally to the costs of O&M. BADC also rented low-lift pumps and shallow tubewells to farmers, who paid a larger share of the O&M costs themselves. In the late 1970s, the government began to ease BADC out of its role as sole provider of equipment to farmers. Subsidies on shallow tubewells were reduced; instead, credit for purchase and installation was provided. Import duties were reduced and the private sector was, for the first time, allowed to import the equipment. Consequently, the number of shallow tubewells shot up from 22,000 in 1980 to 120,000 in 1984.

A drought in 1983 led to an unusually large depletion of groundwater, particularly in the northern districts (Gill 1983, cited in Mandal, Sattar, and Parker 1995). The concerned government agencies reacted strongly, in part to counter the diminution of their authority that was inherent in private groundwater development. It banned new shallow tubewells in the northern districts and within the command areas of publicly operated surface-irrigation schemes, restricted the imports of small diesel engines and other shallow tubewell equipment, and strengthened the enforcement of tubewell spacing regulations. Most of these measures proved unnecessary because the groundwater level returned to normal in 1984, before any of the measures took effect. Nevertheless, the Government did not begin to reverse its policies until 1987. During 1984–1987, the growth of private tubewells was effectively strangled, but it accelerated rapidly thereafter, with shallow tubewell installations growing to 350,000 by 1993. At present, private operators own all the shallow tubewells and most of the deep tubewells, although the popularity of the latter has declined because of their technical complexity and lack of profitability in comparison to shallow tubewells. Informal markets for irrigation water have emerged, with pumped water being sold either for cash or in exchange for a share of the crop.

The growth in tubewells made a major contribution to the rapid expansion of the *boro* (dry season) rice crop. As will be further discussed in Chapter VI, market-oriented reforms in the distribution of fertilizer and other inputs and gradual liberalization of output markets also contributed to dynamism in Bangladesh's foodgrain sector (Ahmed 1995; ADB 1996a). With greater control of water during dry-season cultivation, the boro crop has made extensive use of high-yielding varieties and fertilizer. Boro yields are about double what is achieved during the wet season, and production increased from 2.6 million tons in 1981 to 6.5 million tons in 1995. As a result, there was optimism that foodgrain self-sufficiency was within reach in Bangladesh. Unfortunately, progress toward this goal has been erratic since then because of the combined results of periodic flooding, political unrest, ill-advised government interventions in the fertilizer market, and farmer response to adverse changes in their terms of trade. Bangladesh nonetheless presents one of Asia's clearest examples of what can be achieved if prices are "right" and markets are allowed to work.

In Indonesia, shallow groundwater that can be extracted by simple tubewell technology is much scarcer than in Bangladesh: the estimated potential area of groundwater development constitutes less than 4 percent of Indonesia's present surface-irrigation area. Most of the area under pump irrigation has been developed privately, usually using shallow groundwater. In contrast, public and donor-assisted efforts to exploit groundwater in Indonesia have focused on deep-tubewell technology, often in the country's drier regions where surface irrigation is difficult to develop.

From the early 1970s to the late 1990s, most of the documented groundwater development was under the responsibility of the central Directorate General of Water Resources Development. The approach involved central responsibility for the groundwater resource investigations, tubewell siting, installation, and initial O&M, including repair and most fuel costs. Considerable effort also went into establishing and nurturing WUAs, with the goals of eventually turning the O&M over to them under the devolved guidance of the provincial irrigation service and using the WUAs as focal points for agricultural extension. As this transfer occurred, the large central subsidies, initially almost 100 percent of the cost, were to be withdrawn.

In a detailed evaluation of this program, Johnson and Reiss (1993) concluded that with the withdrawal of subsidies, the deep wells are unlikely to remain financially viable unless farmers switch from food crops to higher-value commercial crops such as vegetables and tobacco. Where this substitution has occurred spontaneously, the deep wells have been only marginally attractive investments, even though the WUAs have often proved cohesive and backstopping has been provided by central and local irrigation agencies after management transfer. More often, however, the sophistication of the technology, combined with the scarcity of agricultural extension and credit services, has led to the prognosis that the tubewells would be sustainable only with the continuation of public technical and financial support.

The Bangladesh and Indonesia cases clearly show that farmers, when left to themselves and where the water table permits, have a strong preference for relatively cheap, simple, and flexible technologies. Even in drought-prone areas, deep tubewells have usually proven to be too technically sophisticated and financially unsustainable in the absence of significant subsidies. A basically similar conclusion emerges in India; see the studies on deep tubewells in Gujarat and Uttar Pradesh in FAO (1995). Deep tubewells require a much higher level of maintenance expertise, often exceeding local skills. Effective cooperation among a much larger group of farmers is needed than for shallow tubewell technology. Moreover, the deep tubewells are permanent structures, whereas shallow tubewell engines can be readily moved from place to place, thus allowing more efficient use of capacity. The lesson is that the State should promote, or at least not restrict, a range of environmentally sound technology choices by farmers.

Unregulated groundwater extraction can rapidly lower the water table and, in coastal areas, contribute to salt water intrusion. Both agricultural and nonagricultural users will suffer, particularly rural households that often draw a large share of their water needs from the ground. The more intensive use of agrochemicals associated with groundwater development and natural geologic characteristics can also adversely influence water quality. For example, natural arsenic content exceeds the concentration permissible for drinking water in a significant share of the tubewells in Bangladesh. For these reasons, private groundwater development must be complemented by a suitable State role in water table and water quality monitoring, backed up, as required, by regulatory mechanisms. Possible approaches to the latter include well and pump licensing, pricing, and legal and institutional interventions (Rosegrant 1997). Such approaches, however, are difficult to apply in the case of shallow tubewells, which are private, widely scattered, mobile, and therefore inherently difficult to monitor.

BASIN-WIDE CONSIDERATIONS

It is well known that water is becoming increasingly scarce in Asia. Water scarcity is hardly new, but it has traditionally been primarily a seasonal phenomenon. ADB's developing member countries are mostly in the monsoon zone, with a long dry season during which there is little rainfall. Water shortages during the dry season can be severe, while at the same time the risk of flooding during the wet season is significant. The desire to balance water supply across the wet and dry seasons has prompted massive investments in water storage and flood control. Increasingly, though, and apart from the seasonal dimension, spatial and sectoral dimensions of scarcity have come to the fore. As irrigation takes up much the largest share of the water in most Asian countries, and as agriculture's share in national income declines, it is not surprising that the agriculture sector is under increasing pressure to release water to meet expanding industrial and household demand.

The international community has increasingly drawn the attention of policymakers to the need for the holistic and participatory integration of multisectoral water policy, development, and management. The World Bank, ADB, and other donors have recently adopted, or are in the process of preparing, comprehensive water-resources policies. To its credit, ADB (1996b) has made the recent development of its own water-resources policy as participatory as possible, involving officials of all member countries in a truly consultative process. There will nevertheless be substantial obstacles to the hands-on application of holistic principles in developing-country environments. Carter (1998) includes the following:

- The perception that water rights are "God-given," i.e., water is not seen as an economic good;
- The short planning horizons and political uncertainty;
- The widely accepted authoritarianism and paternalism of Government; and
- The lack of community empowerment, both among rural communities generally and among specific stakeholders, such as women.

To the above should be added the natural resistance of bureaucracies to relinquishing power, either through decentralization or through the reallocation of power to higher policy-making bodies. To overcome these cultural and institutional obstacles, the international community—and the donors in particular—will need to be both patient and persistent in using their leverage to encourage the effective adoption of broad agendas and policies for water resources.

Asia's success in finding ways to manage water scarcity will be a key determinant of agricultural and rural growth in the future. Chapter IV showed that part of the solution should come at the farm level through research and technology development for resource-constrained agriculture. The main concern of the present chapter is the management of water before it reaches the farm. The annual supply of fresh water is largely fixed. Groundwater is part of that supply and can be mined temporarily, but ultimately its use cannot exceed the recharge. Desalinization of seawater is not considered an economically viable option. That said, within a given water basin, there are three interrelated ways by which water scarcity can be addressed: (i) more infrastructure can be developed to store and control the water supply across and within seasons, (ii) the fixed seasonal supply can be managed through administered rationing, or (iii) demand can be managed through pricing mechanisms.

Supply Augmentation

The traditional approach in Asia, much accelerated by the food and energy crises of 1972–74, has been to build new water-storage capacity, together with downstream works to expand the irrigated area. Since the mid-1980s, however, the rate of investment has slackened considerably for a variety of reasons. With regard to irrigation, decisions to invest are made by national governments, often in collaboration with donors, both presumably seeking to maximize social welfare. By methodological convention, the social profitability of irrigation is determined largely by the world prices of the crops produced. Kikuchi and Hayami (1978) showed that irrigation investments have varied in tandem with world rice prices. The huge investments of the 1970s and 1980s doubtless contributed to the secular decline in real world cereal prices that has, with the principal exception of the early 1970s, continued unabated since the 1950s (see Figure VI.1 in the following chapter). With a declining rice price as the numerator in the profitability equation, the denominator—irrigation construction costs—has increased rapidly over time as less and less favorable sites have been developed. Rosegrant (1997) presents figures showing that, on a per-hectare basis, the real capital costs of new irrigation increased by more than 150 percent from 1966 to 1988 in the major countries of South and Southeast Asia.

Social and environmental considerations have also increasingly influenced investment decisions. Most prominently, large storage dams usually face strenuous objections from environmentalists, who have made common cause with involuntarily resettled people (see Vajpeyi and Zhang [1998] for a good summary of the issues involved). In many countries, displaced people have good reason to be opposed (sometimes violently) to the prospect of having to leave their homes, particularly when practices in the matter of compensation have been unsatisfactory.

Thus, with declining returns to investment, rapidly growing nonagricultural competition for water, and much greater weight given to social and environmental factors, the justification for major investment in water storage and irrigation grows steadily weaker. With few cheap water resources left to be exploited, the basic water resources infrastructure, both for irrigation and nonagricultural uses, is largely complete in the "closing" river basins of densely settled Asia.[4] Megaprojects such as the PRC's Three Gorges Dam and Indonesia's Kedung Ombo Dam will certainly be exceptions rather than the rule in the future. The main issues now center, first, on improving and sustaining the performance of existing infrastructure and, second, on the more efficient allocation and use of the available water supply.

Administered Rationing of Supply Among Water Users

The "command and control" system of bureaucratically determined water allocation for irrigation is still overwhelmingly followed to this day, with various ad hoc allocative arrangements made for nonagricultural uses. The flow of water is controlled by officials who may or may not be responsive to the needs of farmers. By rotating the water or by other means, they will distribute whatever water is available among the users, a process that may or may not be perceived as fair by anyone.

Water authorities are generally able to regulate the supply only in irrigated areas. In most countries, there is no regulation

---

[4] Keller, Keller, and Seckler (1996) define a "closed" water system as one in which no usable water leaves the system, e.g., by flowing to the sea. Interdependence among users only becomes a meaningful issue as water systems close and water demand comes to exceed supply.

of extraction outside the irrigation command area. Indeed, some countries protect the rights of citizens (including industrial users) to the water, which thereby becomes an open access resource. Consequently, agricultural uses become a residual, not only by a conscious decision of policymakers, but also because of the poverty of regulatory instruments.

A common complaint has been that, in cases where a storage dam also generates electricity, irrigation is slighted in favor of electricity (Reidinger 1980). Since water that turns a turbine could then, in principle, be used to irrigate crops, such criticism inevitably involves the dimension of seasonality. If the authority controlling a dam were to ignore irrigation and solely maximize the production of electricity, then it would be better to fill the dam up to the highest level and keep it filled. If this were done, the production of electricity per cubic meter of water released would be maximized. But keeping the dam always full would mean that the outflow of water at any moment would, together with evaporation during storage, be equal to the inflow. Such a strategy would mean that, from the point of view of the farmers downstream, it makes no difference whether there is a dam. Hence, to the extent that the release of water is manipulated to provide for irrigation, the level of water behind the dam will fluctuate to levels below its maximum. In fact, in areas where there is a pronounced dry season, the level of water behind the dam is commonly reduced to its minimum just before the onset of the rains. Electricity generation is sacrificed, because at such a low level the amount of power generated per cubic meter of water released is considerably reduced.

There is greater flexibility to release water for irrigation, however, if hydroelectricity from the dam is but a small proportion of the total electricity demand of the country concerned. If this proportion is large, then irrigation requirements tend to give way to the imperatives of electricity generation. Lest this seem unfair, it should be noted that rural development is also fostered by a steady supply of electricity. Hence, any conclusion about the relative merits of the agriculture-hydropower trade-off should be based on an understanding of the relative productivity of water in the two uses in differing seasons of the year.

Demand Management Through Pricing Mechanisms

Demand management focuses on creating the incentives for water to be allocated efficiently among and by competing users and sectors. As mentioned already, water in most Asian countries has traditionally been viewed as a natural "gift of God." Since it is either free or priced well below its opportunity cost, it is not surprising that demand often exceeds the available supply, particularly during the dry season. Where water is costless, it is equally unsurprising that farmers tend to waste a lot of it. Any move to alter demand through pricing mechanisms cannot but have a profound impact on the relative roles of the State irrigation authority (however organized), the private sector, and the individual communities.

Outside of the wholesale privatization of irrigation, which is not considered a realistic option for Asia's large-scale systems during the medium term, there are two generic and interrelated market-based approaches for forcing demand to match supply. The first is to levy a charge for water use. Discussion about user fees usually focuses on the recovery of investment and O&M costs, but consideration may also extend to broader economic, environmental, and social opportunity costs. From both a theoretical and practical standpoint, calculating these costs for what is usually a nontraded good presents significant challenges (Young, 1996).

One technical problem is that for the user fee to be fair, the rate should be based on the volume of water consumed. Water "consumption" is distinct from water "diversion." When water enters farmers' fields, they are said to have "consumed" it, but a great deal of that water will then either flow into neighboring farmers' fields or drain into the soil and become part of the groundwater. The only part of the water that is "consumed" and thereby no longer available to other users is that which either evaporates or is used by the crop for evapotranspiration.[5]

---

[5] In cultivating paddy, farmers have a great deal of standing water in the field, but do not consume it. Rice paddies are kept continuously flooded during the initial growth period not simply because water is a free good, but also because flooding retards weed growth and is necessary for the field-to-field water flows required by the irrigation systems. In contrast, water diversions are much closer to actual consumption under sprinkler or drip irrigation.

Obtaining this measure is almost impossible, but it would be necessary for a fair, efficient allocation to be achieved.

But if some error is tolerable, charging a fee by the volume diverted can serve in lieu of a precise fee for the volume consumed. The more difficult questions with a user fee are legal and administrative. For the government or any authority to charge a user fee, it must first establish a claim to what were traditionally viewed as God-given water rights. This will entail largely doing away with the open-access regime. Furthermore, for the fee to achieve its purpose, it must be levied both inside and outside the irrigated areas. From a practical standpoint, the collection of fees—indeed, even just identifying all the users—is arduous, but there is scope for charging the fees at the level of the community or WUA. All in all, the administrative and political costs of using water fees as an allocative device will be high in most countries.[6] But the results of continuing inaction will be equally unacceptable.

The second possibility is to create a market for tradable rights to water. For this to happen, clear rights to the water must be established. For surface water systems, there are two basic principles as to what kinds of rights can exist.[7] In an advanced (and dry) economy such as the United States, there are complex legal doctrines pertaining to water rights (see Carlson, Zilberman, and Miranowski [1993] for a listing and brief description). In

---

[6] Political objectives—the desire for rural prosperity and stability—have doubtless tended to perpetuate subsidies for irrigation and water throughout Asia. Chapter VI examines these objectives in the context of Thailand, Malaysia, and Indonesia.

[7] The first, called the riparian doctrine, allows users to take water from a river system only for use on land adjacent to the river and only insofar as the water returned to the river is similar in quantity and quality, and so does not reduce downstream use. The second, called the appropriation doctrine, allows a specified quantity of water to be diverted, stored, and used on lands that may or may not be adjacent to the river. The riparian system has been used largely in regions where water supply exceeds demand, while the appropriation system has been adopted more frequently in water-deficit regions. Variants on the appropriation doctrine make specific provision for allocating water during periods of scarcity, i.e., with rights adjusted on either the basis of the seniority of the water claim ("prior appropriation") or in proportion to the available supply ("proportional appropriation") (Simpson and Ringskog 1997).

Asia, detailed legal frameworks for water rights are often nonexistent, but the impetus for legislative change can only grow with the increasing scarcity of water.

Faith in market mechanisms for resource allocation has been "politically correct"—often approaching dogma—for more than a decade. Although attractive in principle, the complexity of establishing markets for tradable water rights should not be underestimated. Simpson and Ringskog (1997) set out the prerequisites for this to occur:

- The demand for water must exceed supply;
- Water rights must be clearly defined in terms of ownership, quantity, measurability, and reliability;
- There must be adequate infrastructure so that supplies derived from use rights can be transferred between locations when needed;
- Property rights to water must have an enforceable legal basis, which requires a system of allocation, property titling, and regulation that is respected by the market;
- The water rights system must be able to resolve conflicts in a manner that is perceived as impartial, predictable, and timely, including situations where water rights are overtaken by eminent domain;
- The system must apportion supply equitably during periods of shortage and excess;
- The system must reflect the cultural and social values of water use; and
- The system must be financially sustainable.

The above list appears daunting. At the very least, it should indicate that the setting up of tradable water rights at the level of the individual farm or water user will be physically and administratively impossible in most of Asia. It may be feasible, however, to split up the jurisdictions of the water authorities into subbasin entities whose officers are accountable to the people living in them. These entities would then be endowed with water rights in conformity with their traditional demands on the water resources and it would be these entities that would engage in trade. Depending upon sociopolitical circumstances, the entities could be public (e.g., elected officials), community-based (associations of WUAs), or even private (water companies working under contract), as long as their accountability is assured.

Whether supply and demand are managed through rationing or price mechanisms, the technical scope for improving water efficiency is considerable in Asian agriculture; the incentives for doing so will be enhanced if there are effective pricing mechanisms. The field efficiency of water use—i.e., the amount consumed in evapotranspiration as a proportion of the amount diverted—probably averages just 50 percent in most of Asia, and is often as low as 25 percent. The establishment of an effective pricing mechanism would be a powerful force to encourage conservation. At least for high-valued crops (but probably never for rice, given its high water requirements), sophisticated techniques such as sprinkler, drip, and surge irrigation will become economically rational if the scarcity value of water is sufficiently high. The diffusion of these techniques would be a very appropriate role for the private sector. In addition, opportunities for conservation also exist at the irrigation-system level through real-time management based upon improved monitoring and information flows about weather, water levels, and field conditions (Rosegrant 1997).

Upper Watershed Management and Common Property Rights

In one way or another, water is at the heart of the major environmental problems associated with Asian agriculture. Deforestation and the cultivation of annual crops on sloping land may reduce natural water-holding capacity and, by accelerating erosion and sedimentation, increase the seasonal variability of downstream water flows.[8] A central problem is that forested upland areas, even if technically governed by the State, are usually *de facto* common property. They are subject to the dispersed decision making of resource-scarce families, who may respond to incentives that provide them with opportunities to improve their welfare but who will not be swayed by unenforceable resource management laws and administrative instructions.

Technical solutions are available to reduce the external costs of forest encroachment and soil erosion (e.g., bench terracing, alley cropping, and agroforestry), but socially acceptable solutions have proven far more elusive. The principles of property rights to land (Chapter II) and greater community empowerment for the management of common resources are now seen as prerequisites for watershed conservation. Finding workable means of implementing these principles has been, and will continue to be, a challenge for governments and donor agencies.

Donor Roles: Doing More by Doing Less?

The above discussion alluded to donor roles in Asian irrigation development. Indeed, donor financing of irrigation development has been far more extensive and instrumental than for the other rural goods and services considered in this volume. Irrigation and irrigation-related projects have accounted, cumulatively, for about 10 percent of the *total* lending of ADB and the World Bank (the total would be considerably larger if projects for flood control, hydropower generation, and urban and rural water supply were included).

---

[8] Calder (1998) examines the conventional wisdom regarding the relationships between forest cover, soil erosion, water runoff, and dry-season flows. He concludes that the many intervening variables, most importantly the use of land after it has been deforested, preclude the widely held generalization that deforestation inevitably reduces water holding capacity.

Irrigation lending peaked in the late 1970s for the World Bank and in the early 1980s for ADB; it remains an important part of their portfolios. Irrigation has also been prominent in many bilateral assistance programs, most notably those of Japan and, historically, the US. In many countries of Asia, it is fair to state that donor financing has been the engine of growth in public-sector irrigation development and policy since the 1970s. It is, therefore, relevant to ask what the donor experiences have been, what lessons have been learned, and what implications can be drawn for the coming 10–15 years.

Both ADB and the World Bank have conducted detailed post-evaluation studies of the performance of their irrigation projects (see the summaries in ADB [1995b] and World Bank [1994]. Both banks acknowledge that a significant number of their projects have not performed as expected. In the case of ADB, *ex post* economic rates of return on all irrigation projects averaged 10 percent, as compared to appraisal estimates averaging 19 percent. Although the evaluation methods differ, the World Bank may have fared somewhat better, averaging an *ex post* 15 percent as compared to 22 percent at appraisal. Nonetheless, common lessons have been learned and applied.

Environmental and social concerns, along with beneficiary participation, are now explicitly incorporated at the outset of project planning. A more integrated river basin perspective is being taken in irrigation development, focusing on both the water resources and the upper watershed management issues. Designs require more reliable resource assessments of geography, soils, and hydrology. Project formulation and design give greater attention to the institutional, social, and cultural environment and to the sources of poverty and unsustainable resource use, rather than focusing on technical and engineering aspects. Sustainable institutional, technical, and financing mechanisms still need to be established for O&M. Greater modesty is required in estimating project economic rates of return, which have proven particularly sensitive to rice prices and to the assumed levels of cropping intensity, input use, and productivity. Finally, a longer-run perspective on the capacity building of executing agencies and community organizations is needed. The application of these lessons is, hopefully, leading to better-performing and more sustainable irrigation projects.

One lesson remains—the incentives of lending momentum—for which the Asian economic downturn may give useful pause. Asia has built many expensive irrigation schemes, only to discover that they are unsustainable. Even so, there has often been continuing replenishment by donors of funding to rehabilitate and "improve" poorly performing schemes. This has reinforced the innate motivation of public irrigation agencies to build rather than to sustain physical capital and to ignore the equally important "software" sides of irrigation. With government capacity to provide counterpart funding for irrigation projects now severely strained in much of Asia, the time is ripe for the developing countries to look to their own resources in order to refocus the agencies on sustainable O&M of the existing systems and, usually at a higher level of government, on the integration of water-resources planning, development, and management.

SUMMING UP

Because of its past investments in the structures of water control and because the legal and institutional mechanisms for allocating water are still undeveloped, the State remains the dominant force in the rural water resources arena (Table V.1). The principal exception has been the growth of groundwater. If any change is to be detected at the moment, it is in the reorganization of State institutions in charge of water basin management, with a broader role now envisaged than that of mere irrigation management. There is, in general, a movement toward having each water basin under the jurisdiction of its own management authority. The challenge will be to work out a system whereby this authority can be made accountable to the basin's water users.

The huge investments in irrigation should be made to pay by better management of the systems. The general trend over the last two decades has been toward various experiments in devolution and user cost recovery. Ultimately some of these experiments will become models for other countries to follow.

Overarching the performance of irrigation is the emerging water shortage, a consequence of the past growth in cropping intensity as well as growing industrial and household use. In monsoon Asia, the main problem will come during the dry season and periodic droughts. This will require a much more careful look at the management of the water resources within entire water basins in many parts of Asia. The role of the central government in allocating water resources will have to be modified to one where it is the referee in a system of trades, not among individual water users, but among large groups of users organized in the various subunits of the larger basins.

Table V.1 Comparative Advantage of Different Actors in Irrigation

Product	Current Situation	Future Comparative Advantage	Developmental Needs
Small-scale irrigation development and rehabilitation	Coproduction by public irrigation agencies and the communities	Increasing design and financing role by the communities, with support from the State	Reorientation of the engineering and project focus of public irrigation agencies
Large-scale irrigation development and rehabilitation	Public agencies	State role will continue. In large *and* small systems, the private sector will dominate the diffusion of water-conserving, farm-level technology if price incentives warrant.	Full application of the "lessons learned," together with demand management policies
Groundwater development	Private sector, with technology advice provided by public agencies	Same, but growing role for private sector in technology diffusion	Legal and institutional frameworks for environmental regulation must be strengthened.
O&M of small systems	Coproduction (farmers in charge of small canals, public agencies responsible for dams, weirs, and headworks)	Communities, with advice by public agencies	Reorientation of public irrigation agencies. WUAs need to be "empowered."
O&M of large systems	Coproduction	Same, with greater financing share by farmers and some management transfer of secondary canals	Transparency and local accountability in the use of water fees, Empowered WUAs
Environmental monitoring	Public agencies	Will remain publicly financed, possibly with monitoring services provided by the private sector or community-based organizations	Laws and institutions for environmental regulation must be strengthened.
Basin-level water allocation	Public agencies, through "command and control"	Public agencies, as mediators of trade across sectors	Laws that define and institutions that enforce water rights, integration of water policies and sectoral water agencies, mobilization of private entities or community-based organizations to engage in trade.

VI THE POLITICAL ECONOMY OF FOODGRAIN AND FERTILIZER DISTRIBUTION

> What is the "right" price for an agricultural commodity? Economists have an easy answer to the question, but only in a world of perfect information, with competitive markets, without other government interventions into the economy, and without political concerns for the impact on income distribution.
>
> – C. Peter Timmer (1986)

INTRODUCTION: WHY ARE FOODGRAINS SPECIAL?

If looked at casually, it might appear that foodgrains possess all of the characteristics required for private markets to function competitively: cereals such as rice and wheat are divisible, relatively homogeneous commodities, free of externalities, and usually have many sellers and buyers who have generally equal access to the market and market information. Given this, why should governments intervene in the private markets that would be expected to produce an economically efficient outcome? To answer this, one must consider the other characteristics of food. That people should have the ability to acquire and consume food of at least the minimum level needed for their sustenance and that of their children is considered to be a basic need. Thus, food is a merit good, one whose effective demand society often deems too important to be limited by purchasing power. Unfortunately, many households in Asia to this day remain too poor to meet their basic food needs, because their effective demand falls short of what is desirable for them to consume. Moreover, unlike industrial production processes, the supply of food is subject to predictable seasonal variability and, more important, to unpredictable fluctuations due to weather, pests, and other factors. These fundamental reasons why food is different from other private goods are accepted by nearly all policymakers as providing a rationale for government intervention in the market.

Assuring that basic needs can be met in an unpredictable world is not the only, nor even the most important, consideration that motivates Asian governments to intervene extensively in the foodgrain markets, as they have almost continuously since World War II. More compelling is the fact that, in most of Asia's developing countries, foodgrain supplies and prices have been instrumental to overall economic performance and to the distribution of income among urban and rural areas. In the urban areas, food constitutes the biggest single item in the budget of poor consumers. Thus, foodgrain prices have a major influence on real wages, which, in turn, are a key determinant of the profitability of industrial investment. Governments intent on rapid industrialization would therefore wish to keep urban food prices low. This is the "wage-good argument" for government intervention, and it is inherently urban-biased. Political considerations also figure into the calculus: when food is scarce, urban consumers have often exerted strong and effective political pressure for the Government to prevent food prices from rising.

In most of Asia, foodgrain pricing policies have generally tended to favor consumers, often with an explicit urban bias in South Asia.[1] In general, if rural producers had a stronger political voice, the pressure would naturally be greater for higher food prices, since foodgrains constitute the single biggest component of their income. But as explained in Chapter II, rural people generally have a poor record of articulating their political views and thereby influencing government policy. Notwithstanding the lower rural political voice, however, when the green revolution opened up the opportunity, governments, as

---

[1] It should be kept in mind that "consumers" does not necessarily mean "urban," since many rural families also depend upon market purchases of food during some seasons of the year.

never before, lavished resources on the rural areas in the form of subsidies on fertilizer, irrigation, and other inputs. These subsidies served the dual purpose of keeping urban retail prices low and supporting rural incomes. Fertilizer, in particular, became a strategic commodity and, therefore, one for which State market interventions were almost as widespread as those for the foodgrains themselves.

This chapter is divided into two main sections, each providing a distinct perspective on government objectives and strategies for intervening in foodgrain and fertilizer markets. As in much of this volume, the discussion is placed in the historical context of Asia's green revolution, the rapid expansion of the region's urban industrial sector, and the growing importance of electoral politics as a consideration in government decision making. The perspective of the first section is largely economic. Although it is sprinkled, as economists are wont, with the jargon of political economy, the main focus is on the economic efficiency of alternative interventions.

The second section asks why, if relatively cost-effective interventions can be found, have governments often chosen much less efficient approaches? To answer this question, it is necessary to delve deeply into the structure of political institutions and the political incentives faced by policymakers. Since these institutions, incentives, and other relevant characteristics vary widely in Asia, the section presents a detailed comparison of the evolution of food policies in Thailand, Malaysia, and Indonesia during the green-revolution years of the 1970s and early 1980s.

ASIA'S MODELS OF MARKET INTERVENTION AND FOOD PRICE STABILIZATION IN A RISKY WORLD

Intervention in Foodgrain Markets before 1970

Many of the foodgrain programs and agencies currently in place in Asia derive from measures introduced during World War II or immediately afterward, when there was the simple need to ensure that people had sufficient food. These measures were implemented by the colonial powers, which then ruled most of South and Southeast Asia, through State enterprises that often evolved into the organizations being used by today's independent governments to intervene in the food markets. (country studies of this evolution are contained in Mears [1961, Indonesia]; Mears et al. [1974, Philippines]; Ahmed [1979, Bangladesh]; and Gavan and Sri Chandrasekera [1979, Sri Lanka]).

Because of their origins during a time of scarcity, these institutions were mainly interested in procuring sufficient food to feed the crowded cities. In South Asia, the food (mainly rice and wheat) was distributed through ration shops at below-market prices. The need to keep these distribution channels operating then became the driving force for the State enterprises and indeed also for the food markets that remained outside the government system. In particular, procuring enough food from the producers, or through imports, became the central obsession of the State enterprises.

It would be obviously wrong to conclude that it was only the imperative to provision the cities that drove foodgrain policies for decades. That the system of interventions in their various forms lasted so long meant that there were other considerations leading many otherwise market-oriented governments to intervene extensively. In addition to the merit- and wage-good rationales given above, there were thought to be problems in foodgrain markets as well. These problems lead to three further explanations for the persistence of State interventions: one sociological, the second economic, and the third political-economic:

- First, the colonial experience of many Asian countries left many of their domestic trading systems in the hands of nonnatives: Indians in Myanmar, Vietnamese in Cambodia, and Chinese everywhere else in Southeast Asia. In India, trade was mostly in the hands of a few specific castes or of individuals from a particular region. The instinctive ethnic animosity toward these

The Political Economy of Foodgrain and Fertilizer Distribution 217

groups was combined with a class animosity and led to the claim that traders conspired to keep marketing margins high—a claim that research has consistently proven to be erroneous (e.g., by Lele in India [1971][2]; Mears et al. in the Philippines [1974]; and by Mears in Indonesia [1981]).
- Second, it was felt that, if left to its own devices, the market could not ensure price stability—and price stability usually meant asymmetric protection against a sharp upward movement in prices. Price stability will be discussed at length below.
- Third, in bypassing—and in some cases, explicitly prohibiting—private market activity, the State interventions in effect became self-perpetuating. As noted above, the need to keep open the pipeline of public food distribution led governments to engage in various procurement systems. The easiest was a monopoly on imports, both through food-aid and through commercial channels—in the latter case to be sold below cost. The general impact was to keep domestic food prices below border prices. More distortionary steps included compulsory delivery to the State procurement system, usually at prices well below market. South Asia and the PRC practiced different versions of this system. Such compulsory measures extracted resources from (i.e., taxed) the agricultural sector.

Even exporting countries were not immune to the pressure to stabilize their domestic markets, although the policy

---

[2] Lele found the degree of concentration in Indian grain trading to be quite high at the local level but not at the interregional level. She also detected an increase in concentration in some states, but that could be attributable to the growth of monopoly procurement in those states. Mears (1981), on the other hand, found that with government intervention, marketing margins in Indonesia narrowed. The difference in the impact of government arises because of the different objectives and instruments of policy.

instruments were far simpler. All they had to do was to limit exports by means of quantitative restrictions, by State trading and export monopolies (as in present-day Myanmar and in the past, Thailand and Viet Nam), by simple export taxation, or all three.

Malaysia—because of its peculiar ethnic makeup—was the only Asian country to reverse the taxation of food grain producers before 1970 (Goldman 1975). That did not preclude the Government from intervening extensively in the rice market and setting up a State enterprise to procure and distribute rice, but the objective in Malaysia's case was to protect farmers from the full brunt of foreign competition. The end result was to drive down the private sector's share of trade and processing activities (Tamin and Meyanathan 1988). The political and institutional context of Malaysia's food policy will be discussed in this chapter's second section.

Similarly, the Republic of Korea and Taipei,China began to take a protectionist stance in the early 1970s, again with a prominent State role. The Government procured rice in order to support prices, using cooperatives as its handling agents (Myoung and Lee 1988).

In most countries, however, the wage-good argument was used to justify an extractive policy. A corollary to this argument was the notion that the supply effects of such a policy would be small, since it was widely believed (at least among its proponents) that the elasticity of supply of agricultural products was near zero.

Intervention in the Fertilizer Market

Emergence of the Fertilizer Subsidy

While many of the assumptions underlying the extractive policies were indubitably wrong, it was not the economic research refuting these assumptions that led to the change in the earlier policies of extraction. Rather, it was the combination of the green revolution and the Asian food crisis of the early 1970s.

These two developments did not reduce the interventions by Asian governments in the markets for foodgrains. In fact, the scope of the interventions expanded to the input markets as well. What the green revolution did was to overturn the perception of policymakers that there was an absolute limit on food production. For the first time, they realized that food production could be made to respond to policy inducements. With the new high-yield crop varieties, farmers could be induced to produce more food for the Government to procure to feed the cities: that was and remains the central imperative. While policymakers could continue to believe that the own-price elasticity of food supply is zero or near zero, they could also be persuaded to believe that the elasticity of foodgrain supply with respect to fertilizer prices was significantly negative (Suprapto 1988). Coupled with the belief common among urban policymakers that farmers were technologically backward, this concept of negative elasticity became the germ of a subsidy to fertilizer prices.

Indeed, Barker and Hayami (1976) made precisely this case. A well-known proposition from economic theory is that the relationship specifying the value of the marginal product (VMP) of an input determines (indeed is the same as) the demand curve for that input. Barker and Hayami inserted the assumption that the demand curve for fertilizers lay to the left of the VMP curve, i.e., farmers underestimated the value of fertilizers in production. From there it was easy to show that the amount of fertilizer used by the farmers was below what was optimal for them and for society as a whole. Under these circumstances, a fertilizer subsidy increased welfare, thus in effect making fertilizer a merit good.

As a policy option for increasing grain production, a fertilizer subsidy is said to be superior to a higher price for output, because it targets the money on those farmers whose production is more responsive because they use fertilizers. By contrast, an output subsidy benefits all farmers, including those who are not so responsive, with a smaller net benefit in terms of added grain. At the same time, the fertilizer subsidy encourages fertilizer to leak from foodgrains to other crops, which may require the Government to undertake countermeasures (see below).

It was not surprising that the Barker-Hayami analysis struck a chord, as it emerged at the time of the food crisis, when policymakers all over Asia suddenly found it very expensive to procure rice and wheat in the international market (Fig. VI.1). The green revolution and the food crisis therefore led to the emergence of a widespread policy of input subsidies. These came in various forms, but, given the complementarity of the green revolution inputs, it was common to provide a "package" that included credit, seed, and fertilizers, all at subsidized rates. Examples include the Masagana 99 program in the Philippines and the BIMAS program in Indonesia. For programs with a credit component, there was also an additional assumption: that the preexisting credit market was imperfect (Rosegrant and Herdt 1981).

It is debatable how much benefit these programs brought to the countries in the long term. They could be justified at the onset of the green revolution, because farmers could be assumed to underestimate the productivity of fertilizers. Note the similarity of this argument to the "infant-industry" rationale for protecting or subsidizing industry in its early stages. As with infant-industry protection, beyond a certain point, i.e., after farmers had become fully familiar with the use of fertilizers, the continuation of fertilizer subsidization led to a real distortion. And if the devastation wrought to rural financial markets by the subsidized credit programs is added (see Meyer and Nagarajan [1999]), then there are grounds for believing that over all, the persistence of credit and fertilizer subsidies caused significant net losses.

If the purpose of the policy was to reduce the price of fertilizers to farmers, then a fertilizer subsidy could, in principle, have been administered easily, without the Government having to take over the function of marketing itself or engaging in elaborate forms of market intervention, such as uniform pricing (and attendant arrangements to subsidize transport) and the like. The subsidy could have been given at the border if the fertilizer were imported, or at the few factories where it was

Figure VI.1 Real Prices of Rice, Wheat and Corn 1950–1997 (1990 $)

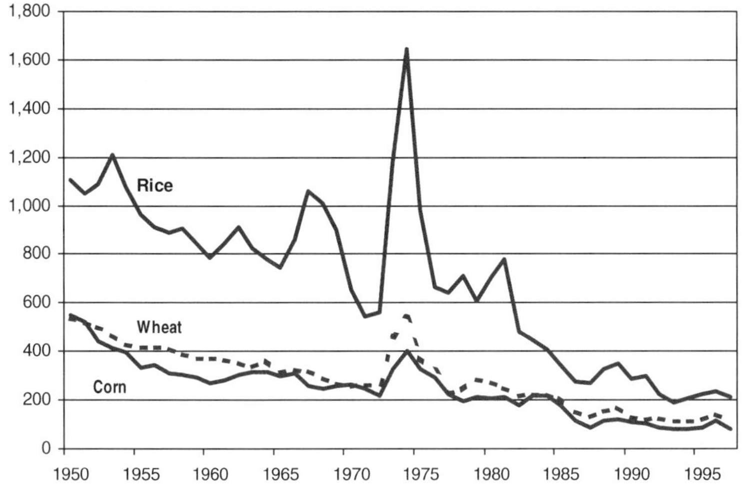

Notes: Thai rice, 5% broken, milled, f.o.b. Bangkok; US wheat, No. 2, Soft Red Winter, f.o.b. Gulf Ports; US corn, No. 2 Yellow, f.o.b. Gulf Ports; Deflated by G-7 consumer price index (1990=100)
Sources: IRRI (1990); World Bank (Various Years).

produced, and a competitive market should have ensured that the subsidy was passed on to the farmers. However, many governments first of all did not believe that the marketing chain would pass on the subsidy to the farmers (another version of the exploiting middleman problem) and, second, governments also wanted to economize on the subsidy by targeting it specifically to food crops.

The Fertilizer Subsidy Becomes Fertilizer Distribution

In Indonesia, the Government arranged the delivery of fertilizer to the farmers. Under the BIMAS program, the credit and fertilizer subsidy was initially administered through the cooperatives, in coordination with the Bank Rakyat Indonesia. By making them agents of the Government, the Government added to its generally heavy-handed attitude toward the cooperatives and caused their development to be stunted.

In Bangladesh, the Government tightly controlled fertilizer distribution. The Bangladesh Agricultural Development Corporation (BADC), a State enterprise, had an absolute public monopoly in fertilizer procurement and distribution, down to the level of the *thana* (comprising 50–150 villages). Below that level, it licensed a set number of dealers (usually 15 per Union, a unit consisting of about 6–12 villages), fixed the retail price, and set the dealer's commission. The control was relieved somewhat in 1978, when dealers were permitted to set up shop by merely registering with BADC, and the dealers' commission was increased to provide more of an incentive. In particular, BADC reduced its distribution points to a smaller number of viable locations. In 1983, the price control below these distribution points was lifted (Mudahar and Kapista 1987). Liberalization of the fertilizer market continued through the early 1990s; by 1993, a vibrant private import and marketing system had developed and public subsidies to fertilizer had been largely eliminated (detailed assessments are provided in Ahmed [1995] and ADB [1996a]). Unfortunately, the ill-advised reintroduction of government controls beginning in late 1994 seriously disrupted the fertilizer market, illustrating the importance of consistent, predictable application of policy in food and input markets.

In the Philippines, a State enterprise was established in 1973 (the Fertilizer Industry Authority, to be renamed in 1977 the Fertilizer and Pesticide Authority). Its functions included the control and regulation of prices, production, imports, marketing, and extension of financial assistance to the fertilizer industry. In the beginning, the Government administered a higher level of subsidy for what were considered the highest priority crops (rice, corn, feed grains, and vegetables). However, because of massive diversion of fertilizers from these priority crops to others, the subsidies were eventually equalized. All subsidies were abolished in 1982 on account of fiscal difficulties (Balisacan 1990).

The way the subsidy was administered in the Philippines is worth dwelling upon, for it shows how the Government's entry into the fertilizer business can have unintended consequences. When the Masagana 99 program was launched, the country's four fertilizer companies were required to sell the fertilizers below cost, with the loss covered by cash subsidies. These were never paid in full and the arrears accumulated over the years. When one of the companies (Planters Products Inc. [PPI]) failed in 1984 (apparently for other reasons), the Government undertook, with the company's foreign bank creditors, to pursue a fertilizer pricing policy that would enable PPI to cover its costs and to repay its creditors (Balisacan 1990). This undertaking was tantamount to making the farmers pay back in the 1980s part of the subsidies that they obtained in the 1970s.

The Indian Government's intervention in the domestic fertilizer sector was extensive. Fertilizer prices were fixed under the "retention price scheme," whereby prices were set factory by factory so as to ensure a 12 percent rate of return on post-tax net worth, provided the plant was run at 80 percent of capacity and certain efficiency norms were met. Despite the provisos, however, such a cost-plus formula for price regulation was not conducive to the optimal efficiency of the firms (Mudahar and Kapista 1987).

Probably the costliest component of the fertilizer subsidy was the insistence of some governments on ensuring supplies of fertilizers by promoting the establishment of domestic production, much of which turned out to be inefficient, absorbing the bulk of the subsidy. Thus, in the Philippines during the crucial period 1973–1982, despite the direct cash subsidies to importers and producers, the implicit tariffs whose burden was eventually borne by the farmers averaged 20 percent (Balisacan 1990). In India, 86 percent of the fertilizer subsidy during the crop year 1983/84 went to domestic producers and 14 percent went to importers, although in this case, unlike that of the Philippines, farmers were still receiving their fertilizers at below-world prices (Mudahar and Kapista 1987).

Fertilizer marketing in most countries remained multichannel, involving the participation of firms from the public, private, and cooperative sectors. In some cases, however, governments adopted a policy of uniform pricing, which required them to take over more of the marketing functions, either directly or through administrative interventions to cross-subsidize transport costs. A study of India, Indonesia, and Bangladesh (Mudahar and Kapista [1987]) suggested that this cross-subsidization was relatively easy to administer.

By taking over some or all of the functions of the distribution, the Government also took on the responsibility of ensuring that the fertilizer arrived at the farm gate on time. At the same time, what was delivered was not to exceed requirements. Fertilizer has a short shelf life, particularly if the storage facilities are poor, as would be the case in rural areas, so it is expensive to store over the season. The logistics of fertilizer distribution are thus more demanding than would appear at first sight. Many governments did not fare well in this operation.

Does the market fare any better in this respect? After all, there are inherent risks in the fertilizer trade. Planting intentions cannot be forecast precisely, either by the Government or by private traders, nor can the weather. In Thailand, where the Government role in fertilizer distribution is smaller than elsewhere, importers and domestic producers normally sell warehouse certificates to local distributors or to groups of farmers a few months before the planting season, with payment expected at the time of delivery. In this way importers and producers have a reasonably firm idea as to planting intentions, since local distributors would have a better idea of what the needs are. When the time comes for taking delivery, the buyers arrange for the transport themselves, saving the importers or producers the complex logistical task of planning. Of course, the risks of weather remain. But at least mistakes in forecasting the weather can be met by storage in the better warehouses of the importers or producers. The Thai Government, it should be noted, did not subsidize fertilizers to nearly the same degree as other Asian countries (see the following section). With less government interference, fertilizer prices were higher in Thailand than in the rest of Asia, while the private sector was provided with an adequate economic incentive to participate in the market. Although Thailand has been somewhat unusual in giving the private sector a dominant role in fertilizer distribution, there is no reason why innovations such as the system of warehouse receipts could not be employed elsewhere.

The Retreat of the Fertilizer Subsidy

During the 1980s, country after country began to dismantle the fertilizer subsidies and the Government's roles in distribution. The changes that took place in the Philippines and Bangladesh have been touched on above, but the trend was Asia-wide, with India being the major exception.[3] Three interrelated reasons combined to bring an end to the era of subsidies.

The first and most important was that the food crisis of the 1970s was easing: indeed, cereal prices were sinking to all-time lows (see Figure VI.1). Asian importing countries were achieving their goal of self-sufficiency and therefore the drive to produce more, which pushed governments to put money into the subsidy in the first place, was no longer so urgent. After almost a decade of exposure to the new technology, the Barker-Hayami rationale, based on the assumption of an imperfect perception of the new technology by farmers, began to look less plausible.

The second reason was the developing countries' debt crisis of the early 1980s, which brought their governments into IMF or World Bank structural adjustment programs. By this time, the fertilizer subsidies were taking hefty chunks of some governments' budgets, so they were ripe targets for donor conditionality. The subsidies, besides entailing direct financial costs, had generated many forms of inefficiency that had become intolerable as the 1970s atmosphere of food crisis was replaced in many countries by the 1980s' debt and fiscal crisis. Mudahar and Kapista (1987) summarize these inefficiencies, most of which have already been alluded to:

---

[3] Even as late as 1993/94, India was spending as much as $1.4 billion annually, or 3 percent of the national budget, on fertilizer subsidies (Bumb and Baanante 1996), a figure that in absolute terms is about the same as what it was in the mid-1980s.

- High-cost domestic plants;
- Poor administration and implementation of subsidies;
- Poor accounting on how much is was actually spent on the subsidies; and
- Absorption of the subsidies by the high-cost marketing system, leaving less to benefit the farmers.

The third reason arose from the linking of the fertilizer subsidy with the provision of credit in countries like the Philippines and Indonesia. In the Philippines, the government even guaranteed the loans that were provided by the rural banks. This created an obvious moral hazard problem that soon led to the collapse of the credit program and, eventually, the end of Masagana 99 and the almost total disappearance of rural banks. In both the Philippines and Indonesia, the arrears in credit repayment provided additional impetus to end the fertilizer subsidy as well.

Stabilizing Output Prices: the Southeast Asian Style of Intervention

The withdrawal of governments from the fertilizer market was not, in general, followed by a parallel withdrawal from the foodgrain market. The latter has come about more gradually, despite the achievement of self-sufficiency, which should have lessened the burden on the government agencies involved in food procurement and distribution.

Government intervention in the markets for foodgrains has taken two broad forms: one prevalent throughout South Asia and the other more common in Southeast Asia.[4] The South Asian form builds upon a public distribution system, often

---

[4] The PRC has a tradition that places it closer to the South Asian form. The Republic of Korea and Taipei,China, on the other hand, follow a mode of stabilization like that of Southeast Asia, but in these countries the policy of price support to the farm sector is so dominant that stabilization is automatically achieved as part of that policy.

down to the retail level, which tries to ensure that consumers, or at least the poorest among them, can receive a ration of foodgrains at a low price. The Southeast Asian form, on the other hand, focuses more on stabilizing the market price of foodgrains, with little or no retail distribution. From the point of view of the governments, the Southeast Asians set prices (for both producers and consumers) as targets, while the South Asians manipulated the supply of foodgrains, including procurement (or import) of a targeted quantity. The Southeast Asian price-targeted form of intervention includes a floor price to protect producers and a ceiling price to protect consumers. To achieve these targets, governments have two instruments at their disposal: storage and variations in the volume of trade.

Storage

Storage of agricultural goods stabilizes prices within three time frames (Ammar 1988). The first is short-term, involving precautionary stocks to prevent spikes in prices due to unforeseen interruptions in supply. Since supply interruptions of this kind occur most often in international trade, this motive makes storage complementary to trade. The second is the normal seasonal variation in the flow of production; this is the phenomenon that private and public storage usually focus on. The third is year-to-year, arising from production fluctuations that are often met by variations in the volume of imports or exports rather than through storage.

The Southeast Asian style of intervention in the rice market starts with the setting of a floor price, usually for paddy, and a ceiling price for rice. The floor price is defended by the relevant State enterprise buying the paddy or rice in the open market, usually at the beginning of the season, and storing it until the latter part of the marketing year, when it is released to defend the ceiling price. The size of the State operation (i.e., how much is procured and how much released) depends essentially on whether the gap between the floor and ceiling prices provides enough spread to induce the private sector to store over the season. Where that gap is small, the State enterprise has to engage in a major operation, buying a large share of the supply in the beginning of the season to be stored for later release.

A crucial requirement for the success of the operation is that the State enterprise must have access to finances—both foreign and domestic—that are, in principle, unlimited. Scarcity of financing for procurement must never send a signal to the market that the State enterprise is "running out of money." If imports are necessary, the State enterprise must have access to foreign exchange to bring in sufficient supplies to defend the ceiling price. Similarly, it must have adequate domestic currency to defend the floor price. Inasmuch as Southeast Asia's food agencies typically buy small shares (less than 10 percent) of domestic supplies (Islam and Thomas 1996), the market's confidence in their commitment is critical and has important consequences for their performance.

For example, Indonesia's National Logistics Agency, known by its Indonesian acronym BULOG, had almost unlimited access to concessional central bank credit for its operations, at least until the late 1990s. In contrast, the Philippines' National Food Authority (NFA) has its resources constrained by annual appropriations from the Government. In some years, the resources supplied were insufficient for NFA to conduct its own operations and the inadequacy became obvious to the market. Hence, its success in defending the target prices was less than that of its Indonesian counterpart.

A primary objective of government intervention has been to reduce the seasonal spread in prices. Some seasonal spread is necessary, of course, to cover the real resource cost of the storage, which is often quite high in Asia. Its components include the transportation from the countryside to the storage facility, the costs of physical storage (including losses), and interest, of which the last is the largest

In Indonesia, Mears (1981) undertook a detailed analysis in which he found BULOG's monthly interest cost to be about 1.2 percent during the early 1970s. Rates were often higher in the private sector, as much as 2.6 percent per month. BULOG's physical cost of transport and storage came to approximately 0.5 percent per month, a figure that was somewhat higher than that of the private sector. In total, therefore, storage costs were about

1.7 percent for BULOG and about 2–3 percent for the private sector. For the years 1969/71, a period during which rice production was more or less on trend and BULOG's operations were small relative to the market, the seasonal (roughly, semiannual) spread ranged between 13 percent and 28 percent, with the rice-deficit areas at the upper end of this range. Thus, Mears concluded that rice storage in Indonesia was profitable *on average*, although the probability of a loss was not negligible: if the interest rates had been much higher, storage would have been unprofitable.

Conceding that the real carrying cost and therefore the seasonal spread are quite high is not the same thing as proving that middlemen do not exploit farmers at harvest time. But Mears' detailed analysis showed that it is difficult to turn a consistent profit from storing rice (or most other cereals), since years in which the seasonal spread is high are interspersed with years in which it is low or even negative. His research on rice in Indonesia and the Philippines is buttressed by Lele's work on sorghum in India (Lele 1971). Other research has shown that the levels of seasonal price rise and the uniformity of price seasonality at the farm, wholesale, and retail levels are influenced by the quality of storage facilities at the farm and wholesale levels, as well as the patterns of international trade (see, for example, the studies of maize in the Philippines by Mendoza and Rosegrant [1995] and of rice, maize, and root crops in Ghana by Southworth [1981]).

From the late 1970s onward, NFA and BULOG were able to reduce the seasonal spread by expanding and improving their operations. Bouis (1983) reported that between 1974 and 1978, NFA reduced the seasonal spread in the Philippines to only 6 percent. Since the seasonal spread reflects real resource costs and, as has already been argued, the private sector does not appear, on average, to make excess profits from storage, public intervention to reduce the price movement could only succeed by subsidizing the carrying cost. How big was the subsidy? The answer depends primarily on two variables: the gradient of monthly storage costs and the "squeeze," i.e., the extent to which policymakers wished to contain prices at levels below the normal seasonal price rise.

Direct measurement of the subsidy is very difficult, since the financial accounts of State enterprises like BULOG and NFA are not always transparent. Ammar (1988) attempted an indirect measurement of the subsidy component of BULOG for a single marketing year (April 1979/March 1980). Based on the actual movements of rice into and out of BULOG storage and estimates of the seasonal spread with and without BULOG intervention, he calculated that the implied subsidy by BULOG came to only $7.2 million, a small amount in relation to the total value of Indonesia's rice marketings. Domestic procurement in 1979/80 was abnormally low, but even at the much higher level of intervention the following year, when procurement expanded more than fivefold, the subsidy was still relatively small, primarily because BULOG's operations allowed for a reasonably wide price spread. Moreover, BULOG accounted for less than 10 percent of the rice produced in Indonesia and, on average, it stored rice for only a few months during the year.

Ammar's estimate represents only the difference between the carrying costs of the private sector and those of the subsidized BULOG. There are other costs associated with the nature of State grain procurement, the most important arising from price variations due to differences in quality. Rice, in particular, has many qualities and the quality-price gradient is fairly steep. Valuation of rice quality is done on a transaction-by-transaction basis by the private sector and requires considerable skill and judgment. A bureaucratic organization may not be well equipped to handle such valuations, often subjecting rice and paddy to only the most superficial grading standards, such as moisture content. Because of their inadequacies in this respect and, just as important, because they are buyers of last resort, State enterprises in most countries (including South Asia) tend to end up with the lowest quality of rice, with the better-quality rice flowing into private channels. This became apparent during the mid-1980s, when the Philippines and Indonesia started to export rice and quickly discovered that the prices obtainable for State-procured rice were very low. Thus in setting a procurement price for anything better than low-quality rice, the State enterprises may provide an additional subsidy to producers.

Another cost—and one that defies documentation—is mismanagement within the State enterprises. Large, vertically-integrated grain-trading operations are very difficult to administer because systems of internal control and accountability are difficult to institute.[5] When these enterprises are working in a highly volatile price environment, the problem of control becomes acute. The international trade in rice is relatively informal and is often conducted on a personalized, government-to-government basis. When the State enterprises have a monopoly in trade, it is very difficult for outsiders to gain an accurate idea of the price at which individual transactions are concluded. The problem of control is compounded by the fact that there is no clear reference price for rice, such as exists for corn at the Chicago Board of Trade.

Nonetheless, it is fair to say that BULOG's domestic rice operations have been conducted efficiently, with relatively favorable outcomes in terms of the price stability achieved. However, this conclusion should not be extended to BULOG's monopolies of wheat, sugar, and soybean imports.

As this chapter was drafted, rapidly evolving developments beginning in 1998 led to significant changes in Indonesia's food economy. In the wake of the economic and political crisis that began in 1997, private imports of rice were first allowed in September 1998 and, by 1999, accounted for more than half of the rice import total. BULOG's monopoly of wheat, soybean, and sugar imports has also ended. The copious, State-backed "liquidity credit" used to finance BULOG's market operations has been curtailed; the organization must now obtain most of its credit on a commercial basis. In order to bring public procurement

---

[5] In the private sector, vertically integrated grain trading operations exist only in developed countries, where there are other market institutions (e.g., futures markets) that help in their internal control structure. In Thailand, where the Government has had relatively little substantive impact on the grain trade (except through the rice export tax), vertical integration has taken place only in the highly specialized fragrant rice market.

closer to the farmer, BULOG's purchase operations have shifted from milled rice to paddy. The role of the cooperatives as the front line in procurement has become moribund, while the ethnic Chinese are reported to have a reduced presence in the domestic foodgrain trade as a result of the country's political and economic instability. Thus, the food economy is in flux at the present time. As was noted above for the Bangladesh fertilizer market, considerable disruption of traditional market relationships has occurred in Indonesia as the result of these rapid, unpredictable shifts in policy. Nonetheless, these changes do not diminish the point of this discussion: BULOG's roles during the decades of the 1970s and 1980s illustrate the objectives, performance, and limitations of what has been one of Southeast Asia's stronger and better-functioning food buffer stock agencies.

BULOG shows what can be achieved by a State agency if there is a clear, sustained direction to policy and firm supervision of its implementation. BULOG's place in the political infrastructure of Indonesia is discussed in the second part of this chapter. Is BULOG a model for other Asian countries to emulate? It is debatable whether a Government that has not yet established a food buffer stock mechanism should embark on this kind of operation. There do exist other methods by which the Government can achieve price stability with a much smaller management requirement; a discussion of them follows.

Variations in Trade

If a country is an importer of foodgrains, then in addition to the use of storage to keep the seasonal spread within policy-prescribed limits, managing the timing of imports would help reduce the storage burden further. The State enterprise could bring in the imports late in the marketing year, saving the country from having to store for year-end consumption. This strategy would pay if the seasonal movements in the world market are narrower than in the domestic market, which is normally the case because the world market has many sources of supply that tend to even out the flow of rice through the year.

In actual operations, the size of the seasonal spread is not the only consideration. The correct timing of imports vis-a-vis the seasonal fluctuation of domestic harvests obviously matters too. Between 1961 and 1974, before the Philippines' NFA (or rather, its predecessor organization) had had a major effect through its storage operations, but after it had acquired the import monopoly, it frequently mistimed import arrivals. Indeed, the timing of imports had a greater impact on seasonal price movements than did the fluctuations in wet- or dry-season harvests (Bouis 1983). This implies that for trade to play its proper role, it must be well executed. In addition, an adequate amount of precautionary storage is absolutely essential, as hitches can generally be expected in procuring supplies from overseas. It is in this sense that precautionary storage is complementary to trade.

But when it comes to annual fluctuations in the volume of output due to harvest failures, then trade and storage are substitutes for each other; in an important group of countries—those that regularly import foodgrains—trade may be superior as a means of stabilizing domestic prices. A regular importer has the option to vary the volume of trade in order to achieve a given level of price stability. Depending upon trade is likely to be cheaper, on average, than maintaining buffer stocks. With buffer stocks, the country is locking up resources as grain in storage, which has a positive carrying cost. Instead, the country could set aside a foreign exchange reserve to provide for imports. In contrast to holding grain in storage, carrying foreign exchange earns revenue. This, ultimately, is the logic behind the use of foreign trade to even out fluctuations in domestic availability and to cope with fluctuations in world prices.

Of course, complete dependence on trade passes on to the domestic market any price instability in the world market. Therefore, to achieve what are considered strategic food security goals, most Asian importing countries have chosen some balance between domestic storage and government trading monopolies that can insulate the domestic market by selling foodgrain at subsidized prices. Provided the foreign exchange is well managed, the wherewithal both to purchase the grain and to subsidize its domestic sale should be at hand.

But the above measures all rely on government decision making. A more market-oriented approach, which has never been tried in Asia but which would avoid the pitfalls (and the management demands) of both the buffer-stock operations and variability in trade, would be a variable border tax. Under such a scheme, the Government sets a price target and imposes a variable levy (or subsidy), but the trading decision is left to private importers and exporters. This would minimize management by the Government and lead to automatic and transparent decision making.[6] This does not quite let the Government off the hook, however, for even with the decisions left to the private sector, better statistical information still has to be obtained by the Government and made available. Accurate information regarding harvest and grain movements is essential, regardless of whether the Government or the private sector is making the decisions to import.

Rationing and Targeted Consumer Subsidy: the South Asian Model

As stated above, most of the patterns of intervention in grain markets, both in South and Southeast Asia, have their origins in the procurement, distribution, and rationing systems established during World War II. In South Asia, unlike in Southeast Asia, these systems remained in place well into the postcolonial era and were designed primarily for the urban areas. Indeed, in most cases, ration shops only existed in urban areas. Relative to the Southeast Asian approach, three basic problems with the South Asian model can be identified: its instability, its inequitable urban bias, and its high public cost.

---

[6] It remains unclear what the GATT's ruling on variable levies will be. Offhand it would appear that as long as the absolute level of the levy at any time exceeds the country's bound tariff rate, then a variable levy should be acceptable. As of now, the matter has yet to be resolved.

South Asia's rationing systems essentially make procurement (and import) policies follow a quantity target, as compared to the price-targeting approach that has been described for Southeast Asia. In normal times, the difference between the two is only of academic interest. But during a crisis, the quantity target becomes much more rigid and demanding—and peculiarly unstable. Except implicitly, by their urban location, the availability of food from the ration shops was nearly universal. At times there was not even a quantity restriction. Under such circumstances, if a shortage developed, the gap between ration and free-market prices could quickly widen, causing increased offtake from the public system and requiring greater effort at procurement, which in turn would drive free-market prices further upward. To break the spiral, the Government had to obtain foodgrains from outside the system, usually from abroad and often from food aid. If domestic sources had to be relied on, then some form of squeeze on the farmers was almost inevitable. Thus, in India during the 1960s and onward, a compulsory rice levy was imposed on farmers (implemented through the rice mills), although this was managed without inducing too much impact on prices.

If the purpose of ration shops was to protect the poor, then, in bypassing the rural poor, the structure that evolved in the decades after World War II became increasingly and manifestly unfair. Moreover, in bypassing market mechanisms through which supply and demand both respond efficiently to changes in prices, the South Asian systems entailed enormous and unsustainable public budgetary costs. In the few cases, notably Sri Lanka and Kerala, India, where the ration shops were open in both rural and urban areas, these costs continually increased. As in the case of fertilizer, with the debt crisis of the early 1980s and considerable prodding from donors, many governments took the opportunity to reform their systems. The cases of Bangladesh and Sri Lanka illustrate the nature and impacts of these reforms.

In Bangladesh, the evolution of food policy during the past two decades has involved an as yet unfinished search for a suitable balance between the often contradictory goals of food security for consumers (both nationally and among vulnerable groups), producer income support, and greater efficiency of public interventions in foodgrain markets (ADB 1996a). In the early 1980s, State interventions in the foodgrain marketing system of Bangladesh were among the most extensive in Asia. State enterprises held monopolies in international trade (including the country's considerable food aid), grain exports were effectively banned, private domestic storage was stifled, and a massive Public Food Distribution System (PFDS) was responsible for procuring grain from millers, storing a large share of the country's annual grain supply (more than 20 percent in 1988), and distributing this through a variety of often inefficient, poorly targeted rationing and program channels. The budgetary and efficiency costs of these interventions were enormous.

Reforms were initiated gradually in the mid-1980s and accelerated in the early 1990s. Legal barriers to private foodgrain trade and storage were reduced, prohibitions against private imports and exports were largely dismantled, the most egregious of the public rationing channels were abolished while the others were streamlined, and significant cutbacks in PFDS staff began. To replace the traditional millgate procurement system, which had awarded rents in the form of price premiums to grain millers, two somewhat competing new mechanisms were introduced to improve the efficiency of domestic procurement: a farmer floor price and a market-based open tender system for milled grain. By the mid-1990s, the private sector had taken over a major share of domestic and international trade in foodgrains. As a result, the reforms reduced the Government's annual budgetary costs for PFDS operations from $199 million in 1990/91 to $93 million in 1994/95 (ADB 1996a). Although conceptually sound, the reforms met considerable administrative and, at times, political resistance, with the former often being most vocal in the State agencies under the PFDS. As of the late 1990s, Bangladesh's food policy—encompassing strategies both for production and marketing—was still evolving and subject to fits and starts as the result of political unrest, weather-related production fluctuations, and other factors. Nonetheless, the tangible achievements of market liberalization were so obvious as to make them appear irreversible.

Sri Lanka gave up its universal food distribution system beginning in 1978 and introduced a means test to target the subsidy toward poorer groups. This reform was occasioned by trade liberalization accompanied by a large devaluation, which increased the fiscal burden of the food subsidy. The reform therefore had as its primary objective the reduction of this burden. It was achieved in three phases. The first phase introduced a mild means test for eligibility to receive rations: families simply declared whether their monthly income was less than 300 rupees (about $15). Despite openness to abuse, this immediately reduced the roll of those eligible to about 50 percent of the population, although this share later increased steadily (because inflation made the rationed food more attractive) until a freeze was declared in 1980. The second phase, implemented in 1979, converted the ration scheme into a food-stamp program. This allowed consumers the option of choosing the mix of goods (kerosene was also included) that could be purchased with the subsidy. Here a trick was inserted to control the level of food subsidies: the allocation of the budget for the food stamps was fixed at a *nominal* level for the future, automatically ensuring the erosion of the real resources transferred through the program. The third phase freed food prices altogether.

As in Bangladesh, the Sri Lankan reforms significantly reduced government expenditures and had a positive impact on the fiscal balance (Ederesinghe 1988). Agricultural incomes rose substantially because of price liberalization. But the precision of the program's targeting mechanism was still poor, illustrating one of the major inefficiencies of the South Asian model: according to a survey by the Central Bank of Ceylon, 30 percent of the nonpoor received food stamps, while 30 percent of the poor did not. The share of food subsidy expenditures captured by the poor rose from 50 percent with the ration system to 60 percent under the food stamps, but this was mostly through the elimination of items such as wheat and dairy products from the subsidy programs. Of course, with the declining real value of the subsidy, the Government's contribution to a poor household's budget declined steadily. The most disturbing impact of the reforms was a decline of some 8 percent in the calorie intake of the bottom income quintile. Their intake prior to the reform was already perilously low (about 1,500 calories per day). This result appeared to be due to the decline in real income that resulted from the increase in general food prices (Ederesinghe 1988).

The whole issue of targeting deserves some elaboration. In an economy where people do not have regular salaries or income that can be easily measured or documented, it is very difficult to single out the poor for special attention. This is especially true if better nutrition is the objective, since almost all households—rich and poor—partake of the consumption of basic starchy staples. More stringent means tests than that used in Sri Lanka are possible, but they are still open to abuse.[7] Self-targeting mechanisms are therefore desirable. Often, self-targeting results from the way in which the distribution is handled. For example queuing for food tends to exclude the rich, whose opportunity cost of time is higher. Similarly, if the public distribution system provides only the poorest grades of food (aesthetically, although not nutritionally), then the system will better target the poor. Bangladesh is well known for having pioneered the food-for-work program, which may be considered an even more efficient approach to self-targeting. A public-works program is self-targeting if it creates jobs for the most unskilled among the labor force and if food, particularly low-grade food, is provided in lieu of monetary payment. In Bangladesh in the 1980s, the food-for-work program distributed wheat that came in as food aid. Wheat at that time was less preferred than rice among the Bangladeshis and therefore enhanced the self-targeting mechanism.

The justification for using food instead of money is that when a labor-intensive public-works program is initiated in a given area, the local demand for food may suddenly rise, putting upward pressure on prices. The Government can avoid this

---

[7] For example, Bangladesh introduced a means test based on the union council taxes paid by households.

by paying the workers directly in food. In contrast, if the share of the workers' budget spent on food is small, or if the marketing system is well developed, then wage payment in money instead of food would suffice.

Assessment of the State Roles

Three questions can be asked about the role of the Government in the area of foodgrain and fertilizer marketing:

- Should it have any role at all?
- Given that it has played a major role and will continue to do so, has it been "excessive," at least in an economic sense?
- Could the State's social and economic objectives be met by more efficient means?

A Marketing Role for Government?

With respect to fertilizer, a clear answer can be given: the governments had a role to play in the 1970s in the wake of the food crisis and with the advent of the green revolution technology that required a period of adaptation by farmers. But by the late 1980s, there was little reason for continuing the fertilizer subsidy anywhere in Asia.

The response is more complex with respect to foodgrains. Superficially, it can be argued that food is a private good and providing it is best done by the private sector. But food is also a merit good of strategic importance. The Government has a clear role to ensure that vulnerable households have adequate access. At the same time, the Government should confine its role to well-targeted subsidization as much as possible. In this respect, some of Asia's experiments in efficient targeting should be continued.

Can a price stabilization role be justified? Here a more complex argument is required. There is no question that society benefits if foodgrains are purchased when supplies are abundant and stored until they are scarce. However, if the interest component of the storage cost reflects the social opportunity cost of capital, and if expectations in the private sector are rational, then the market mechanism, not the Government, will, from *the standpoint of economic efficiency*, arrange for the optimal amount of storage at all times (given the information available), and therefore the optimal degree of price stabilization.

Of these two conditions, it is common for the interest costs facing middlemen to be higher than those of the Government. This may constitute a rationale for the Government to intervene, as it can lay hands on cheaper funds. But caution is in order here. First, if constraints in the financial system limit the credit that is available to private traders, one way out may be for the Government to support the strengthening of the banking system rather than engaging directly in the grain trade.[8] However, this should definitely not be taken as suggesting that the Government should become directly involved in lending to middlemen, particularly given Asia's generally dismal record of State-directed credit to agriculture. Second, even if the banking system is efficient, it is possible, even likely, that the private sector faces a high cost of capital because there is a risk premium attached. A potential policy prescription would be to develop market mechanisms for risk bearing, (e.g., a futures market), rather than for the Government to wade in and become a market stabilizer directly. "Potential," is stressed here because not all countries have the legal and regulatory infrastructure ready for the development of such markets.

It is easy to be skeptical about the second condition, that all actors in the market have rational expectations. To justify government intervention to stabilize markets, however, it must also be claimed that the Government is more rational (has better

---

[8] In some cases, solutions may be straightforward. In Bangladesh, for example, antihoarding laws were left on the books well after the Government embarked on liberalizing the grain trade. Although no longer enforced, these laws nevertheless provided a real disincentive for commercial lending to private grain traders through the mid-1990s.

information or makes better forecasts from the information at hand) than private actors. There may be cases when Government superiority can be justified, for example, when markets and prices are so volatile that private actors cannot form reasonable expectations about the future. In practice, however, this probably occurs only rarely.

In conclusion, there is a clear case for government intervention to ensure that society's nutrition objectives are attained, but a less clear case for the Government to intervene to stabilize prices of foodgrains. There is no longer any case for intervention in the fertilizer market.

Has State Intervention Been Excessive?

There can be no simple answer to this question. A brief (and not very satisfying) answer is simply to say that it all depends! It depends on how much society values price stability; on the nature of the intervention; on a country's size in relation to the world market; on its levels of income, human capital, and other economic resources; on the slopes of the food supply and demand curves; on the extent of poverty and malnutrition; on the level and variability of food supply in the absence of intervention; on the macroeconomic environment; and, last but not least, on all of the market distortions and various natural risks that may lead outcomes in private food markets to depart from what is judged to be socially optimal. During the past decade, economists have become very clever at incorporating these variables in computable general equilibrium models that estimate the distortionary costs of policy. However, a review of this literature is well beyond the scope of this volume.

What can be offered more constructively is the observation that governments have at times misdirected their efforts, doing too much in some areas and not enough in others. By concentrating on price stabilization, governments have expended a great deal of their resources on one objective. While the measurable resource costs of providing price stability may not be very large—at least in relatively normal years—the intangible costs may turn out to be significant: many governments have invested a great deal of their scarce managerial capacity in grain-trading enterprises, and, as will be seen below, the methods they have deployed to achieve their objectives have been especially management-intensive. At the same time, very serious problems related to poverty and malnutrition are not getting the attention they deserve because resources are being diverted to activities for which there is much more political clamor. To correct this resource misallocation, a general recommendation is to seek—consistent with the bounds of society's food policy objectives—market-based solutions, let the private sector do its job, monitor the market carefully, and provide very selective, targeted support to nutritionally vulnerable groups.

Could the Objectives Be Achieved More Efficiently?

Here the answer is unambiguous. In many instances, and particularly in South Asia, the management-intensive enterprises that were created and maintained over the entire postwar era to ensure food security have become extravagant anachronisms.

In addition, now that trade and exchange-rate regimes are increasingly liberalized, the rationale for a foreign-trade monopoly has declined. Fortunately, more efficient, market-based mechanisms exist and are being applied in Asia. The principal suggestion of this volume, for countries that are regular foodgrain importers, is for measures like a variable-levy regime, whereby the Government exerts itself only through the taxation mechanism, without engaging in trading operations. As alluded to above, other government measures to increase market efficiency include the provision of timely market information, monitoring of the marketing system, and efforts to encourage the growth of a healthy financial system.

THE POLITICS OF AGRICULTURAL POLICY MAKING

The Importance of Institutions and Political Dynamics

The economics of Asian agriculture and agricultural policy making are increasingly well understood. As suggested above, theoretical and methodological advances in the discipline of economics, combined with rich applied research on rural Asia, have yielded increasingly powerful insights into the welfare, productivity, and efficiency implications of particular policy measures.

Much less impressive is our understanding of *why* governments make the policy choices they do. All Asian governments face similar circumstances in making decisions about intervening in foodgrain markets, as noted above: the need to ensure adequate food supplies at the lowest possible prices for the urban poor, the desire to avert social and political unrest over constricted food supplies or precipitate food-price rises. Notwithstanding heightened attention to political economy by economists and political scientists, most observers' grasp of why governments opt for one policy instrument over another remains weak.

Repeatedly one encounters writings by policy analysts making vague references to "politics" undermining this or that initiative or obstructing policy reform. Although not wrong, such statements conceal as much as they reveal and are of little utility to practitioners, who are left with the daunting task of crafting economically rational policy measures while at the same time navigating the theoretically uncharted waters of the politically feasible.

The one major innovation of the past 15 years has been the work on the political economy of urban bias. Much (but not all) of this literature grows out of the work of Olson (1965, 1982) on collective action and distributional coalitions. The most influential studies have been those of Lipton (1977), Bates (1981, 1983), Anderson and Hayami (1986), and Lindert (1991).

The central insight of this body of literature is that farmers are likely to suffer policy discrimination in poor countries; but as countries industrialize, as food costs come to constitute a smaller share of living costs and as the obstacles to collective action (lobbying) by farmers decline, reflecting the correspondingly smaller and more concentrated profile of the agricultural sector, the bias will swing to protecting farmers. The Republic of Korea, Malaysia, and Taipei,China have already been cited as examples of this evolution. Among the main subsidiary points is that the potential for collective action by rural producers varies by industry, reflecting the number of players and the incentives to free-ride. Rice farmers, for instance, are less likely to mobilize for effective political action than, say, rice millers or sugar growers.

These are important advances that provide some basis for predicting change over the long run and, more immediately, for anticipating the influence of political dynamics between economic actors and across sectors. Correctly handled, these conceptual advances have real practical implications for policy analysts.[9]

Rather than dealing with the strengths and weaknesses of the urban bias literature, the focus here is instead on what it omits. All this work—like so much of the so-called "new political economy"—is very much demand-side political economy. That is to say, it concentrates on the preferences of a given coalition, sector, or industry and infers policy outcomes from them. Societal preferences or interests—the demands—are assumed to be the critical causal determinants of policy outcomes.

There is much to be gained from such an approach, but also much that is left out. Policymakers—politicians and bureaucrats—are reduced to passive respondents to public pressures (with the partial exception of predatory rent-capturing behavior). Such an approach tells us little or nothing about why agricultural policymakers in different countries who

---

[9] For an important critical review of the literature on urban bias, see the special issue of the *Journal of Development Studies* (Varshney 1993).

are contending with similar constellations of economic interests make very different policy choices. To gain some purchase on these issues it is necessary to factor in the institutional environment, that is, the political architecture of a country. The central proposition of this section is that in order to anticipate more effectively the political feasibility of a given economic strategy for promoting rural development, analysts need to focus on the incentives facing not just economic actors, but policymakers as well. Powerful, if not perfect, insight into the incentives of politicians and bureaucrats can be gained from an understanding of how the political structure within which they must function constrains their actions in designing and implementing policy.

There is a growing and rich literature concerned with the impact of political institutions on economic governance.[10] This literature has been primarily concerned with North America and Europe. Increasingly, however, it is expanding to embrace Latin America and parts of East Asia (principally Japan and Taipei,China). As yet, little attention has been paid to the rest of Asia, and even less to linking political institutions to the particular circumstances of agricultural policy. This section offers an initial attempt to connect this literature to food policy in rural Asia.

Three country case studies are offered: Thailand, Malaysia, and Indonesia. Two interrelated policy issues are investigated across these countries: the handling of rice-price stabilization and the handling of farmer income support. The focus is on the 1970s and early 1980s. There are several reasons for this choice of time frame. First, this was the period during which green revolution technologies were introduced and rice agriculture in Asia was changing most rapidly. Second, it is a period for which the data and the broad outlines of the economic stories are reasonably clear. Third, the institutional framework of Government in these three countries that was

---

[10] For a review that contrasts this literature with the broad interests-based political economy literature, see Haggard (2000). Cox and McCubbins (2000) provide a powerful synthesis and extension of the institutionalist literature.

in place (or took shape) during this period remained largely unchanged until the upheavals linked to the current regional financial and economic crisis.

It should be emphasized that for the purposes of this exercise, the time frame, the countries, and the policy issues are not in themselves important; any or all of these three variables could be changed. The focus here is on the policy process rather than the policy outcomes. The aim is not to illuminate the economics of these issues and cases—that is the topic of the first half of this chapter, as well as other volumes of ADB's Rural Asia study—but rather to highlight the impact of political institutions on the way the issues were handled in these three countries.

Thailand, Malaysia, and Indonesia make it possible to see three quite different political systems at work. From the early 1970s, Thailand had an increasingly competitive political process in place—one that was evolving, to be sure, and not without setbacks, but nonetheless one in which elections and civilian politicians came to play a steadily larger role (even as they shared the stage with military officers and bureaucrats). Malaysia had a more clearly competitive political system in place, even though a range of political controls was introduced in the wake of the race riots of 1969. While electoral competition is of fundamental importance in both Malaysia and Thailand, this section will show that their differing institutional configurations had important consequences for policy making. In political terms, Indonesia presents a very different case, for although the electoral process was not insignificant, it was clearly much more closely managed than Malaysia's or Thailand's. The weakness of the electoral imperative and, moreover, the particular institutional characteristics of Indonesia's presidential system had important consequences for food policy.

Apart from highlighting the impact of differing political frameworks, the wider rationale for this approach is that we can observe three countries, in the same time period, all located in the same neighborhood, all having strong natural resource sectors but undergoing rapid industrialization. In all three, rice is a key crop and rice farmers are an economically and politically important segment of the labor market. All three countries intervened in rice markets to stabilize prices and each took at least some measures (as part of the stabilization process and/or through subsidies for direct inputs) to support farmer income.

There are also critical differences among the three countries that need to be recognized at the outset. A basic difference for policy orientation is that through the period examined here Thailand was a rice exporter while Malaysia and Indonesia were rice importers. Similarly, it makes a difference for fiscal flexibility that Indonesia and Malaysia were oil exporters and Thailand was an oil importer during a period when oil prices were rapidly rising. It matters, too, that Malaysia's income per capita was roughly three times that of Indonesia's.

There can be no doubt that intervening variables such as these have a direct bearing on whether a country will seek to stabilize rice prices above or below world prices and the extent to which it can it can afford to provide subsidies to farmers. The focus here is on *how* governments sought to achieve their policy objectives given these structural economic constraints. Put differently, given the economic circumstances they faced, why did they choose the policy techniques or instruments they did? And more specifically, what does the institutional configuration of politics have to tell us about the choice of instruments?

Thailand

Rice production has long been a central part of the Thai economy. Unlike Malaysia or Indonesia, Thailand was able to enjoy easy expansion of output through the 1950s and 1960s on the basis of its underutilized land. So important was rice to Thailand in the post-World War II period that taxes on rice exports loomed large in the country's fiscal profile, constituting 32 percent of budget revenue in 1953 but declining steadily to just 7 percent by 1969 as other sources of revenue grew in importance (Panayotou 1989). As might be expected, during the early era of authoritarian politics the core priorities for rice-pricing policy were clear: collecting tax revenue and ensuring that consumer prices for the urban elite in Bangkok were neither too high nor too volatile for fear of the economic and political consequences. Price stabilization was a relatively straightforward matter, involving the imposition of export taxes and quantitative controls at the border that were adjusted to keep domestic prices comfortably below world prices. There was little consideration given to boosting farmer income during this early period.

By the early 1970s, however, several important aspects of this picture were shifting. First, the global food crisis of 1972–74 brought the whole question of rice-pricing policy much more sharply into focus. Second, rice taxes had become a minor part of budget revenue. Third, although there were bumps in the road, authoritarian government was replaced by democratic government; from 1973 onward, elected politicians became pivotal in policy-making. Following a coup in 1976, a military regime again came to power, but this was short-lived. From 1978 onward elected politicians were integral to all governments, initially in a power-sharing arrangement with the military and appointed officials and then on their own, with a brief interruption following another coup in 1991.

Pinning down the key elements of the institutional framework of Thai politics during this period is a particularly slippery task, as the framework was undergoing continuous evolution. If we set aside the brief return of strongly authoritarian politics in 1976–78, a stylized sketch of the reasonably democratic years on either side of this would highlight several features. First, Thailand had a parliamentary system of government, but one that featured two fully functional chambers (even if the Senate was unelected). Another key feature that separated Thailand from the classical Westminster (or British) model of parliamentary government was the electoral system: although Thailand did have the plurality (or simple majority) vote-counting rule, instead of having a single member of parliament for each electoral district, Thailand frequently had two or three members per district.

This seemingly mundane fact is often overlooked, but carries very important implications. Instead of tending toward a small number of strongly disciplined parties, Thailand's electoral system encouraged multiple and weak parties. The key to this result is the fact that multimember districts with plurality voting pit members of the same party against one another. Because of this, politicians are unable to differentiate themselves and campaign on the basis of party affiliation and so have to develop personalized strategies that tend to center on the delivery of services and benefits to voters and opinion leaders in their districts.[11] By contrast, in the classical British model, there is only one seat per district to be contested, so parties field only one candidate, as illustrated here by the Malaysian case. Accordingly, candidates tend to campaign on the basis of party affiliation, striving to deliver broader public goods-type policies to voters rather than divisible benefits.

Thus, Thailand had a bicameral parliamentary system in which there were many weak parties. Governments were constructed on the basis of shaky multiparty coalitions; the Prime Minister faced constant battles to hold a coalition together. Ministers (and members of parliament more generally) were encouraged under this system to pursue strongly pork-barrel-style policy measures. This contributed to and was reinforced by the widespread pattern of vote buying in a number of rural areas.

As to Thailand's approach to rice price stabilization, a number of earlier studies (Ammar 1975; Ammar and Kanok 1985; Ammar and Suthad 1989; Panayotou 1989) have provided careful explanations for the country's economic performance in this area. Apart from their operational effectiveness, the striking feature of Thailand's price-stabilization efforts is their disjointedness.

---

[11] The key work in this area on Thailand is important new research being undertaken by Allen Hicken, a doctoral student at the University of California at San Diego. For development of the wider logic of electoral systems that promote intraparty competition, see Cox (1984, 1987) and Carey and Shugart (1995).

A range of taxes was deployed to counterbalance fluctuations in world prices. The Ministry of Commerce collected a tax known as the rice export premium. This was the heaviest of the export taxes and was regularly adjusted in response to global market conditions. The Ministry of Finance collected a separate flat 5 percent export duty. A third tax was the rice reserve requirement, whereby exporters were obligated to sell a varying amount of rice to the Government at below-market prices for every ton of rice exported. This tax was also administered by the Ministry of Commerce and along with being an effective stabilization instrument, it was also nominally used as a modest consumer subsidy for the Bangkok market. A fourth de facto tax instrument was the requirement that all exports be licensed, enabling the Ministry of Commerce to impose quotas.

In 1974, in the wake of the global food crisis and the emergence of democratic government in Thailand, the management of rice export taxes was overhauled as part of the Farmers' Aid Act—a major legislative reform passed by the newly invigorated parliament. Henceforth, although the Ministry of Commerce's administration of the rice premium was formalized, it effectively lost control of the tax, since adjustment of the premium now required Cabinet approval. The revenue raised from the premium was channeled into a special nonbudgetary fund, the Farmer's Aid Fund. Control of the Farmers' Aid Fund was given to the Ministry of Agriculture for the purpose of assisting farmers (of which more below).

Because of these changes, the management of price stabilization shifted. In this case, the end result was the same—effective price stabilization—but with a very different confluence of policy preferences. Prior to this, the Ministry of Commerce had clear leadership in pricing policy and the export premium was its principal instrument. Now the approval of the Cabinet was required to vary the level of the premium, thus shifting the decision-making authority to a loose coalition of diverse and competing political parties, as well as such members of the military and the wider bureaucracy as were included in the Cabinet at the time. Whether the Commerce

Minister could persuade his Cabinet colleagues about a particular export premium adjustment depended on the vagaries of his party's standing in the shifting politics of coalition government, In addition, he had to contend with the entry of a new player, the Ministry of Agriculture.

Denied flexible control of its traditional instrument for price stabilization, the Ministry of Commerce increasingly relied instead on the rice reserve requirement. As Ammar and Suthad (1989) explain, had it not been for the Ministry of Commerce's loss of control of the premium tax, the rice reserve requirement might well have been allowed to wither in the 1970s, since its role in subsidizing Bangkok consumers had become largely a charade. Nevertheless, it quickly became the lead instrument for shielding domestic prices from global fluctuations until its eventual abolition in 1982, in the face of the collapse of global commodity prices and a wider process of economic liberalization. The rice export premium was removed in 1986.

If the primary effect of Thailand's political framework on rice price-stabilization efforts during this period is the disjointed nature of policy interventions, the impact of policy initiatives for farmer income support is more striking and more consequential. In broad terms, a rice-exporting country would usually be reluctant to maintain domestic prices above the world level, as to do so would entail a net fiscal burden, regardless of how the price support was implemented. Nonetheless, the Thai Government from the mid-1970s directed increasing efforts to support for farmer income. This came at a time when rice prices were declining sharply, as were rice export taxes, which fell to just 4 percent of budget revenue in the 1970s and 2 percent in 1982 (Panayotou 1989). At least in part, the efforts were an immediate result of elected politicians' coming to hold executive power (Ammar and Suthad 1989).

Two income support initiatives deserve special attention: rice price-support schemes and subsidization of farmers via the price of the principal industrial input, fertilizer. In the case of the former, a floor price for paddy had in fact been in place in Thailand since 1966, but it was rendered irrelevant because it was set below the market price. In the early 1970s, the market price moved below the floor price, but the floor price still had negligible impact, since the volume of rice procured was too small to influence the domestic market price. With the coming of democracy in the mid-1970s and increased attention to farmer welfare (read: rural constituents), increased (but fluctuating) support for a meaningful floor-price program could be seen. This intensified in the early 1980s with the collapse of commodity prices and the emergence of real hardship among farmers.

The fragmented nature of government in Thailand was reflected in the choice of instruments and implementation of the rice price-support schemes. Rather than a standard procurement and stockpile operation, there was variation, depending on whether the Minister of Agriculture or the Minister of Commerce was designated as the lead player (and which parties controlled these ministries). If Agriculture was in the lead, it bought up rice from millers using a parastatal agency under its control called the Marketing Organization for Farmers. Conversely, if Commerce was in charge it bought up rice from millers using its preferred parastatal agency, the Public Warehouse Organization. During 1981–82, political competition between the two ministers (who were from different parties) was so strong that *both* agencies were involved. Agriculture would fund its operations from the premium revenue in the Farmers' Action Fund, while Commerce would fund its operations from the proceeds of official government-to-government rice trade (supplemented by the rice reserve requirement).

More notable than this disjointedness, as Ammar and Suthad (1989) demonstrate, is that the procurement was not conducted in a way designed to defend a floor price or to benefit farmers. In order to maximize the public profile of the price-support program, the funds available to support procurement were recycled in locations scattered across the country, with the result that the purchased stock did not exert any significant upward pressure on prices. The principal beneficiaries of such rents as were to be had were rice millers rather than farmers.

Why should this be so? Bear in mind that the focus here is on how Thai policymakers chose to use resources, rather than the level of resources or the efficiency with which they were deployed. It is not that senior Thai policymakers were unusually venal or incompetent. Their actions directly reflect the incentives of the political framework in which they operated. As noted above, Thailand's electoral system strongly discouraged politicians from campaigning on the basis of party reputation and strongly encouraged them to generate policies that provided for divisible goods that could be delivered to particular electorates. Rice millers were among the leading economic figures and vote mobilizers at election time in many rural districts (indeed, a number were also members of parliament), so they were natural allies for politicians with rents to award. These were not rents being transferred from farmers to urban consumers. These were public (though nonbudgetary) resources being transferred to politically influential constituents in rural districts.

A parallel story can be seen in the history of direct subsidies to agricultural inputs. Fertilizer subsidies are the typical instrument for direct transfers to rice farmers. Thailand began to subsidize fertilizer, which had previously been subject to significant taxes, under the Fertilizer Act of 1975, (a parallel initiative to the Farmers' Aid Act of 1974). Under the auspices of the Ministry of Agriculture, the fertilizer was distributed through the Marketing Organization for Farmers. The subsidies only affected about 13 percent of the fertilizer sold and amounted to 35 percent of the wholesale price, but Panayotou (1989) reports that less than half of the rent was actually received by farmers, with the rest again being captured by local intermediaries.

The clear point is that this is not a simple story of corruption and administrative leakage (though, no doubt, those were present too). The pattern of rent creation and distribution is strongly consistent with politicians responding to the incentives of an electoral system based on multimember districts with plurality voting. Thailand was unlikely to spend much on farmer income support, but that policymakers should choose these instruments over others reflects the impact of the specific institutional framework of politics then in place. Policymakers could, after all, have opted for a more universalistic or public goods-type method of income support much more simply by easing export taxes slightly. Recall that it was revenue from export taxes (via the Farmers Action Fund and the government-to-government sales of the Public Warehouse Organization) that was funding the rents that were nominally to be distributed to farmers. Policymakers did not opt for a direct nondivisible transfer via lowering export taxes. Nor did they simply steal all the rents themselves. Instead they opted for a strategy that would transfer rents to local power brokers in various electorates. This outcome was a direct consequence of the specific form of Thailand's political institutions

Malaysia

Malaysia is a rice importer with a long history of State intervention in rice markets to promote price stability and protection for rice farmers, as well as direct measures to support rice-farmer income. From 1970, State intervention rapidly intensified, with levels of direct and indirect support for the rice sector becoming very high by the mid-1980s. As in Thailand, the institutional framework of politics helped shape the choice of instruments adopted by policymakers, although these choices differed from Thailand's as a result of Malaysia's different political architecture and socioeconomic circumstances.

Ethnic politics have been a powerful factor in Malaysia's political economy: deep Malay sensitivity about the economic dominance of the ethnic Chinese has been a major determinant of the behavior of Government. At the same time, with the exception of the brief but powerful upheaval of Malaysian politics as a result of the race riots of 1969, competitive elections have been a constant and fundamental element of the country's political architecture. Political authority in Malaysia is much more concentrated than in Thailand. This is not just a function of the tight political controls that have accumulated since the 1970s (Crouch 1996). As compared to Thailand, the parliamentary structure and electoral system of Malaysia tend to generate much stronger and more centralized governments. Not only is executive authority concentrated in one chamber of parliament (rather than spread over two) but the electoral system of single-member districts with plurality voting tends to produce fewer, more coherent, and more strongly disciplined political parties. In this regard, even allowing for its ethnically-based coalition of parties, Malaysia exhibits the core features of centralized, British-style Westminster parliamentary government. Thus, provided a prime minister continues to command majority support with the dominant Malay party, the United Malays National Organization (UMNO), his powers are great and far-reaching.

Two other important institutional features require amplification. In stark contrast to Thailand, Malaysia's electoral system, when combined with its parliamentary government, *did* encourage politicians to campaign on the basis of party affiliation. Where Thailand's electoral system forced members of the same party to compete against each other, thus placing a premium on their ability to deliver particularistic goods to constituents, Malaysian politicians faced far fewer pressures of this sort. This does *not* mean that patronage systems and rent-seeking behavior were rare in Malaysia; the literature on Malaysia's political economy is replete with accounts of patronage and rent-seeking activities in the rural sector (Scott 1985), in the industrial sector (Gomez and Jomo 1997), and in politics more generally (Crouch 1996). But it does mean that the political system was less heavily geared towards enabling politicians to generate divisible rents. In short, in *relative* terms, Malaysia's system of government was institutionally more disposed to generate public goods and to allocate rents in a broader-based fashion.

Also significant is that, according to most observers, Malaysia's electoral boundaries were redrawn to increase the number of electoral districts in rural areas, thereby strongly favoring the largely-rural, ethnic Malay voters (Crouch 1996). Quite apart from the advantages this conferred on particular political parties (principally UMNO), it also forced the Government to be more responsive to rural Malay interests than it might otherwise have been. Along with being rural, rice farmers are almost all Malay.

As to the specific issue of rice price stabilization, Malaysia, like Thailand, has been quite successful at stabilizing domestic rice prices. But where Thailand stabilized prices below world prices, Malaysia—except for years of unusually high world prices—stabilized its prices *above* world prices. The bias has thus been clearly and consistently in favor of rural producers at the expense of urban consumers.

Since Malaysia was and is an importer, the stabilization task was daunting. The year after the traumas of the 1969 race riots, a major review of rice policy was undertaken; it resulted in refocused and intensified market interventions. One immediate result of this overhaul was the creation of a new superagency, the National Paddy and Rice Institute (LPN from its Malay initials), that centralized all existing stabilization measures. Until then, the key stabilization instruments had been a rice stockpile and a floor price. Once the international price hikes of 1973–74 eased, the LPN began to use these instruments much more aggressively. The floor price was raised and the LPN began to soak up a growing share of local production. The LPN bought paddy either directly from farmers or as rice from millers, provided the mill could demonstrate that it purchased the paddy at the guaranteed floor price. Previously, the impact of the floor price and the stockpile had been undercut by rice imports by private traders. To overcome this problem, beginning in 1974 the LPN monopolized all rice imports, enabling it to enforce an effective floor price above world prices.

The LPN was also granted wide-ranging, and in some instances draconian, regulatory powers (Fredericks and Wells 1983). In addition to controlling farm-gate and border prices, it also set wholesale and retail prices. The effect of these price controls was to squeeze private millers and traders. Further pressure was applied on private operators during the 1970s, when the LPN entered into direct competition with millers and traders by rapidly expanding the number of public integrated milling operations. In 1969 there were four State-owned mills; in 1982 there were 31 (Pletcher 1989). With the expansion of its own direct milling operations, the LPN bought up an increasing share of domestic production. Between 1973 and 1985, the private sector's share of the paddy market fell from 88 percent to 54 percent (Tamin and Sahathavan 1988). With an import monopoly and fixed domestic prices, price stabilization could now be achieved by administrative decree and budgetary subsidy. Henceforth, the stockpile ceased to be a stabilization instrument and became primarily a strategic reserve for food-security purposes.

The LPN's import monopoly and domestic price controls, together with its expanding share of the paddy market, implied a growing subsidy from consumers and the Malaysian Treasury to rice farmers. Hardest hit by these measures were the Chinese millers and traders forced out of the market by the expansion of the LPN's activities (Jenkins and Lai 1991). An intriguing puzzle, which ties back directly to discussion in the first half of this chapter concerning the efficiency implications of different policy measures, is why the Government chose to intervene so heavily in rice milling itself. Although no solid explanation is offered here, a number of hypotheses come to mind. Was it simply a function of ethnic politics and the Government's desire to redistribute wealth from the Chinese to the Malays? Was it a function of Malaysia's having a porous border with Thailand and thus being vulnerable to smuggling? Or was it a function of Malaysian paddy being of generally low quality and LPN having to pick it up itself because the market would not set a politically acceptable price?

In the area of farmer income support, the Government's pricing policy clearly had important implications for farmer income. In spite of the substantial subsidies to farmers via the floor price system and other direct subsidies and income-support measures, the incidence of poverty among rice farmers remained stubbornly high through the 1970s. The number of rice-farming households below the official poverty line at the end of the 1970s was higher than for the rural sector overall and very much higher than the national average (Pletcher 1989).

With the second oil boom in 1979, fertilizer prices began to rise rapidly. To prevent this from accentuating the poverty problems among rice farmers, the Government intensified its efforts to provide direct assistance. In this, it was of course greatly aided by the fact that Malaysia was an oil producer. Without doubt, the most important of the Government's farmer income-support measures was the Paddy Price Support scheme introduced in 1980. In effect, this was a supplement to the subsidy provided through the floor price for rice. In January 1980 the Government announced that there would be an automatic bonus of M$2 per *pikul* (60 kgs.) of rice sold.

The launch of this program was badly mishandled, however. Under the original plan, the M$2-per-pikul subsidy was to be transferred to farmers via a coupon for deposit in a long-term savings account with a government bank. This, it was thought, would both boost farmer income and aggregate savings. However, the immediate market reaction was for millers and traders to cut the prices they offered farmers by M$2 per pikul. This triggered farmer outrage and on January 23, in the largest political unrest since the 1969 riots, some 10,000 farmers demonstrated in Alor Setar. The protest was contained only by the use of tear gas and the imposition of a curfew. The protest was notable both for the sharp reminder it provided to the Government about conditions in the rice sector and for the fact that the demonstrations took place in the home district of the deputy prime minister (soon to be Prime Minister) Dr. Mahathir Mohammed. Dr. Mahathir and the UMNO leadership generally were particularly sensitive to the possibility of PAS, a Muslim-based Malay opposition party, making electoral inroads amongst Malay rice farmers.

The protests forced the Government to redesign the program and, in the process, raise the value of the bonus to M$10 per pikul and make it cashable immediately. Once in operation, the Paddy Price Support program amounted to a very substantial subsidy to farmers (Pletcher 1989). Reviewing government interventions in the rice sector over several decades, Jenkins and Lai (1991) conclude that it was not until the Paddy Price Support scheme was introduced that farmer incomes increased significantly.

Other policy instruments provided subsidies to inputs. The most important was the fertilizer subsidy (others included agricultural chemicals, cultivation machinery, and, less directly, drainage, irrigation, and rice research). The Government had experimented with a number of fertilizer subsidies, but the most focused initiative came in 1979 in response to the jump in market prices for fertilizer. Coming at the same time as the Paddy Price Support program, this new initiative provided a 100 percent subsidy: fertilizer was free up to the requirements of the average rice farm (2.4 hectares). For the 1979–82 period the value of this subsidy was estimated to be M$211 per hectare—making it a significant bonus for farmers (Pletcher 1989).

Malaysia's interventions to support farmer income during this period, like its pricing policy instruments, were very intensive. This is consistent with the broad character of Malaysia's political economy at the time: strongly interventionist policy measures launched in the name of building up local economic capabilities and of redistributing income and economic opportunities in favor of the Malay population. But within this context, how do Malaysia's political institutions tie into this policy outcome? We have seen how in Thailand the political architecture produced very weakly coordinated interventions and predisposed politicians to seek policy measures that generated divisible rents. Malaysia's demographic and political architecture encouraged different, indeed opposite, outcomes.

Regardless of their very different economic circumstances, the types of policy action taken by Malaysia in rice pricing and farmer income support would have been very difficult to carry out in Thailand, given its often shifting party coalitions. Policies such as Malaysia's required solid, sustained political consensus on issues having major fiscal and distributive implications. Malaysia's highly centralized system of Government was very "permissive": it made it relatively easy for the Government to take strong and decisive policy action on these issues. The LPN was invested with high-level political and economic backing from the Malaysian Government and given a clear and strong mandate to stabilize prices and support farmers. Malaysia's electoral system encouraged fewer and much more cohesive political parties, which greatly increased the executive autonomy of the Government. This effect was intensified by the fact that Malaysia's upper house of parliament had no effective veto authority. In short, the heavy centralization of authority arising from the political structure meant that there were few institutional constraints on government action.

There is a third and subtler dimension to this. As noted earlier, the combination of parliamentarism and single-member electoral districts with plurality voting places a very much lower premium on the ability of politicians to deliver special pork-barrel type benefits to their constituents. This is typical of Westminster systems: politicians campaign primarily on the basis of their party affiliation. By contrast, Thailand's different electoral system meant that party affiliation was of much less significance and that politicians were typically forced to rely on their own independent electoral strategies. It is not surprising therefore that the policy instruments adopted by Malaysia, both to control prices and to support farmer income, were more arms-length or universalistic in nature. By design at least, rents were to be distributed broadly across the rice sector.

This is not to suggest that all farmers benefited equally or that there were not real problems of rent diversion through State agencies. Indeed, it takes little imagination to sense how much inefficiency was built into many of the LPN's operations (Tan 1987). There is also certainly evidence of some subsidies being slow to reach some areas or of village officials discriminating against farmers known to be PAS supporters (Scott 1985; Jenkins and Lai 1991).

Clearly, while the Malaysian and Thai policy measures differ starkly, the choice of policy preferences in both countries was strongly shaped by the institutional framework in which the policymakers functioned. In Thailand, the whole logic of the policy instruments was to permit the distribution of discreet and selective benefits to particular districts. Malaysia's political architecture did not predispose the country to such an orientation. Rather than being determined by the framework of Government, the preferences of Malaysia's political leaders are exogenously determined by a range of factors, including economic circumstances and ethnic politics.

Indonesia

From the 1970s to the early 1980s, Indonesia was an importer of rice (although it became self-sufficient in rice in the mid-1980s). Having exhibited very strong urban bias in its policy towards the rice sector in the 1950s and 1960s, from the 1970s on the balance was gradually reversed until, in the early 1980s, domestic rice prices moved above world prices. The path Indonesia followed during this period was perhaps the most challenging in policy terms of the three country cases considered here. The Indonesian Government intervened in the market strongly and directly, but in a manner that was reasonably market-conforming in important respects. In broad terms, its stabilization record was marked by success, except for a few exceptional years (such as 1973–74) when the Government lost control of prices. Like Malaysia, Indonesia was also very active in the area of farmer income support.

Indonesia's political architecture was, without question, the most heavily centralized in this sample of countries. Electoral competition was a much less potent constraint on government behavior than in either Malaysia or Thailand. At the center of the Indonesian political framework stood a very powerful presidency: because of the way the political laws were constructed, President Suharto had little to fear from other institutions of government. Nor did he have to bargain with the legislature, since he had formal control over the leadership and membership of all parties. Similarly, he had no need to worry about bureaucrats with loyalties divided between the executive branch and the legislature. And not only was the presidency not subject to direct elections, the whole presidential appointment process was carefully stage-managed, with the President himself effectively appointing more than half of the body (the legislature) responsible for appointing him. More broadly, the President enjoyed far-reaching powers of appointment, as well as extensive monitoring and oversight mechanisms. In short, none of the "problems" often associated with presidential systems—legislative gridlock, control of the bureaucracy, etc.—pertained in Indonesia.

Further, as with parties and the legislature, interest groups were also heavily centralized and controlled, officially organized under a vast and elaborate corporatist, or State-dominated, network. In an effort to contain political demand-making by societal actors, interest groups were, in effect, regulated by the State. An official State-sanctioned organization existed for each sector or industry and virtually all were formally organized under the wider political umbrella of the corporatist State political "party," GOLKAR. And GOLKAR itself of course came under the direct control of the President. In sum, this was a massively centralized political system, with a supremely powerful presidency (MacIntyre [forthcoming]).

The final aspect of Indonesia's political framework that requires some comment was the pervasive presence of patronage relations, the informal and personalized self-help and political-exchange relationships that were often indistinguishable from simple cronyism and corruption. Although these problems were by no means unknown in Thailand or Malaysia, it is not surprising (even if unverifiable) that Indonesia should be seen as being much more prone to this pattern of political representation and exchange. In political systems where the electoral mechanism is weak or nonexistent, patron-client relationships usually proliferate. As is now well understood, this typically results in widespread diversion of public resources, as officials from the top to the bottom of the political hierarchy seek to capture rents created by regulatory initiatives for themselves and their networks of supporters.

Being a massively centralized state, Indonesia unsurprisingly was thoroughly permeated during this period by personalized patronage networks.

If the position of the Malaysian Prime Minister was considerably stronger than that of his Thai counterpart, the position of the Indonesian President during this period was stronger still. Indonesia's political architecture was the most permissive of all; Indonesia exhibited the fewest institutional constraints on executive action in this sample of countries. This is not to say that the President was subject to *no* constraints on policy action: he did need to maintain the support of the armed forces, he did need to avoid food riots or mass discontent, and (as has recently been graphically illustrated) he did need to maintain the confidence of local and foreign investors. But these were not institutional constraints. The critical point about the architecture of Indonesia's political system is that it afforded the President enormous freedom of policy action.

As to the specific issue of rice-price stabilization, it is immediately apparent that the Government played a pivotal role. The policy instruments employed were a monopoly on imports and exports by BULOG, as well as the maintenance by BULOG of a national rice stockpile used to support a floor price for farmers and a ceiling price for consumers. BULOG stabilized farm prices from fluctuations before and after the rice harvest and protected consumers against fluctuations in world prices. Importantly, however, BULOG worked very much with and through the private sector. In Indonesia, there was no strong policy drive to squeeze out Chinese millers or traders. During the 1970s, BULOG procured between 2 and 5 percent of domestic production, a figure that rose to 10 percent in the 1980s (Ali 1986). Contrast this with the figure for Malaysia, which approached 40 percent in the early 1980s, and for Thailand, which was around 5 percent. All the rice that BULOG did buy up for its stockpile was purchased through the network of farmer cooperatives spread throughout rural Indonesia.

In addition to maintaining a much smaller rice stockpile than Malaysia, Indonesia managed it in a different way. Market forces played a greater role. Unlike the LPN in Malaysia,

BULOG did not fix prices rigidly. They were reviewed more frequently and the pricing calculations in setting them were more complex because of the large role allowed for private millers and traders in the food system. The size of the stockpile was constantly being adjusted upwards or downwards depending on price pressures at the production and retail levels, with international trade operations making up the difference as necessary (Timmer 1993). BULOG did not attempt to displace the millers or wholesalers and retailers.

In common with Malaysia, however, BULOG received very high-level political support. In the late 1960s it was completely overhauled and beefed up for the urgent task of reining in rice prices. It was given substantially increased economic resources as well as priority political attention. BULOG came to be headed by an influential general who had easy access to the President and all the key economic ministers. As in Malaysia, key pricing decisions were not made without top-level political guidance. Arguments about appropriate levels for BULOG's floor and ceiling prices would be made before the President by the heads of relevant agricultural and economic agencies, with the President then making a determination (Timmer 1993).

The consideration of the impact of political institutions on the management of price stabilization measures in Indonesia has a number of interesting dimensions. First, as in Malaysia, it is apparent that the heavily centralized nature of the political system greatly facilitated the task of bringing together the necessary economic and political resources to make such a massive enterprise possible. Such a complex and multidimensional undertaking was enormously facilitated by the ability of the President to direct that diverse resources be focused on the task. Such an undertaking would have been extremely difficult in a political system such as Thailand's, in which executive authority was spread across a shifting coalition of players.

Also interesting is the decision to adopt a model that, although having a large role for the State, nonetheless relied heavily on the actions of private actors. Why did Indonesia not adopt the more statist approach of Malaysia? After all, in broad terms, Indonesia's economy during this period was more heavily regulated than Malaysia's.

There are a number of factors that appear to have been at work here, including Indonesia's searing economic experiences with socialist-style economics in the 1960s and the influence of the World Bank in the early days of President Suharto's regime. Also important, however, was a dimension of institutional politics that has not been discussed at length to this point: administrative capacity. The anticipated political costs of failure in rice stabilization were extremely high. The ethnic sensitivities about the role of Chinese middlemen in rice markets were no less strong in Indonesia than in Malaysia. This was overlooked, however, in part because of a recognition that the Government simply did not have the administrative capacity to ensure that it could manage the process efficiently on its own. Rice price stabilization was too politically important to be allowed to fail. Accordingly, one reason why Indonesia did not proceed along an even more heavily interventionist policy path of the sort Malaysia did was because the country's administrative capacity was simply not up to the task.

The final factor to be noted here is the decision to use the farmer cooperatives as a key actor in the implementation of the price-stabilization scheme. Technocratically inclined officials in economic agencies such as Finance, Economic Planning (Bappenas), and even BULOG would have preferred to buy directly from farmers rather than work through the cooperatives. President Suharto, however, was insistent on the role of the cooperatives. Although the reasoning behind this strategy is inevitably speculative, his choice was very much in keeping with the logic of the country's vast corporatist network of representative organizations. Although typically passive or even idle bodies in terms of articulating and advancing collective member interests, these corporatist organizations were an integral element in the overall framework of political management in Indonesia. They both served to contain independent sectoral demand making and also promoted support for GOLKAR at election time. Of all sectors of society, rice farmers were the last that the Government wished to see become politically active or outspoken; the Communists had been able to attract widespread political support among farmers in the 1960s and the Government was desperate to avoid this happening again. Insisting that the rural cooperatives be involved in the marketing of rice was an effective way of maintaining the corporatist structure for managing interest-group activity and channeling support towards GOLKAR.

Turning from price stabilization to the issue of support for farmer income, the broad picture roughly parallels that in Malaysia. From the early 1970s and then particularly in the late 1970s and the 1980s, the Indonesian Government directed very considerable resources to support the incomes of rice farmers, with a view to making rice farming a more profitable undertaking (and thereby lifting production) and to redressing the income imbalances between rural and urban areas. Various measures were adopted, including cheap credit and subsidies on seeds, water, pesticides, fuel, and machinery. As in Malaysia, the largest subsidization effort was directed at fertilizer. Fertilizer subsidies grew through the 1970s on the back of the oil boom, rising very rapidly from the late 1970s. Between 1977 and 1984 the total value of the fertilizer subsidy rose from 32 billion rupiah to 732 billion rupiah (Hill 1996). Use of fertilizer by farmers picked up quickly: per hectare use in irrigated rice grew by 12 percent annually between 1972 and 1983, reflecting, as Timmer (1989) notes, both heavy subsidization and a distribution system capable of getting the fertilizer to farmers effectively. The fertilizer was produced by a State enterprise, PT Pusri, and, from the late 1970s onward, distributed in rural areas primarily by private traders, though the cooperatives and a State-owned rural distribution company also had considerable involvement, particularly during the early years of rice intensification.

Indonesia's remarkable success during this period with both price stabilization and income support for rice farmers has been the subject of much acclaim. Implicit in such acclaim is surprise that these huge undertakings did not become ensnared in the usual web of problems involving patronage, cronyism, administrative leakage, and corruption that came to characterize so many areas of State activism in Indonesia during these years.

Why is it, for instance, that the rents attaching to the fertilizer subsidy did—in large measure—make it through to rice farmers? Certainly this was not true of subsidies to other areas of agriculture or indeed, to the industrial sector; typically, they were largely captured and diverted. Why was support for rice farmer income different? Or, one might equally ask, why was BULOG's rice price-stabilization program run on a remarkably technocratic basis when other parts of its operations (such as the wheat, sugar, and soybean monopolies) were notorious rent-seeking operations?

The answer to this question that is most often heard is that Suharto was determined to avoid a resurgence of rural radicalism and political instability of the sort that had gripped the country in the mid-1960s—in short, that the success of these initiatives was a function of his keen political survival instincts. There is much to accounts of this sort; undoubtedly this extraordinary feat of effective State intervention could not have taken place if it had not been powerfully in the President's interests for it to do so.

But again, as has been consistently emphasized in this discussion, political interests are only part of the story. Also integral was the institutional framework of politics. The massive concentration of authority in the office of the President gave him the ability both to focus resources intensely on this policy challenge and to monitor it closely. There is no reason to believe that BULOG officials and others scattered down through the hierarchy from Jakarta to the districts were more public-spirited than any other officials. They did not make a special exception for rice and restrain normal rent-seeking practices out of any sense of commitment to the national good. Rent-seeking and theft were contained at relatively low levels because it was universally understood that this was a high priority of the Government's and that any significant meddling would be a risky undertaking, possibly inviting severe sanctions from above.

There is of course an irony here, for in large measure it was the very centralization of power that gave rise to the President's ability to monitor and deter large-scale rent-seeking in the rice sector. This circumstance in turn also contributed directly to the persistence of the patron-client-type political behavior that had given rise to the high risk of diversion and capture to begin with. Further, it may seem odd to suggest that the massive centralization of power in Indonesia helped to produce an economically efficient and equity-enhancing outcome, yet empirically there is no other plausible explanation for the rents' not being diverted as they were in other countries.

Models for understanding the dynamics of heavily centralized political frameworks are less well theorized than are models for political systems with competitive elections. One innovative foray into this area is the work on corruption by Shleifer and Vishny (1993). MacIntyre (1999) has applied this to Indonesia to show how the country's very heavily centralized political framework enabled the President for many years both to allow corruption to flourish and to "contain" it at levels that were tolerable to investors. Put simply, on matters of very high priority, the strongly centralized framework of Government in Indonesia gave the President the ability to deter serious transgressions and abuse in policy implementation by virtue of his ability to monitor that implementation and to punish offenders. Plainly, however, rice (along with a few other areas of very high priority) was the exception rather than the rule in Indonesia.

Political Institutions and Agricultural Policy: Lessons for Policy Analysts

Policy analysts have always known that "politics matter." Taking politics into consideration in the design of programs, however, has been much more difficult. The aim of this section has been to make the challenge of incorporating political realities into program design more tractable. To this end, it has attempted to push beyond the familiar and very general ideas associated with the urban-bias thesis. Specifically, the central proposition advanced here is that by focusing on the structure of political institutions in a country—the national political architecture—it is possible to obtain powerful insight into the incentives and choices available to policymakers.

It is standard practice to examine the economic incentives of market actors when designing food policy and agricultural development programs. Indeed, it is widely accepted that failure to take account of economic incentives is likely to doom a program. The argument here is that this same logic needs to be extended to include consideration of the political incentives of policymakers. By and large, international development agencies cannot escape working with and through governments. Yet little attention is routinely given to such incentives.

The handling of price stabilization and farm income support has been examined in three countries in order to demonstrate the powerful incentives that differing political and institutional frameworks exert on policymakers, shaping their approach to a problem and the types of instruments they select to deal with it. A critical part of the reason why policymakers in different countries handle common problems in different ways is that the political frameworks within which they function put different pressures on them.

Little research has been undertaken on the impact of political institutions on agricultural policy making in Asia, so this discussion is illustrative rather than definitive. Nevertheless, the insights of this approach are strong and its relevance to policy and program formulation is obvious. There has been no attempt to demonstrate all the possible ways in which different political and institutional configurations constrain policy behavior. That is a very much larger enterprise and is the subject of an emerging body of scholarly research. Nevertheless, some strongly indicative examples of the impact of institutions have been provided. It is clear, for instance, that the making of coherent policy is much more difficult when authority is dispersed among a large number of institutions. It is also clear how and why some political frameworks place a much greater premium than others on policies that generate divisible and targetable rents. This analytical approach could readily be extended to cover the extent to which authority is delegated from national to local units of government, the ways in which the bureaucracy is structured, and the extent to which the legal system is empowered to review and pass judgment on the actions of government.

The general lesson is that in order to maximize the effectiveness of their policy dialogues and the likelihood of efficient program outcomes, international agencies must have due regard for the institutional framework of government. Of course, institutions are not everything: a policymaker's preferences—what he or she *wants* to do—will have a prior bearing on what he or she seeks to do. But the preferences of policymakers in any given country are forced through an institutional filter that exerts a powerful and, more importantly, predictable, bearing on what they *can* do. As research in this area advances, the ability to predict the policy consequences of institutional configurations can only grow (Haggard and McCubbins [forthcoming]).

It makes little sense to proceed as if all policymakers, whether they are politicians or the officials who support them, function in a standardized operating environment. They simply do not. Indeed, national political frameworks vary widely. To ignore this is to doom policy recommendations and program initiatives to a highly intermittent or patchy impact. It is unrealistic to think that policy recommendations or programmatic initiatives can be tailored perfectly to the political framework of every individual country. Nonetheless, some movement in this direction and some sensitivity to the institutional context in which policymakers function is likely to yield an appreciable increase in the social and economic return on development interventions.

VII Rural Human Capital

"Economists have long known that people are an important part of the wealth of nations. Measured by what labor contributes to output, the productive capacity of human beings is now vastly larger than all other forms of wealth taken together. What economists have not stressed is the simple truth that people invest in themselves and that these investments are very large."

—Theodore W. Schultz (1961)

"There is an intimate and transparent relation between investments in human capital and the alleviation of poverty."

—Gary S. Becker (1995)

RATIONALE FOR STATE INTERVENTION

The three previous chapters examined the most conspicuous components of Asia's green revolution: seed, water, fertilizer, and grain marketing. Rural development depends on more than land and agricultural technology, however. Human capital—the intellectual and physical capacities, skills, and knowledge of the rural population—will be crucial in several areas of rural development. Just to take one example, Chapter IV explained how disembodied knowledge is coming to set the pace of agricultural growth: as agricultural markets diversify and the profit-seeking private sector takes center stage as a marketer and disseminator of technology, farmers must be able to evaluate the costs and benefits of alternative crops and commercial inputs more critically and, based on their knowledge of the natural resource base, to apply inputs appropriately.

In addition, as agriculture's share of national income declines, changes in the *stock* of human capital will influence the pace of the economic transition to nonagricultural sources of growth. The *distribution* of human capital will determine the equity of this transition. In contrast to Asia's agricultural development, which, because of the green revolution, was largely scale-neutral and, on balance, pro-poor,[1] Asia's rural poor have generally lagged behind in the development of human capital.

Finally, the physiological and social aspects of human capital—health, life expectancy, and the sophistication and richness of the individual's interactions with society—are essential elements of the quality of life. In addition to being important in their own right, they will underpin the completion of the demographic transition, which is critical to the sustainability of Asia's future development. The demographic transition involves the move from high to low human mortality and fertility. Usually (but not always) mortality declines first, with the result that population growth rises until a matching decline in fertility occurs. The age distribution also influences population growth. Although many Asian countries have achieved significant declines in fertility, their populations continue to grow rapidly because of the concentration of the age distribution within the reproductive years as the result of past high fertility while child mortality was declining.

Fertility began to decline most noticeably in East Asia in the late 1950s; the decline accelerated throughout the region in the 1970s and continues today at widely varying rates in different regions. It constitutes one of Asia's most remarkable

---

[1] Detailed discussions of the equity impacts of the green revolution and of gender and other social issues in rural Asia are contained in the respective companion volumes in this Rural Asia series by Rosegrant and Hazell (1999), and Bloom, Craig and Malaney (1999).

socioeconomic phenomena and reflects a variety of forces, none more important than lower child mortality and greater female education. Lower mortality means that parents do not have to have so many children in order to ensure that a given number survive to adulthood. Education has encouraged higher labor-force participation by women, their later age at marriage, and, for both sexes, greater desire to control birth spacing and better receptivity to, and knowledge of, family planning practices.[2] As is true in other aspects of Asian development, however, the underlying social and economic determinants of fertility decline have been weaker in rural areas than in the more rapidly growing towns and cities.

Purely market-based approaches to human capital development are unlikely to be optimal from the standpoints of either equity or growth. In part, this is because education and health care share the dual character of private and public (or merit) goods. They also embody closely interlinked externalities. From society's point of view, education provides a more adaptable and productive work force that is able to move with the times and adjust to technological change. Similarly, improved and more secure health allows people to play a fuller role in the economy by helping them become a more active and reliable work force. Historically, governments have recognized this. As measured by the public shares of total health and education financing, the Government's role in human capital development tends to increase with national income (World Bank 1993b and 1995). Note, however, that this does not preclude expanded, vibrant contributions by the private sector, including community-based organizations, in the provision and financing of these social services.

As seen in the previous chapters, it is appropriate, as economies develop, for the private sector to take greater responsibility in areas such as agricultural technology,

---

[2] Schultz (1993) provides a powerful statistical analysis of the relationship between female education and fertility in a cross-country sample of developing countries. Sanderson and Tan (1995) review the Asian fertility decline, concluding that effective family planning programs make a significant contribution *if* the inherent demand for birth control exists.

marketing, and water management. While advocacy has been largely eschewed so far in this volume, this chapter argues that enhanced government roles are needed to redress a number of biases in human capital development:

- Considerable attention is devoted to the inherent *urban bias* in the provision of many social services that promote human development.
- Closely related to this, there is, in general, an *anti-poor bias* in access and quality; indeed, this bias so cuts across sectors that the rural-urban distinction is often blurred in the discussion.[3]
- Society's traditional norms also lead to *gender bias* in access to education, health care, and good nutrition, which is reflected in lower educational attainment and higher mortality for girls than for boys.
- Finally, because of the inherent vulnerability of children, there is *age bias*. Lower child mortality has been a major Asian accomplishment, but it nonetheless remains true that more than seven million mainly poor and underprivileged preschool children die each year of largely preventable causes (ADB 1999a). Many millions more have their futures diminished by malnutrition, illness, and retarded intellectual growth. Despite the progress in improving the aggregate food supply, child malnutrition remains unacceptably high in many countries. Mounting evidence demonstrates that interventions to promote early child development—encompassing nutrition, health, and psychosocial growth—can have a high economic return and contribute profoundly to poverty alleviation in the long run.

---

[3] It must be admitted that part of the blurring is due to the paucity of data that disaggregate education, health, fertility, and so on, by rural and urban area. Lee (1998) provides statistics on education and literacy by gender and rural-urban residence for a few of ADB's member countries. The Appendix provides aggregated social statistics for a larger number of countries.

TRENDS IN EDUCATION AND HEALTH

In Asia as a whole, education and health services have improved significantly over the last few decades, reflecting the rapid economic progress of the region. Primary schooling levels have risen dramatically, with enrollments approaching 100 percent in many countries. There has also been considerable expansion of secondary and tertiary education. In health, there have been major improvements in the provision of facilities, particularly hospitals, as well as in the harnessing of innovative technologies to bring about massive immunization campaigns. Measles immunization alone has saved a half-million lives a year during the last decade (ADB 1998). Mortality rates have declined considerably in the last 35 years. The average Asian can expect to live more than 40 percent longer, about 66 years in 1997 as compared to 46 years in 1960.

These changes are not uniform across countries, however. East Asia has advanced more than Southeast Asia, and far more than South Asia. East Asia had achieved nearly 100 percent primary schooling even before its economic takeoff, but South Asia has not even come close. With the notable exception of Sri Lanka, one half of all South Asians cannot read, as compared to just one eighth of Southeast Asians. In health, differences among regions and individual countries are just as large. Fueled by income growth, East and Southeast Asia have advanced rapidly, but even relatively poor countries like Viet Nam, the PRC, and Sri Lanka have made dramatic strides in improving their health systems by investing their limited resources in countrywide primary health care. South Asia, however, still has a major share of the world's malnourished children, together with infant and preschool mortality rates are among the highest in the world outside of sub-Saharan Africa. In Cambodia and the Lao PDR, war devastated the already weak health systems, and mortality rates remain high.

In Central Asia, the breakdown of social services has been one of the most glaring areas of collapse since the dissolution of the former Soviet Union. The world's experiments in central planning proved economically unsustainable, but nonetheless excelled in the mass provision of social services. Sadly, in many cases, these services have not survived the economic decline and the privatization of State enterprises, including farms. Many children now face a bleak future because of restricted access to education and other social services during their childhood and considerably more uncertain employment opportunities when they reach adulthood (Bauer et al. 1998). Life expectancy in Central Asia actually declined during the 1990s.

Within countries, there are significant differences among regions and income groups. In the PRC and Indonesia, for instance, one can see very different education and health standards between the more isolated, resource-poor provinces and those that are better-endowed. The poorest counties of the PRC have infant mortality rates three times higher than the national average. Similarly, the incidence of infectious disease and mortality are usually far higher in the lowest income groups than in the population as a whole (ADB 1999a).

Besides these broad regional differences, five interrelated features of education and health development can be observed. First, Asia's income growth has been a driving force in both sectors. Both for the direct utility they provide and as longer-term investments, consumer willingness to pay for education and health care usually grows rapidly with income, as illustrated in Table VII.1 with household expenditure data from Indonesia. In the case of health care, not only does total expenditure grow rapidly, but the composition of demand moves away from traditional and public services in favor of modern private providers.

Second, in response to consumer demand, the private sector has grown rapidly as a provider of education and health services. In education, where community roles have long been important in much of Asia, recent for-profit private investment has been greatest at the secondary and tertiary levels. In Indonesia, for example, some 40 percent of secondary-school enrollment is now in private schools; in the Philippines, 85

Table VII.1. Household Expenditure Elasticities for Health Care, Education and Printed Media in Indonesia, 1996

	Rural	Urban
Total Health Care	1.49 (.99)	1.32 (.96)
Private facilities (traditional)	0.98 (.90)	0.31 (.48)
Public facilities	1.56 (.97)	1.12 (.94)
Private facilities (modern)	2.33 (.98)	1.85 (.92)
Reproductive Health & Immunization	0.95 (.95)	1.02 (.97)
Medicines & Vitamins	1.23 (.99)	1.26 (.99)
Education	1.19 (.99)	1.24 (.99)
Newspapers, Magazines & Books	2.79 (.95)	2.78 (.94)

Notes: Elasticities show the percentage change in per capita expenditure on each item with respect to a 1-percent change in total household expenditure per capita. Estimates were derived from grouped expenditure data, with observations weighted by each group's population share. Figures in parentheses are R-squares.
Source: derived from data in Indonesian Central Bureau of Statistics (1997).

percent of tertiary education is privately funded. Similarly, private provision of health services has grown rapidly.

Third, as alluded to above, there is a marked urban bias in the availability of these services. Most tertiary education facilities are located in the cities, which have no significant shortage of schooling at the primary and secondary levels, as there is in rural areas. Similarly, hospitals are numerous in the cities, but health facilities are both scarcer and less well-equipped in the countryside. The urban bias has several causes. Naturally, it is much cheaper on a per capita basis for governments and the private sector to serve densely settled urban and periurban areas than it is to accommodate isolated rural populations. For the Government, it is also politically advantageous. Even more important, the income growth that justifies private investment has been most rapid in the towns and cities.

Fourth, because the private sector inherently responds to opportunities for private profit, some of Asia's most pressing social needs are being neglected. Primary education, primary health care, many poor and disadvantaged groups, and the rural areas in general have benefited relatively little from private-sector investment. As will be seen below, however, community groups and nongovernment organizations (NGOs) are becoming increasingly involved in education and health; this is redressing the urban and anti-poor bias to some extent.

Following from the above, a fifth feature is the changing role of the Government in both sectors. Satisfying the growing demand for secondary and higher education, and for health services, entails rapidly escalating costs, particularly in providing modern health technologies. The Government has limited capacity to satisfy all the demands directly. Hence, as the substitution of public- and private-sector provision takes place, three responses are required by the State. First, the Government will have to regulate the private sector, particularly in the area of health care. Second, the Government will need to reconsider its comparative advantage in providing the services. If the Government's goal is to maximize social welfare, then its comparative advantage may lie in serving those niches of the "market"—i.e., poor and bypassed regions and social groups, particularly girls and women—for whom limited consumer wherewithal and persistent social biases prevent a satisfactory market response. Third, since the communities that are increasingly expected to pay must participate actively, the Government must find ways to encourage local participation in the design and management of social services.

THE PROVISION OF EDUCATION

The great diversity of Asian societies, cultures, and educational systems precludes "cookie cutter" approaches to education development. Education, particularly basic education, does not simply provide specific literacy and numeracy skills; its function is also to impart the cultural, moral, and, often, religious and political values of society. Besides the wide variety of cultures, there is wide diversity in the organizational arrangements for public and private education across Asia. Hence, it would be ill-advised to generalize about the design of specific interventions in the education sector; appropriate interventions must be context-specific. Nonetheless, it is both possible and fitting to generalize about the fundamental access and quality issues arising from rural-urban inequity, poverty, and gender biases. Some countries and regions have grappled with these issues very well despite having relatively low per capita incomes, notably Sri Lanka and Kerala state in South India. Much can be achieved when equity is made the prime objective.

In general, the present focus of education development varies among countries depending on their stage of overall economic development. In the high-income economies of East Asia, which achieved high attendance in primary schools relatively early, the recent emphasis has been on tertiary education. Elsewhere, notably in the lower-income countries of Southeast and South Asia, the primary and secondary levels are still emphasized, although it is nonetheless true in many countries that a disproportionately large share of public funding goes for tertiary education. Although there are exceptions, public funding of education has increased rapidly in many countries (Figure VII.1), growing significantly as a share of total government expenditure in Asia overall between 1980 and 1992 (Lewin 1998). On average, education accounts for about 12–15 percent of total government expenditure in Asia, and is often the largest sectoral allocation in many government budgets.

Except for the most elite social groups and aside from community-based, largely religious training, the provision of primary education has overwhelmingly remained the responsibility of the Government. Even though the schools are publicly owned and managed, however, households pay a substantial share of the total cost of primary education in the form of fees, transportation, books, and uniforms, which amount to 10–15 percent of total education costs in Indonesia and Mongolia, and 50 percent or more in Viet Nam and Cambodia (Bray 1998). Household contributions are even greater at the post-primary levels.

The involvement of the private sector has grown most rapidly at the tertiary level. At present, the private sector provides about one third of higher education in Asia (Mingat 1995), but this has been largely urban-oriented. As the basis for improving public-sector policies, two key

Figure VII.1. Central Government Expenditure on Education as a Share of Total Government Expenditure

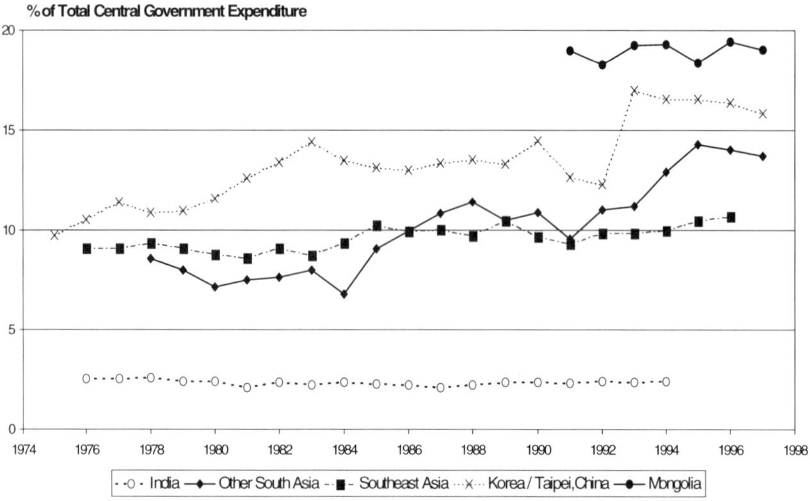

Notes: Other South Asia includes Bangladesh, Nepal, and Sri Lanka. Southeast Asia includes Indonesia, Malaysia, and the Philippines. Grouped countries are weighted by GDP.
Sources: data compiled from (all various years) ADB Statistical Database System; ADB *Key Indicators of Developing Asian and Pacific Countries*; and IMF, *Government Finance Statistics Yearbook*.

dimensions of rural disadvantage must be recognized: *access* and *effectiveness*. In turn, the search for better ways to provide education requires a digression on the issues of financing, efficiency, decentralization, and management.

Access

Who is getting, and who is not getting, access to education? This is among the most fundamental questions in assessing the performance of an educational system. At present, it is clear that most rural populations are not getting adequate access for a number of interrelated reasons:

- *Physical facilities and distance.* The per capita costs of providing schools for widely dispersed rural populations are high. Thus, with the principal exception of Central

Asia,[4] there are not enough rural schools and existing schools are too distant for many children to reach. It is usually economic to build secondary schools, which need to be larger and better equipped, mainly in urban or periurban areas.
- *Lack of affordability.* Public schools may be nominally free, but poor families, whether rural or urban, cannot afford the incremental costs of books, uniforms, and so on. Given the seasonality of many rural activities, even relatively well-off rural households may not have cash for school expenses at certain times of the year.
- *Gender bias.* Girls, particularly in traditional rural societies, often find it difficult to attend school for religious or other cultural reasons. When money for schooling is limited, parents tend to give priority to boys.
- *Parental preferences.* In traditional communities, parents may not be convinced of the value of schooling, particularly for girls, who usually make an economic contribution to the household even at a very young age. In addition, during peak seasons of the agricultural calendar, parents need to have their children working on the farm rather than attending school.
- *Culture and language bias.* The caste system of India and Nepal has traditionally restricted access to schooling by the poor, although, to its considerable credit, India has made a substantial effort over the last three decades to improve the socioeconomic lot of the "scheduled castes." The combined effects of parental preferences, gender bias, and ethnic exclusion tend to be most severe in isolated or mountainous regions of rural Asia. For example, some Nepalese ethic groups tend to see education as being irrelevant to their socio-

---

[4] Basic education and health facilities were traditionally a core part of the social infrastructure of all State farms in the former Soviet Union. However, many of these facilities went into disuse in the aftermath of farm privatization and the overall macroeconomic decline in the newly independent countries.

economic conditions (Barjarcharya et al. 1997); similar attitudes characterize the hill tribes of Indochina. Even if there is motivation, the lack of curricula and instruction in local languages, particularly in isolated areas, is often an effective barrier to access.

Effectiveness and Quality

As measured by educational outcomes—school completion rates and learning accomplishment—the effectiveness and quality of teaching and school facilities are generally lowest in rural areas. Teaching materials and curricula are often irrelevant to rural needs, while facilities are unconducive to learning. Poor quality is a "push" factor contributing to the high percentage of dropouts in Asia's primary schools, both rural and urban. The sad result is that many primary school students leave school without functional literacy or numeracy. Although improvements are gradually occurring, about 30 percent of Indonesian and Philippine children who enter Grade 1 fail to finish Grade 6. The problem is even more severe in South Asia. Among the factors that diminish educational effectiveness and quality:

- *Poor physical conditions in schools.* Many rural schools lack electricity, toilets, potable water, and even chairs and walls. Overcrowded, chaotic classrooms are common. In such conditions, pupils neither learn well nor want to continue their schooling.
- *Poor quality of instruction.* Poor teacher training and low salaries are the main causes. While these failings also exist in urban areas, they are compounded in rural areas by the fact that teachers are reluctant to remain in the countryside because of the hard conditions. Inevitably, the best leave. The majority of primary school teachers in Bangladesh and Laos have no formal training. If they have training, it is difficult for

them to upgrade their skills through further in-service training. In Pakistan, teachers earn less than unskilled workers and enjoy few chances for promotion (Warwick and Reimers 1995). Thus, it is not surprising if teachers, particularly in primary schools, lack mastery of the subjects they are teaching, have limited teaching skills, and are frequently absent. In linguistically diverse countries, teachers assigned to rural schools may not even speak the language of their pupils.
- *Centrally determined and nationally oriented curricula.* Adaptation to local conditions is rare. Curricula, textbooks, and teaching materials usually have an inherent urban bias, making the examples used and the particular skills taught less relevant to rural children. Overly complex, standardized curricula are often not understood in rural areas or even aligned with the available textbooks. Rural students perform less well on national examinations based on such curricula. This, in turn, affects their ability to continue on to secondary school, even when one is available.
- *Scarcity of appropriate textbooks.* Even when produced, transportation and distribution problems limit their use. Libraries are bare or nonexistent. In many cases, books are unsuitable for local use because they reflect only national or otherwise socially dominant languages. Some countries allow the use of local languages in lower primary grades, but the cost of producing local-language textbooks for small numbers of students is often prohibitive.
- *Lack of supervision and monitoring.* This problem is especially prevalent at the lower levels of the educational system. In some cases, educational officials, including inspectors, visit rural schools only once a year (Chapman 1998).

Improving Access and Quality

Remedying the lack of rural schools is complicated by constraints on public funding and the general lack of private-sector interest in investing in rural areas. Simply providing more schools is not even the best way out if the schools continue to be of low quality. Satellite and multigrade schools are alternative approaches to improve access to education in thinly populated rural areas and allow a rationalization of public expenditures. Satellite schools at the junior secondary level can be set up in villages surrounding the town where the main school is situated. Multigrade schools are suited to rural areas with small populations: each teacher teaches more than one grade, thus reducing the total number of teachers needed. However, this approach can only work if there are extra teacher training, salary incentives, and other resources.

Lower-cost strategies can be employed. Primary among these is distance learning, since most rural areas now have access to radio and television. With the rapidly declining costs of computer hardware, educational software and the Internet should, at least in Asia's middle-income countries, be aggressively exploited to truly revolutionize the accessibility, effectiveness and quality of rural education. Unfortunately, poor countries, and rural areas generally, are usually not yet equipped with the necessary infrastructure and other resources to use the most modern technology in a sustainable fashion.

Where isolation and ethnolinguistic differences are severe constraints to school attendance and learning, there may be little option but to produce curricula and textbooks in local languages if minority groups are to be enabled to study. Nepal, the PRC, Viet Nam, and Papua New Guinea (PNG) are already including the production of curricula in local languages in their national educational planning. Better-designed and more flexible curricula that reflect rural and other local conditions are also feasible. Many improvements in access and effectiveness can and are being achieved through greater involvement of NGOs and local communities, as well as better education management, about which there is further discussion below. Where parental attitudes are a constraint, public information campaigns to convince parents of the value of schooling could improve access to education in general, and for girls and isolated ethnic groups in particular.

To improve education quality and effectiveness, it is necessary to begin by considering the capacity of the student. Hungry or malnourished children who suffer from illness or chronic parasitic diseases are more likely to attend school irregularly, to repeat grades, and to perform less well overall. The health of the incoming student is thus a crucial complementary input in any educational system. Indeed, the issue of early childhood development is of such importance that a later section of this chapter is devoted to it.

Quality will also be improved by providing better teachers through more thorough pre-service and in-service training and better incentives and conditions of service for rural teachers. Rural Asians have educational needs that are inherently different from those of the urban population. These were reflected above in the various constraints faced by the rural population in accessing traditional, formal types of education. More attention should be given to preparing teachers to meet the special needs of rural communities. Indeed, rural education should be recognized as a legitimate subfield for education research and training. Better materials, libraries, and more time spent in classroom instruction and homework are also known empirically to be significant determinants of school achievement (Fuller and Clarke 1994, cited in World Bank 1995).

Improving these education inputs should be a priority goal, but with funding constraints there is necessarily a trade-off between access and quality. Confronted with this choice, most Asian countries have apparently opted to improve access by building more rural schools, albeit poorly equipped with material and human resources. Thus, part of the solution requires a much greater concern with education *outcomes*—the actual skills and capacities imparted to school leavers—rather than with the mere numbers of schools and students. From an economist's perspective, finding ways out of the dilemma requires consideration of allocative efficiency in the use of scarce resources, both public and private.

Resource Allocation, Efficiency, and Mobilization

The fundamental problems of education in Asia do not merely reflect financing constraints, since public and private budgets, including household contributions, are all growing rapidly.[5] Clearly there are also fundamental allocation and efficiency issues. The relatively affluent urban population has benefited most from improved access and quality in public and private education. Public education subsidies for primary schooling tend to be pro-poor (World Bank 1995), but, because relatively few poor children are enrolled at the higher levels, subsidies to secondary and higher education—where costs per pupil tend to rise sharply—overwhelmingly benefit the upper-income groups. To redress this inequity, the challenge for the public sector will be to rank social priorities, critically analyze the returns to alternative education investments, and then decide what the Government can and should fund in light of what is likely to be funded privately. Consideration must also be given to improving the effectiveness of education so that the available resources, whether public or private, have maximum impact.

Returns to Education as a Guide to Resource Allocation

Empirical support for a greater emphasis on primary education comes from a body of studies that estimate the rates of return to education investment via the statistical relationship

---

[5] Data on trends in real total expenditure *per student* would substantiate this point, but there are no time series on private enrollments or on private and household education expenditures. Moreover, the data that exist do not permit any comparison of trends in rural and urban areas, for which spending increases in the latter are suspected to have almost literally left rural areas in the dust in most of Asia.

between education, age (reflecting years of work experience), and income, net of the opportunity costs of time spent in school. Table VII.2 formed the empirical cornerstone of a recent World Bank review of education in the developing countries (Psacharopoulos [1994], cited in World Bank [1995]). The estimated social and private returns to education investment are highest at the primary level, clearly implying that resources should be concentrated on primary education. Because the social rates of return adjust primarily for public subsidies to education, they are invariably lower than private returns. The returns to education are generally highest in the poorest countries and decline with national income, a plausible "production function" result given the much greater investment in education in the developed countries. Overall, these estimates provided, in the World Bank's view, powerful evidence in support of strategies focused on primary and lower secondary education.[6] Moreover, since the private returns to education are so high, it is quite reasonable to expect the recipients to contribute to the cost.

The figures presented by Psacharopoulos are compelling, but they are not without their critics, who note that there is wide cross-country variability in the estimated returns to primary and secondary education. In addition, because many of the country studies used by Psacharopoulos were based on data collected well in the past—often two decades or more—the estimated returns to education may not reflect current demands for different skills in the labor market. The estimates are in many cases biased upward by omitted variables (e.g., student ability and self-selection biases) and the failure to consistently incorporate factors such as the opportunity costs of time spent in school, the leakage costs of school dropouts, and the probabilities of unemployment or nonparticipation in the labor force (Bennell 1996a and 1996b; Bray 1998).

---

[6] This emphasis is toned down somewhat in the World Bank's most recent education strategy paper (World Bank 1999), which would target basic education interventions more specifically on the poor and on girls, particularly in South Asia and Sub-Saharan Africa.

Table VII.2. Internal Rates of Return to Investment in Education by Region and Level of Schooling (in percent per completed school level)

	Social			Private		
Region	Primary	Secondary	Higher	Primary	Secondary	Higher
Sub-Saharan Africa	24.3	18.2	11.2	41.3	26.6	27.8
Asia	19.9	13.3	11.7	39.0	18.9	19.9
Europe/Middle East/N. Africa	15.5	11.2	10.6	17.4	15.9	21.7
Latin America/ Caribbean	17.9	12.8	12.3	26.2	16.8	19.7
OECD	n.a.	10.2	8.7	n.a.	12.4	12.3

Notes: The above figures, synthesized by Psacharopoulos (1994) and reproduced in World Bank (1995), average some 78 sets of individual country estimates. OECD comprises the developed-country members of the Organization for Economic Cooperation and Development. Estimates for Asia and Europe, the Middle East, and North Africa exclude OECD member countries. "n.a." indicates not applicable.

The counterargument is that returns are, in fact, downwardly biased because it is impossible to quantify many of the private and social benefits of education, including improved health, lower fertility, the intergenerational benefits passed on to children (all other things being equal, children whose parents have better education tend themselves to achieve higher education and income), and the external effects of a more adaptable labor force and more socially-responsible individual behavior. Moreover, while the criticisms may justify caution in interpreting the absolute magnitude of the estimates, they fail to deflect convincingly the conclusions that education is a sound private investment and that the returns to education are especially high in the low-income countries. At least within Asia, where the results summarized by Psacharopoulos were quite consistent across countries (Bennell 1996a), returns are highest at the lower educational levels.

Given public financing constraints, a shift of funding toward primary schools would entail a reduction in subsidies to largely urban-based secondary and higher education and, perforce, require greater reliance on user fees at the higher levels. Mobilizing political will for such a reallocation of resources will be a challenge for Asia. Measures to attract additional local funding and to encourage the private sector to take a larger role in post-primary education are also warranted. Decentralization and greater community involvement could contribute positively both to efficiency and effectiveness by reducing the aggregate administrative costs of public education and by fine-tuning educational programs and curricula to meet local needs. Decentralization has its caveats, however (see below).

Efficiency and Effectiveness of Public vs. Private Schools

A further challenge is to make the education system more efficient while raising, or at least maintaining, its effectiveness. Here, "efficiency" is used in the traditional economic sense of the amount of various inputs (e.g., teacher hours) needed to produce a given output (e.g., one school graduate). "Effectiveness" is related to achievement and quality (e.g., the graduate's literacy score). The two concepts are interrelated but not interchangeable: "efficient" does not necessarily imply "effective," or vice versa. Moreover, both concepts are relative rather than absolute. All other things being equal, educational efficiency can be improved by reducing the unit cost of producing a school graduate of a given "quality." Particularly at the primary level, teacher salaries tend to be the major component of school costs, so efforts to optimize pupil-teacher ratios and the actual classroom time of teachers will improve efficiency, as will reductions in the wastage caused by students who drop out or repeat grades unnecessarily. Changing these parameters will require improving teacher motivation and performance and making schooling more attractive for students and their parents, both of which entail the need for additional investment in education quality. It will, in many cases, also require greater delegation to local school administrators of responsibility for school resource management.

Privatization has been widely espoused as the best way to promote efficiency in many economic sectors, so it is logical to ask whether this could be true of education as well. Factors that would potentially underlie greater relative efficiency of private schools include their more stringent management, greater accountability to parents, and greater cost-effectiveness in recruiting teachers (e.g., fewer long-term social obligations) and in choosing curricula and materials. At the same time, one could hypothesize that the private sector's natural inclination to minimize costs would tend to sacrifice education quality.

To test the relative efficiency and effectiveness of public and private schools in the developing countries, various analysts have assembled data on student socioeconomic background, school expenditures, and education effectiveness as measured by student performance on standardized tests, usually at the secondary level. Table VII.3 summarizes some of the results of this research. In five studies synthesized by Jimenez, Lockheed, and Pacqueo (1991), private schools were found to operate at lower unit cost, as measured by the schools' total expenditure per student (the single exception being the elite and relatively expensive "F-type" schools in the Dominican Republic). After controlling as well as possible for student background and socioeconomic characteristics, the private schools were also found to have, in many cases, a significant advantage over public schools in terms of student achievement. The authors concluded that, for their sample at least, private schools were superior in efficiency and effectiveness.

However, in examining the data on school and teacher characteristics, they could find little consistent cross-country evidence to explain why private schools have such an advantage. Teacher salaries and qualifications, pupil-teacher ratios, school facilities, and curricula all varied too widely for meaningful patterns to emerge. Unfortunately, many of the studies relied on data that were originally collected for purposes other than the comparative analysis of efficiency and effectiveness (Jimenez, Lockheed, and Pacqueo 1991).

Riddell (1993) provides a critique of these and similar studies, concluding that because of data and methodological limitations, they have failed to adequately capture the complex interactions between student characteristics and the

Table VII.3. Cost-Effectiveness of Public and Private Secondary Schools in Selected Countries, early 1980s

Country	Sample (Schools/ Students)	Achievement Indicator	Ratio of Private to Public Unit Cost[a]	Relative Achievement Advantage[b]
Columbia	129/1,004	Average math and verbal	0.69	1.13
Dominican Republic	76/2,472	Math, F-Type [c]	1.46	1.47
		Math, O-Type	0.65	1.31
Philippines	n.a./446	Math	0.83	1.00
		English	0.83	1.18
		Filipino	0.83	1.02
Tanzania	57/1,124	Average math and verbal	0.69	1.16
Thailand	99/4,030	Math	0.39	2.63

Notes: Source: Jimenez, Lockheed, and Pacqueo 1991. [a] Based on school expenditure data. [b] Estimated statistically, this is the expected relative gain in achievement score if a randomly selected student, having the characteristics of the average public school student, attends private rather than public school, holding constant the student's background. [c] The more prestigious "F" schools are authorized to give Ministry of Education examinations; "O" schools are not. "n.a." indicates not available.

organization, financing, teaching, and learning processes in different schools. In addition to the factors that complicate rates-of-return analysis, such as a student's innate ability and socioeconomic status, analysts have been unable to control for the strong peer group effects of schooling: a student's performance is strongly affected by the behavior and performance of his or her classmates. Riddell argues that, if adequately modeled, peer effects might reduce or even reverse the apparent advantage of private schools.

Overall, then, these studies provide an intriguing indication of the possible advantages of *private schools*, but they do not provide a firm foundation for a policy of *school privatization*. Hence, even if the greater efficiency of private schools could be substantiated—a hypothesis that warrants more systematic research—efforts to improve public education and to better focus the use of government resources may be a preferable strategy from the standpoint of access and equity. After all, private schools may improve access and educational outcomes for those who can afford the fees, but this brings little direct benefit for those who cannot.

Even within the domain of public funding, there are several possible ways to exploit the private sector's greater potential efficiency. One approach involves continued public financing of education, but with the provision of services to be contracted to the private sector. In addition, a number of countries have had some success in introducing education vouchers that allow families to choose between public and private schools. Alternatively, local communities, provided with central government grants and tax incentives, could supervise the recruitment of teachers and monitor their performance. For such solutions to be sustainable, local capacity for decentralized management needs to be strengthened, as does government regulatory capacity. All these approaches would also require a willingness to innovate on the part of Asia's often highly centralized education ministries.

New Approaches for Mobilizing Education Resources

Between the extremes of financing education solely by either the central Government or the private sector, other funding sources can and should be mobilized. Alternative approaches, some already being applied in individual countries, need to be explored:

- *Community support should be mobilized.* Although exceptions can be found and gender bias remains pervasive, by and large rural Asian parents see education as the key to their children's future. Consequently, local communities are often willing to support rural education in a variety of ways. Communities not only help set up and run rural schools; they also provide interested local groups that will help maintain quality. In Bangladesh, for instance, communities run 22 percent of the rural primary schools that are not *madrasah* (Islamic schools usually run by ministries of religious affairs). In Cambodia, communities, faced with the collapse of government support, run some 75 percent of primary schools. The Government of Pakistan has engaged in formal coproduction with village organizations to set up

community-based schools with support from the Aga Khan Foundation: about 250 local groups have received modest endowments (about $2,000) to establish schools, conditional upon the village organization's providing a room, recruiting a local female teacher, and establishing a local education committee (World Bank 1996b).
- *NGOs*, including religious organizations, have long supported rural education in many countries. Notable examples include the Bangladesh Rural Advancement Committee, which provides primary education to thousands of rural girls. In Indonesia, Islamic groups run many rural *madrasah* schools, which follow the State curriculum in addition to providing religious instruction. India, Pakistan, and the Philippines provide further examples. NGOs can play a useful role in the future, particularly where community interest is strong. They should be both encouraged and suitably monitored.
- *Local taxes* may be earmarked specifically for education and would be highly complementary to programs to decentralize education (see below). The use of local taxes is most prevalent in the PRC, where education taxes are levied on a variety of sources, including farmers, government employees, and state and collective organizations (Lewis and Wang 1994). Burgess (1997) argues that broad-based indirect taxes such as value-added taxes are probably most sustainable. Whatever the form, it is important to ensure that the tax is specifically earmarked for education and does not simply disappear into the general treasury. Moreover, to the extent that local taxes must replace central budgetary allocations, the dependence of education upon local revenues will be biased against relatively poor regions.
- *Entrepreneurial activities* can augment educational funding. Schools in Mongolia, for instance, keep flocks of sheep, while those in the PRC run cafeterias and

discos (Bray 1998). Tertiary institutions are, at times, quite creative in their financing methods: in India, central and state universities have a wide range of income-generating activities, including farms and printing presses (Tilak 1997). The risk of such activity, however, is that it comes to take precedence over a school's basic functions.

- *Long-term student loans* can, in principle, improve education access for the poor, particularly at the post-primary levels. Such loans also offer the distinct advantage of shifting the burden of cost recovery to the direct beneficiaries of education. In general, however, loan programs have entailed substantial administrative costs and large subsidies. Repayment rates have often been disappointing (Ziderman and Albrecht 1995).

Education Management and Decentralization

In addition to new financing approaches, improving rural education will require the rationalization and strengthening of education management, including a clearer delineation of responsibilities,[7] improved relevance of curricula and teaching materials, the setting of clearer standards for measuring educational outcomes, the introduction of performance monitoring systems, and the recruitment, training, and retention of higher-caliber staff. Administrators have to understand and deal with new technology and information systems, and with the new private and community actors in education. Management capacity has not kept pace with the

---

[7] In countries as diverse as Cambodia and Kazakhstan, responsibility for education does not always rest with one ministry, but may be distributed across several ministries that do not coordinate well. Even within unified education ministries, multiple offices may have overlapping jurisdiction in specific areas, e.g., girls' education in Indonesia. In addition, there is often no clear delineation of functions between the various levels of management, with national, provincial, and district offices often duplicating functions (Chapman 1998).

rapid expansion of educational systems in the last decade. Indeed, little administrative training is provided to headmasters, who thus have trouble managing the available resources effectively. In a world where the actors and the technology are changing rapidly, administrators have to keep pace. Management deficiencies are a general concern in the education sector, but isolation and the generally low level of capacity particularly affect rural schools.

Under the proper circumstances, decentralization could also contribute to better rural and local education by allowing greater community involvement (see Chapter III). Numerous countries are decentralizing many educational services for political as well as educational reasons. While this should allow greater community participation and make educational systems more responsive to local conditions and needs, decentralization is not necessarily an optimum course. It requires much greater responsibility and accountability from teachers, headmasters and local government administrators, many of whom lack the relevant training and experience. The Government must also retain overall responsibility for regulation and quality control. In relation to financing, decentralization may increase inequity if the burden of costs is shifted entirely to local communities. For example, Lewin and Zhao (1993) have shown that in the Philippines, scarcity of resources after decentralization, together with inadequate management capacity, have weakened the effectiveness of local secondary schools as compared to national and private schools. Similarly, recent articles in the international press have dramatically highlighted the inequities of decentralization in poor inland regions of the PRC (see, for example, IHT [1999b]). In general, rural areas are relatively poor and rural public administrations may be particularly hard-pressed to find the necessary sources of new revenue.

Decentralization will make new demands on education management capacity at the local level. The strengthening of management capacity should begin before decentralization. Such strengthening should cover all activities related to the administration of educational programs, including planning and programming, personnel management, the operation and maintenance (O&M) of facilities, and monitoring and evaluation, both in individual schools and within the school system as a whole.

Nonformal Education

Rural people have many educational needs other than academically-oriented degree training. Many of these needs can be met through nonformal means that often lend themselves nicely to community-based or NGO approaches. Target groups for nonformal education include illiterate adults, women, dropouts from primary and lower secondary school, and farmers. Adult literacy programs can usefully be combined with basic health messages and may also include training in income-generating activities. Similarly, women and, indirectly, their families can benefit from nonformal training in child health care, nutrition, and family planning. Young rural people frequently fail to complete formal primary education because of economic pressures and the gamut of push factors discussed above in relation to access and quality. They could still benefit substantially from nonformal training so that they can achieve minimal standards of literacy and numeracy. Farmers also have a strong need for ongoing education in improved agricultural practices. Traditionally in most of Asia, this has been the responsibility of public extension services provided by ministries of agriculture, but it should nonetheless be seen as an important subcomponent of rural educational needs.

THE PROVISION OF HEALTH SERVICES

Over the past few decades, socioeconomic change in Asia has entailed two interrelated transitions in health care needs (ADB 1998). The first is epidemiological: there has been a gradual decline in the *relative* importance of infectious, communicable, and parasitic diseases that warrant the provision, at relatively low cost, of mass public goods by the Government. Growing in incidence are chronic, noncommunicable diseases related either to aging (e.g., cardiovascular disease and cancer) or individual behavior (e.g., smoking, drug and alcohol abuse), as well as sexually transmitted diseases such as acquired immunodeficiency syndrome (AIDS). In contrast to the first group of diseases, treatment of the latter entails largely private benefits and much higher per capita costs. In addition, there has been (largely during the 1990s) a disturbing emergence of new types of tuberculosis, malaria, and pneumococcal diseases that have proven resistant to standard forms of treatment. Considered largely under control just a few years ago, these diseases have potentially grave implications for Asia's poor and, therefore, warrant a renewal of government and international attention.

The second transition is demographic. As fertility declines and life expectancy improves, there will be a gradual aging of the population, which in turn will influence the composition of disease and, in the long run, lead to a higher dependency burden for cost recovery in health care.

Although most of Asia has been affected by these transitions to one degree or another, they are not occurring uniformly either among countries or, within countries, among population groups. This unevenness leads to a process of *epidemiological polarization*, which should increasingly focus the attention of policymakers in discussions about private- and public-sector roles in health development. Stout et al. (1997) describe the implications of this process succinctly (italics added):

> ...Health systems (*of developing countries*) must develop the capacity to deal with the high incidence of communicable diseases, primarily among rural and poor groups, as well as significant increases in adult health problems and noncommunicable diseases among the urban and wealthier populations. The epidemiologic transition brings not only polarization, but also prompts an important shift in the burden of disease... The combination of these shifts requires corresponding shifts in the services delivered through the health care system.

As with education, changes in the health sector reflect rising consumer demand, rapid growth of the private sector, the urban biases of access and quality, and a growing need for the Government to reprioritize its interventions. In the aggregate, Asia's income growth has had a positive impact on health, tending to improve nutrition, other living standards, and health awareness and knowledge, all of which have contributed to lower mortality and longer life expectancy. Widespread infrastructure development has included the construction of hospitals and clinics. Overall, health services have become more accessible. With higher incomes and improved availability of services, there has also been a shift in utilization patterns. The demand for health care has increased both quantitatively and qualitatively. People have come to demand more modern, professional, and institutional care in place of their earlier reliance on traditional medicine and self-care.

The changing awareness, preferences, and expectations of the public have two implications for public policy. On the one hand, the public is, potentially, a more constructive partner in health affairs and in local health-care development. This is particularly important in the case of primary health care, comprising essential preventive services, including communicable and infectious disease control and health education, together with basic, cost-effective curative services. Communities can now become involved in management, instead of just using the services, and in helping local health authorities with health information dissemination. At the same time, higher incomes and better facilities do not always lead to better-informed decisions by consumers. There is an emerging risk of excessive dependence on professional care and more modern, curative, but not always necessary, technologies, with inadequate attention given to more cost-effective measures, including disease prevention. The role of the Government in promoting good health is a topic that is discussed further below.

With all of these changes, governments are under pressure to reassess their health policies, particularly those relating to expenditures. As compared to education, government spending on health is lower and has grown less rapidly over time (Figure

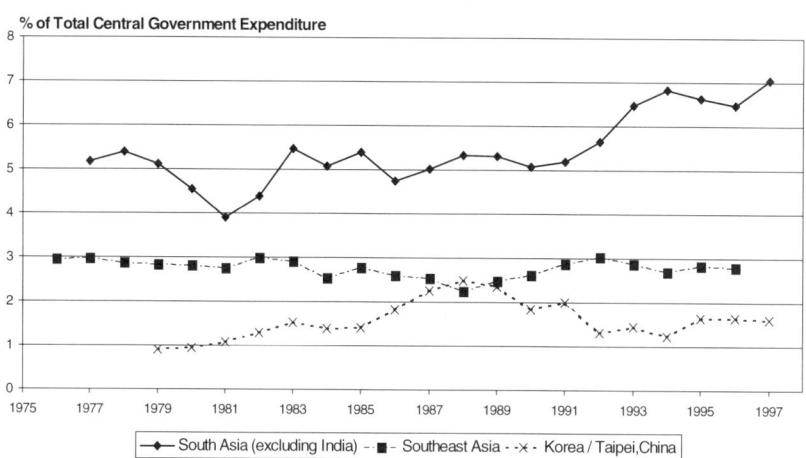

Figure VII.2. Central Government Expenditure on Health as a Share of Total Government Expenditure

Notes: Other South Asia includes Bangladesh, Nepal, and Sri Lanka. Southeast Asia includes Indonesia, Malaysia, and the Philippines. Grouped countries are weighted by GDP.
Sources: data compiled from (all various years) ADB Statistical Database System; ADB *Key Indicators of Developing Asian and Pacific Countries*; and IMF, *Government Finance Statistics Yearbook*.

VII.2). Moreover, public health spending has often been concentrated on interventions of relatively low cost-effectiveness, such as tertiary (hospital-based) care and cancer treatment, rather than critically needed and far more cost-effective interventions for primary health care and the communicable diseases (World Bank, 1993b). This reflects the pronounced urban, anti-poor bias in health expenditures: governments now spend 70 percent of their health budgets on hospitals, mainly in urban areas, and less than 15 percent on primary health care (ADB 1999a). Redressing these biases will require a reexamination of the roles of the public and private sectors in financing, in human-resource development, and in the provision of new technologies.

Reform in Public-Sector Financing

The focus of debate on the public sector's role in health is on how to contain growing government costs while at the same time achieving the goal of improved health for all. A number of interrelated approaches have been proposed. One is for governments to reduce subsidies that tend to be captured disproportionately by the better-off. In Indonesia, for example, it is estimated that the population's highest income quintile captures a larger proportion of public subsidies for outpatient and inpatient care than is received by the bottom two income quintiles combined (World Bank 1993a). Another is to let the private sector provide what are largely private health goods, namely curative and discretionary services, so that public funds can be focused more on ensuring access by the poor to primary health care. A third is to increase direct cost recovery from the beneficiaries of discretionary public health services. As with education, mobilizing the political commitment for these forms of resource reallocation will be a challenge for Asia.

User fees at public facilities are a logical means of rationalizing health services. Although seeming at first glance to restrict access by the poor, user fees may actually improve access by financing the provision of new services not previously available locally, thereby reducing the substantial costs often borne by the poor for travel to distant health centers. The World Bank (1993b) cites evidence that patients in India, Indonesia, and Viet Nam pay 2–3 times the low official fees at public health facilities in the form of transportation costs and the opportunity costs of time away from work. The collection of user fees in the Lao PDR, Myanmar, and Indonesia has also freed funds for support in other areas, such as the purchase of drugs by underfunded public hospitals.

Moreover, user fees serve an important allocative function by discouraging unnecessary use of public health services. If combined with targeted exemptions for the poor—a task easier said than done from the standpoint of efficiency—user fees need not be anti-poor. Thailand, for instance, has had a low-income card program for over two decades to help the poor with user charges. Although still far from perfect, the issuance of the low-income cards to eligible households has helped to ensure that the poor have access to essential health services.

If additional financial resources become available from user fees, they need to be accompanied by improvements in hospital and clinic management to ensure that adequate services are being provided. This requires better financial systems with proper auditing, better O&M of physical facilities, and a greater delegation of authority for hospital and clinic management, especially in remote rural areas.

Decentralization and Health

Changing the way the public sector deals with the population to which it provides health services through user fees and improved management may require some degree of decentralization. Decentralization has numerous implications for the organization of health systems, including the question of who should be providing health services as well as who should be paying for them. However, while some may argue that health care should be decentralized along with everything else, there is clearly a need to retain some centralized services (e.g., immunization) in order to ensure uniform national coverage and avert possible neglect at the local level.

Decentralization of social services thus presents a dilemma. On the one hand, decentralized decision making about the allocation of health resources should make it possible to meet local needs more effectively. On the other hand, how is the State to ensure that local governments continue to give primary health and other social services due priority and not allow them to sink below the horizon of political visibility? As was noted for education, decentralization can be inequitable if excessive costs must be borne by relatively poor communities. Moreover, any decentralization of health management must involve participation by communities to ensure that providers are responsive and accountable. Overall, the argument for decentralizing health services has more caveats than is the case with education and other public services. Considerable care is needed in designing and implementing any major health decentralization program.

Given the complexity of the decentralization issue, it is not surprising to see quite different approaches taken by individual Asian countries (Chapter III). The lessons from those countries make it clear that if decentralization of social services is going to work, full administrative authority needs to be given to local levels of government, along with adequate funds and training to build up the necessary capacity of staff to handle their new responsibilities. If decentralization is also intended to shift more of the cost burden to local governments, then poor regions are likely to need special central budgetary support to preserve essential services until such time as local revenues are sufficient for the task.

The Private Sector, NGOs, and Village Health Workers

The private sector is the major actor in Asia's health sector. With the principal exception of the transitional economies, private expenditure accounts for more than half of the total health spending in most countries (see the Appendix). A wide range of actors provides private health care. Doctors often work privately on a part-time basis outside of their regular employment in public health facilities. Private hospitals are mushrooming in many urban areas. Private providers also include pharmacies, traditional practitioners (e.g., midwives), NGOs, and other nonprofit organizations. Although often organized and given rudimentary training by the Government, village health workers offer voluntary services and may, therefore, also be considered part of the private sector. All of these actors serve social needs and reduce pressure on the public budget; all therefore need to be nurtured and regulated. Although there is scope for private regulation by local professional societies, the Government must play the lead regulatory role in most of Asia.

Private pharmacies play a crucial role in areas where professional care is scarce. They often act as *de facto* health-care providers even though they are not staffed with qualified personnel. Drug outlets are often little more than village convenience stores. They are largely unregulated and their personnel often have little, if any, formal training. Overprescription of medicines by pharmacies and even by physicians is widespread in Asia. In Thailand, for example, where drugs such as steroids can be found in most village outlets, there is believed to be a significant incidence of drug-induced illness resulting from the distribution of inappropriate drugs to the rural population (Suwit 1994). The overuse of over-the-counter drugs in self-care is also common. Private pharmacies can be fostered as a front line in health care, but their licensing, the enforcement of minimum qualifications for their personnel, and the provision of regularly updated information on essential drugs and treatment procedures are roles that must be played effectively by the Government.

NGOs are often involved in strengthening community roles in health or helping with disaster relief and in the aftermath of armed conflict, often delivering crucial health services in regions where governments are unable to function effectively. In India, for example, the Bengal Rural Welfare Service (BRWS) in Calcutta provides direct services for poor rural and urban communities (BRWS 1998). In the northern provinces of Thailand, where the AIDS infection is widespread, community-based organizations and many NGOs work together to provide various types of services for people who have AIDS or are susceptible to it. These include public education, self-help groups, psychological and social support, and home-based care when required.

A number of Asian countries have seen a shift towards closer cooperation between NGOs and governments. These partnerships are at times grudging on both sides, with State workers seeing in the NGO role a *de facto* admission of the ineffectiveness of public-sector outreach. Recent moves towards more participatory government, and the active involvement of communities in many other areas, suggest that more civic health groups will emerge in the future. This form of social capital has close links with the local community, even closer than those of conventional NGOs. Whatever type of community-based organization emerges, however, there is a need for most Asian governments to adopt a more positive attitude towards these actors and to facilitate the strengthening of local community capacity. As their role grows, it will be appropriate for the Government to strengthen its regulatory supervision of NGOs and other community organizations to ensure that standards are maintained.

Finally, village health workers—often working voluntarily—have been significant rural health actors in a number of countries. The PRC under Mao introduced barefoot doctors as service providers at the commune level. They were trained by the Government but paid for by the communes. They made basic services available in rural areas where previously there had been none, but their role declined with the disintegration of the commune system after the economic reforms of the late 1970s. Similarly, Thailand has village health volunteers who are trained by the Government to treat simple illnesses. They are expected to provide services free of charge. To supply medicines, these volunteers set up village drug cooperatives in which villagers own shares. The Government initially provides matching funds, which are revolved. The villagers then set up drug stores supervised by local public health personnel. Any profits from the cooperative go to the shareholders. Although these cooperatives were active during the 1980s, they are not so common now.

Overall, the potential impact of village health workers is likely to be greatest in rural communities where isolation and poverty limit access to formal health services. At relatively low cost to the Government for training, basic supplies, and supervision, they can, together with the village drug dispensaries, provide essential primary care and referral services. However, experience shows that rural household demand will tend to shift toward more modern care providers as incomes grow and isolation is reduced. In anticipation of this transition, PNG provides a model that other countries might apply to avoid loss of the Government's sunk investment in village workers. Beginning in the late 1970s, PNG implemented an innovative program to create a new class of rural health professionals through training to upgrade the knowledge of primary health-care workers. They were placed in 75 percent of the provinces, where they look after the rural health centers, managing both nurses and community health workers (ADB 1999a).

Community Financing

As demonstrated above, there is considerable potential to tap the energy of local communities, which see health care as being in their self-interest. The health sector has witnessed various experiments in community-based financing. The introduction of community-based health funds became popular after the 1978 joint World Health Organization (WHO)/United Nations Children's Fund conference on future health priorities, held in Alma-Ata. Primary health care was made a key strategy in the conference's statement on "Health for All by the Year 2000." Various types of funds were proposed, including drug, sanitation, and nutrition funds. In addition to community contributions, the aim was often to mobilize additional funds from donors and other sources for use at the community level in meeting basic health needs.

Thailand has initiated a variety of efforts consistent with the Alma-Ata conference. Drug funds are now used locally to buy medicines, while sanitation funds enable villagers to build latrines. More comprehensive schemes have emerged in regions that have gained experience in managing community funds. Often, funds were initially set up for general savings purposes and then evolved to provide health services. The Klongpier Community Fund in Southern Thailand, originally a savings fund, now offers a 60 percent reimbursement of hospital charges incurred by its members (Vichit 1998). Other funds with a microfinance background have also taken on health activities; these have often outlived programs set up only for health purposes. Overall, the experience in Thailand shows that financial mobilization and management by the community has its strengths and should be encouraged.

Human Resource Leakage in Rural Health Care

Pharmacies, traditional practitioners, and village health workers offer important support services, but modern professional health care in rural areas is—excepting the few private clinics and NGOs—usually provided by the public sector. Governments have found it difficult to attract health professionals, whether doctors, nurses, pharmacists, or dentists, to work in rural areas; once they are there, it is difficult to retain them. In many cases, these personnel are highly motivated to address pressing social needs, so it is easy to imagine the frustration they feel if patients suffer for simple want of medicines, facilities, and operational budgets. At the same time, the rapid, demand-driven growth of private urban health care has naturally attracted medical personnel to the better job opportunities, facilities, and salaries offered in the cities. In Thailand, the number of doctors in rural districts has stagnated. At its most extreme, countries like the Philippines and India have suffered a brain drain of doctors and nurses who emigrate for better jobs in other countries.

Many Asian governments require a term of compulsory rural health service for graduates of public medical schools and have also attempted to improve conditions at rural health facilities. Contractual incentives have been offered to attract new graduates to work in rural areas, including support for further education. While these strategies have certainly increased the presence of rural health personnel relative to what it would have been otherwise, they have not succeeded in keeping health professionals in the countryside over the longer term. This is unfortunate, since it is often only after one or two years of service that fresh medical graduates gain a real understanding of local needs and develop a rapport with their rural clients.

In Indonesia, the Philippines, and Thailand, doctors are provided with specialist training by the Government after they have satisfactorily completed a contracted period of rural service. Rural service has thus come to be seen as the necessary stepping stone to highly-paid urban employment. In Thailand, this policy has been followed for the past 30 years for medical graduates and nurses and for some ten years for pharmacists and dentists, but few stay on in the rural areas after their contracted period; more than half of all the graduates leave the district level after completing their compulsory service and less than 20 percent remain in the countryside after five years. The situation has not been any better for pharmacists and dentists. Unfortunately, it appears that until rural incomes have risen to the point where they can more directly support the costs of modern private services, public policymakers will be challenged to find appropriate incentives to keep health personnel in rural areas.

Health Research and the Distribution of Health Technology

Modern medicine mostly applies the biological sciences to solve the problems of human health. The total resources expended by Asian countries on medical research are probably much less than what is spent on agricultural research, a topic covered extensively in Chapter IV. Across a wide spectrum of the sciences, Asia is an importer of the results of research from the more developed countries. Agriculture is an exception to this pattern. Being more dependent on environmental conditions, agriculture requires considerable adaptive research suited to farm problems in a particular locality. In the case of health, however, there is less variation in the physiology of the human body than there is in the environment of the farm. As a result, the fruits of medical research are potentially more of an international public good than those of agricultural research. Thus, prima facie, one could conclude that developing countries can free-ride on the work that is done elsewhere, particularly in developed countries, and therefore do not need to invest much in medical research. This would not be an accurate generalization, however. For one thing, international patents may force consumers in the developing countries to end up paying for the research. As with agricultural biotechnology (again, see Chapter IV), the Government will have to consider its stance on intellectual property protection, a rather weightier matter when human health and welfare are involved.

In addition, while there has been a plethora of studies on the returns to agricultural research, little work has been done to calculate the returns to public medical research. Private research in developed countries appears to be financially viable, and may actually be quite profitable,[8] but that does not prove that the total expended is socially optimal. Indeed, as patents are increasingly required to ensure financial viability, and as patents introduce market distortions, there are grounds to suspect that the worldwide total spent on medical research will be somewhat less than socially optimal. More to the point of this volume, even that suboptimal amount will almost certainly bypass the medical problems that are specific to rural Asia. Since dependence on private funding for research will bias the effort toward those areas for which cost recovery is relatively easy, the health problems of the well-off in advanced countries would naturally lay first claim to attention, while those of the rural poor would have the last.

The pharmaceutical industry in Asia remains technologically weak, even in the newly industrialized countries, so it may not be able to contribute much to the needs of the rural poor. Besides, in this most globalized of industries, even if the local industry has the capability, it should not be expected to behave differently than in the developed world. Insofar as the local industry will spend money on research and development, it will focus primarily on the health problems of the rich, rather than the problems that are peculiar to the poor. Seen from a global perspective, the lopsided allocation of research funds is captured well in the following quote:

---

[8] Comanor (1986) surveyed costs and returns studies for the US pharmaceutical industry. His study was prompted by the controversy surrounding claims of excessive profits made in a 1961 report by the US Senate (the Kefauver Committee). As the findings of that report were refined by economists, the estimated rates of return were whittled down from 22 percent—twice the average for all manufacturing at that time—to less than 8 percent. Moreover, at least until the 1980s, returns were declining over time. Despite this, outlays for research and development expanded in real terms by 3 percent annually between 1965 and 1980.

> Of the $50–$60 billion spent worldwide each year on health research and development by the private and public sectors, less than 10 percent is devoted to the health problems of 90 percent of the world's population (GFHR 1999).

For the health problems of the poor, it is difficult to avoid the conclusion that the public sector has to take the lead role in research. As with the "orphan commodities" discussed in Chapter IV, it will be appropriate to target public and internationally-funded research on problems that affect the poor disproportionately but do not have sufficient profit potential to attract private-sector interest. Indeed, given the scarcity of public funds for research, there is a strong case to be made for placing the health problems that are specific to the rural poor at the top of the priority list. Specificity is the essential criterion. Many of the health problems from which the rural poor suffer are shared with the better-off (e.g., AIDS). If, as in the case of AIDS, global research is already ongoing, a lower priority for public research would be justified unless a local public research facility has a clear comparative advantage in a given area.

Placing priority on the problems of the rural poor does not mean that every Asian country must expend resources on every problem. This would be impractical and wasteful for most Asian countries, except perhaps for very large countries like the PRC and India. Clearly, efforts should be made to pool resources across countries, just as with agricultural research, so that each country can carve out an area of work according to the availability of expertise and exchange results with its neighbors.

What health problems are specific to the rural poor? To answer this question, we are assisted by the priority-setting exercise conducted by the Global Forum on Health Research (GFHR), a group whose Steering Committee consists of government policymakers, multilateral and bilateral development agencies, foundations, international NGOs, women's associations, research institutions, and the private sector. Although the answers they give are not specific to the rural poor of Asia, they are certainly relevant because of the GFHR emphasis on the 90 percent of the world population that is shortchanged in health research. GFHR (1999) identified four critical health problems:

- *The unfinished agenda* of preventable death, illness, and disability. Specific recommendations include (i) better understanding of the relative importance of increased nutrient intake, (ii) control of infectious diseases as means of reducing malnutrition, and (iii) maximizing opportunities for disease control through immunization.
- *New and reemerging microbes.* Of particular concern are drug-resistant strains of microbes that are leading to the reemergence of tuberculosis, malaria, and pneumococcal diseases. Specific goals for research include an effective prophylactic for tuberculosis and new malaria drugs and vaccines. Also recommended is strategic research on the genetic composition of the major pathogens.
- *Increased research on noncommunicable diseases.* Specific recommendations include studies of the burden of noncommunicable diseases in developing countries and greater concentration on epidemiological and behavioral research (arguing from the premise that laboratory-based research is already well-supported in the developed countries).
- *More equitable and efficient health-service delivery.* Specific recommendations include better research, data collection, and capacity building in health systems policy.

Although directing more resources to research on the health of the rural poor is to be encouraged, there is no guarantee that even publicly funded research will lead to forms of medical treatment that are easily affordable by the poor. In general, recent health technology development, emerging largely in the private sector, has brought rapidly escalating costs for new medicines and equipment. Although the most modern technologies are reaching many Asian countries, they are usually not available in rural areas. Furthermore, their cost is prohibitive for the poor, whether they are rural or urban. Thus, a critical question for the future is, how can drugs and technologies be more equitably distributed? In the case of AIDS, for which new drugs are expensive, drug manufacturers are donating them or making them available at lower prices in countries like Thailand. In other countries, international organizations and NGOs are negotiating the bulk procurement of drugs at reduced cost. Competitive tendering could also be more widely utilized for the procurement of essential drugs by public agencies.

Several government roles are appropriate to regulate and support drug and technology distribution. Stronger regulatory mechanisms are needed for drug imports, registration, quality control, and distribution. Some countries have begun to establish mechanisms for technology assessment to bring about better control of imports and distribution. Even with drugs and technologies that are deemed to be safe, the Government can play a lead role in educating the public about their proper use and effectiveness. In countries where the market is large enough to support domestic pharmaceutical production, the Government should ensure that this industry is both competitive and safe.

Finally, it is appropriate for the Government to facilitate the efficient access to basic drugs that are essential for primary health care (WHO 1997). WHO introduced the concept of an essential drug list to help countries ensure that important drugs are made available to the population, especially in rural areas. As a result, many countries implemented essential drug programs, with varying degrees of success. In order to reduce wasteful duplication in distribution, WHO has helped countries to distinguish among drugs that may not be significantly different from one another. Related programs were also introduced to improve public knowledge through the use of generic labeling, the establishment of village drug outlets with trained village health workers, and the regulation of drug advertising. However, these programs at times face resistance from professional organizations, private pharmacies, and drug manufacturers, all of whom prefer to profit from the use of brand names and the latest technologies (Reich 1993).

Health Insurance

The major share of health costs in the developed countries is financed through health insurance, through both public and private schemes. In theory, group insurance pools resources to reduce individual exposure to catastrophic loss from predictable population-wide risks. But because information is imperfectly distributed, an unfettered private market for insurance is fraught with moral hazard and selection bias. Those seeking insurance have the incentive to conceal information about preexisting health problems. Once insured, consumers may have little incentive to reduce health costs. Similarly, insurance providers will tend to deny coverage to risky groups most in need. Given the risk of market failure, should a prominent government role in health insurance be promoted in the developing countries? Little more than caution can be offered on this question.

Particularly in the low-income countries, the main concern with public, or social, insurance is that it would, potentially at very high cost, exacerbate the urban bias and other inequities that already exist in health care. In part, this is because the supply of many public-health inputs, particularly physicians, is inelastic in the short run. By increasing the demand for discretionary services among the insured, insurance will tend to raise the scarcity and cost of health services for the uninsured, including the rural population and the poor generally. For the foreseeable future in most of Asia, the financing of insurance through obligatory payroll deductions will only be practical in formal labor markets. Any subsidies in its provision will inevitably tend to benefit the relatively affluent wage-earning population. Nonetheless, the roles for public and private insurance and the need for their efficient, equitable provision will grow as national income grows and, over the longer run, as the demographic and epidemiological transitions lead to higher per capita costs of health treatment.

Private provision of health insurance is growing in Asia, mainly in urban areas and at times in association with medical services provided at designated facilities. In principle, private coverage could reduce the demand for public health services by the insured population, thereby freeing public resources for more socially pressing needs. In turn, the Government will need to regulate the industry to ensure that it operates fairly and in the best interests of consumers. This is because of another asymmetry in information on health: patients rarely have complete knowledge about alternative approaches to treating a given medical problem. Whether through public campaigns or private advertising, provision of information to the public about insurance options will facilitate informed choice by the relatively literate, well-to-do population.

Promoting Good Health

The conventional belief has been that better health would be achieved through the development of better health services. Hence, the focus has been on expanding medical facilities and improving the distribution of health personnel, medicines, and other resources. However, Asia's epidemiological and demographic transitions are leading to a strategic reorientation toward sustaining good health and preventing, rather than simply curing, illness. On the one hand, this is because the increasing number of older and wealthier individuals has led to growing health-care demands related to aging and chronic, noncommunicable diseases for which medical treatment has relatively low cost-effectiveness. At the same time, there has been growing recognition that many largely preventable health problems are related to individual behavior and the environment, e.g., smoking and pollution. These concerns and the resulting shift in strategy are not unique to the urban population but also pertain to rural areas. Public education can mitigate many preventable rural health problems that arise from infectious disease, poor hygiene, and malnutrition (particularly micronutrient deficiencies).

Thus, while health services contribute to good health, public awareness, healthy behavior, and environmental quality are also important. Operationally, the Government can play an important role in disseminating information on good health. Because such information is a public good, and moreover, because the private health sector profits little from a decline in the demand for its services, it behooves the Government to take the principal responsibility in this arena. Controlling advertisements for tobacco products and breast-milk substitutes and promoting more ethical marketing of pharmaceutical products are examples of good public practices in regulating the private sector (WHO 1990). Moreover, one need only drive briefly over the roads and bridges of any bustling Asian city to recognize that the Government's role in protecting environmental quality clearly needs to be strengthened.

WATER SUPPLY, NUTRITION, AND CHILD DEVELOPMENT

The health status of the rural population is determined by the interaction of the environment, nutrition, health awareness and behavior, and health services. These must be examined holistically. The environment and nutritional status are important determinants of the efficacy of curative and preventive health services, including vaccinations. The environment, particularly water supply, exposes people to many communicable, infectious, and parasitic diseases. The potential translation of this exposure into morbidity, and the subsequent severity of illness, depend upon nutrition and health status: healthy, well-nourished individuals are better able to resist disease or to recover from its effects. Water and nutrition are particularly important for the welfare of rural Asia's most vulnerable groups, children and women.

Rural Water Supply and Sanitation

Cleanliness of water is essential in order to prevent the spread of fecally-borne diseases such as diarrhea and intestinal worm infections. Inadequate or unsanitary water supplies also increase the risk of skin and eye infections and diseases like schistosomiasis. In total, some 1.3 billion people in the developing world lack access to clean and plentiful water and nearly two 2 billion lack sanitation systems (World Bank 1993b). Despite the region's rapid growth, rural Asia—weighted heavily by India, where the problem is most acute—generally ranks high in the need for clean water compared with other regions of the developing world.

Less obvious, but of considerable importance, the collection of water is a major determinant of time allocation within rural households. In dry or mountainous areas, the collection of household water requires arduous daily effort, usually by women and children. Since water is an essential human need, rural families have no choice in the matter. Surveys in Indonesia have measured rural family time inputs for water collection ranging from 10–30 hours *per person* per month depending upon the region and season. In discussing the possibilities for establishing bench terraces and permanent cropping in a severely deforested, shifting cultivation area of upland Lao PDR, a group of rural women once bluntly told the first author of this chapter: "Before we have the time to help you with your agricultural project, you will need to help us with water supply." Although not discussed here, the collection of firewood for the household is also time-intensive.

Readier access to water potentially frees a substantial amount of time for more productive activities, including child care and study, in addition to farm and market labor. Because people strongly desire safe water and sanitation, they are usually willing to pay for them. Costs are not necessarily high. Water and sanitation services cost as little as $15 per person per year for a simple rural system (World Bank 1993b).

Water supply and sanitation projects have been implemented throughout Asia, often with donor support. Many of these projects have tapped the considerable potential that exists for community mobilization. One unique evaluation of these projects provides powerful quantitative evidence of the scope for effective coproduction involving communities, local public agencies, and donor organizations. Using information from 121 completed small- and medium-scale rural water projects in Asia, Africa, and Latin America, Narayan (1995) carefully assembled a database covering various dimensions of project outcomes, technical quality, and sustainability; indexes of the depth and phasing of community participation; and a range of determinants of project outcome unrelated to participation, such as socioeconomic, cultural, and environmental characteristics, project size and complexity, and the capabilities of project staff. A range of statistical and qualitative analyses was undertaken.

Several striking findings emerged. The depth of participation proved to be the most important determinant of project benefits. Participation was most effective when it occurred throughout the project cycle, from identification and design to O&M. Participation must therefore be seen as a process, not a discrete event. It had greatest impact when the communities were given real control over major project decisions. Such a policy required an unusual openness and client orientation on the part of local government staff, who, in turn, needed to have adequate autonomy to manage their agency's affairs. Where participation was most successful, the project experience strengthened longer-term social capital, as manifested in community empowerment, enhanced organizational and management skills, and the capacity to undertake other development activities. However, the wide range of project environments precludes pat conclusions about standardized approaches to participation. Rather, effective project outcomes require flexibility, demand-responsiveness, and substantial investment to build the capacity of community-based organizations. Special efforts are needed to give voice to all the stakeholders, particularly women and minority groups, so that project activities are not co-opted by the dominant local elites.

Many donor organizations are applying the above lessons. As just one example, CARE, an international NGO, has been involved in rural water supply since the mid-1970s in four provinces of Indonesia. CARE initially managed all stages of the projects, but over time it learned that the local communities had to take responsibility for financing and managing the systems if sustainability was to be achieved. This lesson was applied with remarkable results, including a dramatic shift in financing contributions: in 1979, CARE and the Government of Indonesia provided 80 percent of the project costs; by 1990, this share had dropped to 30 percent, with most of the local communities managing to operate and maintain their systems successfully, some for up to 10 years. Moreover, many of the communities assisted by CARE were subsequently able to help neighboring communities develop their own systems (Narayan 1995).

Intensive participation becomes more difficult as project scale and technical complexity increase. For very large projects, an alternative approach is that of transferring water supply and sanitation to private commercial operation. If properly regulated, the private sector has a number of potential advantages over the Government. It may be technically more efficient and, if the investment is demonstrably profitable, it can often raise the needed funds without much trouble. It may also tend to keep the public better informed than government departments on performance data. Finally, it can bring in specialist skills relatively quickly and can more rapidly introduce new and improved technology (United Nations 1997). In rural Asia, privatization would probably be most feasible in higher-income communities or periurban areas.

In Malaysia, for example, the states of Johor and Kelantan have privatized their water authorities. In a third state, Selangor, a private company operates treatment plants for drinking water. The Malaysian Government has also signed a long-term concession agreement with a group of private companies to undertake the construction and maintenance of national sewage systems.

However, there are critics of market orthodoxy in regard to the privatization of water supply. Thomas and Clegg (1998) note that water, both as a commodity and in the rights to its use, lacks the characteristics identified by Tietenberg (1992) as essential if market mechanisms are to work with full efficiency:

- universality and enforceability (i.e., clear property rights that lead to unambiguous ownership and entitlement);
- exclusivity of benefits and costs (i.e., no externalities); and
- transferability (i.e., ready exchange).

They also argue that the sourcing and physical infrastructure required for water supply (e.g., the installation of pumps and pipes) lead to natural monopolistic features that preclude efficient, equitable delivery by the private sector. Finally, they assert that market solutions are often anti-poor, since poor households are, empirically, least likely either to receive good water service or to benefit when rationing and subsidies inevitably creep into the system.

These arguments point to the need to improve the Government's regulatory capacity as part of any large-scale program of water supply privatization. To ensure that water delivery is equitable, the Government's role may extend to pro-poor pricing policies, such as sliding scales and cross-subsidization of poor households by wealthy consumers. As with all redistributional measures, such policies require political will.

Nutrition and Early Child Development

Nutrition, health, and cognitive growth during early childhood are fundamental, interrelated determinants of an adult's ultimate stock of human capital. Poor nutrition during the preschool years significantly raises the risks of child mortality and lowers intellectual capacity and subsequent school achievement. There is accumulating scientific evidence that preschool malnutrition also has a lasting impact later in life in the form of reduced work productivity, lower income-earning potential, and higher associated risks of chronic disease and early death.

The relationships between nutrition and human capital also extend to mothers. Maternal nutrition, health, knowledge, and attitudes all influence fetal development, birth outcomes, and the subsequent health and growth of the child. Because mothers are the primary care givers, their illness or diminished capacity due to malnutrition can in turn adversely affect the child's growth. Thus, human capital has intergenerational origins and carryovers over and above genetic lineage and wealth transfers.

Unfortunately, satisfactory nutrition still eludes many children and women despite Asia's aggregate success in raising incomes and increasing the food supply. Infant and child mortality have declined significantly through mass campaigns to control the communicable and parasitic diseases, but for many children improved survival odds have not been enough to bring about healthy growth and development. Poverty is a root cause of the problem. Throughout Asia, the rates of malnutrition, infectious disease, and mortality among poor preschool children are two to three times higher than among the wealthy. Poor children struggle in circumstances that are often incompatible with healthy development.

The data in Table VII.4 reflect fairly typical patterns and were derived from a survey of more than 27,000 Indonesian preschool children and their families. Vulnerable children live in families characterized by relatively low parental education. The mother's fertility tends to be high, meaning that each child competes with more siblings for scarce household resources, including parental childcare time. Food security is limited, as indicated by both the quantity and quality of the diet. Limited parental knowledge and access to medical care are reflected in relatively low rates of immunization. The relative risk of malnutrition is high as compared to children from wealthier homes.

In general, rural children are at a disadvantage along almost all of these dimensions as compared with urban children. Food availability is the one area in which Table VII.4 suggests that rural families have an edge, but it should be noted that urban families often obtain a high share of their food outside the home. Such consumption tends to be underrecorded in household consumption surveys. In any event, the table suggests that the

Table VII.4. Indonesian Health and Nutrition Indicators by Expenditure Quintile, 1987.

	Household Characteristics					Preschool Child Characteristics		
	% < Primary Education[a]		Achieved Fertility[b]	% Food Insecure[c]	% Calories from:		% Vaccinated		% Malnourished[d]	
	Father	Mother			Cassava	Meat/Dairy	Polio	Measles	Moderate	Severe
Rural										
Lowest	70.6	73.2	3.7	23.9	8.5	1.9	24.3	7.2	15.9	2.0
2nd	60.3	65.1	3.5	8.7	5.4	2.8	28.5	9.1	13.8	1.9
3rd	53.4	58.0	3.2	4.9	4.2	3.5	32.7	9.8	13.3	1.3
4th	46.9	54.3	2.9	2.4	3.3	4.4	31.9	8.7	11.6	1.6
Highest	32.9	41.5	2.4	1.2	2.3	6.5	38.9	14.1	9.5	0.6
Urban										
Lowest	38.9	49.1	3.8	28.4	2.1	3.7	51.4	15.9	10.9	1.4
2nd	28.6	35.8	3.2	14.3	1.5	5.5	57.5	22.8	8.4	0.9
3rd	21.2	30.5	2.9	9.6	1.5	6.5	61.3	23.0	7.8	0.7
4th	15.8	21.1	2.5	4.7	1.2	8.3	67.0	24.9	6.6	0.5
Highest	8.1	12.3	2.1	1.7	0.9	11.2	74.3	32.1	5.8	0.1

Notes: [a] Share *not* having completed primary schooling. [b] Average number of children born per family. [c] Share of households with less than 2,000 food calories available daily per adult equivalent during the week before the survey. [d] Share of children aged 1–59 months falling below 70 percent (moderate) and 60 percent (severe) of standardized weight-for-age.
Source: Derived from data in Indonesian Central Bureau of Statistics (1987)

better level of food security in rural households does not translate into better nutritional status among rural preschool children.

When incomes are low and variable, demand-driven market responses often do not produce socially desirable outcomes. Government interventions to promote the healthy growth of young children are among the most proactive ways to jointly foster equitable long-run economic growth and poverty alleviation. It is apposite for the Government to provide leadership, not only because the needed interventions improve welfare, but also because, when designed and implemented efficiently, they are a sound long-run social investment. Successful intervention also depends critically upon household-level knowledge, attitudes, and behavior. Close collaboration and coproduction among national and local public agencies, communities, and community-based organizations is essential. This collaboration is working well in a number of developing countries (excellent reviews are provided in Heaver and Hunt [1995], and Young [1995]).

Table VII.5 summarizes the state of knowledge about the impacts of nutritional deficiencies in Asia and the potential economic returns to intervention.[9] The "macro" nutritional problem of protein-energy malnutrition (PEM) is still the major policy concern. Outside of the Central Asian Republics (where PEM is reportedly rare), the incidence of mild or more serious PEM in preschool children ranges from 13–68 percent across Asia's developing countries and is concentrated in South Asia. PEM interventions range from nutrition education programs in high-risk areas to general food subsidies. As was discussed

---

[9] The methodology used in Table VII.5 deserves note. The benefit-cost (B/C) ratios were calculated by Jay Ross in a methodological appendix to Horton (1999). The estimates of the returns to intervention are based on scientifically documented relationships between malnutrition and adult labor productivity. The assumptions about benefits were conservative. The low discount rate (3 percent) is a standard "rate of social time preference" accepted by most multilateral agencies for investments in the social sector (Horton 1999). Naturally, the B/C ratios are sensitive to the discount rate since much of the benefit stream is obtained so far in the future. At the same time, all B/C ratios would be higher, in some cases significantly so, if the economic benefits of deaths averted had been imputed. However, doing this would inevitably have entailed complicated, often subjective, judgments about the net value of future income streams.

Table VII.5. Estimated Incidence, Impacts, Costs and Benefits of Mitigating Nutritional Deficiencies in Asia

Deficiency	Incidence	Impacts	Mitigation Costs	Benefits of Intervention
Protein and Energy (primarily preschool children)	Mild and moderate: ranges from 38–68% of children in South Asia; 13–45% in East and Southeast Asia. South Asia alone has 75% of the world's malnourished children. Severe: 1–7% across Asia, concentrated in South Asia.	Moderate PEM can retard physical and mental growth by 2–10%. The risks of illness and mortality grow exponentially with increasing severity. PEM is related to more than 50% of all child deaths in low-income Asia. Lower work capacity and productivity in adults cause the loss of 2–3% in GDP. PEM leads to poor reproductive outcomes in women. The efficacy of micronutrient interventions is adversely affected by PEM.	Low (US$2–$10 per child per year) if focus is on nutrition education. Costs are higher (US$100 or more per child) for food supplementation or food subsidies, for which efficient targeting is difficult.	Assuming a targeted program of intensive nutrition education and breastfeeding promotion, costs per death averted range from US$103–$1,112 in low-income Asia. Based on the estimated impacts on adult productivity and wages in the labor market, benefit-cost (B/C) ratios range from 1.6:1 to 8.6:1.
Vitamin A	Mild: 10–40% in low-income Asia. Severe: 1–2% for Asia as a whole.	Leading cause of acquired blindness in children. Increases risks of death from other causes. Where the prevalence of vitamin A deficiency is high, 23% of mortality among children aged 6–72 months is attributable to it.	Supplements cost US$0.20 per year per child and US$0.10 per birth for women post-partum. Food fortification is possible, with the costs borne by consumers.	Costs per death averted range from US$76–$493. B/C ratios not calculated because of difficulty in estimating the deficiency-productivity relationships.

[Continued on following page]

Table VII.5. Estimated Incidence, Impacts, Costs and Benefits of Mitigating Nutritional Deficiencies in Asia (cont'd.)

Deficiency	Incidence	Impacts	Mitigation Costs	Benefits of Intervention
Iron	Anemia affects more than 50% of all women and children in South Asia and more than 18% in East Asia. 88% of pregnant women are anemic in India, 40% in PRC, and 60% elsewhere.	Anemia, for which iron deficiency is a leading cause, is associated with 23% of all maternal mortality, in part due to risks of hemorrhage during childbirth. May reduce physical work productivity of women and men by 5–17%. Childhood deficiency is associated with a 4% impairment of adult cognitive ability.	Iron supplements for women cost US$2.50 per pregnancy. Food fortification for much of the remaining population is possible at low cost (<US$0.10 per capita per year).	Costs per death averted are high because not all maternal deaths from anemia can be prevented by supplementation. B/C ratios range from 0.9:1 to 10.3:1 depending primarily on the level of labor market participation by women.
Iodine	Some 680 million people in Asia suffer risks of iodine deficiency, the leading preventable cause of mental impairment. The incidence of goiter probably averages about 20% in low-income Asia.	About 14% of the children born to iodine-deficient women will suffer mild to severe mental impairment. At its most extreme, maternal deficiency leads to cretinism in children. Some intellectual handicap occurs among virtually all children born to women with goiter.	Capsules for pregnant women cost US$0.50 per pregnancy. Salt fortification for the entire population costs US$0.04 per capita per year.	Cost per death averted not calculated because the impact of iodine deficiency on mortality has not been well established statistically. However, B/C ratios range from 2.7:1 to 28.7:1 due to high productivity impacts.

Notes: Low-income Asia includes Bangladesh, Cambodia, PRC, India, Pakistan, Sri Lanka and Viet Nam. Estimated B/C ratios and program costs per averted death, reported in Horton (1999), are for low-income Asia and calculated for interventions that would reduce the prevalence of nutritional deficiencies by 50 percent over a 9-year period. In the B/C calculations, a 3 percent discount rate is used and the benefits were measured entirely in terms of the effects of reduced prevalence on labor productivity; no monetary benefit is imputed for deaths averted.
Sources: ADB (1999a), Horton (1999), and World Bank (1993b).

in Chapter VI, the latter are notoriously difficult to target efficiently, often subsidizing the well-off. However, carefully targeted interventions for nutrition education and breast-feeding promotion, complemented in extreme cases by food supplementation, show high estimated returns as measured by the expected gains in work capacity and labor income.

Deficiencies of the micronutrients—particularly vitamin A, iron, and iodine—are widespread and contribute to severe adverse health impacts that disproportionately affect women and children, again mainly in South Asia. The socioeconomic and social consequences of micronutrient deficiencies are large, but the costs of prevention or alleviation are in general very low, often just pennies per child each year. Where critical deficiencies exist, appropriate government interventions include programs for dietary supplementation, together with public education through the mass media and at the community level. Of course, the efficient long-run solution is to pass costs on to the consumer through the fortification of commercial foods, for which the Government must provide an effective legal framework. In fact, legislation requiring iodine fortification of salt already exists in much of Asia, but its effectiveness is often compromised by the lack of government capacity to monitor and enforce compliance by the numerous small-scale salt producers. Community and household ignorance about the consequences and cures of iodine deficiency complicate the problem. Hence, direct government roles in supplementation and education will be warranted until food fortification is soundly established (ADB, 1999a).

The State's concern with child development should extend beyond food and physical health. Mental growth occurs most rapidly during a child's early years. It has been estimated that one half of an individual's intellectual potential is established by age four (Bloom 1994, cited in Young 1995). The development of cognitive, psychosocial, and motor skills during early childhood has a permanent effect on intellectual capacity, personality, and social behavior. Considerable evidence shows that by increasing the child's capacity and motivation for learning, early education is likely to make later education more effective, thereby providing permanent private and social benefits (Young 1995). Unfortunately, many poor children are deprived of opportunities for early intellectual and emotional growth because they experience only harsh, confined physical environments where the intensity and quality of child care are low.

Comprehensive programs for early child development (ECD)—encompassing health, nutrition, and education—will vary in cost depending on a country's price level and the mix and intensity of ECD interventions. Some indicative examples are provided below, but it would be unwise to generalize from these figures. The presence of a functioning primary health-care system that is already providing vaccinations and other basic services will reduce the menu of ECD needs and will be highly complementary to any type of nutrition and ECD intervention. In the Philippines, a well-designed program for expanded immunization and basic health care, nutrition monitoring and supplementation, early child education, and community information was estimated in 1994 to cost from $10–$11 annually per child, including overhead costs for administration and training, depending on the age groups covered and the level of supplementary feeding (Heaver and Hunt 1995). This program was proposed to build upon existing government interventions in order to achieve the goals of significantly reducing infant mortality, preschool PEM, and iron deficiency; eliminating vitamin A and iodine deficiencies; and preparing children for successful school entry.

In Tamil Nadu, India, similar child health and nutrition interventions cost about $9 per year per beneficiary in 1994, but did not include early child education (Young 1995). In Viet Nam, costs amounted to $12 per year per malnourished child in 1998 for a large-scale program of growth monitoring, supplementary feeding, micronutrient supplementation, and nutrition education. In Bangladesh, where the basic health care system is weak, a program of primary health care, prenatal care, and community nutrition cost $18 per year per child in 1998 (see the citations in Horton

1999). Elsewhere, Horton found that well-designed and carefully targeted programs focusing primarily on nutrition cost between $5 and $10 per child and had demonstrated cost-effectiveness.

Such costs may appear modest, but it must be borne in mind that total public and private spending on health care amounts to about $18 per capita per year in South Asia, even less in the PRC and the low-income countries of Indochina, and often not much more in the rapidly growing economies of Southeast Asia (see the Appendix Table). It is therefore crucial to target interventions efficiently in terms of need and community receptivity. Community mobilization is an essential prerequisite, a role for which NGOs and other social and religious organizations are often ideally suited. If community mobilization is successful, experience shows that it is possible to reduce public costs through partial contributions from participating households. Some form of user fee is obviously desirable, both to reduce the burden on the public budget and to ensure ownership and commitment on the part of beneficiary families.

The scientific evidence suggests that ECD investments have long-term payoffs involving a sequence of linkages between

- nutrition, health, and intellectual growth;
- intellect and subsequent educational performance; and
- education, subsequent income, and other socioeconomic outcomes.

Although many of the individual relationships are well-established (see Table VII.2 above, Heaver and Hunt [1995], and Young [1995]), a vast number of intervening variables will influence the combined result. Some of the complexities were noted above in the discussion of the returns to education investment and to private versus public schools. Sorting out all the interrelationships statistically may never be possible. Nonetheless, longer-term longitudinal studies in the US and

Latin America have followed groups of participating and nonparticipating children, confirming that, at least during the primary school years, the benefits of ECD programs are substantial.[10] Moreover, sufficient experience has been gained to guide the formulation of efficient ECD strategies and programs. Systematic procedures are available for the assessment of community needs, program targeting and design, the selection of components and technologies, the determination of an appropriate level of beneficiary cost recovery, and program monitoring and evaluation (Heaver and Hunt 1995; Young 1995).

Gender sensitivity is essential in all nutrition and ECD programs, first, because mothers are the primary target group for public education messages about children, and second, because one goal of such programs is to rectify gender bias in health and nutritional status. In most of South Asia, preschool girls are less likely than boys to be fully immunized and to be treated properly for respiratory infections or diarrhea (ADB 1999a).[11] Higher prevalence of morbidity and malnutrition among girls reflects their more limited access to health care and, most probably, intrahousehold biases in the allocation of food and other resources. Consequently, mortality among girls is at times significantly higher than for boys in most of South

---

[10] Young (1995) summarizes a wide variety of studies which conclude generally that ECD programs confer long-term benefits in the forms of higher measured intelligence, higher primary school enrollments, fewer dropouts, and less grade repetition. ECD participation also tends to enhance the effectiveness of other health and nutrition programs. In traditional societies where parents do not consider schooling to be a priority for girls, ECD may give girls an important head start. By demonstrating to parents that girls will succeed, ECD can facilitate their continued school attendance later on.

[11] This gender discrepancy is thought to be smaller elsewhere in Asia. For example, the triennial Indonesian survey drawn upon in Table VII.4 showed consistently in the 1980s that nutritional status for preschool girls was higher than that for boys in most age groups and also less variable (lower sample standard deviation) up to the age of about 18 months. Immunization rates for girls and boys were very similar. These patterns were uniform across rural and urban areas.

Asia (Sri Lanka being the principal exception). In fact, for biological reasons, it should be lower. The gender difference in mortality provides the clearest possible indication that consciousness-raising among parents must be an essential element of any early childhood program.

IMPACTS OF THE ASIAN ECONOMIC CRISIS

Beginning in mid-1997 and with ripple effects that continue today, parts of Asia have been battered by an economic crisis that has—through its macroeconomic effects on exchange rates, inflation, employment, income, and government budgets—reduced household purchasing power and the accessibility and quality of many public services. In East and Southeast Asia, the momentum of three decades of sustained growth was arrested. To what extent did the crisis—through changes in nutrition, health, and access to education—affect human capital accumulation? From the perspective of this volume, the answer to this question must first distinguish between socioeconomic groups: rural versus urban and poor versus nonpoor. Second, at the household level, the effects of the crisis must be disaggregated by gender and age group. The available evidence—some quite detailed and much that is anecdotal—points to the resourcefulness of Asia's households, at least in the short run, in adapting to stress by reallocating resources over which they have command. However, the longer-run and intergenerational impacts will potentially be more severe.

At an aggregate level there is little doubt that the incidence of poverty grew during the crisis, probably more in urban than in rural areas. However, estimating the magnitude of the change is complicated by the lack of systematic data on rural-urban prices, employment (both formal and informal), and consumption. Household adjustment to the crisis varied widely among countries, regions, and socioeconomic groups. In the short run, these adjustments were naturally most visible among the poor, who are inevitably forced into the sharpest realignment of consumption patterns when incomes and relative prices change. Nonetheless, the overall increase in poverty has been less extreme than was feared in late 1998.

The specific *linkages* between the crisis and household incomes differed among rural and urban areas. In general, however, when the starting points of relative poverty and the thrust of post-crisis State interventions are factored in, there appear to have been few pronounced rural-urban differentials in the *net effects* of the crisis on household welfare. Whereas urban areas were set back unambiguously by unemployment and higher prices, rural areas both gained and lost. On the one hand, rural producers of many tradable goods benefited from currency depreciation and substantially higher domestic commodity prices. For the goods they purchase in markets, however, and particularly for goods with high foreign exchange content, rural people felt the same inflationary pressures as the towns and cities. In some countries, rural areas appear to have absorbed part of the labor force displaced from urban jobs. Whether higher commodity prices have led to higher farm wage rates and employment is, as yet, unknown; the expansion of farm employment was, in any event, tempered in many countries in 1997/98 by the drought associated with *El Niño*. It is likely that rural areas have benefited less than urban and periurban areas from emergency government provision of subsidized food and other social services.

The Case of Indonesia

Indonesia was perhaps the hardest-hit by the crisis and has been the most intensively studied. Frankenberg, Thomas, and Beegle (1999) provide a detailed analysis of Indonesian panel surveys that compare conditions just before the crisis in late 1997 with the conditions at its peak in the second half of 1998, when inflation of about 60 percent imposed major adjustments on the poor.[12] During the period covered by these surveys, the crisis affected all strata of society, but the lowest and highest expenditure groups experienced the biggest reversals in real income. However, while savings and other assets buffered the wealthy, the poor had fewer safety nets.

Access to Social Services

The crisis reduced the effective demand for health care because of lower household income. In Indonesia, it also reduced the supply of public health services. Public clinics—at least initially, until donor-assisted safety-net programs kicked in—were unable to cope with reduced budgets and sharply higher prices of medicines and equipment. One year after the onset of the crisis, the proportion of preschool children visiting public health posts had declined by more than 40 percent. The proportion receiving vitamin A supplements was also much lower, but no significant change in immunization rates had occurred. Health workers in the Indonesian surveys consistently expressed concern that the health of the poorest respondents had deteriorated the most. However, the survey's clinical and self-reported assessments could not detect this change. Overall, the authors concluded that health status had proven very robust during the period between the surveys (Frankenberg, Thomas, and Beegle 1999).

Changes in access to education could have a lasting impact on the accumulation of human capital. This is because once children leave school, especially at the secondary level, the odds that they will ever return decline

---

[12] A panel (or "longitudinal") survey follows the same group of respondents at different points in time. The surveys in Indonesia covered some 1,900 households and 8,300 individuals and involved interviews with family members, educators, and community health workers; anthropometric measurements of nutritional status; and clinical evaluations of health indicators such as blood hemoglobin content.

quickly. Here, the distinctions between the poor and the wealthy and rural and urban areas are perhaps clearest. In Indonesia's urban areas, a significantly larger share of children aged 13–19 years was out of school in 1998 as compared to 1997, but in rural areas, the decline in enrollment was most significant in the primary grades. The enrollment gap between poor and wealthy children widened significantly. Overall, the share of poor children aged 7–12 years not enrolled in school doubled between 1997 and 1998.

The decline in enrollment reflects several factors, including rapidly rising costs of school materials and fees, lower real household income, and the greater need for children to contribute to household earnings. Among children, there were few statistically significant gender impacts. Changes in school enrollment and in the use of health care affected boys and girls more or less equally.

Household and Intrahousehold Effects

At the household level, the Indonesian surveys illustrated a variety of coping mechanisms. Prominent among these was the reallocation of the household budget, which inflation had significantly reduced in real terms for most families. Households responded by devoting a larger share of their expenditure to food. Within the food budget, more was being spent on relatively cheap starchy staples. As suggested above, significantly small shares went for health, education, and nonessentials. Investments in children—education and preventive health care—declined most noticeably in the poorest households.

The effects of the crisis were more complex at the intrahousehold level. To begin with, consider the encouraging finding that the nutritional status of children proved robust, even improving in some respects between 1997 and 1998 (Frankenberg, Thomas, and Beegle 1999). In contrast, the "body mass" of adults—a measure based on their weight-for-height—declined significantly overall. The decline was uniform among men and women, but more pronounced for people aged 55 and older.[13] Lower weight-for-height among adults may indicate reduced food intake, but would also be likely to reflect greater work effort and energy expenditure in order to compensate for lower real wages.

In contrast to this seemingly sanguine picture of crisis impacts on existing children, a disturbing indication of long-run intergenerational impacts on the newly born has emerged very recently. In April 2000, the Indonesian Minister of Women's Empowerment reported that 30 percent of the 3.5 million Indonesian babies born during 1998–1999 were underweight (less than 2.5 kilograms at birth). This may imply at least a doubling of the prevalence of low birthweight,[14] which the Minister attributed to poor maternal nutrition and health due to the country's economic crisis (JP 2000). Since low birthweight is strongly associated with later child development, such an increase in prevalence, in combination with the reduction in early child health care, may lead to the most onerous long-run impacts of the Asian crisis.

Thus, the gender-disaggregated impacts of the crisis appear to have been both subtle and selectively pernicious. It may be true that adult men and women experienced a uniform decline in weight-for-height, but the ramifications of this change are far more serious for women of childbearing age. Women have borne a disproportionate share of household adjustment to the crisis. In additional to having to stretch tighter household budgets, female employment—both paid and unpaid (household-based)—grew significantly in Indonesia. Working-age women were far more likely than men to have had a transition in employment, i.e., to

---

[13] Because very high body mass constitutes obesity, the decline does not, in and of itself, reflect poorer nutritional status among adults. Obesity is, of course, unhealthy, but the main nutritional concern lies with adults whose body mass has fallen to a very low level.

[14] Given that many births in Indonesia take place outside of formal medical facilities, there are no comprehensive national statistics on birthweight. Based on a variety of provincial and district-level studies, Soekirman et al. (1992) estimated the prevlence of low birthweight to be between 10 and 12 percent in the early 1990s.

have either lost or gained a job. In 1998 as compared to 1997, adult women were less likely than men to use either public or private health care services. In their qualitative assessments, health workers were generally more concerned about the health status of poor women and children than they were about poor adult males.

Evidence from Other Countries

Elsewhere in Asia, the evidence is less detailed, but a similar pattern emerges. Excepting possible interactions between maternal health and the birthweight of their recent babies, for which only Indonesian evidence is presently available, the short-run impacts of the crisis have been smaller than projected in 1998, but for the poor, who have fewer options for coping, the effects of the crisis are expected to be relatively long-lasting. Knowles, Pernia, and Racelis (1999) synthesize a set of country studies in East and Southeast Asia commissioned by ADB. These studies examined secondary statistics and undertook interviews with focus groups and key community-level informants. The results are summarized thus:

> ...Households (and to a lesser extent, governments) have employed a wide range of mechanisms to cope with the adverse impacts of the crisis. Some of these have been relatively harmless and pose little risk to the future welfare of the populations concerned (e.g., working longer hours, substituting cheaper foods for more expensive foods, delaying purchases of consumer durables). However, others simply result in shifting the social impact of the crisis into the future, or from one generation to the next. Examples include: borrowing to maintain current consumption, selling productive assets, delaying needed medical care, and withdrawing children from school. (Knowles, Pernia, and Racelis. 1999).

As in Indonesia, the cross-country evidence suggests that the nutritional, health, and educational status of preexisting children has not suffered serious short-run effects, although declining immunization and health care may come to have more visible medium-term impacts. In education, while there are exceptions among countries, the adjustments have been greatest overall at the secondary and tertiary levels. Children aged 13 and over have experienced the largest setbacks in educational access. The employment impacts of the crisis have disproportionately affected young adults.

As in Indonesia, much of the household-level burden of adjustment has fallen disproportionately on women. Women have engaged in greater formal and informal employment in many countries. There are also some indications of greater domestic violence, particularly against women. Female-headed households—traditionally among Asia's most vulnerable—may have been particularly hard hit by the crisis (Knowles, Pernia, and Racelis 1999).

In most of Asia, there was a shift from relatively expensive private providers of education and health care to public schools and clinics. Indonesia was an exception: except among the very poor, the shift was from public to private health care, which is thought to reflect the marked contraction of the services provided by public facilities. Household expenditure shares for health care declined sharply in some countries, but not in others. In some cases, the decline reflects the shift to cheaper public facilities and not necessarily a decline in the services received. It also illustrates the difficulty of synthesizing the individual statistics reported for various countries. In education, for example, school enrollments actually increased at the secondary and tertiary levels in Thailand and perhaps in the higher socioeconomic groups of other countries. This should not be assumed to mean that there was no crisis impact. Rather, it reflects both the momentum of past enrollment trends and a reaction to slack labor market demand that has lowered the opportunity costs of continuing education (Kakwani 1999).

More generally, several countries saw increasing rates of crime in 1998, particularly theft and drug use, primarily among the young, and presumably the result of higher unemployment. In general, the crisis has eroded the social capital of many communities, as reflected by decreased participation in voluntary and charitable activities (Knowles,

Pernia, and Racelis 1999).

At least initially, deep cuts in public expenditures for social services were widespread across countries. In many countries, massive bailout programs financed by the International Monetary Fund, the World Bank, and ADB supplemented government budgets. These were often tied to labor-intensive public works programs, as well as to the provision of social services, among which grants and loans to keep children in school have been especially noteworthy. In Thailand, the Government expanded its low-income card program for medical care, also with donor support. Such actions by the Government are appropriate to protect the welfare of the poor, but it is too soon to evaluate their effectiveness. However, it does appear that these and other direct government interventions have, often by design, benefited mainly the more politically active urban and periurban areas, particularly when food subsidies have been involved.

DONOR ROLES IN HUMAN CAPITAL DEVELOPMENT

Organizations like ADB and the World Bank have officially embraced poverty alleviation as their paramount development objective. Both institutions have given high priority to basic education and health in their social-sector strategies. Because of these commitments and the links between human development and poverty, these banks and other donor organizations should serve as a font of proactivity in the development of human capital. They will synthesize the lessons learned, disseminate new knowledge and technology, and support innovation in program design, greater community participation, and better governance. In their relations with Asian governments, the donors will also support social priorities through advocacy (somewhat euphemistically called "policy dialogue") and targeted lending. Because of the complexity of Asia's social problems and the wide variety of multilateral, bilateral, and NGO activities related to human capital development, donor coordination will be important to ensure that there is a complementarity of effort.

As noted above, ADB and the World Bank have, during the past two years, financed social safety-net programs to protect the poor from the consequences of the Asian economic crisis, among which various schemes to keep children in school are potentially the most significant from the standpoint of long-run human capital development. The banks have also provided quick-disbursing budgetary support to further macro and sector-level policy reforms. This assistance has, no doubt, cushioned many people from the effects of sharply lower real income, but a more difficult task nevertheless remains. Through their ongoing policy advice and funding of financial-sector and governance reforms, the multilateral institutions will hopefully contribute to sustained recovery and reduce the risks that such a crisis might ever recur. This will obviously be a far more sustainable avenue for promoting poverty alleviation than the massive bailouts and safety-net programs of the last two years.

SUMMING UP

Finding the optimal path to the equitable development of human capital in rural Asia—particularly in South Asia, where the equity problems are most glaring—is much easier written about than accomplished. In very general terms, it will involve the following sequence of steps: first, the State must define its objectives and priorities. If these priorities include equitable access and poverty alleviation, as it is generally conceded they should, then the second step involves the mobilization of political will. If the will can be found, whether through consensus or fiat, then the third step involves a set of decisions about the tasks that need to be undertaken and the most efficient allocation of tasks between the State, local, and private actors. These decisions must be based on an objective, critical assessment of who the stakeholders are, which actors—individually or collectively through coproduction—have comparative advantage in undertaking the various tasks, and how the provisioning and financing responsibilities should be apportioned. Based on the recent trends in Asia, Table VII.6 shows a suggested allocation of tasks.

More schools and growing enrollments attest to Asia's progress in rural education during the last two decades. While most of this progress has been due to public-sector support, community participation in establishing and running schools is playing an important and growing role in many countries. Nonetheless, the various sources of urban bias need to be addressed in order to improve the accessibility and effectiveness of rural schooling. To some extent, the public sector could reallocate funds to further this objective if the private sector could finance more of the tertiary and secondary education, especially in the urban areas. This chapter has given little attention to specialized education, such as vocational training (including agriculture) and nonformal education (especially for adult literacy). These have admirable objectives and a specific clientele, which in turn will influence the optimal allocation of public, private, and community resources.

As with education, health services suffer from a strong urban bias in the use of funds and provision of facilities. The private sector will take responsibility for a larger share of tertiary health care provision, but this will be concentrated in urban and periurban areas. Various innovative approaches are under way to find new funding and management systems for rural and primary health care outside the public sector. The key roles for the State will be to nurture and guide these approaches (through decentralization, where appropriate), to provide the necessary regulatory frameworks, and to shift the allocation of public funding to areas where the private-sector response is inadequate. Either explicitly or by default, the State's decisions will determine whether the problems of health, nutrition, and early child development among the rural poor are dealt with proactively or left to the confluence of low incomes and the market place.

Table VII.6 Roles of Different Actors in Rural Human Capital Development

Service	Current Roles	Future Roles	Developmental Needs
Primary education	Largely financed and managed by public agencies, although religious and community-based organizations have also been active.	Increasing management role by communities, with continued financing by the State. The potential for contracting of services to private sector and NGOs should be explored.	Local capacity building to begin before decentralization of management. Improved incentives to attract and retain rural teachers. State regulatory capacity to be strengthened.
Secondary and tertiary education	Public agencies, with rapidly growing private sector roles in urban areas.	State's role in provision will diminish in relative terms as the private sector grows, while its regulatory and monitoring roles will grow.	Stronger public capacity to monitor and regulate the private sector. State roles appropriate to redress urban bias and improve access and quality.
Primary health care	Public agencies, with growing private sector role in urban and periurban areas.	Same, with public resources focusing increasingly on rural areas and the poor if the political will can be mobilized. The State will take the lead role in public education for "good health."	Local capacity building for decentralized ownership and management. Better incentives to attract and retain rural health care personnel. Stronger State role in regulating private pharmacies and health care providers.
Tertiary health care	Public agencies, with rapidly growing private sector role in urban areas.	Private sector will continue to grow and may eclipse the role of public hospitals in serving affluent urban populations. Private health insurance will grow as a financing source. The State will lead in promoting good health.	Stronger State regulatory capacity. Tertiary care centers likely to remain urban-based, but new financing approaches, including cross-subsidization, would promote access by the rural population.

Service	Current Roles	Future Roles	Developmental Needs
Communicable and parasitic disease control, vaccinations, and family planning	Largely public agencies, although NGOs have been active in some countries.	Continued public financing, but provision could be privatized under State guidance.	Regardless of who provides the services, the State will continue to determine the required service levels and choice of technology.
Water supply and sanitation	Largely households or communities, but with some State-community coproduction.	Same, with larger financing share by communities. Probably only a limited role for the commercial private sector in rural areas.	Mobilize awareness and involvement of community. NGOs to be encouraged. Greater State role in monitoring and regulating water quality.
Nutrition and early child development	Public agencies and community-based organizations or NGOs.	State to retain financing and monitoring roles, possibly with greater provision by private sector and NGOs.	Educate parents. Mobilize involvement by families and communities in high-risk areas.

CHAPTER VII APPENDIX. ASIAN HEALTH AND EDUCATION INDICATORS

(for sources, see final page)

	1998 Population (millions)	Crude Birth Rate (per 1,000 population) 1980	1990	1997	Crude Death Rate (per 1,000 population) 1980	1990	1997
Southeast Asia							
Indonesia	203	34	25	24	12	9	8
Malaysia	22	31	29	26	6	5	5
Philippines	75	35	31	29	9	7	6
Thailand	61	28	20	17	8	6	7
Total/Weighted Average[b]	361	33	26	24	10	8	7
South Asia							
Bangladesh	126	44	33	28	18	12	10
Bhutan	1	39	38	41	19	16	14
India	955	35	29	27	13	10	9
Nepal	22	43	40	34	20	13	11
Pakistan	135	47	41	36	16	11	8
Sri Lanka	19	28	21	19	6	6	6
Total/Weighted Average	1,257	37	31	28	14	10	9
Transitional East Asia							
Cambodia	11	40	41	34	27	15	12
Lao People's Democratic Republic	5	45	45	38	20	16	14
People's Republic of China (PRC)	1,243	18	20	17	6	7	8
Viet Nam	77	36	29	21	8	7	7
Weighted Average (with PRC)	1,336	19	21	17	6	7	8
Weighted Average (without PRC)	93	37	31	23	11	8	8
Central Asia and Former Soviet Union							
Kazakhstan	16	24	22	14	8	8	10
Kyrgyz Republic	5	30	29	22	9	7	7
Mongolia	2	38	31	23	11	8	7
Tajikistan	6	37	39	23	8	6	6
Uzbekistan	24	34	34	27	8	6	6
Total/Weighted Average	53	31	30	22	8	7	7
Newly Industrialized Countries							
Hong Kong	7	17	12	10	5	5	6
Korea, Republic of	46	22	16	15	6	6	6
Singapore	4	17	18	13	5	5	4
Taipei, China	22	23	17	15	5	5	6
Total/Weighted Average	79	22	16	14	6	6	6
Papua New Guinea and Pacific Islands							
Total/Weighted Average[c]	6	37	34	31	12	10	8
TOTAL ASIA	3,092	28	25	23	10	8	8

Please see p. 345 for notes and sources.

	Natural Increase Rate (% per year)			Total Fertility Rate (births per woman)		
	1980	1990	1997	1980	1990	1997
Southeast Asia						
Indonesia	2.2	1.6	1.6	4.3	3.0	2.8
Malaysia	2.5	2.4	2.1	4.2	3.8	3.2
Philippines	2.6	2.4	2.3	4.8	4.0	3.6
Thailand	2.0	1.4	1.0	3.5	2.2	1.7
Total/Weighted Average[b]	2.3	1.8	1.7	4.3	3.1	2.8
South Asia						
Bangladesh	2.6	2.1	1.8	6.1	4.2	3.2
Bhutan	2.0	2.2	2.7	5.9	5.9	5.9
India	2.2	1.9	1.8	5.0	3.7	3.3
Nepal	2.3	2.7	2.3	6.1	5.6	4.4
Pakistan	3.1	3.0	2.8	7.0	5.8	5.0
Sri Lanka	2.2	1.5	1.3	3.5	2.5	2.2
Total/Weighted Average	2.3	2.0	1.9	5.3	4.0	3.5
Transitional East Asia						
Cambodia	1.3	2.6	2.2	4.7	4.9	4.6
Lao People's Democratic Republic	2.5	2.9	2.4	6.7	6.3	5.6
People's Republic of China (PRC)	1.2	1.3	0.9	2.5	2.1	1.9
Viet Nam	2.8	2.2	1.4	5.0	3.6	2.4
Weighted Average (with PRC)	1.3	1.4	0.9	2.7	2.2	2.0
Weighted Average (without PRC)	2.6	2.3	1.6	5.1	3.9	2.8
Central Asia and Former Soviet Union						
Kazakhstan	1.6	1.4	0.4	2.9	2.7	2.0
KyrgyzRepublic	2.1	2.2	1.5	4.1	3.7	2.8
Mongolia	2.7	2.3	1.6	5.4	4.1	2.6
Tajikistan	2.9	3.3	1.7	5.6	5.1	3.5
Uzbekistan	2.6	2.8	2.1	4.8	4.1	3.1
Total/Weighted Average	2.3	2.4	1.5	4.3	3.8	2.8
Newly Industrialized Countries						
Hong Kong	1.2	0.7	0.4	2.0	1.3	1.3
Korea, Republic of	1.6	1.0	0.9	2.6	1.8	1.7
Singapore	1.2	1.3	0.9	1.7	1.9	1.7
Taipei, China	1.8	1.2	0.9	2.5	1.8	1.8
Total/Weighted Average	1.6	1.0	0.9	2.5	1.8	1.7
Papua New Guinea and Pacific Islands						
Total/Weighted Average[c]	2.5	2.4	2.2	5.5	4.9	4.2
TOTAL ASIA	1.9	1.7	1.4	4.0	3.1	2.7

	Maternal Mortality Rate (per 100,000 births)		Infant Mortality Rate (per 1,000 live births)			Human Development Index[a]		
	1990	1997	1980	1990	1997	1990	1994	1995
Southeast Asia								
Indonesia	450	390	90	63	47	0.515	0.668	0.679
Malaysia	40	34	30	15	11	0.790	0.832	0.834
Philippines	209	180	52	44	35	0.603	0.672	0.677
Thailand	270	155	49	38	33	0.715	0.833	0.838
Total/Weighted Average[b]	344	285	71	52	40	0.584	0.707	0.715
South Asia								
Bangladesh	n/a	449	132	95	75	0.189	0.368	0.371
Bhutan	770	380	159	117	107	0.150	0.338	0.347
India	460	437	116	83	71	0.309	0.446	0.451
Nepal	n/a	n/a	132	101	83	0.170	0.347	0.351
Pakistan	600	340	124	99	95	0.311	0.445	0.453
Sri Lanka	90	30	34	19	14	0.663	0.711	0.716
Total/Weighted Average	471	421	118	85	73	0.300	0.440	0.445
Transitional East Asia								
Cambodia	500	900	201	122	103	0.186	0.348	0.422
Lao People's Democratic Republic	200	660	127	108	98	0.246	0.459	0.465
People's Republic of China (PRC)	n/a	115	42	33	32	0.566	0.626	0.650
Viet Nam	110	105	57	45	38	0.472	0.557	0.560
Weighted Average (with PRC)	n/a	123	45	35	33	0.556	0.619	0.642
Weighted Average (without PRC)	163	232	78	58	49	0.425	0.526	0.538
Central Asia and Former Soviet Union								
Kazakhstan	56	80	33	26	29	0.802	0.709	0.695
Kyrgyz Republic	110	80	43	30	28	0.689	0.635	0.633
Mongolia	156	145	82	63	52	0.578	0.661	0.669
Tajikistan	n/a	88	58	41	30	0.657	0.580	0.575
Uzbekistan	46	43	47	35	24	0.695	0.662	0.659
Total/Weighted Average	61	67	45	34	28	0.717	0.664	0.658
Newly Industrialized Countries								
Hong Kong	6	7	11	6	4	0.913	0.914	0.909
Korea, Republic of	42	30	26	12	9	0.872	0.890	0.894
Singapore	11	10	12	7	4	0.849	0.900	0.896
Taipei, China	129	10	5	6	n/a	n/a	n/a	n/a
Total/Weighted Average	29	21	20	9	8	0.875	0.893	0.896
Papua New Guinea and Pacific Islands								
Total/Weighted Average[c]	n/a	n/a	64	56	51	0.376	0.544	0.537
TOTAL ASIA	234	259	77	57	50	0.466	0.564	0.577

	Life Expectancy at Birth (years)						Daily Per Capita Food Calorie Availability		
	Female			Male					
	1980	1990	1997	1980	1990	1997	1980	1990	1996
Southeast Asia									
Indonesia	56	64	66	53	60	62	2,158	2,602	2,930
Malaysia	69	73	74	65	68	70	2,743	2,772	2,899
Philippines	63	66	68	60	63	64	2,282	2,408	2,356
Thailand	66	71	72	61	66	67	2,224	2,235	2,334
Total/Weighted Average[b]	60	66	68	57	62	64	2,231	2,510	2,708
South Asia									
Bangladesh	48	56	59	49	55	57	1,904	2,076	2,105
Bhutan	43	52	54	42	49	51	n/a	n/a	n/a
India	54	60	62	55	59	62	1,961	2,267	2,415
Nepal	47	53	57	49	54	57	1,889	2,400	2,339
Pakistan	56	62	65	55	60	62	2,124	2,410	2,408
Sri Lanka	70	74	75	66	69	71	2,313	2,221	2,263
Total/Weighted Average	54	60	62	54	59	62	1,976	2,264	2,379
Transitional East Asia									
Cambodia	42	52	55	39	49	52	1,688	1,950	1,974
Lao People's Democratic Republic	45	51	54	42	49	52	2,083	2,115	2,143
People's Republic of China (PRC)	68	70	71	66	67	68	2,311	2,680	2,844
Viet Nam	65	69	70	61	64	66	2,120	2,204	2,502
Weighted Average (with PRC)	68	70	71	65	67	68	2,294	2,644	2,814
Weighted Average (without PRC)	61	66	67	57	61	64	2,065	2,168	2,418
Central Asia and Former Soviet Union									
Kazakhstan	72	73	70	62	64	60	n/a	n/a	3,007
KyrgyzRepublic	70	73	71	61	64	62	n/a	n/a	2,489
Mongolia	59	64	67	57	61	64	2,398	2,212	2,098
Tajikistan	69	72	72	64	67	66	n/a	n/a	2,129
Uzbekistan	71	72	72	64	66	66	n/a	n/a	2,550
Total/Weighted Average	70	72	71	63	65	64	n/a	n/a	2,613
Newly Industrialized Countries									
Hong Kong	77	80	81	71	75	76	2,888	3,233	3,282
Korea, Republic of	70	74	76	64	67	69	3,102	3,254	3,336
Singapore	74	77	79	69	72	74	n/a	n/a	n/a
Taipei, China	75	77	78	70	71	72	2,882	2,943	3,076
Total/Weighted Average	72	75	77	66	69	71	3,019	3,162	3,256
Papua New Guinea and Pacific Islands									
Total/Weighted Average[c]	56	60	62	55	57	60	2,151	2,199	2,253
TOTAL ASIA	61	65	67	60	63	65	2,136	2,441	2,631

	Child Malnutrition (% under age 5 with low weight-for-age)		1992–95 Population % with		
	1980–85	1990–96	Safe Water Urban	Rural	Sanitation
Southeast Asia					
Indonesia	48	40	78	54	51
Malaysia	27	23	100	74	91
Philippines	33	30	93	77	77
Thailand	36	13	89	72	70
Total/Weighted Average[b]	42	32	84	63	62
South Asia					
Bangladesh	70	68	42	80	35
Bhutan	n/a	n/a	75	54	41
India	n/a	66	85	79	29
Nepal	70	49	64	49	20
Pakistan	n/a	40	77	52	30
Sri Lanka	48	38	43	47	52
Total/Weighted Average	n/a	n/a	79	75	30
Transitional East Asia					
Cambodia	20	38	20	12	n/a
Lao People's Democratic Republic	37	40	40	39	19
People's Republic of China (PRC)	n/a	16	93	89	21
Viet Nam	52	45	53	32	21
Weighted Average (with PRC)	n/a	18	90	85	21
Weighted Average (without PRC)	47	44	48	30	21
Central Asia and Former Soviet Union					
Kazakhstan	n/a	1	n/a	n/a	n/a
Kyrgyz Republic	n/a	n/a	n/a	n/a	53
Mongolia	n/a	12	n/a	n/a	n/a
Tajikistan	n/a	n/a	n/a	n/a	62
Uzbekistan	n/a	4	n/a	n/a	18
Total/Weighted Average	n/a	n/a	n/a	n/a	n/a
Newly Industrialized Countries					
Hong Kong	n/a	n/a	n/a	n/a	n/a
Korea, Republic of	n/a	n/a	n/a	n/a	100
Singapore	n/a	14	100	n/a	97
Taipei, China	n/a	n/a	n/a	n/a	n/a
Total/Weighted Average	n/a	n/a	n/a	n/a	n/a
Papua New Guinea and Pacific Islands					
Total/Weighted Average[c]	35	30	84	17	22
TOTAL ASIA	n/a	n/a	n/a	n/a	n/a

| | \multicolumn{6}{c|}{Adult Literacy Rate (%)} |
| | \multicolumn{3}{c|}{Female} | \multicolumn{3}{c|}{Male} |
	1980	1990	1995	1980	1990	1995
Southeast Asia						
Indonesia	58	75	78	78	88	90
Malaysia	60	74	78	80	87	89
Philippines	n/a	93	94	91	94	95
Thailand	n/a	91	92	92	96	96
Total/Weighted Average[b]	n/a	82	84	83	91	92
South Asia						
Bangladesh	17	23	26	41	47	49
Bhutan	15	23	28	41	51	56
India	25	34	38	55	62	66
Nepal	15	11	14	31	37	41
Pakistan	45	21	24	38	46	50
Sri Lanka	72	85	87	91	93	93
Total/Weighted Average	27	31	35	52	59	62
Transitional East Asia						
Cambodia	n/a	n/a	n/a	n/a	n/a	n/a
Lao People's Democratic Republic	28	39	44	56	65	69
People's Republic of China (PRC)	53	68	73	79	87	90
Viet Nam	78	87	91	90	95	97
Weighted Average (with PRC)	54	69	74	79	87	90
Weighted Average (without PRC)	75	84	88	88	93	95
Central Asia and Former Soviet Union						
Kazakhstan	n/a	n/a	n/a	n/a	n/a	n/a
Kyrgyz Republic	n/a	n/a	n/a	n/a	n/a	n/a
Mongolia	63	73	77	82	87	89
Tajikistan	84	n/a	n/a	n/a	n/a	n/a
Uzbekistan	n/a	n/a	n/a	n/a	n/a	n/a
Total/Weighted Average	n/a	n/a	n/a	n/a	n/a	n/a
Newly Industrialized Countries						
Hong Kong	77	85	88	94	96	96
Korea, Republic of	90	95	97	98	99	99
Singapore	n/a	83	86	92	95	96
Taipei, China	n/a	84	91	92	96	98
Total/Weighted Average	89	91	94	95	98	99
Papua New Guinea and Pacific Islands						
Total/Weighted Average[c]	89	57	n/a	70	78	n/a
TOTAL ASIA	37	55	58	68	75	77

	Gross Primary School Enrollment Ratio (%)					
	Female			Male		
	1980	1990	1996	1980	1990	1996
Southeast Asia						
Indonesia	100	114	112	115	117	117
Malaysia	92	93	92	93	93	90
Philippines	110	112	119	114	114	116
Thailand	97	99	88	100	100	88
Total/Weighted Average[b]	101	110	108	111	112	110
South Asia						
Bangladesh	46	64	78	75	74	90
Bhutan	n/a	n/a	n/a	n/a	n/a	n/a
India	67	84	90	98	110	110
Nepal	50	81	84	119	132	125
Pakistan	27	39	51	51	82	109
Sri Lanka	100	104	108	105	106	110
Total/Weighted Average	61	77	85	91	104	108
Transitional East Asia						
Cambodia	157	106	99	187	130	119
Lao People's Democratic Republic	104	85	97	123	114	125
People's Republic of China (PRC)	104	121	120	121	132	121
Viet Nam	106	100	112	111	106	118
Weighted Average (with PRC)	104	120	119	121	130	121
Weighted Average (without PRC)	112	100	110	121	109	118
Central Asia and Former Soviet Union						
Kazakhstan	84	87	96	85	88	95
Kyrgyz Republic	114	111	107	117	111	110
Mongolia	107	98	92	107	96	88
Tajikistan	78	90	92	79	92	95
Uzbekistan	80	81	78	83	82	80
Total/Weighted Average	85	87	88	87	88	89
Newly Industrialized Countries						
Hong Kong	106	103	98	107	102	96
Korea, Republic of	111	105	95	109	105	94
Singapore	106	102	93	109	105	95
Taipei, China	100	100	102	99	99	100
Total/Weighted Average	107	103	97	106	103	96
Papua New Guinea and Pacific Islands						
Total/Weighted Average[c]	51	66	73	66	78	85
TOTAL ASIA	**86**	**100**	**103**	**107**	**116**	**113**

Rural Human Capital

	Gross Secondary School Enrollment Ratio (%)					
	Female			Male		
	1980	1990	1996	1980	1990	1996
Southeast Asia						
Indonesia	23	40	48	35	48	56
Malaysia	46	60	66	50	56	58
Philippines	69	74	80	60	73	78
Thailand	28	30	57	30	31	58
Total/Weighted Average[b]	35	46	57	40	51	61
South Asia						
Bangladesh	9	14	13	26	28	24
Bhutan	n/a	n/a	n/a	n/a	n/a	n/a
India	20	33	39	39	55	59
Nepal	9	20	25	33	46	49
Pakistan	8	15	21	20	30	38
Sri Lanka	57	77	78	52	71	71
Total/Weighted Average	18	29	35	36	49	53
Transitional East Asia						
Cambodia	1	19	20	3	44	35
Lao People's Democratic Republic	16	18	23	25	29	36
People's Republic of China (PRC)	37	42	67	54	56	74
Viet Nam	40	31	40	44	33	41
Weighted Average (with PRC)	37	41	65	53	54	72
Weighted Average (without PRC)	34	29	36	38	34	40
Central Asia and Former Soviet Union						
Kazakhstan	93	99	89	92	97	80
Kyrgyz Republic	108	101	70	112	99	89
Mongolia	94	88	65	88	77	48
Tajikistan	100	102	72	100	102	81
Uzbekistan	94	95	88	117	104	98
Total/Weighted Average	96	97	84	106	100	88
Newly Industrialized Countries						
Hong Kong	65	82	77	63	78	73
Korea, Republic of	74	89	102	82	91	102
Singapore	60	66	74	60	71	72
Taipei, China	80	97	99	81	93	96
Total/Weighted Average	74	89	98	79	89	96
Papua New Guinea and Pacific Islands						
Total/Weighted Average[c]	8	10	11	15	15	16
TOTAL ASIA	31	39	53	46	54	64

	Total Health Expenditure per capita (1990 $)	Health Expenditure as % of GDP (1990)			Private %
		Total	Public	Private	
Southeast Asia					
Indonesia	12	2.0	0.7	1.3	65
Malaysia	59	2.5	1.3	1.2	48
Philippines	20	2.8	1.0	1.9	68
Thailand	73	5.0	1.1	3.9	78
Total/Weighted Average[b]	27	2.7	0.9	1.9	67
South Asia					
Bangladesh	7	3.2	1.4	1.8	56
Bhutan	n/a	n/a	n/a	n/a	n/a
India	21	6.0	1.3	4.7	78
Nepal	7	4.5	2.2	2.3	51
Pakistan	12	3.5	1.8	1.6	46
Sri Lanka	18	3.7	1.8	1.9	51
Total/Weighted Average	18	5.4	1.4	4.0	72
Transitional East Asia					
Cambodia	n/a	n/a	n/a	n/a	n/a
Lao People's Democratic Republic	6	2.9	1.0	1.9	66
People's Republic of China (PRC)	11	3.5	2.1	1.4	40
Viet Nam	2	2.1	1.1	1.0	48
Weighted Average (with PRC)	10	3.4	2.0	1.4	41
Weighted Average (without PRC)	2	2.1	1.1	1.1	49
Central Asia and Former Soviet Union					
Kazakhstan	153	4.4	2.8	1.6	36
Kyrgyz Republic	117	5.0	3.3	1.6	32
Mongolia	n/a	n/a	n/a	n/a	n/a
Tajikistan	100	6.0	4.4	1.6	27
Uzbekistan	116	5.9	4.3	1.6	27
Total/Weighted Average	120	5.4	3.7	1.6	30
Newly Industrialized Countries					
Hong Kong	699	5.7	1.1	4.6	81
Korea, Republic of	377	6.6	2.7	3.9	59
Singapore	219	1.9	1.1	0.8	42
Taipei, China	n/a	n/a	n/a	n/a	n/a
Total/Weighted Average	404	6.2	2.4	3.8	61
Papua New Guinea and Pacific Islands					
Total/Weighted Average[c]	36	4.4	2.8	1.5	34
TOTAL ASIA	28	4.2	1.7	2.6	57

"n/a" indicates data not available or not calculated.

[a] Computed by the United Nations Development Programme, the Human Development Index (HDI) is a composite measure of life expectancy, adult literacy, school enrollment, and adjusted real per capita Gross Domestic Product. The HDI potentially ranges from 0.0 to 1.0 in value.

[b] Population in the subregion is totaled and is then used to weight the calculations in the succeeding columns.

[c] Figures for calorie availability, child malnutrition, safe water, literacy, and school enrolment are for Papua New Guinea, which accounts for two-thirds of the total population of this county group.

Sources: Data on health expenditure from World Bank (1993). All other data are from the statistical database maintained by ADB's Statistics and Data Systems Division.

VIII Conclusion

RESPONDING TO HISTORICAL EXPERIENCE

Two major developments have shaped Asian society in the last thirty 30 years. The first is the green revolution, which has transformed those areas of rural Asia where the new technology was adopted. There, the transformation increased the standard of living of the people, leading them to demand more consumer goods, but also putting pressure on the public sector to provide more basic infrastructure, such as roads and electricity, as well as better education and health care. It also led to a significant increase in food production and seemed to solve the perennial food-shortage problem.

The second is the rapid industrial growth in many Asian economies, mostly in East and Southeast Asia, which has impacted on rural areas through the enormous migration from villages to the factories and urban areas and through the development of rural nonfarm industrial and service businesses. In a few countries, where the labor surplus in agriculture was small to begin with (such as Malaysia and Thailand), acute shortages of labor for agriculture began to appear. A key consequence of this industrialization for the public sector has been the increased demand by parents for their children's education, as they realized that the future of their children lies more in the towns and cities than in the agricultural sector.

The result of both of these changes is the diminishing role of agriculture. Although agriculture continues to be very important from the standpoints of employment, poverty and the environment, it no longer makes nearly as large a contribution to

Asian GDP as it did in the 1950s and 1960s. Indeed, agriculture's share of GDP has shrunk to developed-country levels in some of Asia's fastest-growing economies (Figure VIII.1). Governments today are taking a sanguine view about food security, assuming that the existing research and extension systems are well positioned to sustain the growth of production. The view that agriculture is a "sunset industry" has even received implicit support from many donors. Two major analyses of the East Asian success story, from no lesser authorities than the World Bank (1993c) and the Asian Development Bank (1997), paid little attention to the agricultural sector. This would have been incomprehensible to the planners of the 1950s and 1960s.

As a result, the government's attention has shifted to other sectors. Meanwhile, the productivity increases following upon the green revolution have tended to ameliorate somewhat the problems of poverty among landless laborers and small farmers in the resource-rich areas, but there remain large areas of deep poverty and malnutrition. In general, there has been relative neglect by governments of the needs of rural people in respect to many important social services, such as education and health, the provision of which has mainly benefited urban populations. The private-sector response to the increased demand for education and health care has been dramatic, but even more urban-biased.

NEW ACTORS IN OLD ROLES

Seen in the 1960s as the main provider of funding for all of society's collective needs, the State has changed its role over time. In part, this is because changing conditions, both domestically and internationally, have revealed its limitations: governments simply cannot provide for every need. More importantly, the trends toward market liberalization, privatization, and decentralization have led to a multiplicity of actors in Asian rural development. Thus, Asia has seen the

Figure VIII.1. Agriculture as a Share of Gross Domestic Product

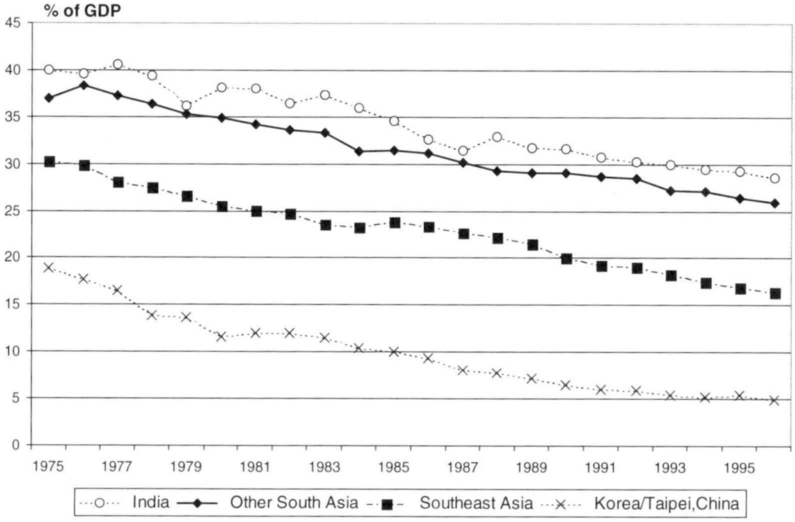

Notes: Other South Asia includes Bangladesh, Nepal, Pakistan, and Sri Lanka. Southeast Asia includes Indonesia, Malaysia, the Philippines, and Thailand. Grouped countries weighted by GDP.
Source: ADB Statistical Database System.

expansion of the competitive private sector as well as the emergnce of local communities and NGOs, buttressed by the moral and financial suasion provided by donors. These actors are not always alternative providers. It is increasingly accepted that various actors can jointly provide for society's collective needs with greater efficiency and accountability. Gone are the days when public- and private-sector activities were largely separate.

There has been in recent years growing pressure for devolution and decentralization, with many countries starting to devolve public administration to local governments at various levels. From the study of this process in Indonesia and the Philippines earlier in this volume, two somewhat conflicting lessons can be drawn.[1] First, the process of devolution—

---

[1] The PRC was also studied in Chapter III, but its circumstances and process of devolution are unique and unlikely to be replicable elsewhere.

including whether it is necessary at all—should be carefully thought through, but once the political decision is made, its implementation should be rapid. Second, decentralization takes time to achieve, particularly for local authorities to acquire a full understanding of their responsibilities and to become wholehearted participants. This dilemma of the simultaneous needs for urgency and caution underscore a third lesson, that both political will for decisive initiation and commitment to a long-drawn-out process of implementation are crucial for decentralization to succeed.

The transitional economies are engaged in the most significant processes of market reform and privatization. Although property rights in land are not yet fully secured, the farm sectors are now effectively in private hands in the PRC and Viet Nam and are well on the way to being so in the Central Asian Republics, particularly Kazakhstan and the Kyrgyz Republic. In the PRC, decentralization of the economy engendered rapid growth of the township and village enterprises, entailing quite substantial rural industrialization. The efforts of other Asian governments to industrialize the countryside have, however, been largely unsuccessful.

In countries that have evolved along a democratic—or at least more participatory—path, the greater voice of civil society, NGOs and local communities has tended to diminish the authority of the civil service. In many countries, the NGOs have yet to work out a fully satisfactory relationship with the organs of the State, including both the civil service and the political parties. Despite the uneasy relationship, NGOs have contributed in many areas, most notably in microfinance, extension, health care, and, traditionally in many countries, education. More visibly, of course, they now play a major role as advocacy groups, and it is in this connection that their relationship with the State is prickliest.

New actors can also be seen in the area of agricultural technology. The public research system used to have a monopoly in research, but two factors have altered this. The first is the rise of biotechnology, which introduces the multinational corporations as significant new players. Although these new actors will no doubt add to the pool of knowledge and technology for future agriculture, their entry onto the scene is also introducing inherent biases in favor of proprietary technologies and away from most tropical crops, including many food crops grown by the poor. It is, therefore, the conclusion of this volume that the central Government should increase its capability in biotechnology, both to correct these biases and also to equip itself with the capability to oversee and regulate biotechnology applications.

The second factor in agricultural technology is the need to move toward more research on resource management and away from the overwhelming concentration on genetic improvement. Resource management is highly location-specific, making the concentration of work in centralized research and experiment stations less relevant. Similarly, in extension, the top-down package approach for public extension was appropriate during the green revolution, but no longer has as great a role to play. In the future, since technology will be much more knowledge-based and location-specific, the need for extension services will be of a different kind. In particular, it is proposed that the extension system should be devolved away from the center as much as possible, with local governments taking charge of the public system and the private sector (particularly the NGOs) being encouraged to participate.

In irrigation, which received the lion's share of public agricultural funding up to the mid-1980s, there is considerably less scope for new construction in the great flood plains. There, the largely private development of groundwater has to some extent circumvented the inefficiencies resulting from poor management of surface water within the public systems. Within the upper valleys, there is scope for irrigation management to improve if it is transferred as much as possible away from State organizations to the user communities. Similarly, new investments within these areas should incorporate from the design stage the knowledge and experience of the communities that are to be served by the irrigation systems.

In regard to water more generally, the dominant issue for the coming decades will be increasing water scarcity. This will require enhanced State regulatory roles in water allocation and, in the distant future, a gradual evolution of a market for water, which will necessitate extensive legal reforms. As an increasingly residual claimant of water, agriculture will come under ever greater pressure to economize.

The situation in irrigation reflects the more general trend toward reducing subsidies, which, in agriculture, have traditionally covered inputs like fertilizer and credit. In direct contrast to this, on the output side, there has been a general move away from the policy of taxing agriculture in favor of supporting prices, sometimes above world levels. Whatever pricing strategy is followed, there is much less need than before for a State grain-trading operation in most Asian countries. This conclusion holds even more strongly with respect to fertilizer distribution. More efficient market-based approaches exist, but their application will be tempered by the political scene, in particular, the structure of political and institutional incentives facing policymakers and the balance of voting power between rural and urban areas.

Almost all Asian governments recognize the need to improve education and health services, but they have, with few exceptions, been relatively unsuccessful in serving the widely dispersed, heterogeneous rural populations. Urban bias is a dominant theme in the discussion of these services. In rural education, primary schooling is the priority in South Asia, but the main need in Southeast Asia is now at the secondary level. Given the enormity of the tasks in both education and health, it is difficult to foresee any lessening of the role of the public sector in providing these "merit goods," at least as far as funding to serve the poor and the rural areas is concerned. Education and health are highly desired goods for almost all households, so it is fully appropriate that consumer willingness to pay be exploited as incomes rise. The argument for greater allocation of public resources to the needs of rural areas stems from the likelihood that rural incomes will continue to grow more slowly than urban incomes and that private-sector investment will continue to be concentrated in urban areas. Moreover, while some countries are experimenting with the use of NGOs and other community-based approaches to provide and finance education, this is unlikely to meet the pressing needs of the rural poor during the foreseeable future, particularly in South Asia.

In rural health, the traditional emphasis since colonial times has been the prevention of infectious and communicable diseases. The problem with the delivery of curative health services is the urban bias that still exists in many parts of Asia. This problem has become both easier and more difficult over time. It has become easier because new knowledge and medicines have come into existence that prolong the lives of rural people significantly. But as people live longer, as incomes have risen, and as shifts away from traditional medicine have taken place, the increased demands are threatening to overwhelm the public system. At both the micro and macro levels, imaginative solutions will have to be sought for the issues of provision and financing.

NEW ROLES FOR AN OLD ACTOR

Even with the entry of new actors into the scene, it would be a mistake to believe that the task of the State will be lightened. On the contrary, the need to ride herd on the various actors, to ensure that they perform with the public interest in mind, and to coordinate their roles with others, requires a cadre of policymakers with savvy and considerable foresight. For Asian societies to come up with such leaders will be a challenge for the 21st century.

The old roles of the State, for which there remains an unambiguous need despite the appearance of new actors, include

- taxation and macroeconomic stabilization;
- provision of pure public goods, for example, basic agricultural research and much rural infrastructure;

- creation and facilitation of new markets, for example in water, which at times require...
- provision of enabling legal frameworks, including the establishment of property rights;
- monitoring of the markets for private goods, including the establishment and enforcement of quality standards for goods such as food and agricultural inputs, and for private services such as health care and education; and
- establishment of disclosure requirements for civil society organizations.

Even in those tasks that remain squarely in the public sector's domain, the central Government's performance will have to be more nuanced and sensitive to the existence of other actors than the top-down approach to which it has been accustomed. Thus, in the area of fiscal policy generally (including its role in macroeconomic stabilization), it will have to reconsider local taxes and expenditures. The provision of basic agricultural research has to be designed to fit in with the more applied agricultural research that should be devolved to the regions. The provision of property rights in land in ecologically fragile areas (whether to communities or to individuals) must be accompanied by appropriate instruments for land-use regulation. At the same time, future water scarcity may require that the State grant property rights in water (probably to communities or groups of users) or sharpen its command and control mechanisms. Whatever it chooses to do, it has to become more responsive to the needs of the users. Finally, the State has to be sensitive in its handling of civil society organizations, navigating carefully between, on the one hand, smothering them with too much attention (benign or malignant) and, on the other, a completely laissez-faire approach that would allow such organizations to be co-opted by vested interests.

There are some tasks that the central Government will increasingly have to share with other actors:

- It will continue to be charged with ensuring that every individual in society, particularly among the poor, is able to meet his or her basic food needs. In this area, the Government will have to work closely with local governments, to increase the accuracy of targeting, and with the for-profit private sector, to ensure the efficiency of the physical distribution mechanism.
- It will continue to manage "large" irrigation structures, but in doing so it will have to work closely with communities of water users, perhaps turning over lower-level operations and maintenance functions to them.
- It will continue to provide (or finance the provision of) elementary education and primary health care, again working closely with local communities and perhaps with NGOs to ensure that the quality standards of both are maintained.
- It will, of necessity, play a lead role in devolving powers to local levels of government and will hopefully take the initiative in building local capacity when this is still very weak. In doing so, it will need to engage in a long and complex process requiring careful preparation, extensive consultation, and meticulous planning, followed by firm political commitment, steady implementation, and above all adequate finance.

The institutional challenges facing Asian states that seek to accelerate rural development are far from trivial. To tackle these challenges, the State will need to marshal new skills for itself as well as financial resources. Both the skills and resources need not "belong" to the State, as was naturally assumed in the 1960s and 1970s. Indeed, the countries that will rise most successfully to the challenge are likely to be those with a vibrant private sector, an active civil society, and a competent, professional bureaucracy. The final requirement is a political leadership that can harness the skills and resources of these three components to improve the lives and welfare of rural people.

The future Asian political leader who can do the job does not need to be charismatic or visionary. Asia has had its share of leaders who claim to possess such qualities, but the results of their rule have been mixed. Some have succeeded in achieving material progress, but in too many instances, this has come at the expense of the development of civil society. Of course there is no harm if political leaders do possess charisma and vision, provided that these do not get in the way of their ability to constructively marshal the resources of the private sector and civil society.

FITTING ACTORS INTO ROLES: A GUIDE FOR THE POLICY ANALYST

The last several paragraphs took a very broad-brush approach to the issue of what can be done by a central Government to further sustainable growth and improved quality of life in rural areas. Unfortunately, it provides little guidance for the policy analyst, who has to start with a role, a project, or a policy; figure out whether it can be implemented; and—the most important lesson from this volume—decide on which actor(s) would be best suited to implement it. The following is an attempt to generalize from the cases discussed in Chapters III through VII, in the form of a series of questions to be asked about the assignment of actors to particular roles.

Before proceeding, it is necessary to make a point of principle: it is necessary to resist the temptation to automatically apply practices that work in one country to any other country. Similarly, success at assigning an actor to a particular role in one country does not necessarily ensure that the same actor will perform well somewhere else. In other words, the answers to the questions must be location- and function-specific.

The process therefore starts with a role, to which the following questions and actions should be addressed:

i. Does the role need to be filled at all?
ii. Who are the stakeholders in that role?
iii. Into how many separate and clearly defined tasks can the role be broken down?
iv. Which actors could potentially undertake each task? In answering the question the net should be cast as widely as possible.
v. Who among the actors has the comparative advantage to undertake each task at hand? If the question has already been implicitly answered in the definition of the task, or in the way that task has been performed in the past, this should put the analyst immediately on guard, for it probably implies that little thought has been given to analyzing options for that role.
vi. Who among the actors identified in iv. above appears to be most suitable to perform the lead function? Actors that fill the lead function are ultimately accountable to the stakeholders for the performance of the role. Suitability should be judged with this in mind.
vii. How is the implementation of the role to be financed?
viii. Given the system of financing, what is the incentive structure facing the lead actor? And given the incentive structure, what are the possibilities for that actor to shirk in his performance?
ix. How is the system of accountability to stakeholders to be implemented? In particular, what mechanisms are to be set up for performance monitoring? What penalties can realistically be imposed on the lead actor if he or she fails to perform as expected?
x. Can the arrangements devised under ix. above be implemented under existing laws and regulations? If the laws and regulations to impose the incentive structure or to set up the system of

monitoring (see ix.) have to be changed, how expensive will this be, in terms of time and resources?
xi. If other actors are to perform the various tasks attached to a role, what systems of accountability, monitoring, and penalties are in place?
xii. What is the overall cost of this particular arrangement?
xiii. Experiment by using other lead actors, go back to steps vii. through xii., and see if costs can be reduced.

REFERENCES

ADB (Asian Development Bank). 1977. *Rural Asia: Challenge and Opportunity*. Manila: Asian Development Bank.
———. 1995a. *Governance: Sound Development Management*. Manila: Asian Development Bank.
———. 1995b. Sector Synthesis of Postevaluation Findings in the Irrigation and Rural Development Sector. Post-Evaluation Office. Manila.
———. 1996a. Program Completion Report on the Foodcrops Development Program to Bangladesh. Manila: Asian Development Bank.
———. 1996b. *Towards Effective Water Policy In the Asian and Pacific Region: Overview of Issues and Recommendations*. Manila: Asian Development Bank.
———. 1997. *Emerging Asia: Challenges and Opportunities*. Manila: Asian Development Bank.
———. 1998. *Financing Human Development*. Manila: Asian Development Bank.
———. 1999a. *Policy for the Health Sector*. Manila: Asian Development Bank.
———. 1999b. *Statistical Tables for Member Countries*. Economics and Development Resource Center. Asian Development Bank. Manila: Asian Development Bank.
———. Various Years. *Key Indicators of Developing Asian and Pacific Countries*. Manila: Asian Development Bank.
———. Various Years. Statistical Database System.
Ahmed, Raisuddin. 1979. Foodgrain Supply, Distribution, and Consumption Policies within a Dual Pricing Mecha-

nism: a Case Study of Bangladesh. *Research Report* No. 8. Washington, DC: International Food Policy Research Institute.

———. 1995. Liberalization of Agricultural Input Markets in Bangladesh: Process, Impact, and Lessons. *Agricultural Economics* 12 (2).

Ali, I. 1986. *Rice in Indonesia: Price Policy and Comparative Advantage*. Asian Development Bank Economic Staff Paper. Manila: Asian Development Bank.

Amara Pongsapich. 1995. Philanthropy in Thailand. In *Emerging Civil Society in the Asia Pacific Community: Nongovernmental Underpinnings of the Emerging Asia Pacific Regional Community*, edited by Tadashi Tamamoto. Tokyo: Japan Center for International Exchange.

Ammar Siamwalla. 1975. A History of Rice Policies in Thailand. *Food Research Institute Studies* 14 (3).

———. 1988. Public Stock Management. In *Agricultural Price Policy for Developing Countries*, edited by John W. Mellor and Raisuddin Ahmed. Baltimore: Johns Hopkins University Press.

———, and Kanok Wongfranjan. 1985. The Institutional Basis of Thai Rice Price Policies. Background paper prepared for the World Bank, in *Thailand: Pricing and Marketing Policy for Intensification of Rice Agriculture*. Washington, DC: World Bank.

———, and Orapin Sobchokchai. 1998. Responding to the Thai Economic Crisis. Paper prepared for the High-Level Consultative Meeting on "Policy Response to the Economic Crisis and Social Impact in Thailand," sponsored by the United Nations Development Program, 22 May 1998.

———, and Suthad Setboonsarng. 1989. *Trade, Exchange Rate, and Agricultural Pricing Policies in Thailand*. Washington, DC: World Bank.

Anan Ganjanapan. 1998. Philanthropy, Raising Capital for Society. *TDRI Quarterly Review* 13 (e).

Anderson, K., and Y. Hayami (editors). 1986. *The Political Economy of Agricultural Protection: East Asia in International Perspective*. Sydney: Allen and Unwin.

Anderson, Robert S., E. Levy, and B. Morrison. 1991. *Rice Science and Development Politics: Research Strategies and IRRI's Technologies Confront Asian Diversity (1950–1980)*. Oxford: Clarendon Press.

Arndt, Heinz W. 1987. *Economic Development: The History of an Idea*. Chicago: University of Chicago Press.

Axelrod, Robert. 1994. *The Evolution of Cooperation*. New York: Basic Books.

Barjarcharya, H. R., B. K. Thapa, and R. Chitrakar. 1997. *Trends, Issues, and Policies in Education of Nepal: A Country Case Study*. Manila: Asian Development Bank.

Balisacan, Arsenio M. 1990. *Fertilizers and Fertilizer Policies in Philippine Agricultural Development*. Los Baños: Center for Policy and Development Studies, University of the Philippines at Los Baños.

Barker, Randolph, and Y. Hayami. 1976. Price Support versus Input Subsidy for Food Self-Sufficiency in Developing Countries. *American Journal of Agricultural Economics*, Part I 58 (4).

Bates, R. 1981. *Markets and States in Tropical Africa: The Political Basis of Agricultural Policies*. Berkeley: University of California Press.

———. 1983. The Nature and Origins of Agricultural Policies in Africa. In *Essays on the Political Economy of Rural Africa*, edited by R. Bates. Berkeley: University of California Press.

Bauer, Armin, N. Boschmann, D. Green, and K. Kuehnast. 1998. *A Generation at Risk: Children in the Central Asian Republics of Kazakhstan and Kyrgyzstan*. Manila: Asian Development Bank.

Becker, Gary S. 1995. Human Capital and Poverty Alleviation. World Bank lecture in December 1994, reproduced in *Human Resources Development and Policy Working Paper* No. 52. Washington, DC: World Bank.

Bennell, Paul. 1996a. Using and Abusing Rates of Return: A Critique of the World Bank's 1995 Education Sector Review. *International Journal of Education Development* 16 (3).

———. 1996b. Rates of Return to Education: Does the Conventional Pattern Prevail in Sub-Saharan Africa? *World Development* 24 (1).

Bloom, B. S. 1994. *Stability and Change in Human Characteristics*. New York: John Wiley and Sons.

Bloom, David E., P. Craig, and P. Malaney. 1999. *The Quality of Life in Rural Asia*. Hong Kong: Oxford University Press.

Booth, Anne. 1986. Efforts to Decentralize Fiscal Policy: Problems of Taxable Capacity, Tax Effort and Revenue Sharing. In *Central Government and Local Development in Indonesia*, edited by Colin MacAndrews. Singapore: Oxford University Press.

Boserup, Ester. 1965. *The Conditions of Agricultural Growth: The Economics of Agrarian Change under Population Pressure*, London: George Allen & Unwin.

Bouis, Howarth. 1983. Seasonal Rice Prices in the Philippines—Measuring the Effects of Government Intervention. *Food Research Institute Studies* 19(1).

Bray, Mark. 1998. Financing Education in Developing Asia: Patterns, Trends, and Policy Implications. Paper prepared for Regional Technical Assistance No. 5722: Regional Study of Trends, Issues and Policies in Education. Manila: Asian Development Bank.

BRWS (Bengal Rural Welfare Services). 1998. *Annual Report 1997–1998*. Calcutta.

Bumb, Balu L., and Baanante, C. 1996. The Role of Fertilizer in Sustaining Food Security and Protecting the Environment. *Food, Agriculture and the Environment Discussion Paper* No. 17. Washington, DC: International Food Policy Research Institute.

Burgess, Robin. 1997. Fiscal Reform and the Extension of Basic Health and Education Coverage. In *Marketizing Education and Health in Developing Countries: Miracle or Mirage?*, edited by Christopher Colclough. Oxford: Clarendon Press.

Byerlee, D. 1998. Knowledge-Intensive Crop Management Technologies: Concepts, Impacts, and Prospects in Asian Agriculture. In *Impact of Rice Research*, edited by Prabhu Pingali and Mahabub Hossein. Los Baños: International Rice Research Institute.

Byrd, William A., and Lin Qingsong. 1990. China's Rural Industry: an Introduction. In *China's Rural Industry: Structure, Development, and Reform*, edited by William A. Byrd and Lin Qingsong. Oxford: Oxford University Press.

Calder, I. R. 1998. Water Resource and Land-Use Issues. Paper No. 3. Colombo: System-Wide Initiative on Water Management. Inter-national Irrigation Management Institute.

Carey, J., and M. Shugart. 1995. Incentives to Cultivate a Personal Vote: A Rank Ordering of Electoral Formulas. *Electoral Studies* 14 (4).

Carlson, Gerald A., D. Zilberman and J. Miranowski (editors). 1993. *Agricultural and Environmental Resource Economics*. New York: Oxford University Press.

Carter, Richard. 1998. Prospects for Sustainable Water Management Policy in Sub-Saharan Africa, with Special Reference to the Northeast Arid Zone of Nigeria. In *Water Resource Management: A Comparative Perspective*, edited by Dhirendra K. Vajpeyi. Westport, CT: Praeger Publishers.

CCAMD. 1997. *Report of Congressional Commission on Agricultural Modernization and Development*. Manila.

Chambers, Robert. 1988. *Managing Canal Irrigation: Practical Analysis from South Asia*. Cambridge: Cambridge University Press.

Chapman, David. W. 1998. Trends, Issues and Policies in Education Management and Efficiency in Asia. Paper prepared for Regional Technical Assistance No. 5722: Regional Study of Trends, Issues and Policies in Education. Manila: Asian Development Bank.

Che, Jiahua, and Yingyi Qian. 1998. Insecure Property Rights and Government Ownership of Firms. *Quarterly Journal of Economics* (May).

Cheema, G.S., and D.A. Rondinelli (editors). 1983. *Decentralization and Development: Policy Implementation in Developing Countries*. Beverly Hills: Sage Press.

Chenery, Hollis, Montek S. Ahluwalia, C. L. G. Bell, John H. Duloy, and Richard Jolly. 1974. *Redistribution with Growth*. London: Oxford University Press.

CIMMYT (Centro Internacional de Mejoramiento de Maiz y Trigo). 1987. *1986 World Maize Facts and Trends: the Eco-*

nomics of Commercial Maize and Seed Production in Developing Countries. Mexico, D.F.

Comanor, William S. 1986. The Political Economy of the Pharmaceutical Industry. *Journal of Economic Literature* 24 (3).

Coward, E. Walter (editor). 1980. *Irrigation and Agricultural Development in Asia.* Ithaca: Cornell University Press.

———, and G. Levine. 1987. Studies of Farmer-Managed Irrigation Systems: Ten Years of Cumulative Knowledge and Changing Research Priorities. In *Public Intervention in Farmer-Managed Irrigation Systems.* Colombo: International Irrigation Management Institute.

Cox, G. 1984. Strategic Electoral Choice in Multi-Member Districts: Approval Voting in Practice? *American Journal of Political Science* 28.

———. 1987. Electoral Equilibrium under Alternative Voting Institutions. *American Journal of Political Science* 31.

———, and M. McCubbins. 2000. Political Structure and Economic Policy: the Institutional Determinants of Policy Outcomes. In *Structure and Policy in Presidential Democracies,* edited by S. Haggard and M. McCubbins. New York: Cambridge University Press.

Crouch, H. 1996. *Government and Society in Malaysia.* Ithaca: Cornell University Press.

Crook, R., and J. Manor. 1994. *Enhancing Participation and Institutional Performance: Democratic Decentralization in South Asia and West Africa.* Report to ESCOR and the Overseas Development Administration.

David, Cristina C., and Keijiro Otsuka. 1994. Differential Impact of Modern Rice Varieties in Asia: an Overview. In *Modern Rice Technology and Income Distribution in Asia,* edited by Cristina C. David and Keijiro Otsuka. Boulder, CO: Lynne Rienner Publishers.

De los Reyes, Romana P., and S. Jopillo 1987. An Evaluation of NIA's Participatory Communal Program. In *Public Intervention in Farmer-Managed Irrigation Systems.* Colombo: International Irrigation Management Institute.

DILG (Philippines Department of Interior and Local Government). 1998. *Program of Devolution Adjustment and Equalization.* Manila.

Dreze, Jean, and Amartya Sen. 1995. *India: Economic Development and Social Opportunity.* Oxford: Oxford University Press.

Du, Haiyan. 1990. Causes of Rapid Rural Industrial Development. In *China's Rural Industry: Structure, Development, and Reform*, edited by William A. Byrd and Lin Qingsong. Oxford: Oxford University Press.

Echeverria, Ruben G. 1991. Impact of Research and Seed Trade on Maize Productivity. In *Agricultural Research Policy: International Quantitative Perspectives*, edited by Philip G. Pardey, Johannes Roseboom, and Jock R. Anderson. Cambridge: Cambridge University Press.

Edirisinghe, Neville. 1988. Food Subsidy Changes in Sri Lanka: the Short-Run Effect on the Poor. In *Food Subsidies in Developing Countries: Costs, Benefits, and Policy Options*, edited by Per Pinstrup-Andersen. Baltimore: Johns Hopkins University Press.

Edwards, Michael, and David Hulme. 1996. Too Close for Comfort? The Impact of Official Aid on Nongovernmental Organizations. *World Development* 24 (6).

Eggertsson, Thrainn. 1990. *Economic Behavior and Institutions.* Cambridge: Cambridge University Press.

El-Ghonemy, M. Riad. 1990. *The Political Economy of Rural Poverty: The Case for Land Reform.* London: Routledge.

Evenson, Robert E. 1991. IARC, NARC and Extension Investment, and Field Crop Productivity: An International Assessment. In *Research and Productivity in Asian Agriculture*, edited by Robert E. Evenson and Carl E. Pray. Ithaca: Cornell University Press.

———. 1998. Rice Varietal Improvement and International Exchange of Rice Germplasm. In *Impact of Rice Research*, edited by Prabhu L. Pingali and Mahabub Hossain. Los Baños: International Rice Research Institute.

———, Robert W. Herdt, and Mahabub Hossain. 1996. Priorities for Rice Research: an Introduction. In *Rice Re-*

search in Asia: Progress and Priorities, edited by R. E. Evenson, R. W. Herdt, and M. Hossain. Oxford: CAB International.

FAO (Food and Agriculture Organization). 1995a. Investment in Agriculture: Evolution and Prospects. Draft prepared for the World Food Summit. Rome: FAO.

———. 1995b. *Irrigation Management Transfer: Selected Papers from the International Conference on Irrigation Management Transfer*, Wuhan, China, September 20–24, 1994. Rome: FAO, and Colombo: International Irrigation Management Institute.

———. 1998. Guide for the Transfer of Irrigation Management Services. Draft. Rome: FAO and Colombo: International Irrigation Management Institute.

Farrington, John, and D. Lewis (editors). 1993. *Non-Governmental Organizations and the State in Asia: Rethinking Roles in Sustainable Agricultural Development*. London and New York: Routledge.

Feder, Gershon, Tongroj Onchan, Yongyuth Chalamwong, and Chira Hongladarom. 1988. *Land Policies and Farm Productivity in Thailand*. Baltimore: Johns Hopkins University Press.

Frankel, Francine R. 1978. *India's Political Economy 1947–1977: the Gradual Revolution*. Princeton: Princeton University Press.

Frankenberg, Elizabeth, D. Thomas, and K. Beegle. 1999. The Real Costs of Indonesia's Economic Crisis: Preliminary Findings from the Indonesia Family Life Surveys. Labor and Population Program Working Paper Series 99-04. Santa Monica, CA: Rand Corporation.

Fredericks, L. J., and R. J. G. Wells. 1983. *Rice Processing in Peninsular Malaysia*. Kuala Lumpur: Oxford University Press.

Fuglie, Keith O., N. Ballenger, K. Day, C. Klotz, M. Ollinger, J. Reilly, U. Vasavada, and J. Yee. 1996. *Agricultural Research and Development: Public and Private Investments under Alternative Markets and Institutions*. Agricultural Economic Report Number 735. Washington, DC: United States Department of Agriculture,.

Fuller, B., and P. Clarke. 1994. Raising School Effects while Ignoring Culture? Local Conditions and the Influence of

Time in School and Pedagogy. *Review of Educational Research*. 64 (1).
Gavan, James D., and I. Chandrasekara. 1979. The Impact of Public Foodgrain Distribution on Food Consumption and Welfare in Sri Lanka. *Research Report 13*. Washington: International Food Policy Research Institute.
Geertz, Clifford. 1963. *Peddlers and Princes*. Chicago: University of Chicago Press.
GFHR (Global Forum for Health Research). 1999. *The 10/90 Report on Health Research 1999*. Geneva: Global Forum for Health Research.
Gill, Gerard J. 1983. *The Demand for Tubewell Equipment in Relation to Groundwater Availability in Bangladesh*. Dhaka: Bangladesh Agricultural Research Council.
Glover, David, and Lim Teck Ghee (editors). 1992. *Contract Farming in Southeast Asia: Three Country Studies*. Kuala Lumpur: Institute for Advanced Studies, University of Malaya.
Goldman, Richard H. 1975. Staple Food Self-Sufficiency and the Distributive Impact of the Malaysian Rice Policy. *Food Research Institute Studies* 14(3).
Gomez, E. T., and K. S. Jomo. 1997. *Malaysia's Political Economy: Politics, Patronage, and Profits*. Cambridge: Cambridge University Press.
Government of Indonesia. 1997. *Statistical Yearbook*. Jakarta: Central Bureau of Statistics.
Grossman, Ton, A. Linnemann, and H. Wierema. 1991. *Seed Industry Development in a North/South Perspective*. Wageningen, the Netherlands: Pudoc.
GTZ (Deutsche Gesellschaft fur Technische Zusammenarbeit [German Agency for Technical Cooperation]). 1998. Fiscal Decentralization of the Agricultural Sector in Indonesia. GTZ in support of Decentralized Measures Project, Working Paper, Jakarta.
Haggard, S. 2000. Interests, Institutions, and Policy Reform. In *Economic Policy Reform: The Second Stage*, edited by Anne Krueger. Chicago: University of Chicago Press.

———, and M. McCubbins, (editors). Forthcoming. *Political Institutions and the Determinants of Public Policy: When Do Institutions Matter?*.

Harberger, Arnold C. 1984. Basic Needs versus Distributional Weights in Social Cost-Benefit Analysis. *Economic Development and Cultural Change*, 32(3).

Hart, Oliver. 1995. *Firms, Contracts and Financial Structure*, Oxford: Clarendon Press.

Hayami, Yujiro. 1989. Community, Market and State. Elmhurst Memorial Lecture. In *Agriculture and Government in an Interdependent World: Proceedings of the Twentieth International Conference of Agricultural Economists*, edited by Allen Maunder and Alberto Valdes. Dartmouth.

———. 1993. Strategies for the Reform of Land Property Relations. In *Agricultural Policy Analysis for Transition to a Market-Oriented Economy in Viet Nam: Selected Issues*, edited by Randolph Barker. FAO Economic and Social Development Paper 123. Rome: Food and Agriculture Organization.

———, and Vernon W. Ruttan. 1985. *Agricultural Development: An International Perspective*. Baltimore: Johns Hopkins University Press.

Heaver, Richard A., and J. Hunt. 1995. *Improving Early Child Development: An Integrated Program for the Philippines*. Collaborative report by the World Bank and ADB for the Government of the Philippines. Washington, DC: World Bank.

Heller, Patrick. 1996. Social Capital as a Product of Class Mobilization and State Intervention: Industrial Workers in Kerala, India. *World Development* 24(6).

Hill, H. 1996. *The Indonesian Economy Since 1966: Southeast Asia's Emerging Giant*. Melbourne: Cambridge University Press.

Hobbelink, Henk. 1991. *Biotechnology and the Future of World Agriculture*. London: Zed Books Ltd.

Horton, Susan. 1999. Opportunities for Investments in Nutrition in Low-Income Asia. Paper prepared for Regional Technical Assistance No. 5671: Reducing Child Malnutrition in Eight Asian Countries. Manila: Asian Development Bank.

Huang Shu-min. 1998. *The Spiral Road: Change in a Chinese Village Through the Eyes of a Communist Party Leader*. Second Edition. Boulder, CO: Westview Press.

IFPRI (International Food Policy Research Institute). 1995. A 2020 Vision for Food, Agriculture, and the Environment: the Vision, Challenge, and Recommended Action. Washington, DC.

IHT (International Herald Tribune). 1999a. Turkish Quake Stirs Return to Roots. September 4–5.

———. 1999b. In Rural China, Fees Make School a Luxury Item. November 2: 4.

IIMI (International Irrigation Management Institute). 1987. *Public Intervention in Farmer-Managed Irrigation Systems*. Colombo: International Irrigation Management Institute.

IMF (International Monetary Fund). Various Years. *Government Finance Statistics Yearbook*. Washington, DC.

Indonesian Central Bureau of Statistics. 1987. *Susenas* (The National Socioeconomic Survey). Raw data tapes. Jakarta.

———. 1997. *Expenditure for Consumption of Indonesia. Susenas*. Book 1. Jakarta.

IRRI (International Rice Research Institute). 1990. *World Rice Statistics 1990*. Los Baños.

Ishikawa, Shigeru. 1967. *Economic Development in Asian Perspective*. Tokyo: Kinukuniya Bookstore.

Islam, Nurul. 1997a. The Nonfarm Sector and Rural Development: Review of Issues and Evidence. Food, Agriculture and the Environment. *Discussion Paper* 22. Washington, DC: International Food Policy Research Institute.

———, and Saji, Thomas. 1996. Foodgrain Price Stabilization in Developing Countries: Issues and Experiences in Asia. *Food Policy Review* 3. Washington, DC: International Food Policy Research Institute.

James, Clive B. 1997a. Global Status of Transgenic Crops in 1997 *ISAAA Brief*s 5. Ithaca: International Service for the Acquisition of Agri-Biotech Applications.

———. 1997b. Progressing Public-Private Sector Partnerships in International Agricultural Research and Development.

ISAAC Briefs 4. Ithaca, NY: International Service for the Acquisition of Agri-Biotech Applications.

———, and A. F. Krattiger. 1996. Global Review of the Field Testing and Commercialization of Transgenic Plants, 1986 to 1995: The First Decade of Crop Biotechnology. *ISAAA Briefs* 1. Ithaca: International Service for the Acquisition of Agri-Biotech Applications.

Jenkins, G. P., and A. K. Lai. 1991. Malaysia. In *The Political Economy of Agricultural Pricing Policy: Asia*, edited by A. Krueger, M. Schiff, and A. Valdes. Vol. 2. Baltimore: Johns Hopkins University Press.

Jimenez, Emmanuel, M. E. Lockheed, and V. Paqueo. 1991. The Relative Efficiency of Private and Public Schools in Developing Countries. *The World Bank Research Observer* 6 (2) (July). Washington, DC: World Bank.

Johnson, Samuel H., and P. Reiss. 1993. Can Farmers Afford to Use the Wells after Turnover: A Study of Pump Irrigation Turnover in Indonesia. Report No. 1. Short Report Series on Irrigation Management Transfer. Colombo: International Irrigation Management Institute.

JP (Jakarta Post). 2000. Over 1 Million Babies Born Malnourished. 18 April.

Jungbluth, Frauke. 1996. *Crop Protection Policy in Thailand: Economic and Political Factors influencing Pesticide Use.* Hannover, Germany: Pesticide Policy Project, University of Hannover.

Kakwani, N. 1999. Poverty and Inequality during the Economic Crisis in Thailand. In *Indicators of Well-Being and Policy Analysis* 3 (1) (January). Bangkok: National Economic and Social Development Board.

Keller, Andrew, J. Keller, and D. Seckler. 1996. Integrated Water Resources Systems: Theory and Policy Implications. *Research Report No. 3*. Colombo. International Irrigation Management Institute.

Keyes, Charles F. 1977. *The Golden Peninsula: Culture and Adaptation in Mainland Southeast Asia.* New York: Macmillan.

Khilnani, Sunil. 1997. *The Idea of India.* Harmondsworth: Penguin Books.

Kikuchi, Masao, and Y. Hayami 1978. New Rice Technology and National Irrigation Development Policy. In *Economic Consequences of the New Rice Technology*. Los Baños: International Rice Research Institute.

Knowles, James C., E. Pernia, and M. Racelis. 1999. Social Consequences of the Financial Crisis in Asia. Summary paper based on Regional Technical Assistance No. 5799: Social Impact Assessment of the Financial Crisis in Selected Developing Member Countries. *Economic Staff Paper No. 60*. Economics and Development Resource Center. Manila: Asian Development Bank.

Kohli, Atul. 1994. Centralization and Powerlessness: India's Democracy in a Comparative Perspective. In *State Power and Social Forces: Domination and Transformation in the Third World*, edited by Joel S. Migdal, Atul Kohli and Vivienne Shue. Cambridge: Cambridge University Press.

Korten, David. 1990. *Getting to the 21st Century: Voluntary Action and the Global Agenda*. New Haven: Kumerian Press.

Krueger, Anne O., M. Schiff, and A. Valdes. 1988. Agricultural Incentives in Developing Countries: Measuring the Effect of Sectoral and Economywide Policies. *The World Bank Economic Review* 2(3).

Landes, David S. 1958. *Bankers and Pashas: International Finance and Economic Imperialism in Egypt*. New York: Harper & Row.

Lardy, N. R. 1975. Centralization and Decentralization in China's Fiscal Management. *The China Quarterly* 61.

Lee, W. O. 1998. Equity and Access to Education in Developing Asia. Paper prepared for Regional Technical Assistance No. 5722: Regional Study of Trends, Issues and Policies in Education. Manila: Asian Development Bank.

Lele, Uma J. 1971. *Food Grain Marketing in India: Private Performance and Public Policy*. Ithaca: Cornell University Press.

Leskien, Dan, and M. Flitner. 1997. Intellectual Property Rights and Plant Genetic Resources. *Issues in Genetic Resources* No. 6. Rome: International Plant Genetic Resources Institute.

Lesser, William H. 1991. *Equitable Patent Protection in the Developing World: Issues and Approaches*. Christchurch, New Zealand: Eubios Ethics Institute.

Lewin, Keith. M. 1998. Access to Education in Emerging Asia: Trends, Challenges, and Policy Options. Working Paper. Manila: Asian Development Bank.

———, and Wang Ying Jie. 1994. Implementing Basic Education in China: Progress and Prospects in Rich, Poor and National Minority Areas. *Research Report* No. 101. Paris: International Institute for Educational Planning.

———, and Zhao, Qinghua. 1993. The Empty Opportunity: Local Control and Secondary School Achievement in the Philippines. *International Journal of Education Development*. 13 (1).

Lewis, David J. 1993. Overview. In *Non-Governmental Organizations and the State in Asia: Rethinking Roles in Sustainable Agricultural Development*, edited by John Farrington and David J. Lewis with S. Satish and Aurea Miclat-Teves. London and New York: Routledge.

Liamzon, Cristina M. 2000. Civil Society Operations and Their Role in People's Empowerment and Rural Poverty Eradication. Prepared for the International Fund for Agricultural Development. Rome.

Lin, Justin Yifu. 1990. Collectivization and China's Agricultural Crisis in 1959–1961. *Journal of Political Economy* 98 (6) (December).

———. 1991. The Household Responsibility System Reform and the Adoption of Hybrid Rice in China. *Journal of Development Economics* 36.

———, and Funing Zhong. 1996. *Fiscal Decentralization and Rural Development in China*. Draft report. Washington, DC: World Bank.

———, Fang Cai and Zhou Li. 1996. *The China Miracle: Development Strategy and Economic Reform*. Hong Kong: Chinese University Press.

Lindert, P. 1991. Historical Patterns of Agricultural Policy. In *Agriculture and the State: Growth, Employment, and Poverty in developing Countries*, edited by C. P. Timmer. Ithaca: Cornell University Press.

Lipton, Michael. 1977. *Why People Stay Poor: A Study of Urban Bias in World Development*. London: Temple Smith.
MacAndrews, Colin. 1986. *Central Government and Local Development in Indonesia*. Singapore: Oxford University Press.
MacIntyre, A. 1999. Political Parties, Accountability, and Economic Governance in Indonesia. In *Party Systems, Democracy, and Economic Governance in East Asia*, edited by J. Blondel, T. Inoguchi and I. Marsh. Tokyo: United Nations University Press.
———. Forthcoming. Investment, Property Rights, and Corruption in Indonesia. In *Corruption: The Boom and Bust of East Asia*, edited by J. E. Campos.
Mandal, M. A. Sattar, and D. E. Parker. 1995. Evolution and Implications of Decreased Public Involvement in Minor Irrigation Management in Bangladesh. *Report No. 11*. Short Report Series on Locally Managed Irrigation. Colombo: International Irrigation Management Institute.
Manwan, Ibrahim, K. Suradisastra, D. A. Adjid and R. Montgomery. 1998. The Implications of Technological Change. Study B-2 of the *Agricultural Sector Strategy Review*, TA No. 2660-INO, Ministry of Agriculture, Republic of Indonesia, prepared by PT Multi Tehniktama Prakarsa and Hunting Technical Services Ltd., Jakarta.
Mears, Leon A. 1961. *Rice Marketing in the Republic of Indonesia*. Jakarta: P. T. Pembangunan.
———. 1981. *The New Rice Economy of Indonesia*. Yogyakarta: Gadjah Mada University Press.
———, M. H. Agabin, T. L. Anden, and R. C. Marquez. 1974. *Rice Economy of the Philippines*. Quezon City: University of the Philippines Press.
Mendoza, M. S., and M. W. Rosegrant. 1995. Pricing Behavior in Philippine Corn Markets: Implications for Market Efficiency. *Research Report No. 101*. Washington, DC: International Food Policy Research Institute.
Meyer, Richard L., and Geetha Nagarajan. 1999. *Rural Finance in Asia: Policies, Paradigms, and Performance*. Hong Kong, China: Oxford University Press.

Mingat, Alain. 1995. Towards Improving our Understanding of the Strategy of High-Performing Asian Economies in the Education Sector. Paper presented at the International Conference on Financing Human Resource Development in Advanced Asian Economies. Manila: Asian Development Bank.

Mingsarn Kaosa-ard, Kanok Rerkasem, and Chaiwat Roongruangsee. 1989. *Agricultural Information and Technological Change in Northern Thailand*. Bangkok: Thailand Development Research Institute.

———, and Benjavan Rerkasem. 1999. *The Growth and Sustainability of Agriculture in Asia*. Hong Kong: Oxford University Press.

Mishra, Pankaj. 1999. The Other India. *New York Review of Books* XLVI (20).

Moon, Pal Yong. 1975. The Evolution of Rice Policy in Korea. *Food Research Institute Studies* XIV(4).

Morfit, Michael. 1986. Pancasila Orthodoxy. In *Central Government and Local Development in Indonesia*, edited by Colin MacAndrews. Singapore: Oxford University Press.

Mosher, Arthur T. 1966. *Getting Agriculture Moving*. Agricultural Development Council. New York: Praeger Publishers.

Motooka, Takeshi. 1976. The Conditions Governing Agricultural Development in Southeast Asia. In *Southeast Asia: Nature, Society and Development; Contributions to Southeast Asian Studies*, edited by Shinichi Ichimura. Honolulu: University of Hawaii Press.

Mudahar, Mohinder S., and E. C. Kapista. 1987. *Fertilizer Marketing Systems and Policies*. Muscle Shoals, AL: International Fertilizer Development Center.

Myoung, Kwang-Sik, and Jung-Hwan Lee. 1988. Evaluation of the Korean Market Intervention System. In *Evaluating Rice Market Intervention Policies*. Manila: Asian Development Bank.

Nagata, Keijuro. 1994. Evolution of Land Improvement Districts in Japan. *Report* No. 6. Short Report Series on Locally Managed Irrigation. Colombo: International Irrigation Management Institute.

Narayan, Deepa. 1995. The Contribution of People's Participation: Evidence from 121 Rural Water Supply Projects. *Environmentally Sustainable Development Occasional Paper Series*, No. 1. Washington, DC: World Bank.

NIA (National Irrigation Administration). 1995. *Devolution of Locally Funded Irrigation Projects to Local Government Units: The Later Developments*. Manila: National Irrigation Administration.

O'Brochta, David A., and Peter W. Atkinson. 1998. Building the Better Bug. *Scientific American* 279 (6).

Olson, M. 1965. *The Logic of Collective Action*. Cambridge: Harvard University Press.

———. 1982. *The Rise and Decline of Nations*. New Haven: Yale University Press.

Ortiz, Isabel, and Patricia Moser. 1996. New Directions in the Delivery of Public Services. *ADB Review*, September-October.

Ostrom, Elinor. 1992. *Crafting Institutions for Self-Governing Irrigation Systems*. San Francisco: Institute for Contemporary Studies.

———. 1993. Self-Governance, the Informal Public Economy and the Tragedy of the Commons. In *Institutions of Democracy and Development*, edited by Peter L. Burger. San Francisco: Institute for Contemporary Studies.

———. 1994. Neither Market nor State: Governance of Common-Pool Resources in the Twenty-first Century. IFPRI Lecture Series. Washington, DC: International Food Policy Research Institute.

———. 1996a. Incentives, Rules of the Game, and Development. In *Annual World Bank Conference on Development Economics 1995*, edited by Michael Bruno and Boris Pleskovic. Washington, DC: World Bank.

———. 1996b. Crossing the Great Divide: Coproduction, Synergy and Development. *World Development* 24 (6) (June).

———, R. Gardner, and J. Walker. 1996. *Rules, Games and Common-Pool Resources*. Ann Arbor: University of Michigan Press.

Otsuka, Keijiro. 1998. Rural Industrialization in East Asia. In *The Institutional Foundations of East Asian Economic Devel-*

opment, edited by Yujiro Hayami and Masahiko Aoki. London: MacMillan Press.
Panayotou, T. 1989. Thailand: The Experiences of a Food Exporter. In *Food Price Policy in Asia*, edited by T. Sicular. Ithaca: Cornell University Press.
Panggabean, A. T. P. 1997. The Impact of the Intergovernmental Grant System on Interregional Growth and Equity: The Case of Indonesia. Ph.D. thesis, Faculty of Commerce and Social Science, University of Birmingham.
Pardey, Philip G., J. Roseboom, and S. Fan. 1998. Trends in Financing Asian and Australian Agricultural Research. In *Financing Agricultural Research: A Sourcebook*, edited by Steven R. Tabor, Willem Jenssen, and Hilarion Bruneau. The Hague: International Service for National Agricultural Research.
Perez, J.P. 1998. Sectoral Rapid Field Appraisal (Health). Governance and Local Democracy Project. Manila: United States Agency for International Development.
Perkins, Dwight H. 1988. Reforming China's Economic System. *Journal of Economic Literature* XXVI (2).
———, and S. Yusuf. 1984. *Rural Development in China*. Baltimore: Johns Hopkins University Press.
Persley, G. (editor). 1990. *Agricultural Biotechnology: Opportunities for International Development*. Oxford: CAB International.
Philippines Department of Health. 1998. *Transition Report*. Manila.
Pingali, Prabhu L., M. Hossein, and R. V. Gerpacio. 1997. *Asian Rice Bowls: The Returning Crisis?* Oxford: CAB International.
Pletcher, J. 1989. Rice and Padi Market Management in West Malaysia, 1975–1986. *Journal of Development Studies* 23 (3).
Plucknett, Donald L., Nigel J. H. Smith, J. T. Williams, and N. Murthi Anishetty. 1987. *Gene Banks and the World's Food*. Princeton: Princeton University Press.
Popkin, Samuel L. 1979. *The Rational Peasant: The Political Economy of Rural Society in Viet Nam*. Berkeley: University of California Press.
Porio, Emma. 1998. Social Services under the Estrada Administration. Unpublished paper. Manila.

Pray, Carl E. 1991. The Development of Asian Research Institutions: Underinvestment, Allocation of Resources, and Productivity. In *Research and Productivity in Asian Agriculture*, edited by Robert E. Evenson and Carl E. Pray. Ithaca: Cornell University Press.

———, and Ruben G. Echeverria. 1991. Private-Sector Agricultural Research in Less-Developed Countries. In *Agricultural Research Policy: International Quantitative Perspectives*, edited by Philip G. Pardey, Johannes Roseboom, and Jock R. Anderson. Cambridge: Cambridge University Press.

Psacharopoulos, George. 1994. Returns to Investment in Education: A Global Update. *World Development* 22 (9).

Putnam, Robert D. 1993. *Making Democracy Work: Civic Traditions in Modern Italy*. Princeton: Princeton University Press.

Razon-Abad, Henedina. 1998. Rapid Field Appraisal of Decentralization (Agriculture). Manila: Governance and Local Democracy Project, United States Agency for International Development.

Reeve, David. 1985. *Golkar of Indonesia: an Alternative to the Party System*. Singapore: Oxford University Press.

Reich, M. R. 1993. The Politics of Health Sector Reform in Developing Countries: the Case of Pharmaceutical Policy. Paper prepared for the Conference on Health Sector Reform in Developing Countries: Issues for the 1990s. Durham, NH: New England Center.

Reidinger, Richard B. 1980. Water Management by Administrative Procedures in an Indian Irrigation System. In *Irrigation and Agricultural Development in Asia*, edited by E. Walter Coward. Ithaca: Cornell University Press.

Riddell, Abby. 1993. The Evidence on Public/Private Educational Trade-Offs in Developing Countries. *International Journal of Education Development* 13 (4).

Robinson, Mark, J. Farrington, and S. Satish. 1993. Overview. In *Non-Governmental Organizations and the State in Asia: Rethinking Roles in Sustainable Agricultural Development*, edited by John Farrington and David J. Lewis with S. Satish and Aurea Miclat-Teves. London and New York: Routledge.

Roche, Frederick. 1994. The Technical and Price Efficiency of Fertilizer Use in Irrigated Rice Production. *Bulletin of Indonesian Economic Studies*, the Australian National University. April.

Romero Jr., Segundo E., and Rostum J. Bautista. 1995. Philippine NGOs in the Asia Pacific Context. In *Emerging Civil Society in the Asia Pacific Community: Nongovernmental Underpinnings of the Emerging Asia Pacific Regional Community*, edited by Tadashi Yamamoto. Tokyo: Center for International Exchange.

Rosegrant, Mark. 1997. Water Resources in the Twenty-First Century: Challenges and Implications for Action. *Food, Agriculture and the Environment Discussion Paper 20.* Washington, DC: International Food Policy Research Institute.

———, and Robert W. Herdt. 1981. Stimulating the Impacts of Credit Policy and Fertilizer Subsidy on Central Luzon Rice Farms, the Philippines. *American Journal of Agricultural Economics* 63.

———, and Peter B. R. Hazell. 1999. *Transforming the Rural Asian Economy: The Unfinished Revolution.* Hong Kong: Oxford University Press.

Sanderson, Warren, and Tan, Jee-Peng. 1995. *Population in Asia.* Washington, DC: World Bank.

Sasson, Albert. 1988. *Biotechnologies and Development.* Paris: United Nations Education, Scientific and Cultural Organization and Technical Center for Agricultural and Rural Cooperation.

Schultz, T. Paul. 1993. Sources of Fertility Decline in Modern Economic Growth: Is Aggregate Evidence on the Demographic Transition Credible? *Working Paper Series* No. 58. Washington, DC: Institute for Policy Reform.

Schultz, Theodore W. 1961. Investment in Human Capital. *American Economic Review* 51 (March).

———. 1964. *Transforming Traditional Agriculture.* New Haven: Yale University Press.

Scott, James C. 1976. *The Moral Economy of the Peasant: Rebellion and Subsistence in Southeast Asia.* New Haven: Yale University Press.

———. 1985. *Weapons of the Weak: Everyday Forms of Peasant Resistance*. New Haven: Yale University Press.
Shah, Anwar, and Z. Qureshi. 1994. Intergovernmental Fiscal Relations in Indonesia: Issues and Reform Options. *World Bank Discussion Paper*. Washington DC: World Bank.
Shirk, Susan L. 1993. *The Political Logic of Political Reform in China*. Berkeley: University of California Press.
Shleifer, A., and M. Vishny. 1993. Corruption. *Quarterly Journal of Economics* 108 (3).
Shue, Vivienne. 1994. State Power and Social Organization in China. In *State Power and Social Forces: Domination and Transformation in the Third World*, edited by Joel S. Migdal, Atul Kohli, and Vivienne Shue. Cambridge, U.K.: Cambridge University Press.
Sidel, John. 1994. Walking in the Shadow of the Big Man: Justiniano Montano and Failed Dynasty Building in Cavite, 1935–1972. In *An Anarchy of Families: State and Family in the Philippines*, edited by Alfred W. McCoy. Manila: Ateneo de Manila University Press.
Simpson, Larry, and Klas Ringskog. 1997. Water Markets in the Americas. *World Bank Directions in Development* series. Washington, DC: World Bank.
Simpson, R. David, Roger A. Sedjo, and John W. Reid. 1996. Valuing Biodiversity for Use in Pharmaceutical Research. *Journal of Political Economy* 104(1).
Siy, Robert Y., Jr. 1987. Averting the Bureaucratization of a Community-Managed Resource: the Case of the Zanjeras. In *Community Management: Asian Experience and Perspectives*, edited by David C. Korten. New Haven: Kumerian Press.
Small, Leslie E., and I. Carruthers 1991. *Farmer-Financed Irrigation*. Cambridge: Cambridge University Press.
Smoke, Paul, and B. D. Lewis. 1998. Fiscal Decentralization in Indonesia: a New Approach to an Old Idea. *World Development* 24, (8).
Soekirman, Ignatius Tarwotjo, Idris Jus'at, Junawan Sumodiningrat, and Fasli Jalal. 1992. Economic Growth, Equity, and Nutritional Improvement in Indonesia. Coun-

try case study supported by the United Nations Childrens Fund for the 15th Congress of the International Union of the Nutritional Sciences, September 25–October 1, 1993, Adelaide, Australia.

Sompop Manarungsan and Suebskun Suwanjindar. 1992. Contract Farming and Outgrower Schemes in Thailand. In *Contract Farming in Southeast Asia: Three Country Studies*, edited by David Glover and Lim Teck Ghee. Kuala Lumpur: Institute for Advanced Studies, University of Malaya.

Southworth, V. Roy. 1981. *Food Crop Marketing in Atebubu District, Ghana*. Ph.D dissertation, Stanford University, summarized under the same title by V. Roy Southworth, William O Jones, and Scott R. Pearson. 1979. *Food Research Institute Studies* 17 (2).

Stout, Susan, A. Evans, J. Nassim, and L. Raney. 1997. Evaluating Health Projects: Lessons from the Literature. *Discussion Paper* No. 356. Washington, DC: World Bank.

Suprapto, Ato. 1988. *Application of a General Equilibrium Model for Agricultural Policy Analysis: a Case Study of Fertilizer Input Subsidy in Indonesia*. Ph.D. Dissertation submitted to Oklahoma State University. Ann Arbor: University Microfilms.

Suthad Setboonsarng, Saran Wattanutchariya, and Banlu Phutigorn. 1991. *The Structure, Conduct and Performance of the Seed Industry in Thailand*. Research Monograph No. 5. Bangkok: Thailand Development Research Institute.

Suwit Wibulpololprasert (editor). 1994. *Thai Drug System*. Nonthaburi: Health Systems Research Institute.

TAC/CGIAR (Technical Advisory Committee, Consultative Group on International Agricultural Research). 1996. A Strategic Review of Natural Resources Management Research on Soil and Water. Report presented at Mid-Term Meeting of the CGIAR, Jakarta, Indonesia, May 20–24, 1996. Rome: Food and Agricultural Organization.

Tamin, Mokhtar, and Sahathavan Meyanathan. 1988. Rice Market Interventions in Malaysia: Scope, Effects and the Need for Reform. In *Evaluating Rice Market Intervention Policies*. Manila: Asian Development Bank.

Tan, S. H. 1987. *Malaysia's Rice Policy: A Critical Analysis*. Kuala Lumpur: Institute for Strategic and International Studies.

TDRI (Thailand Development Research Institute) 1996. *The Potential for the Development of Contract Farming: the Case of Cotton Production in Thailand*. Final Report. Bangkok.

Thomas, Caroline, and P. Clegg. 1998. Water and the Current Development Orthodoxy: World Bank Policy under the Spotlight. In *Water Resource Management: A Comparative Perspective*, edited by Dhirendra K. Vajpeyi. Westport, CT: Praeger Publishers.

Tietenberg, T. 1992. *Environmental and Natural Resource Economics*. New York: Harper Collins Publishers.

Tilak, J. B. G. 1997. The Dilemma of Reforms in Financing Higher Education in India. *Higher Education Policy* 10 (1).

Timmer, C. Peter. 1986. *Getting Prices Right: The Scope and Limits of Agricultural Price Policy*. Ithaca: Cornell University Press.

———. 1988. Analyzing Rice Market Interventions in Asia: Principles, Issues, Themes and Lessons. In *Evaluating Rice Market Intervention Policies*. Manila: Asian Development Bank.

———. 1989. Indonesia: The Transition from Food Importer to Exporter. In *Food Price Policy in Asia*, edited by T. Sicular. Ithaca: Cornell University Press.

———. 1993. Rural Bias in the East and Southeast-Asian Rice Economy: Indonesia in Comparative Perspective. *Journal of Development Studies* 29 (4).

Trung, Ngo Quoc. 1978. Economic Analysis of Irrigation Development in Deltaic Regions of Asia: the Case of Central Thailand. In *Irrigation Policy and Management in Southeast Asia*. Los Baños: International Rice Research Institute.

Untung, K. 1995. Institutional Constraints on IPM Implementation in Indonesia. In *Institutional Constraints to IPM*, edited by H. Waibel and J. C. Zadoks. Hannover: Pesticide Policy Project, University of Hannover.

UNDP (United Nations Development Program). 1993. Workshop on the Decentralization Process. Bern, Switzerland.

United Nations. 1997. *Guidebook on Private Sector Participation in Water Supply and Sanitation*. New York: United Nations.
UPOV (International Convention for the Protection of New Varieties of Plants). 1999. *States Party to the International Convention for the Protection of New Varieties of Plants*. Geneva. <http:www.upov.int>. Updated 20 December 1999.
U. S. Patent Office. 1997. *Basmati Rice Lines and Grains*. Patent No. 5,663,484. Washington, DC.
Vajpeyi, Dhirendra K., and Zhang, TingTing. 1998. To Dam or not to Dam: India's Narmada River Basin Project. In *Water Resource Management: A Comparative Perspective*, edited by Dhirendra K. Vajpeyi. Westport, CT: Praeger Publishers.
Van Roy, Edward. 1971. *Economic Systems of Northern Thailand: Structure and Change*. Ithaca: Cornell University Press.
Varshney, A.E. 1993. Special Issue: Beyond Urban Bias. *Journal of Development Studies* 19 (4).
Vermillion, Douglas L. 1997. Impacts of Irrigation Management Transfer: A Review of the Evidence. *Research Report* No. 11. Colombo: International Irrigation Management Institute.
Vichit Nantasuwan. 1998. *State of the Art Review on Management of Community Health Funds in Thailand*. Bangkok: Health Systems Research Institute.
Von Braun, Joachim, R. F. Hopkins, D. Puetz, and R. Pandya-Lorch. 1993. Aid to Agriculture: Reversing the Decline. *Food Policy Report*. Washington, DC: International Food Policy Research Institute.
Wade, Robert. 1982. Employment, Water Control and Water Supply Institutions: South India and South Korea. Asian Employment Programme Working Papers. Bangkok: International Labor Organization.
———. 1988. *Village Republics: Economic Conditions for Collective Action in South India*. Cambridge: Cambridge University Press.
———. 1995. The Ecological Basis of Irrigation Institutions: East and South Asia. *World Development* 23 (12).

Warwick, D. P., and F. Reimers. 1995. *Hope or Despair? Learning in Pakistan's Primary Schools*. Westport, CT: Praeger Publishers.

Weber, Max. [1920] 1946. *From Max Weber: Essays in Sociology*. Translated, edited and with a preface by H. H. Gerth and C. Wright Mills. Oxford: Oxford University Press.

West, Loraine A. 1997. Provision of Public Services in Rural PRC. in *Financing Local Government in the People's Republic of China*, edited by Christine P. W. Wong. Hong Kong: Oxford University Press.

WHO (World Health Organization). 1990. Resolution of the World Health Assembly: WHA 41.17.51. In *Handbook of Resolutions and Decisions of the World Health Assembly and the Executive Board*, Vol. 3, Phase 3 (1985–1989). 2nd edition. Geneva: World Health Organization.

———. 1997 *The Use of Essential Drugs: Eighth Report of the WHO Expert Committee* (including the revised model list of essential drugs). Geneva: World Health Organization.

Wong, Christine P.W. 1997. Rural Public Finance. In *Financing Local Government in the People's Republic of China*, edited by Christine P. W. Wong. Hong Kong: Oxford University Press, 167–212.

World Bank. 1990. http://www.worldbank.org/data/databytopic.html. Primary Commodity Prices.

———.1993a. *Indonesia: Public Expenditures, Prices and the Poor*. Washington, DC: World Bank.

———. 1993b. *World Development Report 1993: Investing in Health*. Washington, DC: World Bank.

———. 1993c. *The East Asian Miracle: Economic Growth and Public Policy*. World Bank Policy Research Report. New York: Oxford University Press.

———. 1993d. *Price Prospects for Major Primary Commodities 1990–2005*. Washington, DC: World Bank.

———. 1994a. *A Review of World Bank Experience in Irrigation*. Report No. 13676. Operations Evaluation Department. Washington, DC.

———. 1994b. *Philippines. Devolution and Health Services: Managing Risks and Opportunities*. Report 12343-PH. Country

Department 1, East Asia and Pacific Regional Office. Washington, DC: World Bank.

———. 1995. *Priorities and Strategies for Education: A World Bank Sector Review.* Washington, DC: World Bank.

———. 1996a. *Achievements and Problems in Development of National Agricultural Research Systems.* Processed. Washington DC.

———. 1996b. *India: Primary Education, Achievements and Challenges.* Washington, DC: World Bank.

———. 1996c. *Pakistan: Improving Basic Education.* Washington, DC: World Bank.

———. 1997. *The State in a Changing World.* World Development Report 1997. Washington, DC: World Bank

———. 1999. *Education Sector Strategy.* Washington, DC: World Bank.

———. Various Years. *Price Prospects for Major Primary Commodities.* Washington, DC: World Bank.

Wyke, Alexandra. 1988. A Survey of Biotechnology. *The Economist* 307 (7541).

Young, Mary Eming. 1995. *Early Child Development: Investing in the Future.* Washington, DC: World Bank.

Young, Robert. 1996. Measuring Economic Benefits for Water Investments and Policies. *Technical Paper* No. 338. Washington, DC: World Bank.

Ziderman, Adrian, and D. Albrecht. 1992. *Financing Universities in Developing Countries.* London: Falmer Press.

AUTHOR INDEX

ADB (Asian Development Bank)   3, 12, 18, 22, 78, 95, 196, 199, 208, 221, 236, 274, 275, 276, 280, 296, 299, 304, 323, 324, 327, 349
Ahmed, Raisuddin   196, 216, 221
Albrecht, D.   294
Ali, I.   263
Amara Pongsapich   64
Ammar Siamwalla   18, 227, 230, 249, 250, 251, 252
Anan Ganjanapan   63
Anderson, K.   243
Anderson, Robert S.   129
Arndt, Heinz W.   2, 3
Atkinson, Peter W.   138
Axelrod, Robert   75

Baanante, C.   224
Bajracharya, H. R.   282
Balisacan, Arsenio M.   222, 223
Banlu Phutigorn   131
Barker, Randolph   219
Bates, R.   243
Bauer, Armin   276
Bautista, Rostum J.   60
Becker, Gary S.   271
Beegle, K.   329, 330, 331
Benjavan Rerkasem   5
Bennell, Paul   287, 288
Bloom, B. S.   324
Bloom, David E.   272
Booth, Anne   89
Boserup, Ester   30
Bouis, Howarth   229, 233
Bray, Mark   279, 287, 294
BRWS (Bengal Rural Welfare Services)   303

Bumb, Balu L.   224
Burgess, Robin   293
Byerlee, D.   163
Byrd, William A.   66

Calder, I. R.   207
Carey, J.   249
Carlson, Gerald A.   204
Carruthers, I.   187
Carter, Richard   199
CCAMD (Congressional Commission on Agricultural Modernization and Development   107
Chaiwat Roongruangsee   174
Chambers, Robert   183, 192
Chandrasekara, I.   216
Chapman, David   283, 294
Che, Jiahua   66, 67
Cheema, G. S.   84
Chenery, Hollis   3
CIMMYT (Centro Internacional de Mejoramiento de Maiz y Trigo)   131
Clarke, P.   285
Clegg, P.   317
Comanor, William S.   308
Coward, E. Walter   187, 188
Cox, G.   245, 249
Craig, P.   272
Crook, R.   85
Crouch, H.   255, 256
David, Cristina C.   159
De los Reyes, Romana P.   187
DILG (Department of Interior and Local Government)   111
Dreze, Jean   75
Du, Haiyan   66

Echeverria, Ruben G.   132, 155, 156
Edirisinghe, Neville   237, 238
Edwards, Michael   62
Eggertsson, Thrainn   35
El-Ghonemy   22
Evenson, Robert E.   130, 150, 173

Fan, S.   171
Fang Cai   40
FAO (Food and Agriculture Organization)   5, 8, 191, 197
Farrington, John   63, 177, 178
Feder, Gershon   31
Flitner, M.   152
Frankel, Francine R.   43
Frankenberg, Elizabeth   329, 330, 331
Fredericks, L. J.   257
Fuglie, Keith O.   141
Fuller, B.   285
Funing Zhong   118

Gardner, R.   188
Gavan, James D.   216
Geertz, Clifford   83
Gerpacio, R. V.   160, 167
Gill, Gerard J.   195
Glover, David   175
Goldman, Richard H.   218
Gomez, E. T.   255
Government of Indonesia   320
Grossman, Ton   132, 141
GTZ.   90
Haggard, S.   245, 270
Harberger, Arnold C.
Hart, Oliver   29
Hayami, Yujiro   33, 56, 126, 173, 174, 200, 219, 243
Hazell, Peter B. R.   5, 272
Heaver, Richard A.   106, 321, 325, 326, 327
Heller, Patrick   57, 75

Herdt, Robert W.   150, 220
Hill, H.   266
Hobbelink, Henk   142
Horton, Susan   321, 323, 325
Hossein, M.   150, 160, 167
Huang Shu-min   39, 40, 41
Hulme, David   62
Hunt, J.   106, 321, 325, 326, 327
IFPRI (International Food Policy Research Institute)   4
IHT (International Herald Tribune)   1, 295
IIMI (International Irrigation Management Institute)   190
Indonesian Central Bureau of Statistics   277
IRRI (International Rice Research Institute)   225
Ishikawa, Shigeru   130
Islam, Nurul   10, 228

James, Clive B.   7, 136, 137
Jenkins, G. P.   257, 259, 261
Jimenez, Emmanuel   290, 291
Johnson, Samuel H.   197
Jomo, K. S.   255
Jopillo, S.   187
JP (Jakarta Post)   332
Jung-Hwan Lee   218
Jungbluth, Frauke   162

Kakwani, N.   334
Kanok Rerkasem   174
Kanok Wongfranjan   249
Kapista, E. C.   221, 222, 223, 225
Keller, Andrew   201
Keller, J.   201
Keyes, Charles F.   30, 54
Khilnani, Sunil   44
Kikuchi, Masao   200
Knowles, James C.   333, 334
Kohli, Atul   43, 44, 45
Korten, David   60

Krattiger, A. F.   136, 137
Krueger, Anne O.   53

Lai, A. K.   257, 259, 261
Landes, David S.   76
Lardy, N. R.   115
Lee, W. O.   218, 274
Lele, Uma J.   217, 229
Leskien, Dan   152
Lesser, William H.   145, 146, 150
Levine, G.   188
Levy, E.   129
Lewin, Keith M.   279, 295, 293
Lewis, B. D.   91
Lewis, D.   177, 178
Lewis, David J.   61
Liamson, Cristina M.   62
Lim Teck Ghee   175
Lin, Justin Yifu   40, 66, 114, 118, 130
Lin Qingsong   66, 118
Lindert, P.   243
Linnemann, A.   132, 141
Lipton, Michael   243
Lockheed, M. E.   290, 291
MacAndrews, Colin   93
MacIntyre, Andrew   268
Malaney, P.   272
Mandal, M. A. Sattar   195
Manor, J.   85
Manwan, Ibrahim   96, 165
McCubbins, M.   245, 270
Mears, Leon A.   216, 217, 228
Mendoza, M. S.   229
Meyanathan, Sahathavan   218, 257
Meyer, Richard L.   10, 174, 220
Mingat, Alain   279
Mingsarn Kaosa-ard   5, 174
Miranowski, J.   204
Mishra, Prankaj   23
Moon, Pal Yong   41
Morfit, Michael   89
Morrison, B.   129

Moser, Patricia   72
Mosher, Arthur T.   123
Motooka, Takeshi   54
Mudahar, Mohinder S.   221, 222, 223, 225
Myoung, Kwang-Sik   218

Nagarajan, Geetha   10, 174, 220
Nagata, Keijuro   187
Narayan, Deepa   316, 317
NIA (National Irrigation Administration, Philippines)   107

O'Brochta, David A.   138
Olson, M.   243
Orapin Sobchokchai   18
Ortiz, Isabel   72
Ostrom, Elinor   54, 73, 188, 189, 190, 192
Otsuka, Keijiro   10, 159

Panayotou, T.   248, 250, 251, 253
Panggabean, A. T. P.   93
Pacqueo, V.   290, 291
Pardey, Philip G.   171
Parker, D. E.   195
Perez, J. P.   105, 106
Perkins, Dwight H.   32
Pernia, E.   333, 334
Persley, G.   142
Philippines Department of Health   105
Pingali, Prabhu L.   160, 167
Pletcher, J.   257, 258, 259
Plucknett, Donald L.   126
Popkin, Samuel L.   56
Porio, Emma   105, 108
Pray, Carl E.   128, 132, 155, 168
Psacharopoulos, George   287, 288
Putnam, Robert D.   75

Qureshi, Z.   58

Racelis, M.   333, 334
Razon-Abad, Henedina   107
Reeve, David   89
Reich, M. R.   312
Reid, John W.   154
Reidinger, Richard B.   192, 202
Reimers, F.   2, 83
Reiss, P.   197
Riad, M.   22
Riddell, Abby   290
Ringskog, Klas   204, 205
Robinson, Mark   63
Roche, Frederick   163
Romero Jr., Segundo E.   60
Rondinelli, D. A.   84
Roseboom, J.   171
Rosegrant, Mark W.   5, 198, 200, 206, 220, 229, 272
Ruttan, Vernon W.   126, 173, 174

Sanderson, Warren   273
Saran Wattanutchariya   131
Sasson, Albert   135
Satish, S.   63
Sattar, M. A.   195
Schiff, M.   53
Schultz, T. Paul   273
Schultz, Theodore W.   174, 271
Scott, James C.   56, 255, 261
Seckler, D.   201
Sedjo, Roger A.   154
Sen, Amartya   75
Shah, Anwar   58
Shirk, Susan L.   40, 67, 116, 117
Shleifer, A.   268
Shue, Vivienne   38, 39, 40
Shugart, M.   249
Sidel, John   31
Simpson, Larry   204, 205
Simpson, R. David   154
Siy, Robert Y., Jr.   186, 187
Small, Leslie E.   187
Smoke, Paul   91

Sompop Manarungsan   175, 176
Southworth, Roy V.   229
Stout, Susan   297
Suebskun Suwanjindar   175, 176
Suprapto, Ato   219
Suradisastra, K.   96, 165
Suthad Setboonsarng   131, 250, 251, 252
Suwit Wibulpololprasert   303

TAC/CGIAR (Technical Advisory Committe/Consultative Group on International Agricultural Research)   158, 159
Tamin, Mokhtar   218, 257
Tan, Jee-Peng   273
Tan, S. H.   261
TDRI (Thailand Development Research Institute)   156
Thomas, Caroline
Thomas, D.
Thomas, Saji   228
Tietenberg, T.
Tilak, J. B. G.   294
Timmer, C. Peter   213, 264, 266
Trung, Ngo Quoc   185

UNDP (United Nations Development Programme)   102
United Nations
Untung, K.   162
UPOV (International Convention for the Protection of New Varieties of Plants)   145
US Patent Office   148

Vajpeyi, Dhirendra K.   201
Valdes, A.   53
Van Roy, Edward   30
Varshney, A. E.   244
Vermillion, Douglas L.   190
Vichit Nantasuwan   305
Vishny, M.   268
Von Braun, Joachim   7

Author Index

Wade, Robert 54, 185, 193
Walker, J. 188
Wang Ying Jie 293
Warwick, D. P. 283
Weber, Max 47, 48
Wells, R. J. G. 257
West, Loraine A. 117, 118
World Health Organization 311, 314
Wierema, H. 132, 141
Wong, Christine P. W. 66, 117
World Bank 4, 48, 49, 51, 86, 95, 105, 180, 208, 225, 273, 285, 286, 287, 288, 293, 299, 300, 315, 323
Wyke, Alexandra 139

Yingyi Qian 66, 67
Young, Mary Eming 321, 324, 325, 326, 327
Young, Robert 203
Yusuf, S. 32

Zhang, TingTing 201
Zhao, Qinghua 295
Zhou Li 40
Ziderman, Adrian 294
Zilberman, D. 204

SUBJECT INDEX

Symbols

2-acetyl-1-pyrroline **148**

A

AARD. *See* Agency for Agricultural Research and Development
accountability **18, 50, 78, 99, 122, 231**
Aceh, Indonesia **88, 101**
acquired immune deficiency syndrome (AIDS) **297, 303, 311**
actors **7, 20, 24, 36-70, 269, 360-362**
    collective action **36**
    descriptions **36-70**
    interactions **70**
    private **8**
ADB. *See* Asian Development Bank
Africa **1, 142, 313**
Africa, North **288**
Aga Khan Foundation (Pakistan) **293**
agency costs **71-72**
Agency for Agricultural Research and Development (Indonesia) **96**
agriculture **3, 4, 7, 8, 17, 41, 61, 92, 94, 123, 160, 103**
    as share of GDP (fig.) **353**
    development **3, 123, 183**
    extensification **5**
    extension **21, 62, 95, 103, 173-180, 197**
    external assistance to (fig.) **18**
    extractive approach **2**
    intensification **5, 159-161, 164**
    labor productivity in **6**
    output per capita (fig.) **5**
    research **7, 9, 18, 21, 62, 96, 118, 121, 123, 124, 140, 158-166, 170, 177**
        beneficiaries **170**
        genetic improvement in **170**
        mechanization **170**
        NGO roles in **177**
        resource management **170**
    taxation of **47**
    terms of trade **6**
agrochemicals **7, 136, 198**
agroforestry **177, 207**
AIATs. *See* Assessment Institutes for Agricultural Technology
AIDS. *See* acquired immune deficiency syndrome
Alma-Ata conference (WHO/UNICEF, 1978) **305**
Alor Setar, Malaysia **258**
America, Central **148**
America, Latin **136, 245, 288, 313**
America, North **148, 245**
America, South **142, 148**
Andhra Pradesh, India **193**
animals **128, 130**
    breeding of **126**
        small animals **132**
        large animals **132-133**
    diseases
        foot-and-mouth disease **135**
    vaccines **135**
APEC. *See* Asia Pacific Economic Cooperation
Arbor Acres Company (United States) **175**
areca nut **171**
ASEAN. *See* **Association of Southeast Asian Nations**
Asia **1, 4, 288, 313**
    capital flows **11**
    diversity of political forms of government **37**
    foreign investment **11**
    middle class **16**
    political institutions, change in **16**
    reduction of barriers **11**
    universal liberalization of markets **11**

Asia, Central 4, 14, 53, 275
Asia, East 4, 5, 6, 11, 16, 187, 245
Asia Pacific Economic Cooperation (APEC) 15
Asia, South 4, 11, 13, 34, 287
Asia, Southeast 5, 7, 11, 13, 14, 16, 30, 54, 76, 126, 216
Asian Development Bank (ADB) 11, 67, 70, 199, 207-208, 246, 274, 330, 331, 336, 352
Asian Development Fund (ADF) 70
Asian financial and economic crisis (1997) 6, 16-19, 325, 328-335
  political repercussions 17-18, 329-335
  social repercussions 17-18, 329-335
Asian food crisis (1970s) 41, 186, 218, 250
Asian crisis, debt and fiscal (1980s) 225
Assam, India 30
Assessment Institutes for Agricultural Technology 96
Association of Southeast Asian Nations (ASEAN) 15
autonomy 40, 90, 91, 99
azadirachtin 147

B

Bacillus thuringiensis (Bt) 135, 136, 156
Badan Perwakilan Desa *See* Village Consultative Body (Indonesia)
BADC. *See* Bangladesh Agricultural Development Corporation
Bali, Indonesia 97
Bangkok, Thailand 47, 248
Bangladesh 12, 13, 49, 61, 85, 171, 178, 194, 195-196, 197, 216, 221, 224, 225, 235-236, 238, 280, 292, 293, 299, 322-323, 325, 340-348, (table) 353
Bangladesh Agricultural Development Corporation (BADC) 195, 221, 222
Bank Rakyat Indonesia 221
bappeda. *See* district planning boards

barangays (villages) (Philippines) 102
Barker-Hayami rationale 219, 220, 225
basmati rice 147, 149
Beijing, PRC 116
benefit-cost (B/C) ratios 318
Bengal, India 74
Bengal Rural Welfare Service (BRWS) (India) 303
Bhutan 340-348 (table)
bias
  age 274
  anti-poor 274, 299
  gender 274, 281, 327, 332-333
  language 281
  urban 214, 243, 244, 274, 299
BIMAS (mass guidance) rice campaign (Indonesia) 90, 95, 220, 221
biological agents 140
biological sciences 307
"bioprospecting" 153
biosafety regulations 9
biotechnology 7, 126, 132, 134, 135-138, 143, 308
  adverse effects of 140
  assessment of 142
  risks of 138
birth control 273
birth outcomes 316
birth spacing 273
boro (dry season) 196
bovine somatotropin (BST) 138, 142
Brazil 62, 126, 151
  land tenure security in 62
Bretton Woods institutions 1
BRWS. *See* Bengal Rural Welfare Service
BST. *See* bovine somatotropin
Bt. *See* Bacillus thuringiensis
Bt cotton 136, 156
budgets 36, 50-53, 111
  Balancing 52
  constraints 36, 50-53, 57-60
  integrated system 97
  local government 57-60
  support 333

Subject Index 397

build-operate-transfer arrangements **103**
BULOG (National Logistics Agency) (Indonesia) **228, 231, 232, 263, 264, 265, 267**
Bureau of Local Government Finance (Philippines) **104**
bureaucrats **37, 47-50, 246**

C

calorie intake **238, 346**
Cambodia **47, 62, 216, 275, 279, 292, 294, 322-323, 340-348 (table)**
capacity building **100, 113, 121**
capital **2, 141**
    accumulation **1**
    human **241, 271-339**
    opportunity cost of **240**
    real net external flow **12**
    rural human **21, 271-339**
    social **55-57, 73-77**
CARE, international NGO **314**
Caribbean **148, 288**
cashew **171**
castes (India) **42, 44, 46, 76, 281**
cassava **129, 141, 166**
CBD. *See* Convention on Biodiversity
Central Bank of Ceylon (Sri Lanka) **237**
Centro Internacional de Mejoramiento de Maiz y Trigo (CIMMYT) (International Maize and Wheat Improvement Center) **292, 131**
cereals **4, 213**
    changes in production **6**
    maize **127, 131, 143, 177**
    rice **129-131, 143, 177**
    wheat **143**
CGE. *See* computable general equilibrium
CGIAR. *See* Consultative Group for International Agricultural Research
charitable organizations **60**
Charoen Pokphand company (CP) (Thailand) **176-178**

chemical
    companies **141**
    herbicides **135**
    industry **126**
Chicago Board of Trade (United States) **231**
child development **311, 322, 323, 324-328**
Chile **179**
China. *See* People's Republic of China
Chinese (outside PRC) **76, 216, 223, 254-255, 263, 265**
Chinese Communist Party **39, 40, 76, 115**
CIMMYT. *See* Centro Internacional de Mejoramiento de Maiz y Tri (International Maize and Wheat Improvement Center)
civil service **48, 50**
    British **48, 49**
    growth of **49**
    mandarin tradition **48, 79**
    salaries **48, 89**
civil society **74, 103, 108**
coconut **141, 171**
coffee **171**
collective action **24, 70, 78, 80, 124, 244**
collectivization **14, 40**
Colombia **291**
colonial heritage **2, 78, 169, 216-217, 234**
commodities **172**
    homogeneous **213**
    orphan **142**
communes **32, 38**
communities **3, 8, 18, 54-56, 19-22**
    empowerment **199, 207**
    financing **305**
    local. *See* villages
    paticipation **20, 22**
    support **292**
community health centers. *See puskesmas*
comparative advantage **70-72**

computable general equilibrium (CGE) 241
Congress Party (India) 43, 44
Consultative Group on International Agricultural Research (CGIAR) 7, 124, 130, 140
Convention on Biodiversity (CBD) 151-153, 158
cooperatives 42, 92, 265-266
coproduction 72-73, 190, 210
corn 225
Costa Rica 154
costs
  agency 71-72
  public 190
  user, recovery 210
cotton 129, 137, 171
credit 3, 173, 195, 220, 266
  component 220
  public, subsidized 174
  services 197
crisis, Asian financial and economic 6, 16-197, 327, 328-335
  political repercussions 17-18
  social repercussions 17-18, 332-335
crisis, debt and fiscal (1980s) 225
crisis, food and energy (1970s) 41, 186, 218, 250
cronyism 262, 266
crops 125-134, 137
  cash 172
  cross-pollinating 126, 128, 130-132, 156
  diversified 164
  estate 95
  export (or plantation) 128
  import-competing 172
  nontraded 172
  self-pollinating 128
  spices 141
  tropical fruits 141
  transgenic 135, 136
  tree crops 132
  vegetatively propagating 128

Cultural Revolution, 1966-76 (PRC) 40, 66, 115
curricula, school 282, 283
  in local languages 284
  unsuitability of 283

D

dams 193, 202, 210
DBM. *See* Department of Budget and Management
decentralization 83-121, 178, 289, 295, 334
  administrative 91, 93
  dangers of 86
  definition of 85
  financial prerequisites 21
  financing 99-100, 103, 111-113, 115-117, 120
  fiscal 92, 93, 118
  institutional prerequisites 21
  of agriculture 106-107
  of education 294-296
  of extension 178-179
  of health affairs 97
  of research 9, 96
  of social services 301
  political 21, 120
  social prerequisites 21
deforestation 112, 206
demography 15-16, 297, 310
Deng Xiaoping (PRC) 40, 41, 115
Department of Agricultural Extension (Thailand) 162
Department of Agriculture (Philippines) 107, 178
Department of Budget and Management (DBM) (Philippines) 104, 110
Department of Health (DOH) (Philippines) 104, 105
Department of Interior and Local Government (DILG) (Philippines) 104, 110
Department of Justice (DOJ) (Philippines) 110

Department of Social Welfare and
  Development (Philippines) 108
Department of Watershed Development and Soil Conservation
  (Rajasthan, India) 158
desalinization 200
development 3, 4, 16, 89-90
  industrial 5
  interventions 3
  paradigms 19
  political 15
  rural 2, 18, 19, 22, 53, 89-90
  urban 5, 94-95
devolution 59, 72, 72, 83, 106-107,
  122, 178, 210
  definition of 83
  financial 58
  of management 190-195
Diamond vs. Chakrabarty case
  (United States) 146
DILG 110. *See* Department of
  Interior and Local Government
Directorate General of Water
  Resources Development (Indonesia) 196
disease 123, 161
  chronic, noncommunicable 310
  communicable 296
  fecally-borne 312
  infectious 296, 311
  migration 139
  parasitic 296
District People's Committee (Viet
  Nam) 179
district planning boards (*bappeda*)
  (Indonesia) 93
diversification 165
DNA 139
doctors 302
  barefoot 304
DOH. *See* Department of Health
Dominican Republic 290-291
donors 68, 85 335-336, 353
  evaluation 192
  roles 68, 85, 207-209, 332
  support 332

drugs
  over-the-counter 303
  overpresciption 303

E

early child development (ECD)
  322, 323, 324-328
Earth Summit (Rio de Janeiro, 1992)
  151
East Timor 97
ECD. *See* early child development
economies
  post-Soviet 4
  transitional 36, 52
education 3, 10, 21, 64, 92, 103, 117,
  121, 275-296, 323, 327
  access to 280-282
  and poverty 273-276
  decentralization of 295-296
  effectiveness of 282-286, 289-292
  efficiency 292-286, 289-292
  enrollment (primary) 330-331,
    346 **(table)**
  enrollment (secondary) 347
    (table)
expenditure 280
  management 294
  NGOs and 293
  nonformal 296
  outcomes 285
  primary 275, 277
  privatization 289-290, 291
  public financing 292
  quality 282-286
  secondary 275, 347
  urban bias in 277
electricity 45, 183, 202
employment 6, 14
  female 329
  loss of, in periurban areas 17
  loss of, in urban areas 17
  public-sector 49
enterprises, State-owned. *See* State-
  owned enterprises
entomologists 126
environment 125, 311

environmental management 103
　forest management 103
　institutional 8
　legal 8
　monitoring 210
　preservation 20
　protected areas and wildlife 103
　regulation 210
epidemiological transitions 310
Europe 1, 245, 288
Europe, Eastern 65
Europe, Western
　reconstruction in 68
European Union 139
evapotranspiration 203
exchange rates 11
　depreciated 17
expenditures, government
　government 11-14
　on agriculture 13
　on social services 13
exports
　earnings 6
　levy 172
　sectors 2
　services 15
　tax 169
extension, agricultural 18, 95, 173-180
private contract farming 175-177
externalities 25, 213

F

"F-type" schools (Dominican Republic) 290
family planning 107, 273
FAO. *See* Food and Agriculture Organization
farmers 8
　cooperatives 265
　exemption 147, 156
　welfare 25
　rights 151, 154, 157
Farmers Action Fund (Thailand) 252, 254
Farmers' Aid Act (Thailand) 250

Farmers' Aid Fund (Thailand) 250
farming, contract 175-177
fertility 272
　decline in Asia 15, 273
　rate, total 341 **(table)**
Fertilizer and Pesticide Authority, 1977 (Philippines) 222
Fertilizer Industry Authority, 1973 (Philippines) 222
fertilizers 7, 123, 162, 173, 218-226, 239, 253
　application 163
　distribution 213, 221-224
　marketing 21, 223
　subsidies 2, 215, 218-226, 239, 253
fetal development 316
field trials (plant breeding) **135-136**
financing
　capacity 184
　public constraints 288
firewood 312
fiscal
　balance problem 52
　crisis 225
　flexibility 247
　management problems 53
fisheries 6, 92, 95
fishes 139
flood control 207
floodplains 185, 186, 192-194
food 4
　adequacy 6
　aid 235
　crises (1970s) 41, 186, 218, 250
　daily calorie availability 343 **(table)**
　nonstaple 6
　price
　　stabilization 215, 226-234, 249-254, 256-258, 264-268
　processing 9
　security 2, 4, 233
　staple 6
　supply 3, 4
Food and Agriculture Organization (FAO) 152

foodgrain
  policies **213-269**
  trade **232-234**
Ford Foundation (US) **129**
Ford Motor Company (US) **77**
forestry **92**
forests **5, 9, 207**
fuel, subsidies **266**
Fujian, PRC **116**
funds
  inflow of **89**
  shortage of **107**
  transfer of **92**

G

Gandhi, Indira (India) **43, 44, 45**
Gandhi, Rajiv (India) **45**
GATT. *See* General Agreement on Tariffs and Trade
GDP. *See* gross domestic product
gender **272**
  discrepancy **324**
  equality **3**
  impacts **328**
  sensitivity **324**
gene banks **96, 128, 132, 152**
General Agreement on Tariffs and Trade (GATT) **15, 234**
General Motors (United States) **77**
genetic
  base **125, 126-134**
  improvement **126, 158, 164**
  manipulation **135-138, 148**
  resources **152, 153**
genetics **126-143**
  biotechnology **7, 126, 132, 134, 135-143, 308**
GFHR. *See* Global Forum on Health Research
Ghana **85, 229**
Global Forum on Health Research (GFHR) **309-310**
globalization **15**
GOLKAR (Gologan Karya, functional groups) (Indonesia) **89, 262, 265, 266**

good health **310**
goods **24-27**
  buyers and sellers **26**
  international public **124**
  local public **25**
  merit **26, 72, 213-214**
  private **25, 27**
  public **24-25, 72, 256**
    nonexcludability of **25**
    nonrivalry of **24, 25**
governance **11, 20, 78-79, 80, 84**
  building blocks of **18**
  definitions **78-79**
governments **108**
  authoritarianism **199**
  central **1, 2, 24, 32, 35, 36, 45, 52, 60, 67, 71, 90, 187**
  bureaucratically-run **80**
  local **53-60**
  parliamentary
    bicameral **249**
    electoral system **249**
  revenue-generating capacity **14**
grain
  marketing **72, 213-270**
  trading **217, 231**
grants, bloc **90**
Great Leap Forward (PRC) **40, 66, 114, 115**
green revolution **2, 4, 6, 7, 9, 123, 124, 130, 174, 183, 214, 218, 219, 272, 351**
  technology **57**
gross domestic product (GDP) **6, 17**
groundwater **185, 195-196, 197, 198**
  unregulated extraction **197**
  tubewells **195-196, 197, 198**
growth **2, 17**
  agricultural **2, 4-5**
  economic **2-10**
  rural nonfarm **9-10**
  urban-industrial linkages **9**
Guangdong, PRC **65, 116**
Guizhou, PRC **118**
Gujarat, India **197**

H

health 3, 21, 61, 271-278, 296-313, 315, 316, 323, 330
  and income growth 276, 298
  awareness 311
  disease, nature of 296-297
  facilities 275
  and fertility 297
  research B
health care 92, 94, 103, 117, 271-278, 296-313
  and NGOs 303-304
  and poverty 273-276
  expenditure 29
    per capital (table) 348
    as % of GDP (table) 348
  insurance 26, 312
  private sector 276, 277, 300, 302-303
  human resource leakage 305-307
  urban bias in 277
herbicide 135
  tolerance 136
  varieties 14
Hinduism 88
Hong Kong 340-348 (table)
horticulture 6, 7, 95
hospitals 277
households 3, 18, 32
  budgets 328
housing 9
  projects 103, 117
Huguenots 76
Human Development Index (HDI) (table) 342
human resettlement 28
human rights 16
Hungary 84
hybrid seed
  industry 127
  production 177
hydroelectricity 202
hydrology 208
hydropower 207
hyperinflation 14

I

IARCs. *See* International Agricultural Research Centers
IDA. *See* International Development Association
IMF. *See* International Monetary Fund
immunization 275
inbred lines 127
incomes
  high 51
  inequalities of 27
  low 51
  national 273
  per capita 3
  redistribution 47
  support initiatives
    price-support schemes 252
    subsidization of farmers 252
  support measures 261
India 5, 12, 21, 23, 38, 42-47, 51, 56, 62-63, 74-75, 76, 80, 131, 136, 147, 158-159, 171, 173, 177, 178, 194, 216, 223, 224, 225, 235, 281, 293, 300, 303, 306, 309, 322-323, 325, 340-348
India, South 55
Indian Council for Agricultural Research (India) 178
Indonesia 12, 13, 20, 41, 42-45, 46, 47, 51, 52, 61, 69, 84, 86, 87-101, 163, 171, 181, 194, 196-197, 201, 204, 215, 216, 220, 221, 224, 226, 228, 230, 231, 232, 245, 246, 247, 261-268, 276, 280, 293, 299, 300, 306, 317, 319, 320, 329-333, 340-348 (table), 353
  May 1998, events of 88
  New Order (Order *Baru*) period, 1965 87-88
  NGO activities 61
  reformasi (reform) in 87
  Reformasi Era 88
industrialization
  forced-pace 41
  rural 10, 65-67

infrastructure 10, 22, 118, 200
  flood-control 184
  investments, decline in 40, 109, 118
  irrigation 68
  physical 10, 184
  ports 68
  roads 68
  rural 10
  urban 117
insecticides 25
insects 139
integrated pest management (IPM) 161-163
Integrated Urban Infrastructure Development Program (Indonesia) 94
intellectual growth 323
intellectual property protection (IPP) 9, 128, 143-157
  assessment of 155-157
  benefitsof 145-150
  "natural protection" 143
Internal Revenue Allotments (IRA) (Philippines) 103, 111, 112
International Agricultural Research Centers (IARCs) 124, 142, 143, 164
International Convention for the Protection of New Varieties of Plants (UPOV) 145, 152
International Development Association (IDA) 70
International Maize and Wheat Improvement Center. See Centro Internacional de majoramiento de Maiz 6 Trigo (CIMMYT)
International Irrigation Management Institute (IIMI) 191, 192
International Monetary Fund (IMF) 331
International Rice Research Institute (IRRI) 129, 130, 134, 160, 168
International Undertaking on Plant Genetic Resources (IUPGR) 151, 152

interventions, State 28, 68, 226, 236, 241, 271, 298
  appropriateness 278
  fertilizer market 218-226
  foodgrain markets 213-218
  price stabilization 226-234
IPM. See integrated pest management
IPP. See intellectual property protection
IRA. See Internal Revenue Allotments
Irian Jaya, Indonesia s
IRRI. See International Rice Research Institute
irrigated areas 159
irrigation 2, 7, 18, 21, 107, 121, 141, 159, 165, 183,-210
  community-based systems 107, 187-195
  drip 203, 206
  floodplain systems 190-193
  gravity systems 185
  groundwater 184, 194-197
  large-scale systems 192-194
  management 183-210
  rehabilitation 210
  service feeS 194
  small systems 55, 186
  small-floodplain B
  small-scale 55, 185-191, 192
  sprinkler 203, 206
  subsidies 2
  sustainability 184
  upper-basin 186
  user fees 194
Italy 75, 76, 77
IUIDP. See Integrated Urban Infrastructure Development Program (Indonesia)
IUPGR. See International Undertaking on Plant Genetic Resources

J

Jakarta, Indonesia 267
Japan 9, 130, 187, 245

rural industrialization 9
Java, Indonesia 88, 97
Jews 76
Jiangsu, PRC 115
Johor, Malaysia 314
"jumping genes" 138
jute 171

K

Kalimantan, Indonesia 97
Kazakhstan 53, 294, 340-348 (table), 354
Kedung Ombo Dam, Indonesia 201
Kefauver Committee, US Senate (United States) 308
Kelantan, Malaysia 314
Kerala, India 22, 56, 57, 74-78, 235
   caste self-help 74
   civil society 74
   cooperative societies 74
   density of civil organizations 74
   fair-price shops (public food distribution) 74
   heralth care units 74
   labor-displacing technologies, restricting of 74
   'library movement' 74
   literary associations and film industry 74
   social capital in 74-78
   social upliftment societies 74
   social welfare system B
Klongpier Community Fund (Thailand) 305
Korea 130
Korea, Republic of 5, 9, 41, 42, 47, 51, 52, 187, 217, 226, 244, 340-348 (table)
   presidential system of government 37
   rural industrialization 9
Korean People's Democratic Republic 11
Kyrgyz Republic 53, 340-348 (table), 354

L

labor 16, 92
   absorption 17
   displacement 167
   rural mobility 15
   skills 10
   surplus 2
lac 171
land reform 21, 40, 44, 47
land tenure rights 21, 31
"landraces". *See* cultivars
land 7, 21-22, 32
   surplus 136
   underutilized 247
   unirrigated 165
Lao PDR. *See* Lao People's Democratic Republic (PDR)
Lao People's Democratic Republic (PDR) 14, 47, 185, 274, 300, 315, 340-348 (table)
Leagues of Provinces, Cities, and Municipalities (Philippines) 104
less favored areas (LFAs) 164-167, 276
LFAs. *See* less favored areas
LGUs. *See* local government units
life expectancy 276, 343 (table)
literacy 275, 345 (table)
   programs, adult 296
livestock 92, 95
   production 135
loans 103, 112
   agriculture-sector 69
   grant element 70
   local government 60
   student 294
Local Government Code (Philippines) 102-114
local government units (LGUs) 102-114
   and decentralization 110-111
local legislative bodies (*sangguniang bayan*) 108
longitudinal survey 327
LPN (Malaysia). *See* National Paddy and Rice Institute

M

macroeconomic
  disequilibrium 14
  stability 10-15, 27
  policy 10-15
madrasah schools (Bangladesh) 292, 293
Mahathir Mohammed, Dr. (Malaysia) 258
maize 127, 131, 177
  hybrid producers 155
  hybrid seed 156
Malaysia 12, 13, 20, 41, 42-45, 46, 47, 51, 52, 61, 69, 84, 86, 87-101, 163, 171, 181, 194, 196-197, 201, 204, 215, 216, 220, 221, 224, 226, 228, 231, 232, 245, 246, 247, 261-268, 277, 280, 293, 299, 300, 306, 317, 319, 320, 329-333, 353
  parliamentary system 37
  State intervention in rice markets 254, 261-268
malnutrition 311
  child 344 **(table)**
Maluku, Indonesia 97
mandates
  administrative 86
  legal 86
  unfunded 111
manufactured goods 6
Mao Tsetung (People's Republic of China) 38, 66, 304
Marcos, Ferdinand (Philippines) 41, 42, 102
Marketing Organization for Farmers (Thailand) 252, 253
markets
  economies 36
  future 231
  labor 247
  output 196
  rice 231, 247
Marxist-Leninist ideology 85
Masagana 99 program (Philippines) 220, 222

mechanization (agriculture) 167-168
medicines 123
Mediterranean fruit fly 138
Mekong River basin 185
Mendelian
  biology 165
  genetics 127, 152
Merck 154
merit goods, 26, **213-214**, 216,
micronutrients 321
Middle East 288
millgate procurement system 236
mills
  integrated operations 257
mining 92
Ministry of Women's Empowerment (Indonesia) 329
Ministry for Regional Autonomy (Indonesia) 101
Ministry of Agriculture (Thailand) 250, 251
Ministry of Agriculture (MOA) (Indonesia) 95
Ministry of Commerce (Thailand) 250, 251
Ministry of Finance (Indonesia) 90
Ministry of Finance (Thailand) 250
Ministry of Health (Indonesia) 101
Ministry of Home Affairs (Indonesia) 91, 98
Ministry of Public Works (Indonesia) 94
Ministry for Regional Autonomy (Indonesia) 101
MOA. *See* Ministry of Agriculture
mobilization
  political 43-47
  resource 92
Mongolia 12, 14, 51, 84, 275, 293, 340-348 **(table)**
monopolies 236
Monsanto 140, 156
moral hazard 26
mortality 273
  child 274, 342 **(table)**
  infant 276, 342 **(table)**

life expectancy at birth 343 **(table)**
matenal 342 **(table)**
municipalities 86
Myanmar 185, 216, 217, 300, 340-348 **(table)**

N

National Assembly (Indonesia) 98
National Development Planning Agency (Indonesia) 90, 94
National Food Authority (NFA) (Philippines) 228, 229, 233
National Logistics Agency (BULOG) (Indonesia) *See* BULOG
National Paddy and Rice Institute (LPN) (Malaysia) 256-257, 260
neem 147
Nehru, Jawaharlal (India) 42-43
nematodes 139
Nepal 12, 13, 51, 84, 173, 177, 280, 281, 284, 299, 340-348 **(table)**, 353
New Order period (Indonesia) 87, 88-97, 100
New Zealand 84
NGOs. *See* nongovernment organizations
Nigeria 55
nitrogen (N) 126, 163
nongovernment organizations (NGOs) 20, 56, 60-64, 85, 103, 108-109, 110, 111, 166, 177-178, 277, 293, 302, 332, 353, 354
   advocacy 61, 63, 64
   annual revenue 63
   description of 60-61
   financing 62-64
   foreign funding of 63-64
   government cooperation with 61
   government 61
   restrictions on 61
   service-providing 64
Nusa Tenggara Timor (NTT) (Indonesia) 88, 97
nutrition 107, 311, 315, 316, 318-324
   deficiencies 318, 321-324
   benefits of intervention 319
   impacts 318-319
   mitigation costs 319
   maternal 316

O

O&M. *See* operations & maintenance
obesity 329
OECD. *See* Organization for Economic Cooperation and Development
Official Development Assistance (Philippines) 112
oil
   exporters 247
   boom 25
   crises, (1970s) 52
oil palm 7
oilseeds 171
operation and maintenance (O & M) 186, 295
   large systems 210
   small systems 210
Organization for Economic Cooperation and Development (OECD) 62, 288
"orphan commodities" 309

P

Paddy Price Support program (Malaysia) 258-259
Pakistan 12, 51, 86, 148, 171, 194, 292, 293, 322-323, 340-348 **(table)** 353
palm oil 68, 171
Pancasila (Indonesia) 89
Papua New Guinea 51, 284, 304, 340-348 **(table)**
Park Chung Hee (Republic of Korea) 41, 42
participation 79, 110
   and local governance 110
   growing demand for 84
PAS opposition party (Malaysia) 259
patents (on plants) 146-149
   law 147
   nonobvious inventive step 147

Subject Index

novelty **145**
protection **18, 146-149**
usefulness **146**
patron-client relationships **39, 78**
PEM. *See* protein-energy malnutrition
people's organizations (POs) **108-110**
People's Republic of China (PRC) **9, 12, 14, 20, 21, 34, 38-42, 51, 53, 58, 65-67, 86, 114-119, 130, 132, 136, 145, 185, 187, 201, 226, 275, 276, 284, 293-294, 296, 303, 309, 322-323, 326, 340-348 (table), 353, 354**
   1966-76 Cultural Revolution **115**
   Chinese rural society **38**
   Cultural Revolution **66**
   decentralization **114-119**
   Great Leap Forward **40, 66, 114, 115**
   land reform efforts **22**
   Maoist revolution **38**
   politicians in **38-41**
   property rights, reestablishing **32**
   rural industrialization **9, 65-67, 117**
   tax reform **116**
   township and village enterprises (TVEs) **65-67, 117**
pesticides **147, 160-164, 173, 266**
   hazards **162**
   subsidies **162, 266**
   use **162**
pests **214**
   infestation of **160**
   populations **137**
   use of biotechnology against **137-138**
pharmaceutical industry (US) **308**
pharmacies **302**
philanthropy **63**
Philippines **9, 12, 14, 20, 21, 34, 38-42, 51, 53, 58, 65-67, 86, 114-119, 130, 132, 136, 145, 185, 186, 201, 226, 275, 276, 284, 293-294, 296, 303, 309, 322-323, 326, 340-348 (table), 353**

Local Government Code **102-114**
   problems **109**
   progress **109**
   prospects **109**
local government units (LGUs) **102-114**
NGO activities **61**
presidential system of government **37**
phosphorous **163**
plants
   breeding **126-134, 144-146**
   breeders' rights. *See* plant variety protection
   cross-pollinating **127**
   domestic **226**
   genetic resources **151, 152, 153, 154**
   physiologists **126**
   plant variety protection **144-146, 152, 155**
plantation crops **92**
Planters Products Inc. (PPI) (Philippines) **222**
Poland **84**
policies
   agricultural **243-269**
   divide-and-rule **83**
   extractive **41**
   fiscal **11**
   monetary **11**
   water resources **184**
political
   architecture **245**
   dynamics **243**
   economy **56**
   mobilization **42-47**
   participation **3, 16**
   structure **245**
   support **119**
   uncertainty **199**
   will **86**
politicians **37-47**
  as actors **37-47**
  rural **45-47, 253-254**

population 340 **(table)**
  crude birth rate (table) 340
  crude death rate (table) 340
  density 185
  rural 45
POs. *See* people's organizations
postcolonial era 234
potato 137
poultry 6, 144, 176-178
  farming 176-178
  industry 177
poverty 3, 6, 10, 68
  reduction 3, 20, 27, 28, 271
  rural 3
PPI. *See* Planters Products Inc.
PRC *See* People's Republic of China
price
  ceiling 227
  seasonal spread 228
  stabilization 226-234, 249-254, 256-258, 264-268
  support 226
"prisoner's dilemma"-type games 75, 76-77
private
  enterprises 2
  markets 217
  sector 18, 19, 64-67 103, 179, 279, 292, 302
privatization 11, 65-67, 84, 289
  of education 291
  of health care 302-303
production function 73, 287
productivity 7
  enhancement 158
  of individuals 77
Program for Preventing/Eliminating Child Labor (Philippines) 108
programs
  bilateral assistance 208
  credit 226
  food stamp 237
  food-for-work 238
  public works 238
  training 100
  turnover 190

projects
  construction 45
  design 208
property rights 10, 20 21, 28-32, 35, 207, 315
  assignment 29-30, 31
  communal 29, 207
  control 29
  enforcement of 35
  intellectual 34
  open access 29
  private 28, 34-35, 66
  State 29
  to forestlands 35
  to land 30, 34
  to water 31, 33
protein-energy malnutrition (PEM) 318
PT Pusri (Indonesia) 266
public
  agencies 210
  funding 291
  interventions 7, 18
  research 9
  resettlement schemes 175
  sector
    financing 299
    irrigation development 208
  works 103
Public Food Distribution System (PFDS) (Bangladesh) 236
public sector
financing 299
irrigation developement 208
Public Warehouse Organization (Thailand) 252, 254
puskesmas 97

Q

quality of life 3, 272

R

radios 16
Rajasthan, India 158
Ramos, Fidel V. (Philippines) 105
rapeseed 137

Subject Index

rationing 234-129
  shops 234
  systems 234-239
  water 201-212
Reagan, Ronald (US) 68
Reaganomics 11
reformasi 87
Reformasi Era 97-101
reforms 35, 66, 117
  economic 86
  market-oriented 68, 84
  movements 84
  redistributive 45
regulation 10
  structure 8-9
relationships
  center-province 91
  patron-client 46-47, 263
rents 256
  diversion 260
  divisible 255, 270
  targetable 270
research 156, 158-172
  agricultural 7, 9, 18, 21, 62, 96, 118, 121, 140, 158-166, 170, 177
  biotechnology 142-143, 181-182
  financing of 168-172
  in less favored areas 164-167
  NGO roles in 177
  plant breeding 126-143
  resource management 158-167
  shortcomings in 180-181
resource 69
  allocation 171, 286, 288
  base 125
  common property 9
  constrained areas 164, 177
  management 158-167
  misallocation 242
  open access 29, 202
  scarcities 21
revenues 117
  general tax 171, 172
  oil 88
Riau, Indonesia 101

rice 129-131, 177, 213, 216, 225
  boro (dry season) 196
  fertilizer-responsive variety 130
  Indica 134
  IR-8 123, 126, 158
  Japonica 134
  marketing 21
  millers 244
  mills 235
  paddies 203
  quality 231
  stockpiles 263
  storage of 21
  suwan 131
rice-deficit areas 229
Rice-Tec Company 147, 148, 149
rights
  human 16
  property rights 10, 20, 21, 28-32, 35, 207, 315
    assignment 29-30, 31
    communal 29, 207
    control 29
    enforcement of 35
    intellectual 34, 128, 143-147
    open access 29
    private 28, 34-35, 66
    State 29
    to forestlands 35
    to land 30, 34
    to water 31, 33
  water, tradable 204
riparian doctrine 204
river systems 185
roads 22, 45, 90
Robert McNamara 3
Rockefeller Foundation (US) 129
roles 4, 20, 21, 24-36, 360-362
  descriptions 24-36
  interactions 70
  State 2-3, 166-168, 239, 352-360
    in education 278, 279-280, 284, 288-289
    in health care 278, 298-300, 303, 309, 311-312, 314, 321, 324
    in irrigation 211

in property rights 28-36
in social justice 28
macroeconomic 278
regulatory 10, 183-210
Royal Irrigation Department
(Thailand) 194
rubber 171
transgenic 136
tree 126
rural
areas 214, 282
banks 226
dynamism 4, 9
economy 3
legal frameworks 20
regulatory frameworks 20
elite 46
households 198
industrialization 9
population 40, 311
schools 284
poverty 3
technology 2
Rural Asia study
3, 5, 10, 17, 19, 22
Rural Extension Centers (Indonesia)
95
rural nonfarm
growth 9, 10
production 9

S

salaries
civil service 48
government 48
Samahang Nayon pre-cooperative
(Philippines) 42
sanitation 312, 315-318, 344
schistosomiasis 312
school leavers 16
schools 90, 280, 281
poor physical conditions 282-293.
284, 285
private 289-292
public 289-292

seeds 3, 123, 162, 220
industry 131, 141
laws covering 156
production 156
stations 173
subsidies 266
Selangor, Malaysia B
Semaul Undung organization
(Republic of Korea) 42
semiarid zones 165
services 23, 24, 25, 72-73
buyers and sellers 26
discretionary 300
social 108
urban 94
Shaman Laboratories 154
Shanghai, PRC 116
Sichuan, PRC 116
silk 171
Singapore 51, 340-348 (table)
social
cellularization 38
cohesion 55
justice 27, 28
services 106, 274, 275, 327
health 14
housing 14
welfare 103
social capital 20, 55-57, 73-77, 18
social safety net 11, 14
society, civil 108
SOEs. *See* state-owned enterprises
soil 123, 208
conservation 158, 177
erosion 207
scientists 126
structure 158
sorghum 131, 229
Soviet Union 14, 65, 85, 276
soybeans 129, 137, 174, 231
Sri Lanka 12, 13, 46, 51, 171, 216, 235,
237-238, 175, 280, 299, 322-323,
340-348 (table), 35
stabilization 226
price 226, 234, 239-240, 247-254,
256-258, 262-268, 278

State
  intervention 28, 68, 213-270, 298
  primacy 22
  State 2-3, 166-168, 239, 352-360
    in education 278, 279-280, 284, 288-289
    in health care 278, 298-300, 303, 309, 311-312, 314, 321, 324
    in irrigation 211
    in property right 28-36
    in social justice 28
    macroeconomic 278
    regulatory 10, 183-210
  subsidies 190
  theory of 37-50
state-owned enterprises (SOEs) 14, 221
storage (of grain) 227-232
  burden 232
  costs 229
Sub-Saharan Africa 287, 288
subsidies 117
  component 230
  consumer 234-239, 250
  fertilizer 218-226, 253, 258, 266
  targeted consumer 234-239, 258-259, 263-268
    food for work 238-239
sugar 129, 171
  growers 244
Suharto (Indonesia) 41, 87, 88, 262
Sukarno (Indonesia) 87, 89
Sulawesi, Indonesia 97
Sumatra, Indonesia 97
sunflowers 131
sustainability issue 184

T

Taipei,China 5, 9, 37, 47, 134, 171, 187, 217, 226, 244, 245, 340-348 (table)
  presidential system of government 37, 51
  rural industrialization 9
Taiwan 130

Tajikistan 340-348 (table)
Tamil Nadu, India 322
tariffs
  implicit 223
taxes 2, 50-53, 57-60, 92 169, 170, 172
  assignment system 58-59
  collection of 59-60
  export 169-170, 171, 172
  excise 59
  local 293
  reform 116
  revenues 58, 67
  sales 60
  variable border levy 234
tea 171, 177
teachers 23, 54, 282-283, 285
technology 123, 175
  changes 7
  communications 16
  development 9
  rural 2
  transfer 2
  transgenic 138
telecommunications 10, 22, 103
televisions 16
textbooks
  scarcity 283
  language 283
  unsuitability 283

Thailand 12, 18, 32-33, 37, 41, 42, 46, 48-49, 51, 52, 63, 131, 132, 136, 162, 171, 174, 175-177, 179, 185, 194, 204, 215, 217, 221, 224, 232, 245, 246, 246-254, 255, 256, 260, 261, 262, 263, 291, 300, 313, 305, 306, 311, 334, 340-348 (table), 351, 353
  parliamentary system 37
  policy interventions 251
  property rights in 30-31
Thatcher, Margaret (United Kingdom) 68
Thatcherism 11
Three Gorges Dam, PRC 201
Tianjin, PRC 116

timber 171
tobacco 171
tomato 137
township and village enterprises (TVEs) 65-67, 117
trade 92
  barriers, elimination of 15
  grain 67
  international 14
  liberalization 15
  retail 9
  variations in 232
tranportation 15
transitional countries 37
tree crops
  cocoa 133, 171
  coffee 133
  rubber 133
tubewells 195-196, 197, 198
  subsidized program 195
  technology 196
turmeric 147
TVEs. *See* township and village enterprise

U

UMNO. *See* United Malays National Organization
UNICEF. *See* United Nations Children's Fund
United Malays National Organization (UMNO) (Malaysia) 255, 256
United Nations Children's Fund (UNICEF) 305
United States (US) 7, 68, 139, 140, 146-147, 148, 149, 151, 204, 221 308
UPOV. *See* International Convention for the Protection of New Varieties of Plants
upper basin 185
UR. *See* Uruguay Round
urban
  areas 14, 214
  bias 234, 243, 274
  development 94-95

Urban Development Coordination Team, 1987 (Indonesia) 94
urbanization 10, 15
Uruguay Round (UR) 152
US. *See* United States
US hybrid industry 132, 144
US Patent Office 148
user fees 194, 204, 300
Uttar Pradesh, India 197
Uzbekistan 340-348 **(table)**

V

vaccine research 177
value of marginal product (VMP) 219
Vavilov, Russian botanist 133
Viet Nam 12, 14, 21, 34-35, 53, 58, 179, 216, 275, 279, 284, 300, 322-323, 325, 340-348 **(table)**, 354
  agriculture, decollectivized 33
  cooperatives 33
  forest lands, allocation of 33
  land eform efforts 22
  land law of 1993 33
  land-use classifications 33
  People's Committees 33
  private property rights, reestablishing B
Viet Nam, South 46
village drug dispensaries 304
village health workers 302, 304
Village Representative Body (Badan Perwakilan Desa) Indonesia 99
Village Scout Movement (Thailand) 42
villages 9, 17, 54-57. *See also barangays*
  collective action in 54-57
  irrigation systems in 55
  power of 54
  schools 55
  schoolteachers in 54
VMP. *See* value of marginal product
"vote banks" (India) 43, 46

W

W. R. Grace Company 147
wage-good argument 214, 216, 218
Wahid, Abdurrahman (Indonesia) 101
water 5, 9, 21, 34, 162, 183-210
  allocation
    basin-level 210
  availability 189
  basin 184, 185-194, 209
    floodplains 191-195
    upper-basin 185-191
  collection 312
  conservation 177, 210
  consumption 203
  delivery 315
  demand 188, 201-206
  desalinization 200
  diversion 183, 203
  local accountability 210
  management 182-210
  pricing 203-206
  property rights in 204-207, 210
  quality monitoring 198
  rights 210
    tradable 204-206
  rural nonagricultural 184, 310
  scarcity 5, 184, 198
  storage capacity 200
  subsidies 266
  supply 94, 200-206
  supply, rural 207, 315-318
  supply, urban 207
  user fees 194, 200, 203-204, 300
  water-user associations (WUAs) 191, 193, 196, 197
watersheds 5, 184
weather 206, 214, 224
Weber, Max 49, 193
weight-for-height 329
  bamboo 189
West Bengal, India
  land reform efforts 22
wheat 213, 216, 225
  Soft Red Winter 225
WHO. *See* World Health Organization
women 278, 311, 329, 331
  bias against 274, 281, 332-333
  participation of 273
  roles 28
World Bank (WB) 1, 67-70, 95, 199, 207-208, 287, 300, 331, 337, 352
  structural adjustment programs 225
World Health Organization (WHO) 162, 305, 311-312
World Trade Organization (WTO) 15, 124
World War II 1, 68, 214, 215, 234, 247
WTO. *See* World Trade Organization
WUAs. *See* water-user associations